Copyright © 2021-All rights reserved.

No part of this publication may be reproduced, distributed, or transmitted in any form or by any means, including photocopying, recording, or other electronic or mechanical methods, without the prior written permission of the publisher, except in the case of brief quotations embodied in reviews and certain other non-commercial uses permitted by copyright law.

This Book is provided with the sole purpose of providing relevant information on a specific topic for which every reasonable effort has been made to ensure that it is both accurate and reasonable. Nevertheless, by purchasing this Book you consent to the fact that the author, as well as the publisher, are in no way experts on the topics contained herein, regardless of any claims as such that may be made within. It is recommended that you always consult a professional prior to undertaking any of the advice or techniques discussed with in.This is a legally binding declaration that is considered both valid and fair by both the Committee of Publishers Association and the American Bar Association and should be considered as legally binding within the United States.

CONTENTS

INTRODUCTION 10
MORNING RECIPES 12
    Honey Butternut Squash Cake Oatmeal 12
    French Cheese & Spinach Quiche 12
    Walnut & Pumpkin Strudel 12
    Italian Egg Cakes 12
    Smoked Salmon & Egg Muffins 12
    Breakfast Frittata 12
    Tofu Hash Brown Breakfast 13
    Speedy Soft-Boiled Eggs 13
    Spinach & Feta Pie with Cherry Tomatoes 13
    Strawberry Jam 13
    Ricotta & Potato Breakfast 13
    Light & Fruity Yogurt 13
    Greek Yogurt with Honey & Walnuts 13
EGGS & VEGETABLES 15
    Potato & Salmon Salad 15
    Potato, Green Bean & Egg Salad 15
    Broccoli & Cherry Tomato Salad 15
    Carrot & Broccoli Salad with Hazelnuts 15
    Broccoli & Egg Salad 15
    Cheesy Vegetable Medley 15
    Zucchini & Bacon Cheese Quiche 16
    Asparagus & Tomato Tart 16
    Baby Spinach & Gruyère Gratin 16
    Spinach & Potato Gratin 16
    Mushroom-Potato Hash Casserole 16
    Baby Spinach with Beets & Cheese 16
    Potatoes with Creamy Arugula Sauce 17
    Cheesy Potatoes with Herbs 17
    Dill Potatoes with Butter & Olives 17
    Feta & Onion Layered Potatoes 17
    Crushed Potatoes with Aioli 17
    Rosemary Sweet Potatoes with Butter 17
    Parsley New Potatoes with Radishes 18
    Chive & Truffle Potato Mash 18
    Potato & Carrot Puree 18
    Chipotle & Garlic Mashed Potatoes 18
    Pumpkin & Potato Mash 18
    Creamy Potatoes 18
    Chili Coconut Potatoes 18
    Mediterreanean Asparagus 19
    Thyme & Garlic Potatoes 19
    Rosemary Potato Fries 19
    Sumac Red Potatoes 19
    Steamed Sweet Potatoes with Cilantro 19
    Cheesy Jalapeño Sweet Potatoes 19
    Nutty Potatoes 19
    Hazelnut Brussels Sprouts with Parmesan 20
    Butternut Squash & Kale Pot 20
    Spicy Cauliflower Cakes 20
    Steamed Vegetables with Chile Butter 20
    Steamed Cauliflower with Cheese 20
    Italian-Style Brussels Sprouts 20
    Brussels Sprouts with Cranberries 20
    Chili Corn On the Cob 21
    Provençal Ratatouille 21
    Cauliflower & Kale Curry 21
    Parsnip & Cauliflower Mash 21
    Fall Vegetable Mash 21
    Zucchini with Asparagus 21
    Mango & Pumpkin Porridge 21
    Steamed Asparagus with Salsa Verde 22
    Steamed Artichokes with Salsa Roquefort 22
    Coconut Pumpkin Chili 22
    Mascarpone Mashed Turnips 22
    Tarragon Baby Carrots with Parsnips 22
    Carrot & Beet Medley 22
    Orange Glazed Carrots 22
    Garlic Eggplants with Parmesan 23
    Yogurt Eggplant Dip 23
    Spicy Okra & Eggplant Dish 23
    Winter Root Vegetables with Feta 23
    Orange & Thyme Beet Wedges 23
    Butter-Braised Cabbage 23
    Mushroom & Bell Pepper Casserole 24
    Curried Tofu with Vegetables 24
    Asparagus & Mushrooms with Bacon 24
    Green Vegetables with Tomatoes 24
    Yummy Vegetable Soup 24
POULTRY 25
    Tasty Indian Chicken Curry 25
    Tasty Chicken Breasts with BBQ Sauce 25
    Pumpkin & Wild Rice Cajun Chicken 25
    Avocado Fajitas 25
    Sweet Chicken Carnitas in Lettuce Wraps 25
    Hot Chicken with Coriander & Ginger 26
    Savory Chicken Chili with Chickpeas 26
    Thyme Chicken with White Wine 26
    Easy Chicken with Capers & Tomatoes 26
    Best Italian Chicken Balls 26
    Chicken with Honey-Lime Sauce 26
    Tasty Chicken Breasts 27
    Chicken Alla Italiana 27
    Tarragon & Garlic Chicken 27
    Chicken Drumsticks in Sriracha Sauce 27
    Chicken & Zucchini Pilaf 27
    Rice & Lentil Chicken with Parsley 28
    Rosemary Chicken with Asparagus Sauce 28
    Chicken Wings with Worcestershire Sauce 28
    Grilled Chicken Drumsticks with Salad 28
    Picante Chicken with Lemon 28
    Hot Chicken with Garlic & Mushrooms 29
    Corn & Sweet Potato Soup with Chicken 29

Pea & Rice Chicken with Paprika & Herbs 29	Cuban Mojo Chicken Tortillas 38
Chicken Sausage & Navy Bean Chili................... 29	Creole Chicken with Rice...................................... 38
Savory Tropical Chicken.. 29	Moroccan-Style Chicken 38
Punjabi Chicken in Lemon-Honey Gravy......... 30	Chicken in Creamy Mushroom Sauce................ 39
Awesome Chicken in Tikka Masala Sauce........ 30	Peppered Chicken with Chunky Salsa............... 39
Pesto Chicken with Green Beans 30	Chicken & Bacon Cacciatore................................ 39
Chicken & Vegetable Stew 30	Lemon & Thyme Chicken 39
Colorful Vegetable & Chicken Rice 31	Cumin Chicken with Capers 39
Chicken Thighs with Mushrooms & Garlic...... 31	Feta Cheese Turkey Balls 40
Quinoa Pilaf with Chicken.................................... 31	Chicken with Port Wine Sauce 40
Brussels Sprouts & Zucchini Chicken................ 31	Turkey Cakes with Ginger Gravy 40
Tarragon Whole Chicken...................................... 31	Delicious Turkey Burgers..................................... 40
Tuscan Vegetable Chicken Stew 31	Rigatoni with Turkey & Tomato Sauce............. 40
Bell Pepper & Chicken Stew 32	Sunday Turkey Lettuce Wraps........................... 40
Spicy Chicken Thighs 32	Homemade Turkey Pepperoni Pizza................. 41
Sage Chicken in Orange Gravy 32	Turkish-Style Roasted Turkey 41
Easy Italian Chicken Stew with Potatoes......... 32	Spicy Turkey Casserole with Tomatoes 41
Spiced Chicken Thighs with Garlic 32	Cranberry Turkey with Hazelnuts...................... 41
Chimichurri Chicken 32	Parsley & Lemon Turkey Risotto 41
Quick Swiss Chard & Chicken Stew 33	Sage Turkey & Red Wine Casserole 41
Easy Primavera Chicken Stew 33	Spicy Ground Turkey Chili with Vegetables ... 42
Dijon Mustard Chicken Breast 33	Turkey & Black Bean Chili 42
Festive Chicken with Bacon 33	Turkey Stew with Salsa Verde 42
Country Chicken with Vegetables...................... 33	Potato Skins with Shredded Turkey 42
Saucy Chicken Marsala 33	Turkey Soup with Noodle 42
Garlic Chicken 33	Caribbean Turkey Wings 43
Herby Chicken with Peach Gravy 34	Turkey Meatball Soup with Rice 43
Chicken Wings in Yogurt-Garlic Sauce 34	Hungarian-Style Turkey Stew 43
Spinach Chicken Thighs.. 34	Buffalo Turkey Chili... 43
Thai Chicken 34	Turkey Sausage with Brussels Sprouts 43
Chicken Fricassee 34	Potato & Cauliflower Turkey Soup.................... 44
Spring Onion Buffalo Wings................................ 34	North African Turkey Stew................................. 44
Curried Chicken with Mushrooms 35	Weekend Turkey with Vegetables..................... 44
Chili & Lemon Chicken Wings 35	Turkey with Rice & Peas 44
Sticky Chicken Wings.. 35	Mediterranean Duck with Olives 44
Korean-Style Chicken.. 35	Honey-Glazed Turkey... 44
Chicken & Pepper Cacciatore 35	Roast Goose with White Wine............................ 45
Spicy Honey Chicken... 35	Duck Breasts with Honey-Mustard Glaze........ 45
Chicken & Tomato Curry 36	**PORK 46**
Creamy Mascarpone Chicken 36	Christmas Ham with Honey-Mustard Glaze ... 46
Greek Chicken with Potatoes & Okra 36	Saucy Baby Back Ribs 46
Harissa Chicken Thighs... 36	Steamed Red Cabbage with Crispy Bacon....... 46
Filipino-Style Chicken Congee 36	Rice Chowder with Bacon & Green Peas.......... 46
Famous Chicken Adobo 36	Caribean-Style Pork with Mango Sauce 46
Jamaican Chicken with Pineapple Sauce 36	Pork Chops with Brussels Sprouts 46
Buffalo Chicken with Blue Cheese Sauce 37	Pork Tenderloin with Balsamic & Butter 47
Homemade Chicken Puttanesca........................ 37	Spiced Pork with Orange & Cinnamon 47
Sweet & Spicy BBQ Chicken 37	Pork Loin with Apples & Rutabaga 47
Fennel Chicken with Tomato Sauce.................. 37	Pork Loin with Pineapple Sauce......................... 47
Chicken Gumbo 37	Pork Carnitas Wraps with Lime & Cilantro 47
Sticky Teriyaki Chicken... 37	Pork Shoulder with Honey & Ginger 48
Za'atar Chicken with Baby Potatoes 38	Pork Chops on Puréed Butternut Squash........ 48
Indian-Style Chicken 38	Pulled Pork with Homemade BBQ Sauce........ 48
Chicken with Chili & Lime.................................... 38	Spicy Garlic Pork.. 48

Spring Onion & Pork Egg Casserole 48	Juicy Pork Butt Steaks 57
Maple Pork Carnitas 49	Japanese-Style Pork Tenderloin 57
Tasty Buckwheat & Pork Stew 49	Pork Medallions with Porcini Sauce 58
Sweet & Spicy Pulled Pork 49	Fennel & Rosemary Pork Belly 58
Garlic Pork Meatloaf with Ketchup Glaze 49	Spicy Pork Sausage Ragu 58
Wine Pork Butt with Fennel & Mushrooms ... 49	German Pork with Sauerkraut 58
Short Ribs with Wine Mushroom Sauce 49	Tandoori Pork Butt 58
Pork Chops in Cinnamon Apple Sauce 50	Prune & Shallot Pork Tenderloin 59
White Peas with Jalapeño & Bacon 50	Quick Pork & Vegetable Rice 59
Homemade Braised Pork Belly 50	Mushroom & Pork Stroganoff 59
Pancetta Kale with Chickpeas 50	Cilantro Pork with Avocado 59
Easy Pork Balls with Apple Sauce 50	Parsley Pork with Savoy Cabbage 59
Pork Meatloaf with Chili Tomato Sauce 50	Spiced Pork with Garbanzo Beans 60
Pork with Onions & Cream Sauce 51	Smoky Shredded Pork with White Beans 60
Thyme Pork Loin with Apples & Daikon 51	Pulled Pork Tacos 60
Apple Pork Chops 51	Bacon & Potato Brussels Sprouts 60
Fennel Pork Butt with Mushrooms 51	Spiced Mexican Pork 60
Vegetable Casserole with Smoked Bacon 51	Asian Pork & Noodle Soup 60
Easy Pork Fillets with Peachy Sauce 51	Awesome Pork & Celery Soup 61
Garlic Mashed Potatoes with Sausages 52	Delicious Pork & Vegetables Soup 61
Party Apple-Glazed Pork Ribs 52	Cajun Orange Pork Shoulder 61
Oregano Pork with Pears & Dijon Mustard 52	Garlic & Thyme Pork 61
Pork Tenderloin with Cherries & Apples 52	German-Style Red Cabbage with Apples 62
Tasty Cajun Pork Chops 52	Gruyere Mushroom & Mortadella Cups 62
Pork Belly with Tamari Sauce 52	Asparagus Wrapped in Parma Ham 62
Saucy Barbecue Baby Back Ribs 53	Ranch Potatoes with Ham 62
Savory Pork Chops with Brussel Sprouts 53	**BEEF & LAMB 63**
Italian Sausage & Lentil Pot 53	Beef & Jasmine Rice Porridge 63
Merlot Pork Chops 53	Butternut Squash & Beef Stew 63
Broccoli & Cauliflower Pork Sausages 53	Beef Fillets with Onions 63
Friday Night BBQ Pork Butt 53	Beef Gyros with Yogurt & Dill 63
Cajun Pork Carnitas 54	Ground Beef & Eggplant Casserole 63
Pork Chops & Mushrooms with Tomato Sauce 54	Sirloin Steaks with Red Wine 63
Garlic-Spicy Ground Pork with Peas 54	Chili Beef & Turnip Stew 64
Sweet Mustard Pork Chops with Piccalilli 54	Penne with Beef & Tomato Sauce 64
Chili-Braised Pork Chops with Tomatoes 54	Moroccan Beef & Cherry Stew 64
Chorizo with Macaroni & Cheddar Cheese 54	Traditional Turkish Dolma (Stuffed Peppers) 64
Baby Carrot & Onion Pork Chops 55	Easy Wax Beans with Ground Beef 64
Thai-Style Chili Pork 55	Pesto Beef Sandwiches with Pepperoncini 65
Sweet & Spicy Pork Ribs 55	Creamy Beef & Cauliflower Chili 65
BBQ Pork Lettuce Cups 55	Gingered Beef Pot Roast 65
Beer-Braised Pork 55	Beef Lasagna with Eggplant & Almonds 65
Hoisin Spare Pork Ribs 55	T-Bone Steaks with Basil & Mustard 65
Cinnamon BBQ Pork Ribs 56	Stewed Beef with Potatoes 65
Fruity Pork Steaks 56	Carrot Casserole with Beef & Potato 65
Pork Sirloin Chili 56	Beef Goulash with Cabbage & Potatoes 66
Awesome Herby Pork Butt with Yams 56	Beef Arancini with Potatoes 66
Best Pork Chops with BBQ Sauce & Veggies .. 56	Green Pea & Beef Ragout 66
Chorizo & Tomato Pork Chops 56	Classic Mushroom Beef Stroganoff 66
Tarragon Apple Pork Chops 56	Eggplant & Beef Stew with Parmesan 66
Paprika Pulled Pork Fajitas 56	Tasty Spicy Beef 66
Mexican Pork Chili Verde 57	Red Wine Beef & Vegetable Hotpot 67
Pear & Cider Pork Tenderloin 57	Beef Bones with Beans & Chili Pepper 67
Hot Pork Chops with Cheddar Cheese 57	Beef & Potatoes Moussaka 67

Beef with Potatoes & Mushrooms	67
Chinese Beef with Bok Choy	67
Simple Beef with Rice & Cheese	67
Fall Beef Steak with Vegetables	68
Calf's Liver Venetian-Style	68
Thyme Ground Beef Roll	68
Pino Noir Beef Pot Roast	68
Beer-Braised Beef Short Ribs	68
Maple Beef Teriyaki	68
Beef with Snow Peas	68
Italian Roast Beef	69
Classic Beef Stroganoff	69
Sambal Beef Noodles	69
Beef Tikka Masala	69
Traditional American Beef Meatloaf	69
Savory Herb Meatloaf	70
Beef Steak with Mustard Sauce	70
Thai Beef Short Ribs	70
Mediterranean Beef Stew with Olives	70
Smoky Chipotle Beef Brisket	70
Beef Ragù Bolognese	71
Leftover Beef Sandwiches	71
Rich Beef & Vegetable Casserole	71
Rosemary Braised Beef in Red Wine	71
Beef & Bean Chili	72
Garlicky Herb-Rubbed Beef Brisket	72
Beef & Lentil Stew	72
Beef & Vegetable Stew	72
Beef & Root Vegetable Pot	72
Beef & Butternut Squash Chili	73
Beef Neapolitan Ragù	73
Boeuf Bourguignon	73
Pulled BBQ Beef	73
Beef Meatballs with Tomato-Basil Sauce	73
Vietnamese Beef	74
Greek-Style Stuffed Peppers	74
Chipotle Shredded Beef	74
Veal Chops with Greek Yogurt	74
Easy Lamb & Spinach Soup	74
Roast Lamb Leg with Potatoes	75
Lamb Shanks with Garlic & Thyme	75
Lamb with Tomato & Green Peas	75
Minty Lamb	75
Hot Paprika & Oregano Lamb	75
Mediterranean Lamb	76
Quick French-Style Lamb with Sesame	76
Lamb Stew with Lemon & Parsley	76
Simple Roast Lamb	76
Traditional Lamb with Vegetables	76
Garlic Lamb with Thyme	76
Leg of Lamb with Garlic and Pancetta	76
Savory Irish Lamb Stew	77
Asian-Style Lamb Curry	77
Spicy Lamb & Bean Chili	77
Fennel Lamb Ribs	77
Lamb Chops with Mashed Potatoes	77
Vegetable & Lamb Casserole	78
Balsamic Lamb	78
Lamb Chorba	78
FISH & SEAFOOD	**79**
Pizza with Tuna & Goat Cheese	79
Tuna & Pasta Bake	79
Cheesy Tuna	79
Spicy Haddock with Beer & Potatoes	79
Haddock with Edamame Soybeans	79
Italian Steamed Sea Bream with Lemon	79
Tilapia with Basil Pesto & Rice	80
Tilapia Fillets with Hazelnut Crust	80
Lemon & Leek Tilapia	80
Thyme Sea Bass with Turnips	80
Stuffed Tench with Herbs & Lemon	80
Pollock & Tomato Stew	80
Dijon Catfish Fillets with White Wine	80
Chili Steamed Catfish	81
Mackerel with Potatoes & Spinach	81
Corn & Mackerel Chowder	81
Steamed Halibut Packets	81
Seafood & Fish Stew	81
Vietnamese Fish & Noodle Soup	81
Seafood Medley with Rosemary Rice	82
Seafood Chowder with Oyster Crackers	82
Seafood Traditional Spanish Paella	82
Easy Seafood Paella	82
Seafood Pilaf	82
Seafood Hot Pot with Rice	83
Spicy Pasta with Seafood	83
Creole Seafood Gumbo	83
Shrimp with Chickpeas & Olives	83
Shrimp Boil with Chorizo Sausages	83
Party Shrimp with & Rice Veggies	83
Quick Shrimp Gumbo with Sausage	84
Hot Shrimp & Potato Chowder	84
Shrimp with Okra & Brussels Sprouts	84
Spinach & Shrimp Fusilli	84
Jalapeño Shrimp with Herbs & Lemon	84
Creole Shrimp with Okra	84
Rich Shrimp Risotto	85
Tangy Shrimp Curry	85
Chinese Shrimp with Green Beans	85
Cheesy Shrimp Scampi	85
Indian Prawn Curry	85
Butter & Wine Lobster Tails	86
Ginger & Garlic Crab	86
Herby Crab Legs with Lemon	86
Black Squid Ink Tagliatelle	86
Crab Pilaf with Broccoli & Asparagus	86
Red Wine Squid	86
White Wine Marinated Squid Rings	86

Mussels With Lemon & White Wine	87
Chili Squid	87
Spicy Mussels & Anchovies with Rice	87
Beer-Steamed Mussels	87
Basil Clams with Garlic & White Wine	87
Saucy Clams with Herbs	87
Clam & Corn Chowder	88
Lime & Honey Scallops	88
Octopus & Shrimp with Collard Greens	88
Galician-Style Octopus	88
White Wine Oysters	88

PASTA & RICE 89

Spinach & Anchovy Fusilli	89
Bean Pasta with Vegetables	89
Tomato & Mushroom Rotini	89
Sicilian Seafood Linguine	89
Spicy Rice Noodles with Tofu & Chives	89
Beef Garam Masala with Rice	89
Spinach, Garlic & Mushroom Pilaf	90
Salmon & Tomato Farfalle	90
Vegetarian Wild Rice with Carrots	90
Risotto with Spring Vegetables & Shrimp	90
Stuffed Mushrooms with Rice & Cheese	90
Risotto with Broccoli & Grana Padano	91
Arugula & Wild Mushroom Risotto	91
Yummy Mexican-Style Rice & Pinto Beans	91
Butternut Squash with Rice & Feta	91
Avocado & Cherry Tomato Jasmine Rice	91
Date & Apple Risotto	91
Butternut Squash & Cheese Risotto	92
Spring Risotto	92
Arroz con Pollo	92
Chicken & Broccoli Rice	92
Hawaiian Rice	92
Lime Brown Rice	92
South American Pot	93
Honey Coconut Rice	93
Beef & Brussels Sprout Rice	93
Pork Rice Porridge	93
Broccoli & Ham Risotto	93
Button Mushroom Risotto	93
Provençal Rice	93
Vegetable Paella	94
Coconut Rice Breakfast	94
Prawn Basmati Rice	94
Pomegranate Rice with Vegetables	94
Hazelnut Brown Rice Pilaf	94
Vegetable Green Biryani	94
Wild Rice Pilaf	94
Spicy Indian Rice	95
Pilau Brown Rice	95
Rice & Red Bean Pot	95
Rice & Chicken Soup	95
One-Pot Mexican Rice	95

BEANS & GRAINS 96

Sausage & Red Bean Stew	96
Spinach & Kidney Beans	96
Navy & Pinto Bean Pot	96
Greek-Style Navy Beans	96
Simple Black Bean Soup	96
Pancetta with Garbanzo Beans	96
Chickpea & Jalapeño Chicken	96
Chickpea & Lentil Soup	97
Quinoa Bowls with Broccoli & Pesto	97
Homemade Veggie Quinoa	97
Colorful Quinoa with Red Salsa	97
Almond & Raisin Quinoa	97
Saffron Quinoa Pilaf	98
Chorizo & Veggie Quinoa	98
Cilantro & Spring Onion Quinoa	98
Chorizo & Lentil Stew	98
Easy Red Lentil Dhal with Spinach	98
Traditional Indian Lentil Soup	98
Creamed Lentils	99
Lentil & Chorizo Chili	99
Lime Bulgur with Olives	99
Bulgur Pilaf with Roasted Bell Peppers	99
Kale & Parmesan Pearl Barley	99
Pearl Barley Sloppy Joes	99
Barley & Smoked Salmon Salad	100
Tomato & Feta Pearl Barley	100
Cranberry Millet Pilaf	100
Rich Millet with Herbs & Cherry Tomatoes	100
Feta & Vegetable Faro	100
Harissa Chicken with Fruity Farro	100
Gluten-Free Porridge	100
Broccoli Couscous	101
Couscous with Lamb & Vegetables	101
Salmon & Spinach Couscous	101
Ham & Peas with Goat Cheese	101
Mom's Black-Eyed Peas with Garlic & Kale	101
Apricot Steel Cut Oats	101
Honey Oat & Pumpkin Granola	102
Kiwi Steel Cut Oatmeal	102
Southern Cheese Grits	102
Coconut Cherry Steel Cut Oats	102
Jamaican Cornmeal Porridge	102
Cheesy Polenta with Sundried Tomatoes	102
Garlic Mushroom Polenta	102

APPETIZERS & SIDE DISHES 103

Mediterranean Meatballs with Mint Sauce	103
Saucy Carrots with Crispy Bacon	103
Scrambled Eggs with Cranberries & Mint	103
Four Cheeses Party Pizza	103
Dill Marinated Gherkins	103
Steamed Leek with Parmesan Topping	103
Tomato & Mozzarella Egg Scramble	103
Beef Layer Tart with Yogurt	104

Warm Spinach Salad With Eggs & Nuts 104
Garlic & Herbed Potatoes 104
Chicken Drumsticks with Hot Sauce 104
Poached Eggs with Watercress 104
Chili Poached Eggs with Leeks 104
Egg Pancake with Spinach & Herbs 104
Old-Fashioned Apple Pie 105
Easy Camembert Cakes 105
Goat Cheese & Beef Steak Salad 105
Feta & Potato Salad 105
Healthy Kale & Egg Muffins 105
Potatoes & Tuna Salad with Pickles 105
Grandma's Egg Salad 106
Arugula Salad with Sweet Potatoes & Eggs .. 106
Authentic German Salad with Bacon 106
Delicious Broccoli & Cauliflower Salad 106
Greek-Style Pasta Salad 106

BROTHS & SAUCES 107
Authentic Neapolitan Sauce 107
Cranberry Orange Sauce 107
Herbed Squash Sauce 107
Garlic Red Bell Pepper Sauce 107
Quick Zucchini Sauce with Greek Yogurt 107
Mediterranean Tomato Sauce 107
Caprese Sauce with Goat Cheese 107
Homemade Honey Applesauce 108
Spicy Green Sauce 108

SOUPS 109
Black Bean & Corn Chicken Soup 109
Traditional Italian Vegetable Soup 109
Chipotle Pumpkin Soup 109
Spicy Tomato Soup with Rice 109
Green Immune-Boosting Soup 109
Chowder with Broccoli, Carrot & Tofu 109
Vegetarian Lentil Soup with Nachos 110
White Cabbage & Beetroot Borscht Soup 110
Chorizo Soup with Roasted Tomatoes 110
Mediterranean Carrot & Chickpea Soup 110
Chili Cream of Acorn Squash Soup 110
Cauliflower & Potato Soup with Parsley 110
Squash Soup with Yogurt & Cilantro 111
Simple Carrot & Oregano Soup 111
Garam Masala Parsnip & Red Onion Soup 111
Fall Vegetable Soup 111
Farro & Vegetable Chicken Soup 111
Chili Soup with Avocado & Corn 112
Kimchi Ramen Noodle Soup 112
Quick Mushroom-Quinoa Soup 112
Garden Vegetable Soup 112
Potato-Leek Soup with Tofu 112
Delicious Chicken & Potato Soup 112
Homemade Winter Soup 113
Potato & Broccoli Soup with Rosemary 113
Traditional Cheesy Onion Soup 113
Parsley Noodle Soup with Chicken 113
Creamy Broccoli-Gorgonzola Soup 113
Rustic Soup with Turkey Balls & Carrots 113
Vegetable Beef Soup 113
Modern Minestrone with Pancetta 114
Piri Piri Chicken Soup 114
Turmeric Butternut Squash Soup 114
Vegetarian Soup with White Beans 114
Yellow Beef Soup 114
Spicy Red Kidney Bean Soup 114
Creamy Celery & Green Pea Soup 115
Creamy Bean & Potato Soup 115
Effortless Tomato-Lentil Soup 115
Parsley Creamy Tomato Soup 115
Tasty Asparagus Soup 115
Gingery Squash & Leek Soup 115
Lentil & Carrot Soup 115
Cabbage & Pork Soup 116
Millet & Beef Soup 116
Jalapeño Chicken Soup with Tortilla Chips.. 116
Dilled Salmon Soup 116
Spicy Sweet Potato Soup 116
Quick Beef Soup 116
Pork Soup with Cabbage & Beans 117
Chicken & Potato Soup 117
Smoked Ham & Potato Soup 117
Hearty Beef Soup 117
Lentil & Pork Shank Soup 117
Ukrainian-Style Borscht 118
Chicken & Spinach Soup 118
Mom's Meatball Soup 118
Coconut Chicken Soup 118
Cilantro & Coconut Chicken Soup 118
Spring Chicken Vermicelli Soup 119
Veggie & Elbow Pasta Soup 119
Kale, Bean & Pancetta Soup 119
Navy Bean & Zucchini Soup 119
Turkish-Inspired Lentil Soup 119
Mexican Bean Soup 120
Black-Eyed Pea Soup 120
Greek-Style Fish Soup 120
Chicken & Lima Bean Soup 120
Zuppa Toscana 120
Moroccan Lentil Soup 121
Green Soup 121
Harvest Vegetable Soup with Pesto 121
Mediterranean Soup with Tortellini 121
Creamed Butternut Squash Soup 121
French Onion Soup 122
Peasant Bean Soup 122
Pea & Garbanzo Bean Soup 122
Cauliflower Cheese Soup 122
Minestrone with Fresh Herbs 122
Spicy Pumpkin Soup 122

Corn Soup with Chicken & Egg 123
Mustard Carrot Soup.. 123
Easy Veggie Soup.. 123
Cheesy & Creamy Broccoli Soup 123
Gingery Carrot Soup.. 124
Carrot & Cabbage Soup 124
Scallion Chicken & Lentil Soup 124
Tomato Shrimp Soup 124
Mustard Potato Soup with Crispy Bacon....... 124
Curried Pumpkin Soup...................................... 124
Nutmeg Broccoli Soup with Cheddar............. 125
Kielbasa Sausage Soup 125
Chorizo & Bean Soup... 125
Beet & Potato Soup 125
Vegan Tomato Soup... 125
Asian Tomato Soup.. 125
Tangy Pumpkin Soup... 126
Chicken Soup with Vegetables......................... 126
Celery & Oxtail Soup... 126
Creamy Mushroom Soup with Chicken 126
Cheesy Cauliflower Soup.................................. 126
Spicy Ground Beef Soup................................... 126
Hot Spinach Soup... 127
Asian-Style Chicken Soup................................ 127
Egg & Chicken Soup.. 127
Cheesy Chicken Soup 127
Brussel Sprout & Pork Soup............................. 127
Tamarind Beef Soup.. 127
Cashew & Tomato Soup 128
Pecorino Mushroom Soup................................ 128
Creamy Chicken & Zucchini Soup.................. 128
Quick Chicken Soup.. 128
Chicken & Noodle Soup.................................... 128
Simple Onion Cheese Soup 128

STEWS 129
Curried Sweet Potato Stew............................... 129
Vegetable & Ground Pork Stew 129
German-Style Sauerkraut & Pork Stew 129
Chicken Stew with Bacon & Cheese............... 129
Classic Goulash 129
Kale, Potato & Beef Stew 129
Pea & Beef Stew.. 130
Cauliflower Beef Stew....................................... 130
Rosemary Pork Belly Stew 130
Seafood Stew with Sausage 130
Mushroom & Spinach Chicken Stew.............. 130
Green Pork Chili 131
Cheesy Turkey Stew 131
Chicken Stew with Potatoes & Broccoli 131
Taco-Style Chicken Stew 131
One-Pot Sausages with Peppers & Onions.... 131
Cheesy Duck & Spinach Stew.......................... 131
Sausage & Cannellini Bean Stew 132
Tuscan Chicken Thighs 132

Spicy Pumpkin Curry 132
Vegetables with Veal & Pork............................ 132
Aromatic Lamb Stew 132
Flemish Beef Stew 133
Grandma's Beef & Vegetable Stew.................. 133
Chili Goose Stew.. 133
Delicious Pork & Garbanzo Bean Chili........... 133
Red Wine Pork Stew with Tomatoes.............. 134
Creamy Mushroom Chicken Stew 134
Herby Whole Chicken Stew 134
Rabbit & Veggie Stew.. 134
Thyme Chicken Pot with Cheese 134
Coconut & Cauliflower Curry.......................... 135
Pancetta & Cheese Chicken Thighs 135
Habanero Chicken Stew.................................... 135
Chinese-Style Chicken Stew with Broccoli... 135
Hot Beef Chili... 135
Delicious Thai Vegetable Stew 136
Garbanzo Stew with Onions & Tomatoes...... 136

VEGAN & VEGETARIAN................................137
Mashed Potato Balls with Tomato Sauce...... 137
Weekend Burrito Bowls.................................... 137
Plant-Based Indian Curry................................. 137
Spicy Vegetable Pilaf 137
Quick Farro with Greens & Pine Nuts 138
Quinoa with Brussels Sprouts & Broccoli..... 138
Vegetarian Green Dip.. 138
Cauliflower & Potato Curry with Cilantro 138
Parmesan Topped Vegetable Mash................. 138
Steamed Artichokes with Lime Aioli 138
Buttery Mashed Cauliflower 139
Vegetarian Chili with Lentils & Quinoa 139
Minestrone Soup with Green Vegetables...... 139
Homemade Gazpacho Soup.............................. 139
Easy Tahini Sweet Potato Mash....................... 139
Parsley Lentil Soup with Vegetables 139
Simple Cheese Spinach Dip.............................. 139
Savory Spinach with Mashed Potatoes.......... 140
Coconut Milk Yogurt with Honey 140
Tofu with Noodles & Peanuts 140
Mushroom & Gouda Cheese Pizza 140
Chickpea Stew with Onion & Tomatoes 140
One-Pot Swiss Chard & Potatoes.................... 140
Green Bean Salad with Cheese & Nuts........... 141
Power Green Soup with Lasagna Noodles ... 141
Stuffed with Rice Grape Leaves 141
Spanish-Style "Tortilla de Patatas"................. 141
Parsnip & Cauliflower Mash with Chives 141
Traditional Italian Pesto 141
Mozzarella & Eggplant Lasagna...................... 141
Mushroom & Ricotta Cheese Manicotti 142
Mixed Vegetables Medley................................. 142
Carrot & Chickpea Boil with Tomatoes 142
Amazing Vegetable Paella 142

Delicious Mushroom Goulash 142
Stuffed Peppers with Rice & Mushrooms 142
Celery & Red Bean Stew 143
Penne Pasta with Shiitake & Vegetables 143
Thyme Asparagus Soup 143
Gingery Butternut Squash Soup 143
Vegan Lentil & Quinoa Stew 143
Spinach Tagliatelle with Mushrooms 143
Pasta Orecchiette with Broccoli & Tofu 143
English Vegetable Potage 144
Spicy Split Pea Stew 144
Speedy Mac & Goat Cheese 144
Two-Cheese Carrot Sauce 144
Curly Kale Soup 144
Cauliflower Rice with Peas & Chili 144
Sweet Potato Medallions with Garlic 144
Steamed Artichokes & Green Beans 145
Stuffed Potatoes with Feta & Rosemary 145
Grandma's Asparagus with Feta & Lemon 145
Turmeric Stew with Green Peas 145
Spicy Shiitake Mushrooms with Potatoes 145
Creamy Turnips Stuffed with Cheese 145
Sautéed Spinach with Roquefort Cheese 146
Roman Stewed Beans with Tomatoes 146
Cannellini Beans with Garlic & Leeks 146
Stuffed Avocado Bake 146
Corn & Lentil Hummus with Parmesan 146
Indian Dhal with Veggies 146
Acorn Squash with Sweet Glaze 146
Vegan Sloppy Joe's 147
Sweet Polenta with Pistachios 147
Almond & Cherry Millet 147
Basil Parmesan Sauce 147
Coconut Milk Millet Pudding 147
Blueberry & Quinoa Porridge 147
Carrot & Sweet Potato Thick Soup 147
Coconut Millet Porridge 147
Cheddar Cheese Sauce with Broccoli 148
Hot Tofu Meatballs 148

DESSERTS & DRINKS 149
Vanilla Cheesecake with Cranberry Filling .. 149
Orange New York Cheesecake 149
Pie Cups with Fruit Filling 149
Homemade Lemon Cheesecake 149
Classic French Squash Tart 150
Walnut & Pumpkin Tart 150
Cottage Cheesecake with Strawberries 150
Yogurt Cheesecake with Cranberries 150
Lemon-Apricot Compote 151
Banana Chocolate Bars 151
Cherry & Chocolate Marble Cake 151
Chocolate Glazed Cake 151
Molten Chocolate Cake 151
Best Tiramisu Cheesecake 151
Catalan-Style Crème Brûlée 152
Simple Apple Cinnamon Dessert 152
Easy Lemon Cake 152
Honey Homemade Almond Milk 152
Amazing Fruity Cheesecake 152
Chocolate Quinoa Bowl 152
Simple Apple Cider with Orange Juice 153
Spiced & Warming Mulled Wine 153
Walnut & Dark Chocolate Brownies 153

APPENDIX : RECIPES INDEX 154

INTRODUCTION

Instant Pot is a magic pot which can transform a few, affordable ingredients into the most delicious dinner in the fastest and easiest way. If you are about to start using the Instant Pot that will be one of the best companion in your journey to a healthier and happier life. Even if you have a tight schedule, you can always find 5-10 minutes to prepare a bunch of ingredients and put them in the pot. You can steam the baby carrots, cook the lentils or produce the homemade yogurt from one single touch of the display. Instant Pot will make you love the world of food, so you will be more successful in sticking to your diet with way less efforts.

During the last century, the food industry provided us with too many options of tasty, but unhealthy processed foods full of artificial additives, colors, and preservatives. Long-term consumption of such products resulted in worsening health conditions of the population, so it's time to make a change. Home cooking can prevent the development of diabetes, stroke and heart failure, and it can also normalize blood pressure and cholesterol levels. Moreover, this magnificent cooking appliance can be used as a safe and effective tool for improving weight loss. If you are reading this page, it means that you have already decided to start better eating habits and you chose the one of the healthies and fastest way to prepare the food - the Instant Pot pressure cooker. I congratulate you with the right choice to change your life for the better. This book contains 1000 recipes which will help you enjoy mouthwatering and healthy meals, everyday and for any occasion for the whole family and friends.

Why The Instant Pot is Great to Have

Sometimes it's easier to buy ready-to-eat sausages in the supermarket or a quick cheesy burger at burger king. The combination of various unnatural additives, huge amounts of monosodium glutamate and sugar ruin the digestive system and affect some organs. Nothing bad will happen because of one or two "cheat meals", but repetetive consumption of processed foods over the course of months and years will affect you and your health.

The second thing you should do is to change your shopping behavior and buy fresh, organic and quality products so you can start cooking at home. I promise that you will find tons of mouthwatering recipes in this book which will excite you to cook and forget about the quick sugary snacks.

One-Touch Cooking Modes of Instant Pot

Instant Pot Pressure Cooker is your best friend in the kitchen that will help you immensely to achieve freedom in your kitchen - quickly and effortlessly. Thanks to one-touch cooking modes, the Instant Pot saves a lot of time and energy, and rewards you with tasty and nutritious meals.

- **Soup/Broth**. This pre-set method is for cooking soups or broths.
- **Meat/Stew**. This mode will be useful for stewing almost all kind of vegetables including peas, zucchini, spinach and other leafy veggies along with some juicy beef or park stew meat
- **Beans/Chili**. Lentils and beans are healthy plant-based sources of protein, so this setting will help you cook them in the fastest and hassle-free way.

- **Poultry.** Chicken and turkey should be prepared under this cooking mode. The meat will cook itself becoming tender and juicy.
- **Rice.** While rice is not considered as a part of the 20 healthiest foods, yet you can still utilize this setting for cooking quinoa or other nutritious grains.
- **Multigrain.** Wholegrains are full of the fiber, micro and macro elements, so you must add them to your everyday meals. The Instant Pot significantly reduces the cooking time of whole grains in comparison to a standard oven.
- **Porridge.** Tasty and nutritive oatmeal is a great way to start your day. This mode will help you cook the perfect breakfast.
- **Steam.** Steaming is the safest and the most effective cooking method, since it maximizes the amount of antioxidants and fiber in the food.
- **Sauté.** This mode allows stir-frying, browning or searing veggies, meat, poultry of fish.
- **Yogurt.** The best option for a homemade low-fat yogurt. When cooked at home, the yogurt is a very healthy food, without any added sugars and preservatives.
- **Pressure cook/Manual mode** - this is the most important Instant Pot setting. You can use this function for any kind of food preparation and adjust the pressure and cooking time as needed.
- **Slow cook.** The Instant Pot can also function as a Slow cooker. If you have plenty of time before a dinner, this method will help you to prepare the most delicious and tasty stews.
- **Pressure Level.** Depending on the amount of ingredients and their properties, you can adjust higher or lower pressure level to ensure the best cooking results.
- **Delay start.** You have a busy day and don't want to spend morning time in the kitchen? No problem, just prepare the ingredients, throw them in the Pot and set it to start cooking in 8h. And the dinner will be ready just in time. This function is also handy for soaking beans/grains.
- **Keep warm.** This function keeps the food warm. No need to microwave the meal anymore.

Note! Some Instant Pot models may have slightly different functions or buttons. Always check the manufacturer's manual before using any setting on your pressure cooker.

MORNING RECIPES

Honey Butternut Squash Cake Oatmeal

Serving Size: 4 | **Total Time:** 35 minutes
3 ½ cups coconut milk
1 cup steel-cut oats
8 oz butternut squash, grated
½ cup sultanas
1/3 cup honey
¾ tsp ground ginger
½ tsp salt
½ tsp orange zest
¼ tsp ground nutmeg
¼ cup walnuts, chopped
½ tsp vanilla extract
½ tsp sugar

In the cooker, mix sultanas, orange zest, ginger, milk, honey, butternut squash, salt, oats, and nutmeg. Seal the lid and cook on High Pressure for 12 minutes. Do a natural release for 10 minutes. Into the oatmeal, stir in the vanilla extract and sugar. Top with walnuts and serve.

French Cheese & Spinach Quiche

Serving Size: 5 | **Total Time:** 20 minutes
1 lb spinach, chopped
½ cup mascarpone cheese
½ cup feta cheese, shredded
3 eggs, beaten
½ cup goat cheese
3 tbsp butter
½ cup milk
1 pack (6 sheets) pie dough

In a bowl, mix spinach, eggs, mascarpone, feta and goat cheeses. Dust a clean surface with flour and unfold the pie sheets onto it. Using a rolling pin, roll the dough to fit your Instant Pot. Repeat with the other sheets. Combine milk and butter in a skillet. Bring to a boil and melt the butter completely. Remove from the heat.
Grease a baking pan with oil. Place in 2 pie sheets and brush with milk mixture. Make the first layer of spinach mixture and cover with another two pie sheets. Again, brush with butter and milk mixture, and repeat until you have used all ingredients. Pour 1 cup water into your Instant Pot and insert a trivet. Lower the pan on the trivet. Seal the lid. Cook on High Pressure for 6 minutes. Do a quick release. Place parchment paper under the pie to use it as a lifting method to remove the pie. Serve cold.

Walnut & Pumpkin Strudel

Serving Size: 8 | **Total Time:** 55 minutes
2 cups pumpkin puree
1 tsp vanilla extract
2 cups Greek yogurt
2 eggs
2 tbsp brown sugar
2 tbsp butter, softened
2 puff pastry sheets
1 cup walnuts, chopped

In a bowl, mix butter, yogurt, and vanilla until smooth. Unfold the pastry and cut each sheet into 4-inch x 7-inch pieces; brush with some beaten eggs. Place approximately 2 tbsp of pumpkin puree, sugar, and 2 tbsp of the yogurt mixture at the middle of each pastry, sprinkle with walnuts. Fold the sheets and brush with the remaining eggs.
Cut the surface with a sharp knife and gently place each strudel into an oiled baking dish. Pour 1 cup of water into the pot and insert the trivet. Place the pan on top. Seal the lid and cook for 25 minutes on High Pressure. Release the pressure naturally for about 10 minutes. Let it chill for 10 minutes. Serve.

Italian Egg Cakes

Serving Size: 4 | **Total Time:** 25 minutes
¼ cup ricotta cheese, cubed
½ cup mozzarella, shredded
1 cup chopped baby spinach
6 beaten eggs
1 chopped tomato
Salt and pepper to taste
2 tbsp basil, chopped

Pour 1 cup of water into the Instant Pot and fit in a trivet. Place spinach in small cups. Combine eggs, mozzarella cheese, ricotta cheese, tomato, salt, and pepper in a bowl. Fill 3/4 of each cup with the mixture and top with basil.
Place the cups on top of the trivet and seal the lid. Select Manual and cook for 15 minutes on High pressure. Once ready, perform a quick pressure release. Serve hot.

Smoked Salmon & Egg Muffins

Serving Size: 2 | **Total Time:** 15 minutes
4 beaten eggs
2 salmon slices, chopped
4 tbsp mozzarella, shredded
1 green onion, chopped

Beat eggs, salmon, mozzarella cheese, and onion in a bowl. Share into ramekins. Pour 1 cup of water into your Instant Pot and fit in a trivet.
Place the tins on top of the trivet and seal the lid. Select Manual and cook for 8 minutes on High pressure. Once done, let sit for 2 minutes, then perform a quick pressure release and unlock the lid. Serve immediately.

Breakfast Frittata

Serving Size: 4 | **Total Time:** 25 minutes
8 beaten eggs
1 cup cherry tomatoes, halved
1 tbsp Dijon mustard
1 cup mushrooms, chopped
Salt and pepper to taste
1 cup sharp cheddar, grated

Combine the eggs, mushrooms, mustard, salt, pepper, and ½ cup of cheddar cheese in a bowl. Pour in a greased baking pan and top with the remaining cheddar cheese and cherry tomatoes. Add 1 cup of water to your Instant Pot and fit in a trivet. Place the baking pan on the trivet.

Seal the lid. Select Manual and cook for 15 minutes on High. When ready, perform a quick pressure release and unlock the lid. Slice into wedges before serving.

Tofu Hash Brown Breakfast

Serving Size: 4 | **Total Time**: 21 minutes
1 cup tofu cubes
2 cups frozen hash browns
8 beaten eggs
1 cup shredded cheddar
¼ cup milk
Salt and pepper to taste

Set your Instant Pot to Sauté. Place in tofu and cook until browned on all sides, about 4 minutes. Add in hash brown and cook for 2 minutes. Beat eggs, cheddar cheese, milk, salt, and pepper in a bowl and pour over hash brown. Seal the lid, select Manual, and cook for 5 minutes on High. Once done, perform a quick pressure release. Cut into slices before serving.

Speedy Soft-Boiled Eggs

Serving Size: 4 | **Total Time**: 10 minutes
4 large eggs
Salt and pepper to taste

To the pressure cooker, add 1 cup of water and place a wire rack. Place eggs on it. Seal the lid, press Steam, and cook for 3 minutes on High Pressure. Do a quick release.
Allow to cool in an ice bath. Peel the eggs and season with salt and pepper before serving.

Spinach & Feta Pie with Cherry Tomatoes

Serving Size: 2 | **Total Time**: 35 minutes
4 eggs
Salt and pepper to taste
½ cup heavy cream
1 cup cherry tomatoes, halved
1 cup baby spinach
1 spring onion, chopped
¼ cup feta, crumbled
1 tbsp parsley, chopped

Grease a baking dish with cooking spray and add in the spinach and onion. In a bowl, whisk the eggs, heavy cream, salt, and pepper. Pour over the spinach and arrange the cherry tomato on top. Sprinkle with the feta.
Add a cup of water to the Instant Pot and insert a trivet. Place the dish on the trivet. Seal the lid, press Manual, and cook on High pressure for 15 minutes. Release pressure naturally for 10 minutes. Scatter parsley to serve.

Strawberry Jam

Serving Size: 6 | **Total Time**: 30 minutes
1 lb strawberries, chopped
1 cup sugar
½ lemon, juiced and zested
1 tbsp mint, chopped

Add the strawberries, sugar, lemon juice, and zest to the Instant Pot. Seal the lid, select manual, and cook for 2 minutes on High.
Release pressure naturally for 10 minutes. Open the lid and stir in chopped mint. Select Sauté and continue cooking until the jam thickens, about 10 minutes. Let to cool before serving.

Ricotta & Potato Breakfast

Serving Size: 4 | **Total Time**: 25 minutes
2 tbsp olive oil
1 lb potatoes, chopped
5 eggs, whisked
1 cup ricotta, crumbled
½ tsp dried oregano
1 tsp dried onion flakes
Salt and pepper to taste

Warm the olive oil in your Instant Pot on Sauté. Place the potatoes and cook for 3-4 minutes. Add in eggs, ricotta cheese, oregano, dried onion flakes, ¼ cup of water, salt, and pepper.
Seal the lid, select Manual, and cook for 10 minutes on High pressure.
Once ready, perform a quick pressure release and unlock the lid. Serve immediately.

Light & Fruity Yogurt

Serving Size: 12 | **Total Time**: 24hr
¼ cup Greek yogurt containing active cultures
1 lb raspberries, mashed
1 cup sugar
3 tbsp gelatin
1 tbsp fresh orange juice
8 cups milk

In a bowl, add sugar and raspberries and stir well to dissolve the sugar. Let sit for 30 minutes at room temperature. Add in orange juice and gelatin and mix well until dissolved. Remove the mixture and place in a sealable container, close, and allow to sit for 12 hrs to 24 hrs at room temperature before placing in the fridge. Refrigerate for a maximum of 2 weeks.
Into the cooker, add milk, and close the lid. The steam vent should be set to Venting then to Sealing. Select Yogurt until "Boil" is showed on display. When complete, there will be a display of "Yogurt" on the screen.
Open the lid and using a food thermometer, ensure the milk temperature is at least 185°F. Transfer the steel pot to a wire rack and allow to cool for 30 minutes until the milk has reached 110°F.
In a bowl, mix ½ cup warm milk and yogurt. Transfer the mixture into the remaining warm milk and stir without having to scrape the steel pot's bottom. Take the steel pot back to the base of the pot and seal the lid. Select Yogurt and cook for 8 hrs. Allow the yogurt to chill in a refrigerator for 1-2 hrs. Transfer the chilled yogurt to a bowl and stir in fresh raspberry jam.

Greek Yogurt with Honey & Walnuts

Serving Size: 10 | **Total Time**: 15hr
2 tbsp Greek yogurt
8 cups milk
¼ cup sugar honey
1 tsp vanilla extract
1 cup walnuts, chopped

Add the milk to your Instant Pot. Seal the lid and press Yogurt until the display shows "Boil". When the cooking cycle is over, the display will show Yogurt. Open the lid and check that milk temperature is at least 175°F. Get rid of the skin lying on the milk's surface. Let cool in an ice bath until it becomes warm to the touch.

In a bowl, mix one cup of milk and yogurt to make a smooth consistency. Mix the milk with yogurt mixture. Transfer to the pot and place on your Pressure cooker.

Seal the lid, press Yogurt, and adjust the timer to 9 hrs. Once cooking is complete, strain the yogurt into a bowl using a strainer with cheesecloth. Chill for 4 hours. Add in vanilla and honey and gently stir well. Spoon the yogurt into glass jars. Serve sprinkled with walnuts and enjoy.

EGGS & VEGETABLES

Potato & Salmon Salad
Serving Size: 6 | **Total Time:** 20 minutes
½ lb smoked salmon, chopped
6 eggs
3 lb red potatoes, cubed
2 cups mayonnaise
2 tbsp capers
1 tbsp chives, chopped
Salt and pepper to taste

Pour 1 cup of water into your Instant Pot and fit in a steamer basket. Place in the eggs and potatoes and seal the lid. Select Manual and cook for 5 minutes on High.
Once ready, perform a quick pressure release and unlock the lid. Remove the egg to a bowl with iced water and let cool for a few minutes.
In another bowl, mix cooked potatoes, mayonnaise, smoked salmon, and capers. Peel and chop the eggs and mix them in the salad bowl. Sprinkle with salt and pepper. Serve topped with chives.

Potato, Green Bean & Egg Salad
Serving Size: 4 | **Total Time:** 30 minutes
1 lb potatoes, sliced to 1 inch thick
2 tbsp toasted almonds, chopped
2 large eggs
1 lb green beans, trimmed
Salt and pepper to taste
2 tbsp olive oil
1 tbsp balsamic vinegar
2 tbsp basil, chopped

Cover the potatoes with salted water in your Instant Pot. Seal the lid, select Manual, and cook for 12 minutes on High. Once ready, perform a quick pressure release and unlock the lid. Remove cooked potatoes to a bowl and set aside. Place eggs in the cooking water and fit in a steamer basket. Place in the green beans.
Seal the lid, select Manual, and cook for 6 minutes on High. When over, perform a quick pressure release. Remove the green beans and transfer them into the potato bowl. Combine with salt, pepper, olive oil, and vinegar.
Cool and peel the eggs, then cut them in half lengthways. Top the vegetables with egg halves, almonds, and basil. Serve right away.

Broccoli & Cherry Tomato Salad
Serving Size: 4 | **Total Time:** 20 minutes
2 tbsp olive oil
1 cup mushrooms, sliced
1 tbsp soy sauce
10 oz broccoli florets
1 cup cherry tomatoes, halved
1 cup vegetable broth

Warm the olive oil in your Instant Pot on Sauté. Place the mushrooms and cook for 5 minutes. Add in soy sauce and broccoli and Sauté for 1 more minute. Stir in vegetable broth and seal the lid. Select Manual and cook for 2 minutes on High. Once ready, perform a quick pressure release and unlock the lid. Let cool for a few minutes, top with cherry tomatoes, and serve.

Carrot & Broccoli Salad with Hazelnuts
Serving Size: 4 | **Total Time:** 15 minutes
1 lb broccoli florets
2 carrots, sliced
2 green onions, sliced
1 tbsp lemon juice
1 tsp oregano
1 tsp garlic powder
2 tbsp hazelnuts, chopped
2 tbsp olive oil
Salt to taste

Pour 1 cup of water into your Instant Pot and fit in a steamer basket. Place in the broccoli and carrots and seal the lid. Select Manual and cook for 2 minutes. When done, perform a quick pressure release and unlock the lid. Remove the vegetables to iced water for a few minutes. Drain and place in a serving bowl. Add in green onions, lemon juice, oregano, garlic powder, salt, and olive oil and stir to combine. Serve topped with hazelnuts.

Broccoli & Egg Salad
Serving Size: 4 | **Total Time:** 20 minutes
1 lb small broccoli florets
4 large eggs
1 cup mayonnaise
2 tbsp parsley, chopped
¼ cup onion, chopped
1 tbsp dill pickle juice
1 tbsp yellow mustard
Salt and pepper to taste

Pour 1 cup water into your Instant Pot and fit in a trivet. Place broccoli and eggs on the trivet. Seal the lid, select Manual, and cook for 5 minutes on High. When over, perform a quick pressure release. Remove the eggs and transfer to a bowl with cold water for 2-3 minutes.
Meanwhile, mix mayonnaise, parsley, onion, dill pickle juice, and mustard in a bowl. Sprinkle with salt and pepper. Peel and slice the eggs. Place sliced egg and broccoli into mayonnaise mixture and toss to coat. Serve.

Cheesy Vegetable Medley
Serving Size: 4 | **Total Time:** 20 minutes
2 tbsp canola oil
1 red onion, sliced
1 cup broccoli florets
2 red bell peppers, sliced
2 green bell pepper, sliced
1 yellow bell peppers, sliced
2 tomatoes, chopped
Salt and pepper to taste
2 garlic cloves, minced
2 tbsp parsley, chopped
3 tbsp mozzarella, shredded

Warm the canola oil in your Instant Pot on Sauté. Place the onion and garlic and cook for 3 minutes until softened. Add in bell peppers and Sauté for 5 minutes.

Stir in tomatoes, broccoli, salt, and pepper and seal the lid. Select Manual and cook for 2 minutes on High pressure. When done, perform a quick pressure release and unlock the lid. Remove the vegetables to a bowl and top with mozzarella cheese and parsley. Serve immediately.

Zucchini & Bacon Cheese Quiche

Serving Size: 4 | Total Time: 40 minutes
4 slices cooked and crumbled bacon
1 zucchini, chopped
6 large eggs, beaten
½ cup milk
Salt and pepper to taste
1 cup diced ham
1 cup Parmesan, shredded
2 spring onions, chopped

Pour 1 cup of water into your Instant Pot and fit in a trivet. Mix eggs, milk, salt, and pepper in a bowl. Add in ham, bacon, zucchini, Parmesan cheese, and spring onions and stir. Cover with aluminum foil and place it on top of the trivet. Seal the lid, select Manual, and cook for 20 minutes on High pressure. When done, allow a natural release for 10 minutes and unlock the lid. Serve.

Asparagus & Tomato Tart

Serving Size: 4 | Total Time: 40 minutes
10 eggs
½ cup milk
Salt and pepper to taste
1 lb chopped asparagus
1 cup tomatoes, chopped
4 green onions, chopped
3 tomato slices
¼ cup Parmesan, shredded

Crack the eggs in a bowl and beat them with milk, salt, and pepper. In a separated bowl, mix asparagus, chopped tomatoes, and green onions and transfer to a baking dish. Pour the egg mixture over and toss to combine. Top with tomato slices and Parmesan cheese. Pour 1 cup of water into your Instant Pot and fit in a trivet.

Place the dish on top of the trivet and seal the lid. Select Manual and cook for 20 minutes on High pressure. Once ready, allow a natural release for 10 minutes, then perform a quick pressure release, and unlock the lid. Serve warm.

Baby Spinach & Gruyère Gratin

Serving Size: 4 | Total Time: 25 minutes
¼ cup Gruyère, grated
8 beaten eggs
Salt and pepper to taste
½ cup milk
1 cup tomato, diced
3 cups baby spinach
3 green onions, sliced
4 tomatoes, sliced

Pour 1 cup of water into your Instant Pot and fit in a trivet. Combine eggs, salt, pepper, and milk in a bowl. Place diced tomato, spinach, and green onions in a baking dish. Pour egg mixture over and top with tomato slices and Gruyère cheese. Place the dish on top of the trivet and seal the lid. Select Manual and cook for 15 minutes on High pressure. Perform a quick pressure release.

Spinach & Potato Gratin

Serving Size: 4 | Total Time: 30 minutes
2 tbsp olive oil
2 cups spinach, torn
½ yellow onion, chopped
1 lb potatoes
1 cup cheddar, shredded
Salt and pepper to taste
1 cup breadcrumbs
3 tbsp melted butter

Heat oil in your Instant Pot on Sauté. Place the onions and cook for 5 minutes; reserve. Pour 1 cup water in the pot and fit in a trivet. Place the potatoes on the trivet. Seal the lid. Select Manual and cook for 5 minutes on High.

Mix the breadcrumbs with butter. Once ready, perform a quick pressure release. Peel and slice the potatoes and transfer them to a baking sheet. Mix in the spinach. Sprinkle with cooked onion and cheddar cheese, season with salt and black pepper, and top with breadcrumb mixture. Place under a preheated broiler for about 8 minutes until crisp. Serve.

Mushroom-Potato Hash Casserole

Serving Size: 4 | Total Time: 20 minutes
1 onion, chopped
2 garlic cloves, minced
1 lb potatoes, peeled
1 cup mushrooms, sliced
Salt and pepper to taste
½ tsp paprika
½ tsp porcini powder
¼ tsp chili pepper powder

Place the potatoes in your Instant Pot and cover them with water. Seal the lid, select Manual, and cook for 5 minutes on High. Perform a quick pressure release. Unlock the lid. Remove the potatoes with a slotted spoon, then shred them with a cheese grater into a bowl.

Add in the mushrooms, garlic, onion, paprika, porcini powder, chili pepper powder, salt, and pepper and stir to combine. Transfer the mixture to a greased baking dish. Insert a trivet in the pot over the potato water and place the dish on the trivet. Seal the lid, select Manual, and cook for 7 minutes. Perform a quick pressure release.

Baby Spinach with Beets & Cheese

Serving Size: 4 | Total Time: 32 minutes
2 medium beets
Salt and pepper to taste
¼ cup Goat cheese, crumbled
2 cups baby spinach
1 tbsp apple cider vinegar

¼ tsp brown sugar
2 tbsp extra-virgin olive oil
2 tbsp walnuts, chopped

Pour 1 cup of water into your Instant Pot and fit in a steamer basket. Place in the beets and seal the lid. Select Manual and cook for 12 minutes on High pressure. When over, allow a natural release for 10 minutes, then perform a quick pressure release, and unlock the lid.

Remove the beets to a bowl and let cool. Peel and slice them into wedges. In a bowl, beat the apple cider vinegar, brown sugar, olive oil, salt, and pepper. Place the spinach, beets, and goat cheese in a serving bowl. Drizzle the dressing all over and toss lightly to coat. Sprinkle with walnuts and serve.

Potatoes with Creamy Arugula Sauce

Serving Size: 4 | **Total Time:** 30 minutes
2 lb potatoes, peeled, halved
1 garlic clove, chopped
1 tbsp pine nuts, toasted
1 cup arugula
1 tbsp basil, chopped
¼ cup extra-virgin olive oil
2 tbsp Parmesan, grated
2 tbsp heavy cream

Pour 1 cup water into your Instant Pot and fit in a trivet. Place the potatoes on the trivet and seal the lid. Select Manual and cook for 10 minutes on High. When over, allow a natural release for 10 minutes. Remove to a bowl.

Add garlic, pine nuts, arugula, and basil to a food processor and pulse until smooth. While the food processor is running, gradually pour the olive. Mix in the Parmesan cheese and heavy cream; adjust the seasonings. Pour the arugula sauce over the potatoes and serve.

Cheesy Potatoes with Herbs

Serving Size: 4 | **Total Time:** 30 minutes
½ cup Pecorino Romano cheese, shredded
2 tbsp butter
1 lb potatoes, cubed
1 cup chicken broth
½ tsp rosemary
½ tsp thyme
½ tsp basil
½ tsp cayenne pepper
Salt to taste

Melt the butter in your Instant Pot on Sauté. Place the potatoes and cook for 5 minutes. Add in chicken broth, rosemary, thyme, and basil and seal the lid. Select Manual and cook for 5 minutes on High. Once over, allow a natural release for 10 minutes and unlock the lid. Sprinkle with salt and cayenne pepper and transfer to a plate. Scatter Romano cheese over and serve.

Dill Potatoes with Butter & Olives

Serving Size: 4 | **Total Time:** 40 minutes
1 lb potatoes, chopped
2 tbsp butter
2 tbsp dill, chopped
1 tsp sea salt flakes
3 tbsp sliced Kalamata olives

Cover the potatoes with enough water in your Instant Pot and seal the lid. Select Manual and cook for 12 minutes on High pressure. Once over, allow a natural release for 10 minutes, then perform a quick pressure release, and unlock the lid. Drain potatoes and leave them to dry.

Press Sauté and melt the butter. Put the dried potatoes back and cook for 3-4 minutes until lightly browned. Remove to a serving bowl and add in Kalamata olives; toss to combine. Sprinkle with dill and salt and serve.

Feta & Onion Layered Potatoes

Serving Size: 4 | **Total Time:** 30 minutes
1 tbsp butter, melted
1 lb potatoes, sliced
½ tsp garlic powder
½ lb onions, finely sliced
1 cup feta cheese, grated
Salt and pepper to taste
2 tbsp scallions, chopped

Pour 1 cup of water into your Instant Pot and fit in a trivet. Add a layer of potatoes on a greased baking pan, sprinkle with salt and pepper, then add onions and half of the feta cheese. Top with another layer of potatoes and finish with the remaining feta cheese. Sprinkle with garlic powder and drizzle melted butter all over.

Cover with aluminum foil and lower the pan onto the trivet. Seal the lid, select Manual, and cook for 20 minutes on High. When done, perform a quick pressure release and unlock the lid. Garnish with scallions and serve.

Crushed Potatoes with Aioli

Serving Size: 4 | **Total Time:** 25 minutes
1 lb Russet potatoes, pierced
Salt and pepper to taste
2 tbsp olive oil
4 tbsp mayonnaise
1 tsp garlic paste
1 tbsp lemon juice

Mix the olive oil, salt, and pepper in a bowl. Add in the potatoes and toss to coat. Pour 1 cup of water into your Instant Pot and fit in a trivet. Place the potatoes on the trivet and seal the lid. Select Manual and cook for 12 minutes on High. Once ready, perform a quick release.

In a small bowl, combine the mayonnaise, garlic paste, and lemon juice and whisk well. Peel and crush the potatoes and transfer to a serving bowl. Serve with aioli.

Rosemary Sweet Potatoes with Butter

Serving Size: 4 | **Total Time:** 25 minutes
2 tbsp olive oil
1 tbsp butter, melted
2 lb sweet potatoes, halved
Salt and pepper to taste
½ tsp rosemary

Warm the olive oil in your Instant Pot on Sauté. Place the sweet potatoes and cook for 10 minutes until golden brown. Sprinkle with salt and pepper. Pour in ¼ cup of water and seal the lid. Select Manual and cook for 6 minutes on High pressure. Once over, allow a natural release for 10 minutes, then perform a quick pressure release, and unlock the lid. Adjust the seasonings. Garnish with butter and rosemary and serve warm.

Parsley New Potatoes with Radishes

Serving Size: 4 | **Total Time:** 30 minutes
3 tbsp olive oil
2 lb baby potatoes, washed
2 oz radishes, sliced
2 tbsp parsley, chopped
Salt and pepper to taste
½ cup chicken broth

Warm the olive oil in your Instant Pot on Sauté. Place the potatoes and cook for 6-7 minutes. Make some holes with a fork. Season with salt and pepper. Pour in chicken broth and seal the lid.
Select Manual and cook for 10 minutes on High pressure. When done, perform a quick pressure release and unlock the lid. Remove the potatoes to a serving plate and scatter with radishes and parsley to serve.

Chive & Truffle Potato Mash

Serving Size: 4 | **Total Time:** 35 minutes
1 lb potatoes, quartered
½ cup milk
2 tbsp truffle oil
Salt and pepper to taste
2 tbsp chives, chopped

Pour 1 cup of water into your Instant Pot and fit in a trivet. Place the potatoes on the trivet and seal the lid. Select Manual and cook for 15 minutes on High pressure.
Once over, allow a natural release for 10 minutes, then perform a quick pressure release, and unlock the lid. Remove potatoes to a bowl and mash them until smooth. Stir in milk and truffle oil; season with salt and pepper. Sprinkle with chives and serve.

Potato & Carrot Puree

Serving Size: 4 | **Total Time:** 20 minutes
1 lb potatoes, cubed
2 carrots, chopped
Salt and pepper to taste
½ cup buttermilk
2 tbsp butter, melted

Pour 1 cups of water in your Instant Pot and fit in a trivet. Place the potatoes and carrots on the trivet. Seal the lid. Select Manual and cook for 12 minutes on High.
Once ready, perform a quick pressure release. Remove potatoes and carrots to a bowl and sprinkle with salt and pepper. Add in buttermilk and butter and mash them using a potato masher until smooth. Serve.

Chipotle & Garlic Mashed Potatoes

Serving Size: 4 | **Total Time:** 25 minutes
1 lb potatoes, cubed
2 garlic cloves
1 tbsp chipotle paste
1 cup chicken broth
¼ cup milk
1 tbsp butter
1 tbsp chili oil
Salt to taste

Place the potatoes, garlic, and chicken broth in your Instant Pot and seal the lid. Select Manual and cook for 15 minutes on High pressure. When done, perform a quick pressure release and unlock the lid. Drain potatoes and transfer to a bowl. Add in milk, chipotle paste, chili oil, and butter and mash them using a potato masher until smooth. Sprinkle with salt. Serve.

Pumpkin & Potato Mash

Serving Size: 4 | **Total Time:** 20 minutes
½ lb pumpkin, cubed
½ lb sweet potatoes, cubed
2 garlic cloves
¼ tsp dried tarragon
¼ tsp dried sage
½ cup milk
2 tbsp butter
½ cup Parmesan, grated

Pour 1 cup of water into your Instant Pot and fit in a steamer basket. Place the pumpkin, sweet potatoes, and garlic in the steamer basket and seal the lid. Select Manual and cook for 12 minutes on High pressure.
Once ready, perform a quick pressure release and unlock the lid. Remove the veggies to a bowl. Stir in tarragon and sage. Pour in milk and butter and them using a potato masher until smooth; adjust the seasonings. Sprinkle with Parmesan cheese and serve.

Creamy Potatoes

Serving Size: 4 | **Total Time:** 25 minutes
6 potatoes, sliced
1 tsp scallions
2 tbsp butter
1 cup chicken broth
¼ cup buttermilk
¼ cup milk
2 tbsp potato starch
¼ tsp cayenne pepper

Place the potatoes and broth in your Instant Pot and seal the lid. Select Manual and cook for 5 minutes on High. Once ready, perform a quick pressure release and unlock the lid. Remove potatoes to a greased baking sheet.
Select Sauté on the pot and mix in the remaining cooking liquid with buttermilk, butter, milk, scallions, and potato starch and cook for 2-3 minutes until the sauce thickens. Pour it over the potatoes and place under the broiler for about 4 minutes. Sprinkle with cayenne pepper and serve.

Chili Coconut Potatoes

Serving Size: 4 | **Total Time:** 20 minutes

1 lb new potatoes
½ tsp mustard seeds
2 garlic cloves, diced
3 tbsp coconut oil, melted
1 red chili pepper flakes
Salt and pepper to taste

Pour 1 cup of water into your Instant Pot and fit in a trivet. Place the potatoes in a baking pan with garlic, mustard seeds, coconut oil, salt, and pepper; stir to combine. Lower the pan onto the trivet. Seal the lid, select Manual.

Cook for 4 minutes on High. When done, let sit for 5 minutes, then perform a quick pressure release and unlock the lid. Remove the potatoes to a bowl. Sprinkle with red chili pepper flakes and serve.

Mediterreanean Asparagus

Serving Size: 4 | **Total Time**: 15 minutes
1 lb asparagus, trimmed
3 tbsp butter, melted
2 garlic cloves, chopped
Salt and pepper to taste
3 tbsp feta cheese, crumbled
2 tsp parsley, chopped
¼ tsp red pepper flakes

Pour 1 cup of water into your Instant Pot and fit in a trivet. Place the asparagus on a foil and brush with butter, garlic, salt, and pepper.
Fold up the sides of the foil to seal asparagus. Place the asparagus on the trivet and seal the lid. Select Manual and cook for 4 minutes on High.
Once ready, perform a quick pressure release and unlock the lid. Remove the asparagus from the foil and arrange them on a serving platter. Scatter with feta cheese, red pepper flakes, and parsley and serve.

Thyme & Garlic Potatoes

Serving Size: 4 | **Total Time**: 30 minutes
3 tbsp canola oil
2 garlic cloves
2 lb baby potatoes
1 thyme spring
½ cup stock
Salt and pepper to taste
2 tbsp toasted almonds, chopped

Warm the canola oil in your Instant Pot on Sauté. Place the garlic, potatoes, and thyme and Sauté for 10 minutes, stirring occasionally. Stir in stock, salt, and pepper and seal the lid. Select Manual and cook for 7 minutes on High pressure. Once ready, perform a quick pressure release and unlock the lid. Serve topped with almonds.

Rosemary Potato Fries

Serving Size: 4 | **Total Time**: 15 minutes
1 lb potatoes, cut into ½ inch sticks
Sea salt to taste
4 tbsp olive oil
2 tbsp rosemary, chopped

Place 1 cup of water in your Instant Pot and fit in a steamer basket. Place the potatoes in the basket and seal the lid. Select Manual and cook for 3 minutes on High.
Once ready, perform a quick pressure release. Unlock the lid. Remove potatoes to a bowl and pat them dry. Discard the water and dry the pot. Warm the olive oil in the pot on Sauté. Place the potato sticks and cook until golden brown. Sprinkle with salt and rosemary to serve.

Sumac Red Potatoes

Serving Size: 4 | **Total Time**: 16 minutes
2 tbsp butter
1 lb red potatoes wedges
2 tbsp sumac
Salt and pepper to taste

Melt the butter in your Instant Pot on Sauté. Mix the potatoes, sumac, and ½ cup of water and seal the lid. Select Manual and cook for 6 minutes on High pressure. Once ready, perform a quick pressure release and unlock the lid. Sprinkle with salt and pepper. Serve immediately.

Steamed Sweet Potatoes with Cilantro

Serving Size: 4 | **Total Time**: 20 minutes
2 tbsp butter, melted
1 lb sweet potatoes, scrubbed
2 tbsp cilantro, chopped

Pour 1 cup water into your Instant Pot and fit in a trivet. Place the potatoes on the trivet. Seal the lid, select Manual, and cook for 12 minutes on High. When done, perform a quick pressure release and unlock the lid. Drizzle with melted butter and sprinkle with cilantro to serve.

Cheesy Jalapeño Sweet Potatoes

Serving Size: 4 | **Total Time**: 35 minutes
1 lb sweet potatoes, sliced
2 tbsp olive oil
Salt to taste
1 jalapeño pepper, sliced

Pour 1 cup of water into your Instant Pot and fit in a steamer basket. Place in the sweet potatoes and seal the lid. Select Manual and cook for 15 minutes on High.
Once ready, perform a quick pressure release and unlock the lid. Warm the olive oil in the pot on Sauté. Add in sweet potatoes and Sauté for 3-5 minutes. Sprinkle salt and pepper. Serve scattered with jalapeño slices.

Nutty Potatoes

Serving Size: 4 | **Total Time**: 20 minutes
1 tbsp lemon zest
Sea salt to taste
1 lb baby potatoes
¼ cup butter
¼ cup honey
1 tbsp cornstarch
1 cup mixed nuts, chopped

Mix the potatoes, lemon zest, salt, and 2 cups of of water in your Instant Pot and seal the lid. Select Manual and cook for 10 minutes on High pressure. When done, perform a quick pressure release and unlock the lid. Remove potatoes to a bowl. Melt the butter in the pot on Sauté. Stir in honey, cornstarch, and mixed nuts and cook for 2 minutes. Top the potatoes with sauce to serve.

Hazelnut Brussels Sprouts with Parmesan
Serving Size: 4 | **Total Time:** 15 minutes
1 lb Brussels sprouts, halved
2 tbsp butter
2 garlic cloves, minced
¼ cup hazelnuts, chopped
½ tsp thyme
¼ cup grated Parmesan cheese
Salt and pepper to taste

Pour 1 cup of water into your Instant Pot and fit in a steamer basket. Place in the sprouts halves and seal the lid. Select Manual and cook for 3 minutes on High. Once ready, perform a quick pressure release. Unlock the lid. Clean the pot and melt the butter on Sauté. Add in Brussels sprouts and garlic and Sauté for 2-3 minutes, stirring occasionally. Season with salt, pepper, and thyme and mix in hazelnuts. Serve topped with Parmesan cheese.

Butternut Squash & Kale Pot
Serving Size: 4 | **Total Time:** 25 minutes
2 tbsp olive oil
1 onion, diced
2 garlic cloves, minced
1 tsp cumin seeds
1 tsp coriander seeds
½ tsp hot paprika
1 cup canned white beans
1 lb butternut squash, cubed
1 cup canned diced tomatoes
3 cups vegetable stock
3 cups kale, chopped

Warm olive oil in your Instant Pot on Sauté. Add in the onion, garlic, cumin and coriander seeds and Sauté for 3 minutes until tender. Stir in paprika, butternut squash, tomatoes, white beans, and vegetable stock and seal the lid. Select Manual and cook for 10 minutes on High.
When done, perform a quick pressure release and unlock the lid. Adjust the seasonings. Stir in kale and close the lid. Let it sit in the residual heat until the kale wilts. Serve.

Spicy Cauliflower Cakes
Serving Size: 4 | **Total Time:** 20 minutes
1 cauliflower head, chopped
1 cup panko breadcrumbs
1 cup Parmesan, shredded
Salt and pepper to taste
½ tsp cayenne pepper
2 tbsp olive oil

Pour 1 cup of water into your Instant Pot and fit in a steamer basket. Place in the cauliflower and seal the lid. Select Manual and cook for 3 minutes on High pressure.
Once ready, perform a quick pressure release and unlock the lid. Mash the cauliflower with a fork in a bowl. Add in breadcrumbs, Parmesan cheese, cayenne pepper, salt, and black pepper and mix to combine. Form the meat mixture into patties. Clean the pot and warm the olive oil on Sauté. Fry the cakes for 4-5 minutes, flipping once until golden brown. Serve warm.

Steamed Vegetables with Chile Butter
Serving Size: 4 | **Total Time:** 10 minutes
10 oz broccoli florets
2 red bell peppers, sliced
2 garlic cloves, minced
1 tbsp Italian seasoning
Salt to taste
2 tbsp butter
1 serrano chile, minced

Pour 1 cup of water into your Instant Pot and fit in a steamer basket. Place in the broccoli and bell peppers. Sprinkle with Italian seasoning. Seal the lid. Cook for 1 minute on Steam. When done, perform a quick release.
Clean the pot and melt in the butter on Sauté. Add in serrano chile, garlic, and salt and stir-fry for 1-2 minutes. Drizzle the chile butter over the veggies and serve.

Steamed Cauliflower with Cheese
Serving Size: 4 | **Total Time:** 10 minutes
1 lb cauliflower florets
Salt and pepper to taste
1 cup shredded cheddar

Pour 1 cup water into your Instant Pot and fit in a steamer basket. Place in the cauliflower and seal the lid. Select Manual and cook for 2 minutes on Steam. When done, perform a quick pressure release. Sprinkle the cauliflower with salt and pepper. Top with cheese to serve.

Italian-Style Brussels Sprouts
Serving Size: 4 | **Total Time:** 15 minutes
1 lb Brussels sprouts, halved
2 garlic cloves, minced
1 tbsp mustard seeds
1 cup vegetable broth
Salt and pepper to taste
1 tsp olive oil
2 tbsp rosemary, chopped

Heat the olive oil in your Instant Pot and on Sauté. Cook Brussels sprouts, garlic, and mustard seeds for 2 minutes, stirring often. Pour in vegetable broth, salt, and pepper and seal the lid. Select Manual and cook for 4 minutes on High pressure. When done, perform a quick pressure release and unlock the lid. Serve topped with rosemary.

Brussels Sprouts with Cranberries
Serving Size: 4 | **Total Time:** 20 minutes
1 lb Brussels sprouts, halved
Salt and pepper to taste
¼ cup pine nuts, toasted
2 tbsp dried cranberries
1 tbsp apple cider
½ tsp brown sugar
2 tbsp olive oil

Pour 1 cup of water into your Instant Pot and fit in a steamer basket. Place in the Brussels sprouts and

seal the lid. Select Manual and cook for 4 minutes on High.
Once ready, perform a quick pressure release and unlock the lid. Remove the sprouts to a bowl. Clean the pot and heat in the olive oil. Add in the dried cranberries, apple cider, and brown sugar and cook for 1 minute. Stir in Brussels sprouts and fry for another 2-3 minutes. Sprinkle with salt, pepper, and pine nuts and serve.

Chili Corn On the Cob
Serving Size: 4 | **Total Time:** 10 minutes
4 ears corn on the cob, husked
1 Poblano chili pepper, chopped
4 tbsp butter, softened
2 tbsp parsley, chopped
Pour 1 cup of water into your Instant Pot and fit in a trivet. Mix the chili pepper, parsley, and butter in a blender until smooth. Rub the mixture all over the corn and place on the trivet. Seal the lid, select Manual, and cook for 2 minutes on High pressure. Serve right away.

Provençal Ratatouille
Serving Size: 4 | **Total Time:** 20 minutes
2 tbsp olive oil
1 red onion, sliced
2 garlic cloves, minced
2 eggplants, sliced
3 zucchini, sliced
½ fennel bulb, sliced
2 red bell peppers, sliced
1 cup vegetable broth
14 oz canned tomatoes, diced
½ tbsp herbs de Provence
Warm the olive oil in your Instant Pot on Sauté. Place the onion, garlic, eggplants, zucchini, fennel, and bell peppers and cook for 3-4 minutes. Stir in tomatoes, vegetable broth, and herbs de Provence and seal the lid. Select Manual and cook for 5 minutes on High pressure. When done, perform a quick pressure release. Serve.

Cauliflower & Kale Curry
Serving Size: 4 | **Total Time:** 10 minutes
1 lb cauliflower florets
1 can coconut milk
½ tsp fresh ginger, grated
1 lb kale, chopped
2 tsp garam masala
1 cup tomato sauce
1 cup vegetable broth
Salt and pepper to taste
Mix the cauliflower, coconut milk, kale, garam masala, tomato sauce, ginger, broth, salt, and pepper in your Instant Pot. Seal the lid, select Manual, and cook for 4 minutes on High pressure. When done, perform a quick pressure release and unlock the lid. Serve immediately.

Parsnip & Cauliflower Mash
Serving Size: 4 | **Total Time:** 15 minutes
1 cauliflower, cut into florets
2 parsnips, chopped
Salt and pepper to taste
2 tbsp safflower oil
1 green onion, chopped
Pour 1 cup water into your Instant Pot and fit in a steamer basket. Place in the cauliflower and parsnips and seal the lid. Select Manual and cook for 3 minutes on High.
Once over, perform a quick pressure release and unlock the lid. Mash the cauliflower and parsnips with a potato masher and mix in salt, pepper, and safflower oil. Serve topped with green onion.

Fall Vegetable Mash
Serving Size: 4 | **Total Time:** 25 minutes
1 lb pumpkin, cubed
¼ lb celeriac, cubed
1 parsnip, cubed
2 potatoes, cubed
½ tsp dried thyme
½ tsp dried rosemary
2 tbsp butter
1 tsp garlic powder
¼ cup milk
Salt to taste
Pour 1 cup of water into your Instant Pot and fit in a steamer basket. Place in pumpkin, celeriac, parsnip, and potatoes and seal the lid. Select Manual and cook for 12 minutes on High. Once ready, perform a quick pressure release and unlock the lid. Transfer the vegetable to a bowl and mash them with a potato mash. Mix in milk, butter, garlic powder, rosemary, thyme, and salt. Serve.

Zucchini with Asparagus
Serving Size: 4 | **Total Time:** 15 minutes
1 lb asparagus, trimmed and chopped
2 tbsp olive oil
2 garlic cloves, minced
2 zucchinis, sliced
½ cup whipping cream
½ cup vegetable broth
Salt and pepper to taste
2 tbsp fresh dill, chopped
Warm the olive oil in your Instant Pot on Sauté. Place the garlic and cook for 2 minutes. Stir in zucchinis, asparagus, vegetable broth, salt, and pepper. Seal the lid, select Manual, and cook for 4 minutes on High pressure. When done, perform a quick pressure release and unlock the lid. Stir in whipping cream. Serve topped with dill.

Mango & Pumpkin Porridge
Serving Size: 4 | **Total Time:** 20 minutes
1 lb pumpkin, chopped
1 mango, chopped
1 cup milk
2 tbsp cinnamon powder
2 tbsp maple syrup
2 tbsp walnuts, chopped
A pinch of salt
Mix the pumpkin, mango, cinnamon powder, maple syrup, milk, and salt in your Instant Pot. Seal the lid,

select Manual, and cook for 12 minutes on High pressure. Once ready, perform a quick pressure release and unlock the lid. Serve topped with walnuts.

Steamed Asparagus with Salsa Verde

Serving Size: 4 | **Total Time**: 15 minutes
1 lb asparagus, trimmed
1 tbsp onion, chopped
Salt and pepper to taste
2 tbsp parsley, chopped
4 anchovy fillets, chopped
2 tbsp extra-virgin olive oil
1 tbsp sherry vinegar
2 tsp capers, chopped

Pour 1 cup of water into your Instant Pot and fit in a trivet. Place the asparagus on the trivet. Season with salt and pepper. Seal the lid and cook for 2 minutes on Steam. Once ready, perform a quick pressure release. Add parsley, onion, sherry vinegar, olive oil, anchovies, and capers in a blender and process until everything is well mixed. Drizzle the asparagus with the sauce.

Steamed Artichokes with Salsa Roquefort

Serving Size: 4 | **Total Time**: 25 minutes
1 lb artichokes, trimmed
1 lemon wedge
½ cup Roquefort cheese
1 cup heavy cream

Pour 1 cup of water into your Instant Pot and fit in a steamer basket. Place in artichokes and seal the lid. Select Manual and cook for 10 minutes on High pressure.
When over, perform a quick pressure release. Remove artichokes to a plate to cool. Clean the pot and heat the heavy cream on Sauté. Add in the Roquefort cheese and stir constantly until the cheese melts, about 3-4 minutes. Pour the sauce over the artichokes and serve with lemon.

Coconut Pumpkin Chili

Serving Size: 4 | **Total Time**: 20 minutes
½ lb pumpkin, chopped
2 cups tomatoes, diced
1 cup coconut milk
1 tsp red chili flakes
1 tbsp red curry paste
1 tsp cumin
1 tbsp chili powder
Salt and pepper to taste
2 tbsp cilantro, chopped

Mix the pumpkin, tomatoes, cumin, coconut milk, chili powder, curry paste, salt, pepper, and 2 cups of water in your Instant Pot and seal the lid. Select Manual and cook for 10 minutes on High pressure. Once ready, perform a quick pressure release and unlock the lid. Top with red chili flakes and cilantro and serve.

Mascarpone Mashed Turnips

Serving Size: 4 | **Total Time**: 32 minutes
1 lb turnips, cubed
1 onion, chopped
½ tsp ground nutmeg
½ cup chicken stock
Salt and pepper to taste
¼ cup sour cream
2 tbsp mascarpone

Place the turnips, onion, and chicken stock in your Instant Pot and seal the lid. Select Manual and cook for 12 minutes on High. Once over, allow a natural release for 10 minutes and unlock the lid. Add in sour cream, nutmeg, and mascarpone and mash it using a potato masher until smooth. Sprinkle with salt and pepper.

Tarragon Baby Carrots with Parsnips

Serving Size: 4 | **Total Time**: 25 minutes
1 tbsp olive oil
1 small onion, chopped
½ lb baby carrots, sliced
2 parsnips, sliced
1 tsp ground cumin
1 tsp lemon juice
Salt and pepper to taste
2 tbsp tarragon, chopped

Warm the olive oil in your Instant Pot on Sauté. Place the onion and cook for 3 minutes. Add in baby carrots, parsnips, cumin, and lemon juice and sauté for 1 more minute; season with salt and pepper. Add in 1 cup of water and seal the lid. Select Manual and cook for 7 minutes on High pressure. When done, perform a quick pressure release and unlock the lid. Serve topped with tarragon.

Carrot & Beet Medley

Serving Size: 4 | **Total Time**: 20 minutes
2 tbsp olive oil
2 shallots, chopped
1 lb carrots, sliced
2 beets, peeled and cubed
1 cup vegetable broth
1 tbsp caraway seeds
Salt and pepper to taste

Warm the olive oil in your Instant Pot on Sauté. Place the shallots and cook for 3 minutes. Stir in caraway seeds, carrots, beets, vegetable broth, salt, and pepper. Seal the lid, select Manual, and cook for 8 minutes on High pressure. Once ready, perform a quick pressure release and unlock the lid. Serve warm.

Orange Glazed Carrots

Serving Size: 4 | **Total Time**: 25 minutes
1 tbsp butter
6 carrots, sliced diagonally
¼ tsp orange zest
½ cup orange juice
1 tbsp orange marmalade
Salt and black pepper to taste

Pour 1 cup of water into your Instant Pot and fit in a steamer basket. Place in the carrots and seal the lid. Select Manual and cook for 8 minutes on High. When done, perform a quick release. Remove carrots to a bowl.

Clean the pot and melt in the butter on Sauté. Add in orange zest, orange juice, orange marmalade, salt, and pepper and stir to combine. Add in carrots and cook until they are caramelized and sticky, 5-8 minutes. Serve.

Garlic Eggplants with Parmesan

Serving Size: 4 | **Total Time**: 20 minutes
2 tbsp olive oil
1 onion, chopped
3 garlic cloves, minced
1 lb eggplants, cubed
Salt and pepper to taste
1 cup tomato sauce
½ tsp dried oregano
¼ cup Parmesan, grated

Warm the olive oil in your Instant Pot on Sauté. Place the onion and garlic and cook for 3 minutes. Add in the eggplants, salt, pepper, tomato sauce, oregano, and ½ of water. Season with salt and pepper.
Seal the lid, select Manual, and cook for 8 minutes on High. Once ready, perform a quick pressure release and unlock the lid. Serve topped with Parmesan cheese.

Yogurt Eggplant Dip

Serving Size: 4 | **Total Time**: 20 minutes
3 tbsp olive oil
3 eggplants, chopped
4 garlic cloves, sliced
Salt to taste
1 lemon, juiced
1 cup Greek yogurt
1 tsp ground cumin
1 cup vegetable broth
2 tbsp cilantro, chopped

Warm the olive oil in your Instant Pot on Sauté. Place the eggplants and cook for 3 minutes, stirring occasionally. Add in garlic and Sauté for another 30 seconds. Season with salt and pour in vegetable broth
Seal the lid. Select Manual and cook for 6 minutes on High pressure. When over, perform a quick pressure release and unlock the lid. Transfer the mixture to a food processor and lemon juice, cumin, and yogurt and blend until smooth. Sprinkle with cilantro and serve.

Spicy Okra & Eggplant Dish

Serving Size: 4 | **Total Time**: 25 minutes
2 tbsp olive oil
1 onion, chopped
2 garlic cloves, minced
2 eggplants, cubed
½ lb okra, tops removed
1 tsp ground coriander
½ tsp chili powder
½ cup diced tomatoes
¾ cup vegetable stock
Fresh scallions, chopped

Warm the olive oil in your Instant Pot on Sauté. Place the onion, garlic, okra, and eggplants and cook for 3-4 minutes, stirring often. Add in the coriander, chili powder, tomatoes, and vegetable stock. Seal the lid, select Manual, and cook for 8 minutes on High pressure.
Once over, perform a quick pressure release and open the lid. Adjust the seasonings and serve topped with fresh scallions.

Winter Root Vegetables with Feta

Serving Size: 4 | **Total Time**: 40 minutes
½ lb beets
½ lb carrots
1 tbsp olive oil
1 clove garlic, minced
2 tbsp parsley, chopped
Salt and pepper to taste
3 tbsp raspberry vinaigrette
½ cup feta, crumbled

Pour 1 cup of water into your Instant Pot and fit in a steamer basket. Place in the beets and carrots and seal the lid. Select Manual and cook for 12 minutes on High pressure. Mix the garlic, parsley, salt, pepper, and raspberry vinaigrette in a bowl.
When over, allow a natural release for 10 minutes. Peel and slice the vegetables. Arrange on a greased baking sheet, drizzle with olive oil, and season with salt and pepper. Place under a preheated broiler for 4-5 minutes. Add in the dressing and feta and toss to coat. Serve.

Orange & Thyme Beet Wedges

Serving Size: 4 | **Total Time**: 25 minutes
1 lb beets
2 tbsp butter, melted
2 thyme sprigs
1 orange, juiced

Pour 1 cup of water into your Instant Pot and fit in a steamer basket. Place in the beets and seal the lid. Select Manual and cook for 12 minutes on High pressure. Once ready, perform a quick pressure release and unlock the lid. Remove the beets to a plate and let cool. Peel and cut into wedges. Clean the pot and melt the butter on Sauté. Add in the thyme sprigs and cook for 30-40 seconds. Pour in the orange juice and beets and stir for 2-3 minutes. Discard the thyme sprigs and serve.

Butter-Braised Cabbage

Serving Size: 4 | **Total Time**: 30 minutes
4 tbsp butter
1 head cabbage, shredded
1 ½ cups vegetable broth
½ tsp red pepper flakes
½ tsp herbs de Provence
1 carrot, grated
2 tsp cornstarch

Melt the butter in your Instant Pot on Sauté. Add in the cabbage and 2-3 tbsp of the vegetable broth and cook for 6 minutes, stirring occasionally. Mix in carrots, herbs de Provence, and the remaining vegetable broth.
Seal the lid, select Manual, and cook for 6 minutes on High pressure. When done, perform a quick pressure

release and unlock the lid. Remove the cabbage and carrot to a bowl with a slotted spoon.
Combine the cornstarch with some of the cooking liquid and pour it into the pot. Press Sauté and cook until the sauce thickens, about 3-4 minutes. Stir in red pepper flakes and pour over the cabbage. Serve warm.

Mushroom & Bell Pepper Casserole
Serving Size: 4 | **Total Time**: 30 minutes
1 ½ cups cremini mushrooms, sliced
2 tbsp butter
1 onion, chopped
1 red bell pepper, sliced
½ cup heavy cream
½ cup chicken broth
½ cup crispy onions

Melt butter in your Instant Pot on Sauté. Place in onion, bell pepper, and mushrooms and cook for 3-4 minutes. Stir in heavy cream and chicken broth. Seal the lid, select Manual, and cook for 15 minutes on High pressure. Once over, perform a quick pressure release and unlock the lid. Serve topped with crispy onions.

Curried Tofu with Vegetables
Serving Size: 4 | **Total Time**: 20 minutes
2 tbsp sesame oil
3 green onions, sliced
3 garlic cloves, minced
1 celery stalk, chopped
1 cup mushrooms, sliced
1 red bell pepper, chopped
¼ tsp curry powder
28 oz firm tofu, cubed
1 cup bbq sauce
1 tbsp sesame seeds, toasted

Warm the sesame oil in your Instant Pot on Sauté. Place the green onions, garlic celery, mushrooms, and bell pepper and cook for 3 minutes. Stir in salt and curry powder and cook for 2 more minutes.
Add in tofu, and bbq sauce, and ½ cup of water. Seal the lid, select Manual, and cook for 5 minutes on High. Once ready, perform a quick pressure release and unlock the lid. Serve warm topped with sesame seeds.

Asparagus & Mushrooms with Bacon
Serving Size: 4 | **Total Time**: 30 minutes
1 lb asparagus, trimmed
6 oz bacon, chopped
1 clove garlic, minced
1 yellow onion, chopped
8 oz mushrooms, sliced
Salt and pepper to taste
1 tbsp balsamic vinegar

Place asparagus in your Instant Pot and pour in water. Seal the lid, select Manual, and cook for 3 minutes on High pressure. When ready, allow a natural release for 10 minutes and unlock the lid. Strain asparagus; set aside.
Press Sauté on the pot and add bacon; cook for 1-2 minutes. Stir in garlic and onion and sauté for 2 minutes. Mix in mushrooms and cook until they are soft. Mix in cooked asparagus, salt, pepper, and balsamic vinegar and combine. Serve immediately.

Green Vegetables with Tomatoes
Serving Size: 6 | **Total Time**: 15 minutes
1 tsp olive oil
1 clove garlic, minced
2 cups chopped tomatoes
½ cup vegetable stock
½ lb green beans, trimmed
½ cup green peas
½ lb asparagus, trimmed
Salt and pepper to taste

Warm the olive oil in your Instant Pot on Sauté. Place in garlic and cook for 30 seconds until fragrant. Stir in tomatoes. Pour in vegetable stock, green beans, green peas, and asparagus; season with salt, and pepper. Seal the lid, select Manual, and cook for 5 minutes on High pressure. When done, perform a quick pressure release.

Yummy Vegetable Soup
Serving Size: 4 | **Total Time**: 25 minutes
2 tbsp olive oil
1 cup leeks, chopped
2 garlic cloves, minced
4 cups vegetable stock
1 carrot, diced
1 parsnip, diced
1 celery stalk, diced
1 cup mushrooms
1 cup broccoli florets
1 cup cauliflower florets
½ red bell pepper, diced
¼ head cabbage, chopped
½ cup green beans
2 tbsp nutritional yeast
Salt and pepper to taste
½ cup parsley, chopped

Heat oil on Sauté. Add in garlic and leeks and cook for 6 minutes until slightly browned. Add in stock, carrot, celery, broccoli, bell pepper, green beans, salt, nutritional yeast, cabbage, cauliflower, mushrooms, parsnip, and pepper. Seal the lid and cook on High Pressure for 6 minutes. Release pressure naturally. Stir in parsley to serve.

POULTRY

Tasty Indian Chicken Curry
Serving Size: 6 | **Total Time**: 30 minutes
1 (14.5 oz) can coconut milk, refrigerated overnight
2 lb boneless, skinless chicken legs
2 tbsp butter
1 large onion, minced
1 tbsp grated fresh ginger
1 tbsp minced fresh garlic
½ tsp ground turmeric
1 tbsp Kashmiri chili powder
3 tomatoes, pureed
2 tbsp Indian curry paste
2 tbsp dried fenugreek
1 tsp garam masala
Salt to taste

Melt butter on Sauté in your Instant Pot. Add in onion and cook for 3 minutes until fragrant. Stir in ginger, turmeric, garlic, and red chili powder for 2 minutes. Place the water from the coconut milk can in a bowl and mix with pureed tomatoes and chicken. Pour in the onion mixture.
Seal the lid and cook on High Pressure for 8 minutes. Release the pressure quickly. Stir in coconut milk, fenugreek, salt, curry paste, and garam masala. Simmer for 10 minutes until the sauce thickens on Sauté. Serve.

Tasty Chicken Breasts with BBQ Sauce
Serving Size: 6 | **Total Time**: 20 minutes
2 lb chicken breasts
1 tsp salt
1 ½ cups barbecue sauce
1 small onion, minced
1 cup carrots, chopped
4 garlic cloves

Rub salt onto the chicken and place it in the Instant Pot. Add onion, carrots, garlic, and barbeque sauce; toss to coat. Seal the lid, press Manual, and cook on High for 15 minutes. Do a quick release. Shred the chicken and stir into the sauce. Serve.

Pumpkin & Wild Rice Cajun Chicken
Serving Size: 6 | **Total Time**: 30 minutes
6 chicken thighs, skinless
Salt and pepper to taste
½ tsp ground red pepper
½ tsp onion powder
1 tsp Cajun seasoning
1/8 tsp smoked paprika
2 tbsp olive oil
1 cup pumpkin, cubed
2 celery stalks, diced
2 onions, diced
3 cups chicken broth
1 ½ cups wild rice

Season the chicken with salt, onion powder, Cajun seasoning, white pepper, red pepper, and paprika. Warm oil on Sauté in your Instant Pot. Cook celery and pumpkin for 5 minutes; set aside. In the pot, sear chicken for 3 minutes per side until golden brown; reserve.
Into the cooker, add ¼ cup chicken stock to deglaze the pan, scrape away any browned bits from the bottom. Add in onion and cook for 2 minutes until fragrant. Take back the celery and pumpkin to the cooker and add the wild rice and remaining chicken stock. Place the chicken over the rice mixture. Seal the lid and cook for 10 minutes on High Pressure. Release the pressure quickly. Place rice and chicken pieces in serving plates and serve.

Avocado Fajitas
Serving Size: 4 | **Total Time**: 20 minutes
4 chicken breasts
1 taco seasoning
1 tbsp olive oil
24-oz can diced tomatoes
3 bell peppers, julienned
1 shallot, chopped
4 garlic cloves, minced
Juice of 1 lemon
Salt and pepper to taste
4 flour tortillas
2 tbsp cilantro, chopped
1 avocado, sliced

In a bowl, mix taco seasoning and chicken until evenly coated. Warm oil on Sauté. Sear chicken for 2 minutes per side until browned. To the chicken, add tomatoes, cilantro, shallot, lemon juice, garlic, and bell peppers. Season with pepper and salt. Seal the lid and press Manual.
Cook for 4 minutes on High Pressure. Release the pressure quickly. Move the bell peppers and chicken to tortillas. Add avocado slices and serve.

Sweet Chicken Carnitas in Lettuce Wraps
Serving Size: 6 | **Total Time**: 40 minutes
2 lb chicken thighs, boneless, skinless
2 tbsp canola oil
1 cup pineapple juice
¼ cup soy sauce
2 tbsp maple syrup
1 tbsp rice vinegar
1 tsp chili-garlic sauce
3 tbsp cornstarch
Salt and pepper to taste
12 lettuce large leaves
2 cups canned pinto beans

Warm oil on Sauté in your Instant Pot. In batches, stir chicken in the oil for 5 minutes until browned. Set aside in a bowl. Into your pot, mix chili-garlic sauce, pineapple juice, soy sauce, vinegar, maple syrup, and 1/3 cup water. Stir in chicken to coat. Seal the lid and cook on High Pressure for 7 minutes. Release pressure naturally for 10 minutes. Shred the chicken with two forks.
Take ¼ cup liquid from the pot to a bowl. Stir in cornstarch to dissolve. Mix the cornstarch mixture with the mixture in the pot and return the chicken. Select Sauté and cook for 5 minutes until the sauce

thickens; add pepper and salt for seasoning. Transfer beans into lettuce leaves, top with chicken carnitas, and serve.

Hot Chicken with Coriander & Ginger

Serving Size: 6 | **Total Time:** 45 minutes
2 lb chicken thighs
1 tbsp ancho chili powder
1 tsp fresh basil
Salt and pepper to taste
6 cups chicken broth
1 tbsp ginger, freshly grated
1 tbsp coriander seeds
3 garlic cloves, crushed

Season the chicken with chili powder, salt, and pepper and place in the Instant Pot. Add the chicken broth broth, ginger, garlic, and coriander seeds; stir. Seal the lid and cook on Meat/Stew for 25 minutes on High. Do a natural release for 10 minutes. Serve topped with basil.

Savory Chicken Chili with Chickpeas

Serving Size: 4 | **Total Time:** 25 minutes
1 tbsp olive oil
3 serrano peppers, diced
1 onion, diced
1 jalapeño pepper, diced
1 lb chicken breasts, cubed
1 tsp ground cumin
1 tsp minced fresh garlic
1 tsp salt
2 (14.5 oz) cans chickpeas
2 tbsp chili powder
½ cup chopped cilantro
½ cup grated Monterey Jack

Warm oil on Sauté in your Instant Pot. Add in onion, serrano peppers, and jalapeño pepper and cook for 5 minutes until tender. Season with salt, cumin, and garlic. Stir in chicken for 3 to 6 minutes until no longer pink; add 2 cups water and chickpeas. Mix well. Seal the lid and cook for 5 minutes on High Pressure. Release pressure naturally. Stir chili powder with ½ cup water. Press Sauté. Boil the chili as you stir and cook until slightly thickened. Top with cheese and cilantro to serve.

Thyme Chicken with White Wine

Serving Size: 6 | **Total Time:** 45 minutes
1 cup chicken stock
½ cup white wine
½ onion, chopped
2 cloves garlic, minced
3.5-pound whole chicken
Salt and pepper to taste
½ tsp dried thyme
3 tbsp butter, melted
½ tsp paprika

Into your Instant Pot, add onion, stock, wine, and garlic. Over the mixture, place a steamer rack. Rub pepper, salt, and thyme onto chicken. Put it on the rack breast-side up. Seal the lid, press Manual, and cook for 26 minutes. Release the pressure quickly. Preheat oven broiler. In a bowl, mix paprika and butter. Remove the chicken from your pot. Get rid of onion and stock. Brush butter mixture onto the chicken and cook under the broiler for 5 minutes until chicken skin is crispy and browned. Set chicken to a cutting board to cool for about 5 minutes, then carve, and transfer to a serving platter. Serve.

Easy Chicken with Capers & Tomatoes

Serving Size: 4 | **Total Time:** 35 minutes
4 chicken legs
Salt and pepper to taste
2 tbsp olive oil
1 onion, diced
2 garlic cloves, minced
1/3 cup red wine
2 cups diced tomatoes
1/3 cup capers
2 pickles, chopped

Sprinkle pepper and salt over the chicken. Warm oil on Sauté in your Instant Pot. Add in onion and Sauté for 3 minutes until fragrant. Add in garlic and cook for 30 seconds. Mix the chicken with vegetables and cook for 6 to 7 minutes until lightly browned. Add the red wine to the pan to deglaze, scraping the pan's bottom to eliminate any browned bits of food. Stir in tomatoes. Seal the lid and cook on High Pressure for 12 minutes. Release the pressure quickly. To the chicken mixture, add the capers and pickles. Serve the chicken topped with the tomato sauce and enjoy!

Best Italian Chicken Balls

Serving Size: 4 | **Total Time:** 35 minutes
1/3 cup blue cheese, crumbled
¼ cup Pecorino Romano cheese, shredded
1 lb ground chicken
3 tbsp red hot sauce
1 egg
¼ cup breadcrumbs
1 tbsp ranch dressing
1 tbsp fresh basil, chopped
Salt and pepper to taste
15 oz canned tomato sauce
1 cup chicken broth
2 tbsp olive oil

In a bowl, mix ground chicken, egg, Pecorino cheese, pepper, salt, ranch dressing, blue cheese, hot sauce, and breadcrumbs. Shape the mixture into balls. Warm oil on Sauté in your Instant Pot. Add in the meatballs and cook for 2-3 minutes until browned on all sides.
Add in tomato sauce and broth. Seal the lid and cook on High Pressure for 7 minutes. Release the pressure quickly. Remove meatballs carefully and place them on a serving plate. Top with basil and serve.

Chicken with Honey-Lime Sauce

Serving Size: 4 | **Total Time:** 30 minutes
4 chicken breasts, cut into chunks
1 onion, diced
4 garlic cloves, smashed
1 tbsp honey
3 tbsp soy sauce

2 tbsp lime juice
2 tsp sesame oil
1 tsp rice vinegar
1 tbsp cornstarch
Salt and pepper to taste

Mix garlic, onion, and chicken in your Instant Pot. In a bowl, combine honey, sesame oil, lime juice, soy sauce, and rice vinegar. Pour over the chicken mixture. Seal the lid and cook on High Pressure for 15 minutes. Release the pressure quickly. Mix 1 tbsp water and cornstarch until well dissolved; Stir into the sauce, add salt and pepper to taste. Press Sauté. Simmer the sauce and cook for 2 to 3 minutes as you stir until thickened.

Tasty Chicken Breasts

Serving Size: 4 | **Total Time**: 30 minutes
4 chicken breasts
Salt and pepper to taste
2 tbsp olive oil
2 tbsp soy sauce
2 tbsp tomato paste
2 tbsp honey
2 tbsp minced garlic
1 tbsp cornstarch
½ cup chives, chopped

Season the chicken with pepper and salt. Warm oil on Sauté in your Instant Pot. Add in chicken and cook for 5 minutes until lightly browned. In a small bowl, mix garlic, soy sauce, honey, and tomato paste. Pour the mixture over the chicken. Stir in ½ cup water.
Seal the lid and cook on High Pressure for 12 minutes. Release the pressure quickly. Remove the chicken. Mix 1 tbsp water and cornstarch to create a slurry. Stir it in the sauce for 2 minutes until thickened. Serve the chicken with sauce and chives.

Chicken Alla Italiana

Serving Size: 4 | **Total Time**: 45 minutes
1 lb chicken drumsticks, boneless, skinless
2 tsp olive oil
Salt and pepper to taste
1 carrot, chopped
1 red bell pepper, chopped
1 yellow bell pepper, chopped
1 onion, chopped
4 garlic cloves, chopped
2 tsp dried oregano
1 tsp dried basil
1 tsp dried parsley
1 tsp red pepper flakes
28-oz can diced tomatoes
½ cup dry red wine
¾ cup chicken stock
1 cup black olives, chopped
2 bay leaves

Warm oil on Sauté in your Instant Pot. Season the drumsticks with pepper and salt. In batches, sear the chicken for 5-6 minutes until golden brown. Set aside on a plate. Drain the pot and remain with 1 tablespoon of fat. In the hot oil, sauté onion, garlic, carrot, and bell peppers for 4 minutes until softened. Add red pepper flakes, basil, parsley, and oregano, and cook for 30 more seconds. Season with salt and pepper. Stir in tomatoes, black olives, chicken stock, red wine, and bay leaves. Return chicken to the pot. Seal the lid and cook on High Pressure for 15 minutes. Release the pressure quickly. Top with tomato mixture before serving.

Tarragon & Garlic Chicken

Serving Size: 4 | **Total Time**: 30 minutes
1 ¼ lb chicken breasts
Salt and pepper to taste
2 garlic cloves, crushed
3 tbsp tarragon, chopped
2 tbsp olive oil
1 onion, finely chopped

Warm oil on Sauté in your Instant Pot. Stir-fry the onion and garlic for 3 minutes until fragrant. Add in the chicken, salt, and pepper. Pour in 2 cups of water and adjust the seasoning. Seal the lid and cook on High Pressure for 15 minutes. When ready, do a quick pressure release. Slice the chicken and serve topped with fresh tarragon.

Chicken Drumsticks in Sriracha Sauce

Serving Size: 4 | **Total Time**: 20 minutes
4 boneless, skinless chicken drumsticks
½ cup soy sauce
½ cup chicken broth
3 tbsp honey
2 tbsp tomato paste
1 tbsp sriracha
1-inch piece ginger, grated
3 garlic cloves, grated
1 tbsp cornstarch
1 tbsp water
2 tbsp toasted sesame seeds
1 tbsp sesame oil
2 cups canned black beans
2 green onions, chopped

In your Instant Pot, mix soy sauce, honey, ginger, tomato paste, chicken broth, sriracha, and garlic. Stir until smooth; toss in chicken to coat. Seal the lid and cook for 3 minutes on High Pressure. Release the pressure quickly.
Open the lid and press Sauté. In a small bowl, mix water and cornstarch until no lumps remain, stir into the sauce and cook for 5 minutes until thickened. Stir sesame oil and 1½ tablespoons sesame seeds through the chicken mixture; garnish with extra sesame seeds and green onions. Serve with black beans.

Chicken & Zucchini Pilaf

Serving Size: 4 | **Total Time**: 25 minutes
1 lb boneless, skinless chicken legs
2 tsp olive oil
1 zucchini, chopped
1 cup leeks, chopped
2 garlic cloves, minced
1 tbsp chopped rosemary
2 tsp chopped fresh thyme
Salt and pepper to taste
2 cups chicken stock

1 cup rice, rinsed

Warm oil on Sauté in your Instant Pot. Add in zucchini and cook for 5 minutes. Stir in thyme, leeks, rosemary, pepper, salt, and garlic. Cook the mixture for 4 minutes. Add in ½ cup chicken stock to deglaze, scrape the bottom to get rid of any browned bits of food.

When liquid stops simmering, add in the remaining stock, rice, and chicken with more pepper and salt. Seal the lid and cook on High Pressure for 5 minutes. Do a quick release. Carefully open the lid. Serve warm.

Rice & Lentil Chicken with Parsley

Serving Size: 4 | **Total Time:** 30 minutes
4 boneless, skinless chicken thighs
1 tsp olive oil
1 garlic clove, minced
1 yellow onion, chopped
3 cups chicken broth
1 cup white rice
½ cup dried lentils
Salt and pepper to taste
2 tbsp chopped parsley

Warm oil on Sauté in your Instant Pot. Stir-fry onion and garlic for 3 minutes. Add in broth, rice, lentils, chicken, pepper, and salt. Seal the lid and cook on High Pressure for 15 minutes. Do a quick release. Remove and shred the chicken in a large bowl. Set the lentils and rice into serving plates. Top with chicken and parsley to serve.

Rosemary Chicken with Asparagus Sauce

Serving Size: 4 | **Total Time:** 40 minutes
1 (3 ½ lb) whole chicken
4 garlic cloves, minced
2 tbsp olive oil
4 fresh thyme, minced
3 fresh rosemary, minced
2 lemons, zested, quartered
Salt and pepper to taste
2 tbsp olive oil
8 oz asparagus, chopped
1 onion, chopped
1 cup chicken stock
1 tbsp soy sauce
1 fresh thyme sprig
1 tbsp flour
Chopped parsley to garnish

Rub all sides of the chicken with garlic, rosemary, black pepper, lemon zest, thyme, and salt. Into the chicken cavity, insert lemon wedges. Warm the olive oil on Sauté in your Instant Pot. Add in onion and asparagus, and sauté for 5 minutes until softened. Mix chicken stock, thyme sprig, black pepper, soy sauce, and salt. Into the inner pot, set trivet over asparagus mixture.

On top of the trivet, place the chicken with breast-side up. Seal the lid, select Manual, and cook for 20 minutes on High. Do a quick release. Remove the chicken to a serving platter. In the inner pot, sprinkle flour over asparagus mixture and blend the sauce with an immersion blender until desired consistency.

Top the chicken with asparagus sauce and garnish with parsley.

Chicken Wings with Worcestershire Sauce

Serving Size: 4 | **Total Time:** 35 minutes
8 chicken wings
3 cups chicken broth
1 tsp fresh ginger, grated
1 tbsp honey
2 tbsp olive oil
1/3 cup Worcestershire sauce
2 spring onions, chopped
2 garlic cloves, crushed
1 tsp salt

Add the chicken to your Instant Pot and pour in broth. Seal the lid and cook on Poultry for 15 minutes on High. Do a quick release. Remove chicken and broth and wipe the pot clean. Heat oil on Sauté and stir-fry onions and garlic for 3 minutes. Add Worcestershire sauce, honey, salt, and ginger. Cook for 1 minute and return the wings. Stir for 2 minutes until nice. Serve.

Grilled Chicken Drumsticks with Salad

Serving Size: 4 | **Total Time:** 60 minutes
4 chicken drumsticks
3 cups chicken broth
1 tomato, roughly chopped
2 oz lettuce, torn
1 cup kalamata olives
1 cucumber, chopped
3 tbsp olive oil
1 tbsp Dijon mustard
¼ cup white wine
1 tsp lemon juice
1 tbsp Italian seasoning mix
Salt and pepper to taste

In a bowl, mix mustard, 2 tbsp olive oil, Italian mix, salt, and pepper. Brush the chicken with the mixture. Cover and refrigerate for 30 minutes. Place the tomato, lettuce, cucumber, and kalamata olive in a serving bowl. Season with salt and pepper and add in the remaining olive oil and lemon juice. Stir and set aside.

Remove the drumsticks from the fridge and transfer them to your Instant Pot. Pour in the broth and wine. Seal the lid and cook on Manual for 15 minutes on High. Do a quick release and remove the drumsticks. Preheat a non-stick grill pan over high heat. Brown the drumsticks for 6-7 minutes, turning once. Serve with the salad.

Picante Chicken with Lemon

Serving Size: 2 | **Total Time:** 60 minutes
1 lb chicken breasts, sliced
1 cup olive oil
1 cup chicken broth
½ cup lemon juice
1 tbsp parsley, chopped
3 garlic cloves, crushed
1 tbsp cayenne pepper
1 tsp dried oregano
½ tsp salt

In a bowl, mix olive oil, lemon juice, parsley, garlic, cayenne, oregano, and salt. Add in the chicken slices, toss to coat, and cover. Chill for 30 minutes. Remove from the fridge and place all inside your Instant Pot. Add in the broth. Seal the lid and cook on High Pressure for 7 minutes. Release the pressure naturally for about 10 minutes and serve immediately.

Hot Chicken with Garlic & Mushrooms

Serving Size: 4 | **Total Time:** 30 minutes
1 cup button mushrooms, chopped
1 lb chicken breasts, cubed
2 cups chicken broth
2 tbsp flour
1 tsp cayenne pepper
Salt and pepper to taste
2 tbsp olive oil
2 garlic cloves, chopped

Warm the olive oil in your Instant Pot on Sauté. Add mushrooms, garlic, and chicken, season with salt, and stir-fry for 5 minutes, stirring occasionally until the veggies are tender. Pour in the chicken broth. Seal the lid. Cook on High Pressure for 8 minutes. Release the steam naturally for 10 minutes and stir in flour, cayenne, and black pepper. Cook for 5 minutes on Sauté. Serve warm.

Corn & Sweet Potato Soup with Chicken

Serving Size: 4 | **Total Time:** 25 minutes
4 oz canned diced green chiles, drained
2 chicken breasts, diced
2 garlic cloves, minced
1 cup chicken stock
1 cup corn kernels
1 sweet potato, peeled, cubed
2 tsp chili powder
1 tsp ground cumin
2 cups cheddar, shredded
2 cups creme fraiche
Salt and pepper to taste
Cilantro leaves, chopped

Add chicken, corn, chili powder, cumin, chicken stock, sweet potato, green chiles, and garlic to your Instant Pot. Mix well. Seal the lid and cook on High Pressure for 10 minutes. Release the pressure quickly. Set the chicken to a cutting board and shred it. Return to the pot and stir well into the liquid. Stir in cheese and creme fraiche; Season with pepper and salt. Cook for 2-3 minutes until the cheese is melted. Place chowder into plates and top with cilantro. Serve warm.

Pea & Rice Chicken with Paprika & Herbs

Serving Size: 4 | **Total Time:** 30 minutes
4 chicken breasts, chopped
1 garlic clove, minced
½ tsp paprika
¼ tsp dried oregano
¼ tsp dried thyme
1 tsp cayenne pepper
Salt and pepper to taste
1 tbsp oil olive
1 onion, chopped
1 tbsp tomato puree
2 cups chicken broth
1 cup rice
1 celery stalk, diced
1 cup frozen green peas

Season chicken with garlic, oregano, white pepper, thyme, paprika, cayenne pepper, and salt. Warm the oil on Sauté in your Instant Pot. Add in onion and cook for 4 minutes until fragrant. Mix in tomato puree to coat. Add ¼ cup chicken broth into the cooker to deglaze the pan, scrape the pan's bottom to get rid of browned bits of food. Mix in celery, rice, and seasoned chicken. Add in the remaining broth to the chicken mixture. Seal the lid and cook on High Pressure for 8 minutes. Do a quick release. Mix in green peas, cover with the lid, and let sit for 5 minutes. Serve warm.

Chicken Sausage & Navy Bean Chili

Serving Size: 6 | **Total Time:** 50 minutes
1 (14-oz) can diced tomatoes with green chilies
3 tbsp olive oil
1 shallot, diced
½ cup fennel, chopped
¼ cup minced garlic
1 tbsp smoked paprika
2 tsp chili powder
2 tsp ground cumin
Salt and pepper to taste
28-oz can crushed tomatoes
2 lb chicken sausages, sliced
¾ cup buffalo wing sauce
2 (14-oz) cans navy beans

Warm oil on Sauté in your Instant Pot. Add the sausages and brown for 5 minutes, turning frequently. Set aside on a plate. In the same fat, sauté shallot, roasted fennel, and garlic for 4 minutes until soft. Season with paprika, cumin, pepper, salt, and chili powder.
Stir in crushed tomatoes, diced tomatoes with green chilies, buffalo sauce, and navy beans. Return the sausages to the pot. Seal the lid and cook on High Pressure for 30 minutes. Do a quick pressure release. Serve.

Savory Tropical Chicken

Serving Size: 4 | **Total Time:** 20 minutes
4 boneless, skinless chicken thighs
2 tbsp olive oil
¼ cup pineapple juice
2 tbsp ketchup
2 tbsp Worcestershire sauce
1 garlic clove, minced
1 tsp cornstarch
2 tsp water
2 tbsp cilantro, chopped

Warm oil on Sauté in your Instant Pot. In batches, sear the chicken in oil for 3 minutes until golden brown and set aside on a plate. Mix pineapple juice, Worcestershire sauce, garlic, and ketchup. Add to the pot to deglaze, scraping the bottom to get rid of any browned bits of food. Place the chicken into the sauce

and stir well to coat. Seal the lid cook for 5 minutes on High Pressure.
Release the pressure quickly. In a bowl, mix water and cornstarch until well dissolved. Press Cancel and set to Sauté. Stir the cornstarch slurry into the sauce and cook for 2 minutes until the sauce is well thickened. Sprinkle with cilantro to serve.

Punjabi Chicken in Lemon-Honey Gravy

Serving Size: 4 | **Total Time:** 25 minutes + marinade time
PUNJABI CHICKEN
4 chicken thighs, skinless
½ cup Greek yogurt
1 tbsp olive oil
1 tbsp lemon juice
1 tbsp red chili powder
1 tsp garam masala
½ tsp ground turmeric
½ tbsp grated fresh ginger
½ tbsp minced garlic
CILANTRO GRAVY
A handful of cilantro leaves
1 tsp cumin seeds
½ jalapeño, chopped
2-3 garlic cloves
2 tsp honey
2 tsp lemon juice
¾ cup olive oil
1 tbsp of water
Salt to taste

In a bowl, mix yogurt, lemon juice, garam masala, garlic, turmeric, red chili powder, olive oil, and ginger. Use a paper towel to pat dry the thighs. Place into a resealable plastic bag. Add in yogurt mixture and seal. Massage bag to ensure the marinade coats the chicken completely and place in the refrigerator for 12 hours. Remove 30 minutes before cooking.
Add 1 cup water into your Instant Pot and insert a trivet. Arrange the drained chicken on the trivet. Seal the lid. Cook for 15 minutes on High Pressure. Quick-release the pressure. Unlock the lid. Blend the cilantro, cumin seeds, jalapeño, garlic, honey, lemon juice, olive oil, water, and salt in a food processor until smooth. Pour over the chicken and serve.

Awesome Chicken in Tikka Masala Sauce

Serving Size: 4 | **Total Time:** 30 minutes
2 lb boneless, skinless chicken thighs
Salt and pepper to taste
1 ½ tbsp olive oil
½ onion, chopped
2 garlic cloves, minced
3 tbsp tomato puree
1 tsp fresh ginger, minced
1 tbsp garam masala
2 tsp curry powder
1 tsp ground coriander
½ tsp ground cumin
1 jalapeño pepper, minced
29 oz canned tomato sauce
3 tomatoes, chopped
½ cup natural yogurt
1 lemon, juiced
¼ cup chopped cilantro
4 lemon wedges

Rub black pepper and salt onto the chicken. Warm oil on Sauté in your Instant Pot. Add garlic and onion and cook for 3 minutes until soft. Stir in tomato puree, garam masala, cumin, curry powder, ginger, coriander, and jalapeño pepper; cook for 30 seconds until fragrant.
Stir in tomato sauce and tomatoes. Simmer the mixture as you scrape the bottom to get rid of any browned bits. Stir in chicken to coat. Seal the lid and cook on High Pressure for 10 minutes. Release the pressure quickly.
Press Sauté and simmer the sauce and cook for 5 minutes until thickened. Stir lemon juice and yogurt through the sauce. Serve garnished with lemon wedges and cilantro.

Pesto Chicken with Green Beans

Serving Size: 4 | **Total Time:** 30 minutes
4 chicken breasts
2 tbsp olive oil
¼ cup dry white wine
¾ cup chicken stock
Salt and pepper to taste
1 cup green beans, chopped
FOR PESTO
1 cup fresh basil
1 garlic clove, smashed
2 tbsp pine nuts
¼ cup Parmesan cheese
¼ cup extra virgin olive oil
Salt and pepper to taste

First, make the pesto - in a bowl, mix fresh basil, pine nuts, garlic, salt, pepper, and Parmesan cheese and place in a food processor. Add in oil and process until the desired consistency is attained. Apply a thin layer of pesto to one side of each chicken breast; tightly roll into a cylinder and fasten closed with small skewers.
Press Sauté. Heat oil in your Instant Pot. Cook chicken rolls for 1 to 2 minutes per side until browned. Add in wine and cook until the wine has evaporated, about 3-4 minutes. Add stock, salt and pepper, and top the chicken with green beans. Seal the lid, press Meat/Stew, and cook at High Pressure for 5 minutes. Release the pressure quickly. Serve chicken rolls with cooking liquid and green beans.

Chicken & Vegetable Stew

Serving Size: 4 | **Total Time:** 45 minutes
2 cups fire-roasted tomatoes, diced
½ cup button mushrooms, sliced
1 lb chicken breasts, chopped
1 tbsp fresh basil, chopped
2 cups coconut milk
1 cup chicken broth
Salt and pepper to taste
2 tbsp tomato paste
2 celery stalks, chopped
2 carrots, chopped
2 tbsp coconut oil

1 onion, finely chopped

Warm the coconut oil in your Instant Pot on Sauté. Add celery, onion, and carrots and cook for 7 minutes, stirring constantly. Add tomato paste, basil, and mushrooms. Continue to cook for 10 more minutes. Addin the tomatoes, chicken, coconut milk, chicken broth, salt, and pepper. Seal the lid and cook on Manual for 15 minutes on High. Do a quick release. Serve warm.

Colorful Vegetable & Chicken Rice

Serving Size: 4 | Total Time: 45 minutes
6 oz button mushrooms, chopped
1 lb chicken breasts, cubed
1 cup rice
1 red bell pepper, halved
1 green bell pepper, halved
1 yellow bell pepper, halved
6 oz broccoli florets
½ cup sweet corn
2 carrots, chopped
2 tbsp olive oil
1 tbsp butter
Salt and pepper to taste
1 tsp fresh basil, chopped
Parmesan for topping

Add the rice to your Instant Pot and pour in 2 cups of water. Stir in butter, pepper, and salt and seal the lid. Cook on Manual for 8 minutes on High. Do a quick release. Remove the rice. Heat oil on Sauté and add carrots and broccoli. Sauté for 10 minutes. Add sweet corn and bell peppers and cook for 5 minutes, stirring constantly. Stir in mushrooms and cook for 3-4 minutes.

Remove the vegetables, mix with the rice, and set aside. Add the chicken to the pot and pour in 2 cups of water. Season with salt and pepper. Seal the lid and cook on High pressure for 7 minutes. Do a quick release. Open the lid, stir in rice and vegetables and serve warm sprinkled with Parmesan cheese and fresh basil.

Chicken Thighs with Mushrooms & Garlic

Serving Size: 2 | Total Time: 30 minutes
2 chicken thighs, boneless and skinless
6 oz button mushrooms
3 tbsp olive oil
1 tsp rosemary, chopped
2 garlic cloves, crushed
½ tsp salt
1 tbsp butter
1 tbsp Italian seasoning

Heat a tablespoon of olive oil on Sauté in your Instant Pot. Add chicken thighs and sear for 5 minutes. Set aside. Pour in the remaining oil, and add mushrooms, rosemary, salt, and Italian seasoning mix. Stir-fry for 5 minutes. Add in butter, chicken, and 2 cups of water.
Seal the lid and cook on Pressure Cook for 13 minutes on High. Do a quick release. Remove the chicken and mushrooms from the cooker and serve with garlic.

Quinoa Pilaf with Chicken

Serving Size: 4 | Total Time: 35 minutes
1 lb chicken breasts, chopped
1 cup quinoa
Salt and pepper to taste
Greek yogurt for topping

Add chicken and 2 cups of water to your Instant Pot. Seal the lid. Cook on Manual for 15 minutes on High. Do a quick release; remove the chicken. Add the quinoa to the pot and seal the lid again. Cook on Manual for 8 minutes on High. Do a quick release. Stir in the chicken and adjust the seasoning with salt and pepper. Plate and top with yogurt. Serve immediately.

Brussels Sprouts & Zucchini Chicken

Serving Size: 4 | Total Time: 30 minutes
4 chicken thighs, boneless and skinless
1 cup chicken stock
½ cauliflower head, chopped
2 tomatoes, chopped
½ lb Brussels sprouts
2 zucchinis, chopped
1 onion, chopped
3 tbsp olive oil
1 tsp salt

Heat the olive oil in your Instant Pot on Sauté. Stir-fry onion, cauliflower, tomatoes, sprouts, and zucchinis for 5 minutes until tender. Add in the chicken stock, chicken thighs, and salt and seal the lid. Cook on manual for 15 minutes on High. Do a quick release. Serve warm.

Tarragon Whole Chicken

Serving Size: 6 | Total Time: 45 minutes
1 (3 lb) whole chicken
1 tsp tarragon, chopped
3 tbsp butter, softened
1 tbsp onion powder
1 tbsp garlic powder
1 tbsp paprika
Salt and pepper to taste
1 cup chicken broth
1 tbsp white wine
2 tsp soy sauce
1 minced green onion

Combine butter, tarragon, onion powder, garlic powder, paprika, salt, and pepper in a bowl. Pour the chicken broth, white wine, and soy sauce in your Instant Pot and fit in a trivet. Brush chicken with the butter mixture on all sides and place it on the trivet. Seal the lid, select Manual, and cook for 25 minutes on High pressure. When done, allow a natural release for 10 minutes and unlock the lid. Serve topped with minced green onion.

Tuscan Vegetable Chicken Stew

Serving Size: 4 | Total Time: 60 minutes
14 oz broccoli and cauliflower florets
A handful of yellow wax beans, whole
1 (3 lb) whole chicken
1 onion, peeled, chopped
1 potato, peeled, chopped
3 carrots, chopped

1 tomato, peeled, chopped
¼ cup extra virgin olive oil
Salt and pepper to taste

Warm 3 tbsp olive oil in your Instant Pot on Sauté. Stir-fry the onion for 3-4 minutes on Sauté. Add the carrots and sauté for 5 more minutes. Add the remaining oil, broccoli, potato, wax beans, tomato, salt, and pepper and top with chicken. Add 1 cup of water and seal the lid. Cook on High Pressure for 30 minutes. Release the pressure naturally for about 10 minutes. Carefully unlock the lid. Serve warm.

Bell Pepper & Chicken Stew

Serving Size: 4 | **Total Time:** 30 minutes
1 lb chicken breasts, cubed
2 potatoes, peeled, chopped
5 bell peppers, chopped
2 carrots, chopped
2 ½ cups chicken broth
1 tomato, roughly chopped
2 tbsp chopped parsley
3 tbsp extra virgin olive oil
1 tsp cayenne pepper

Warm the olive oil on Sauté in your Instant Pot. Stir-fry the bell peppers and carrots for 3 minutes. Add in the potatoes and tomato. Sprinkle with cayenne and stir well. Top with the chicken, pour in the broth, and seal the lid. Cook on High Pressure for 13 minutes. When ready, do a quick pressure release. Sprinkle with parsley and serve.

Spicy Chicken Thighs

Serving Size: 4 | **Total Time:** 45 minutes
1 lb chicken thighs
2 tbsp oil
4 cups chicken broth
1 tsp salt
2 tsp lime zest
1 tsp chili powder
½ cup tomato puree
1 tbsp sugar

Season the meat evenly with salt and chili powder on both sides. Warm oil on Sauté and add the thighs. Brown on both sides and then set aside. Add the tomato puree, sugar, and lime zest. Cook for 10 minutes to obtain a thick sauce. Add the chicken and pour in the broth. Seal the lid and cook on Poultry for 20 minutes on High pressure. Do a quick release. Unlock the lid. Serve.

Sage Chicken in Orange Gravy

Serving Size: 4 | **Total Time:** 50 minutes
1 (3.5 lb) whole chicken
¼ cup olive oil
2 tbsp fresh sage, minced
2 tbsp lemon zest
1 tsp garlic powder
¼ tsp red pepper flakes
3 cups chicken broth
1 cup red wine
2 tbsp butter
1 cup orange juice
½ cup flour
Salt and pepper to taste

Mix oil, sage, lemon zest, garlic, salt, pepper, and red pepper in a bowl. Rub the mixture onto chicken. Melt butter on Sauté in your Instant Pot and brown the chicken for 3-4 minutes. Pour in broth and wine. Seal the lid and cook on Manual for 30 minutes on High. Do a quick release and remove the chicken.
In a bowl, mix the orange juice, 1 cup of cooking liquid, and flour. Cook for 5 minutes on Sauté until the sauce has thickened. Scatter the sauce over the chicken to serve.

Easy Italian Chicken Stew with Potatoes

Serving Size: 4 | **Total Time:** 30 minutes
2 fire-roasted tomatoes, peeled, chopped
2 potatoes, peeled, cut into chunks
2 lb chicken wings
1 carrot, cut into chunks
2 garlic cloves, chopped
2 tbsp olive oil
1 tsp smoked paprika
4 cups chicken broth
2 tbsp parsley, chopped
Salt and pepper to taste
1 cup spinach, chopped

Rub the chicken with salt, pepper, and paprika. Warm the olive oil on Sauté in your Instant Pot. Cook the wings for 5 minutes, stirring occasionally. Add in tomatoes, potatoes, carrot, garlic, and chicken broth and seal the lid. Cook on High Pressure for 12 minutes. When ready, do a quick release. Stir in spinach and cook for 5 minutes until wilted on Sauté. Sprinkle with parsley and serve hot.

Spiced Chicken Thighs with Garlic

Serving Size: 4 | **Total Time:** 30 minutes + marinating time
4 chicken thighs
1 cup olive oil
¼ cup apple cider vinegar
3 garlic cloves, crushed
½ cup lemon juice
1 tbsp fresh basil, chopped
2 tbsp fresh thyme, chopped
1 tbsp rosemary, chopped
1 tsp cayenne pepper
1 tsp salt

In a bowl, add oil, vinegar, garlic, juice, basil, thyme, rosemary, salt, and cayenne. Submerge thighs into this mixture and refrigerate for 1 hour. Remove from the fridge and pat dry with kitchen paper.
Pour 1 cup of water into your Instant Pot and set a trivet. Place the chicken on it. Seal the lid and cook on Manual for 15 minutes on High. Do a quick release. Remove the chicken and broth. Warm oil on Sauté and brown the chicken for 5 minutes, turning once until nice and golden.

Chimichurri Chicken

Serving Size: 6 | **Total Time:** 25 minutes
2 lb chicken breasts
1 cup chicken broth
1 tsp smoked paprika

1 tsp cumin
Salt and pepper to taste
2 cups chimichurri salsa

Sprinkle chicken breasts with paprika, cumin, salt, and pepper. Place the chicken broth with chicken breasts in your Instant Pot. Seal the lid, select Manual, and cook for 15 minutes on High pressure. Once done, perform a quick pressure release and unlock the lid. Cut the chicken into slices and top with chimichurri sauce. Serve.

Quick Swiss Chard & Chicken Stew

Serving Size: 4 | **Total Time**: 30 minutes
1 lb chicken breasts, cubed
1 lb Swiss chard, chopped
2 cups chicken broth
2 tbsp butter, unsalted
2 tbsp olive oil
Salt and pepper to taste

Add the chicken, oil, and broth to your Instant Pot. Season with salt and black pepper. Seal the lid and cook on Manual for 13 minutes on High. Do a quick release. Unlock the lid. Add Swiss chard and butter. Cook on Sauté for 5 minutes until the chard is wilted. Serve warm.

Easy Primavera Chicken Stew

Serving Size: 4 | **Total Time**: 55 minutes
4 green onions, chopped
3 garlic cloves, minced
3 new potatoes, chopped
1 cup baby carrots, chopped
4 oz can tomato sauce
Salt and pepper to taste
1 lb chicken breasts, chopped
2 cups chicken broth
2 tbsp olive oil
2 tbsp parsley, chopped

Heat the olive oil on Sauté in the Instant Pot. Stir-fry the onions, garlic, and carrots for 3 minutes until tender. Add in the chicken and brown for 5-6 minutes, stirring occasionally. Pour in the tomato sauce, potatoes, and chicken broth. Season with salt and pepper. Seal the lid and cook on Manual for 15 minutes on High. Do a natural release for 10 minutes. Top with parsley to serve.

Dijon Mustard Chicken Breast

Serving Size: 2 | **Total Time**: 40 minutes
1 lb chicken
¼ cup apple cider vinegar
2 tbsp Dijon mustard
Salt and pepper to taste
2 tbsp olive oil
2 cups chicken stock

Season the chicken with salt and black pepper. Place in your Instant Pot and pour in the stock. Seal the lid and cook on Manual for 20 minutes. Do a quick release and remove the meat along with the stock. In a bowl, mix olive oil, mustard, and vinegar. Pour into the pot and press Sauté. Place the chicken in this mixture and cook for 10 minutes, turning once. When done, remove from the pot and drizzle with the sauce.

Festive Chicken with Bacon

Serving Size: 4 | **Total Time**: 55 minutes
1 whole chicken (3.5 lb)
3 tbsp butter
¼ cup Worcestershire sauce
2 cups chicken stock
6 oz bacon
1 tbsp flour

Place the chicken in your Instant Pot along with stock and Worcestershire sauce. Seal the lid and cook on High Pressure for 40 minutes. Do a quick release and remove to a bowl. Melt butter on Sauté. Stir-fry the bacon for 2 minutes until crispy.
Stir in flour and 1 cup of cooking juices and cook for 4 minutes until the sauce thickens. Transfer the chicken to a platter. Allow cooling for a few minutes, then carve, and serve drizzled with gravy.

Country Chicken with Vegetables

Serving Size: 4 | **Total Time**: 30 minutes
4 boneless, skinless chicken thighs
1 cup quartered cremini mushrooms
Salt and pepper to taste
2 tbsp olive oil
2 chopped carrots
½ lb green peas
1 chopped onion
3 garlic cloves, smashed
1 tbsp tomato paste
10 cherry tomatoes, halved
½ cup pitted green olives
½ cup fresh basil, minced
¼ cup parsley, chopped

Sprinkle chicken thighs with salt and pepper. Warm the olive oil in your Instant Pot on Sauté and cook carrots, mushrooms, and onion for 5 minutes. Add in garlic and tomato paste and cook for another 30 seconds. Stir in cherry tomatoes, chicken thighs, and olives.
Pour in 1 cup of water. Seal the lid, select Manual, and cook for 10 minutes on High pressure. Once ready, perform a quick pressure release and unlock the lid. Select Sauté and mix in green peas; cook for 5 minutes. Serve topped with fresh basil and parsley.

Saucy Chicken Marsala

Serving Size: 4 | **Total Time**: 30 minutes
4 chicken breasts
¼ cup ketchup
¾ cup Marsala wine
½ cup soy sauce
2 green onions, chopped

Place chicken breasts, 1 cup of water, ketchup, Marsala wine, and soy sauce in your Instant Pot and stir. Seal the lid and cook for 15 minutes on Manual. When ready, perform a quick pressure release and unlock the lid. Simmer for 5 minutes on Sauté until the sauce thickens. Top with green onions and serve.

Garlic Chicken

Serving Size: 4 | **Total Time**: 35 minutes
1 lb chicken breasts
Salt and pepper to taste

2 tbsp butter
1 cup chicken broth
2 garlic cloves, minced
2 tbsp tarragon, chopped

Place chicken breasts in your Instant Pot. Sprinkle with garlic, salt, and pepper. Pour in the chicken broth and butter. Seal the lid, select Manual, and cook for 15 minutes on High pressure.
When over, allow a natural release for 10 minutes and unlock the lid. Remove the chicken and shred it. Top with tarragon and serve.

Herby Chicken with Peach Gravy

Serving Size: 4 | **Total Time**: 55 minutes
4 chicken breasts
¼ cup olive oil
1 cup onions, chopped
2 celery stalks, chopped
2 peaches, cut into chunks
½ tsp dried thyme
½ tsp dried sage
2 cups chicken stock
Salt and pepper to taste

Heat oil on Sauté in your Instant Pot and stir-fry the onions for 2-3 minutes until soft. Add celery stalks and peaches and cook for 5 minutes, stirring occasionally.
Rub the meat with salt, pepper, thyme, and sage. Add it to the pot along with the stock. Seal the lid and cook on High Pressure for 35 minutes. Do a quick release. Serve.

Chicken Wings in Yogurt-Garlic Sauce

Serving Size: 6 | **Total Time**: 35 minutes
12 chicken wings
3 tbsp olive oil
Salt to taste
3 cups chicken broth
½ cup sour cream
1 cup yogurt
2 garlic cloves, minced

Heat oil on Sauté in your Instant Pot. Brown the wings for 6 minutes, turning once. Pour in broth, salt, and seal the lid. Cook on Poultry for 15 minutes on High. Do a natural release. Unlock the lid. In a bowl, mix sour cream, yogurt, salt, and garlic. Drizzle with yogurt sauce. Serve.

Spinach Chicken Thighs

Serving Size: 4 | **Total Time**: 40 minutes
1 lb chicken thighs
1 lb spinach, chopped
2 garlic cloves, minced
½ cup soy sauce
½ cup white wine vinegar
2 bay leaves
Salt and pepper to taste

Combine garlic, soy sauce, vinegar, bay leaves, salt, and pepper in a bowl. Add in chicken thighs and toss to coat. Transfer to your Instant Pot. Seal the lid and cook for 15 minutes on Poultry. Once ready, allow a natural release for 10 minutes and unlock the lid. Discard bay leaves and mix in spinach. Cook on Sauté for 4-5 minutes until the spinach wilts. Serve right away.

Thai Chicken

Serving Size: 4 | **Total Time**: 25 minutes
1 lb chicken thighs
1 cup lime juice
4 tbsp red curry paste
½ cup fish sauce
2 tbsp brown sugar
1 red chili pepper, sliced
2 tbsp olive oil
1 tsp ginger, grated
2 tbsp cilantro, chopped

Combine lime juice, red curry paste, fish sauce, olive oil, brown sugar, ginger, and cilantro in a bowl. Add in chicken thighs and toss to coat. Transfer to your Instant Pot and pour in 1 cup water.
Seal the lid, select Manual, and cook for 15 minutes on High. When done, perform a quick pressure release. Top with red chili slices and serve.

Chicken Fricassee

Serving Size: 4 | **Total Time**: 40 minutes
4 chicken breasts
2 tbsp olive oil
1 onion, chopped
2 garlic cloves, minced
Salt and pepper to taste
½ cup dry white wine
½ cup chicken broth
¼ cup heavy cream
2 tbsp capers
1 bay leaf
2 tbsp tarragon, chopped

Warm the olive oil in your Instant Pot on Sauté. Sprinkle chicken with salt and pepper and place in the pot. Cook for 6 minutes on all sides. Add in onion and garlic and cook for 3 minutes. Pour in chicken broth, white wine, and bay leaf. Seal the lid, select Manual, and cook for 15 minutes on High pressure. When ready, perform a quick pressure release. Remove bay leaf and put in heavy cream and capers. Stir for 2-3 minutes and cook in the residual heat until thoroughly warmed. Ladle into bowls, top with tarragon, and serve.

Spring Onion Buffalo Wings

Serving Size: 6 | **Total Time**: 30 minutes
2 lb chicken wings, sectioned
2 spring onions, sliced diagonally
½ cup hot pepper sauce
1 tbsp Worcestershire sauce
3 tbsp butter
Sea salt to taste
2 tbsp sugar, light brown

Combine hot sauce, Worcestershire sauce, butter, salt, and brown sugar in a bowl and microwave for 20 seconds until the butter melts. Pour 1 cup of water into your Instant Pot and fit in a trivet. Place the chicken wings on the trivet and seal the lid. Select Manual and cook for 10 minutes on High pressure.

Once done, perform a quick pressure release and unlock the lid. Remove chicken wings to a baking dish and brush the top with marinade. Broil for 4-5 minutes, turn the wings and brush more marinade. Broil for 4-5 minutes more. Top with spring onions and serve.

Curried Chicken with Mushrooms

Serving Size: 4 | **Total Time**: 25 minutes
1 cup shiitake mushrooms, sliced
1 cup white mushrooms, sliced
1 lb chicken breasts, cubed
2 tbsp olive oil
1 yellow onion, thinly sliced
1 tbsp curry paste
1 cup chicken stock
½ bunch cilantro, chopped

Warm the olive oil in your Instant Pot on Sauté. Add in the chicken breasts and cook for 2 minutes until browned. Stir in onion and mushrooms and cook for another 3 minutes. Mix curry paste and chicken stock in a bowl and pour into the pot. Seal the lid, select Manual, and cook for 15 minutes on High pressure. Once ready, perform a quick pressure release and unlock the lid. Serve topped with cilantro.

Chili & Lemon Chicken Wings

Serving Size: 4 | **Total Time**: 20 minutes
1 lb chicken wings
2 tbsp olive oil
1 tbsp honey
1 lemon, zested and juiced
½ tsp garlic powder
½ tsp cayenne pepper
½ chili pepper, chopped
Salt and pepper to taste
1 ½ cups chicken broth

Combine olive oil, lemon zest, lemon juice, red chili pepper, honey, garlic powder, cayenne pepper, black pepper, and salt in a bowl. Brush chicken wings with the mixture on all sides. Place the chicken broth and chicken wings in your Instant Pot. Seal the lid, select Manual, and cook for 10 minutes on High pressure. When over, perform a quick pressure release. Serve warm.

Sticky Chicken Wings

Serving Size: 6 | **Total Time**: 35 minutes + marinating time
2 lb chicken wings
3 tbsp light brown sugar
2 tbsp soy sauce
1 small lime, juiced
½ tsp sea salt
1 tsp five-spice powder

Combine soy sauce, lime juice, five-spice powder, brown sugar, and salt in a bowl. Place chicken wing and marinade in a resealable bag and shake it. Transfer to the fridge and let marinate for 30 minutes.
Pour 1/2 cup of water and marinate chicken wings with the juices in your Instant Pot. Seal the lid, select Manual, and cook for 15 minutes on High pressure. When done, allow a natural release for 10 minutes and unlock the lid. Cook on Sauté until the sauce thickens. Serve.

Korean-Style Chicken

Serving Size: 6 | **Total Time**: 35 minutes
3 green onions, sliced diagonally
3 chicken breasts, halved
5 tbsp sweet chili sauce
5 tbsp sriracha sauce
1 tbsp grated ginger
4 garlic cloves
1 tbsp rice vinegar
2 tbsp sesame seeds
1 tbsp soy sauce
½ cup chicken stock

Combine chili sauce, sriracha sauce, ginger, garlic, vinegar, sesame seeds, soy sauce, and chicken stock in a bowl. Add in the chicken fillets and toss to coat. Transfer to your Instant Pot. Seal the lid, select Manual, and cook for 15 minutes on High pressure. Once ready, allow a natural release for 10 minutes and unlock the lid. Top with green onions and serve.

Chicken & Pepper Cacciatore

Serving Size: 4 | **Total Time**: 50 minutes
4 chicken thighs, with the bone, skin removed
3 mixed bell peppers, cut into strips
2 tbsp olive oil
Salt and pepper to taste
2 garlic cloves, minced
1 diced onion
1 cup canned diced tomatoes
2 tbsp chopped rosemary
½ tsp oregano
10 black olives, pitted

Warm olive oil in your Instant Pot on Sauté. Sprinkle chicken with salt and pepper and cook in the pot for 2-3 minutes per side; reserve. Add bell pepper, garlic, and onion to the pot and cook for 5 minutes. Stir in tomatoes, oregano, and 1 cup water and return the chicken. Seal the lid, select Manual, and cook for 20 minutes on High pressure. When done, allow a natural release for 10 minutes and unlock the lid. Serve topped with black olives and rosemary.

Spicy Honey Chicken

Serving Size: 4 | **Total Time**: 20 minutes
4 chicken drumsticks
5 tbsp soy sauce
2 tbsp honey
1 cup chicken broth
1 garlic clove, minced
2 tbsp hot chili sauce
2 tbsp cornstarch
1 lime, cut into wedges

Place soy sauce, honey, garlic, and chili sauce in your Instant Pot and stir. Add in chicken drumsticks and toss to coat. Pour in chicken broth and seal the lid. Select Manual and cook for 12 minutes on High pressure. Mix 2 tbsp of water and cornstarch in a bowl.

When over, perform a quick pressure release and unlock the lid. Add in the slurry and simmer on Sauté until the sauce thickens. Serve right away with lime wedges.

Chicken & Tomato Curry

Serving Size: 4 | **Total Time:** 35 minutes
2 lb chicken breasts
16 oz canned coconut milk
1 lb tomatoes, chopped
1 tbsp tomato paste
2 garlic cloves, minced
1-inch piece ginger, grated
1 onion, chopped
2 tbsp red curry paste
1 tsp salt
2 tbsp cilantro, chopped

Place coconut milk, tomatoes, tomato paste, garlic cloves, ginger, onion, curry paste, salt, and cilantro in your Instant Pot and stir. Add in chicken and 1 cup of water and seal the lid and stir. Select Manual and cook for 15 minutes on High pressure. When over, allow a natural release for 10 minutes and unlock the lid. Top with cilantro and serve.

Creamy Mascarpone Chicken

Serving Size: 4 | **Total Time:** 30 minutes
8 bacon slices, cooked and crumbled
1 lb chicken breasts
8 oz mascarpone cheese
1 tbsp Dijon mustard
1 tsp ranch seasoning
3 tbsp cornstarch
½ cup cheddar, shredded

Place the chicken breasts, mustard, and mascarpone cheese in your Instant Pot. Add in ranch seasoning and 1 cup of water. Seal the lid, select Manual, and cook for 15 minutes on High pressure. Once ready, perform a quick pressure release and unlock the lid. Remove the chicken and shred it. Add in cornstarch, shredded chicken, cheese, and bacon and cook for 3 minutes on Sauté. Lock the lid and let chill for a few minutes. Serve.

Greek Chicken with Potatoes & Okra

Serving Size: 4 | **Total Time:** 45 minutes
2 lb chicken thighs, skinless and boneless
1 lb potatoes, peeled and cut into quarters
2 tbsp olive oil
¾ cup chicken stock
¼ lb okra, tops removed
¼ cup lemon juice
2 tbsp Greek seasoning
Salt and pepper to taste

Warm the olive oil in your Instant Pot on Sauté. Sprinkle chicken thighs with salt and pepper. Place in the pot and cook for 6 minutes on all sides. Combine chicken stock, lemon juice, and Greek seasoning in a bowl and pour over the chicken. Stir in potatoes, okra, salt, and pepper and seal the lid. Select Manual and cook for 15 minutes on High pressure. Once ready, allow a natural release for 10 minutes and unlock the lid. Serve warm.

Harissa Chicken Thighs

Serving Size: 4 | **Total Time:** 25 minutes
2 lb boneless chicken thighs
2 tbsp harissa
¼ cup soy sauce
1 tbsp ketchup
2 tbsp olive oil
¼ cup honey
2 tsp garlic powder
2 cups cooked rice
Salt and pepper to taste

Place soy sauce, ketchup, olive oil, honey, garlic powder, harissa, pepper, and salt in your Instant Pot and stir. Add in chicken thighs and pour in 1 cup of water. Seal the lid, select Manual, and cook for 20 minutes on High pressure. Once done, perform a quick pressure release and unlock the lid. Serve with a bed of rice.

Filipino-Style Chicken Congee

Serving Size: 6 | **Total Time:** 55 minutes
6 chicken drumsticks
1 cup Jasmine rice
1 tbsp fresh ginger, grated
1 tbsp fish sauce
4 green onions, chopped
3 hard-boiled eggs, halved

Place chicken, rice, 6 cups of water, fish sauce, and ginger in your Instant Pot and stir. Seal the lid, select Manual, and cook for 25 minutes on High pressure. When done, allow a natural release for 10 minutes. Remove the chicken and shred it. Put shredded chicken back in the pot and cook for 10 minutes on Sauté. Top with eggs and green onions and serve.

Famous Chicken Adobo

Serving Size: 4 | **Total Time:** 50 minutes
4 chicken thighs
Salt and pepper to taste
2 tbsp olive oil
¼ cup white vinegar
¼ cup soy sauce
1 tbsp honey
1 onion, chopped
2 garlic cloves, crushed
2 bay leaves
2 tbsp cilantro, chopped

Warm the olive oil in your Instant Pot on Sauté. Sprinkle chicken with salt and pepper. Place it in the pot and brown for 8 minutes on all sides. Stir in vinegar, soy sauce, honey, onion, garlic, bay leaves, 1 cup of water, and pepper. Seal the lid, select Manual, and cook for 20 minutes on High pressure. Once done, perform a quick pressure release and unlock the lid. Simmer for 10 minutes on Sauté until the sauce thickens. Discard bay leaves and top with cilantro. Serve.

Jamaican Chicken with Pineapple Sauce

Serving Size: 4 | **Total Time:** 40 minutes
1 lb chicken thighs
½ cup coconut cream
2 tbsp soy sauce

1 cup pineapple chunks
1 tsp Jamaican seasoning
1 tsp coriander seeds
¼ tsp salt
½ cup cilantro, chopped
1 tsp arrowroot starch

Place chicken thighs, coconut cream, soy sauce, Jamaican jerk seasoning, coriander seeds, and salt in your Instant Pot and stir. Pour in 1 cup of water and seal the lid; cook for 15 minutes on manual. Once over, allow a natural release for 10 minutes and unlock the lid.

Remove chicken to a bowl. Combine arrowroot starch and 1 tbsp of water in a cup and pour it into the pot. Add in pineapple chunks and cook for 4-5 minutes on Sauté. Top the chicken with cilantro and sauce. Serve.

Buffalo Chicken with Blue Cheese Sauce

Serving Size: 4 | **Total Time:** 30 minutes
1 lb chicken breasts, cut into thin strips
2 tbsp olive oil
1 tsp paprika
1 yellow onion, chopped
½ cup celery, chopped
½ cup buffalo sauce
½ cup chicken stock
¼ cup blue cheese, crumbled
4 tbsp sour cream

Place the chicken breasts, olive oil, paprika, onion, celery, buffalo sauce, and chicken stock in your Instant Pot. Seal the lid, select Manual, and cook for 12 minutes on High.

When ready, allow a natural release for 10 minutes and unlock the lid. In a bowl, combine the crumbled blue cheese and sour cream and add 1 cup of the cooking juice and stir. Pour into the pot. Serve right away.

Homemade Chicken Puttanesca

Serving Size: 6 | **Total Time:** 45 minutes
6 chicken thighs, skin on
2 tbsp olive oil
2 anchovy fillets, chopped
14 oz canned diced tomatoes
2 garlic cloves, crushed
½ tsp red chili flakes
6 oz pitted black olives
1 tbsp capers
1 tbsp fresh basil, chopped
Salt and pepper to taste

Warm the olive oil in your Instant Pot on Sauté. Place in the chicken thighs skin side-down and brown for 4-6 minutes. Remove to a bowl. Place tomatoes, garlic, chili flakes, anchovy fillets, black olives, capers, fresh basil, salt, and pepper into the pot. Pour in 1 cup of water.

Bring to a simmer. Add in back the chicken and seal the lid. Select Manual and cook for 20 minutes on High pressure. When ready, allow a natural release for 10 minutes and unlock the lid. Serve immediately.

Sweet & Spicy BBQ Chicken

Serving Size: 4 | **Total Time:** 35 minutes
6 chicken drumsticks
1 tbsp olive oil
1 onion, chopped
1 tsp garlic, minced
1 jalapeño pepper, minced
½ cup sweet BBQ sauce
1 tbsp arrowroot

Warm the olive oil in your Instant Pot on Sauté. Add in the onion and cook for 3 minutes. Add in garlic and jalapeño pepper and cook for another minute. Stir in barbecue sauce and 1/2 cup of water. Put in chicken drumsticks and seal the lid. Select Manual and cook for 18 minutes on High pressure. When over, perform a quick pressure release and unlock the lid. Mix 2 tbsp of water and arrowroot and pour it into the pot. Cook for 5 minutes on Sauté until the liquid thickens. Top with sauce and serve.

Fennel Chicken with Tomato Sauce

Serving Size: 4 | **Total Time:** 35 minutes
1 lb chicken breasts
½ cup chicken broth
Salt and pepper to taste
1 tbsp fennel seeds
2 tbsp olive oil
2 cups tomato-basil sauce

Place the chicken breasts, olive oil, chicken broth, fennel seeds, salt, and pepper in your Instant Pot. Seal the lid, select Manual, and cook for 20 minutes on High pressure. When done, perform a quick pressure release and unlock the lid. Shred the chicken and add in tomato sauce. Simmer for 5 minutes on Saute. Serve immediately.

Chicken Gumbo

Serving Size: 4 | **Total Time:** 40 minutes
4 chicken thighs
1 onion, diced
2 garlic cloves, minced
2 sticks celery, finely diced
2 green peppers, diced
1 tsp Cajun seasoning
Salt and pepper to taste
2 tbsp olive oil
1 ½ cups tomato sauce
1 jalapeno, halved
2 tbsp sage, chopped

Warm the olive oil in your Instant Pot on Sauté. Place in chicken and cook for 4-6 minutes on all sides; reserve. Add in onion, garlic, celery, and green peppers and cook for 5 minutes. Stir in Cajun seasoning, tomato sauce, salt, pepper, and 1 cup of water. Seal the lid, select Manual, and cook for 20 minutes on High pressure. When ready, perform a quick pressure release and unlock the lid. Top with sage and jalapeño pepper and serve.

Sticky Teriyaki Chicken

Serving Size: 4 | **Total Time:** 30 minutes
1 lb chicken breasts
2/3 cup teriyaki sauce
1 tsp sesame seeds

½ cup chicken stock
Salt and pepper to taste
3 green onions, chopped

Set your Instant Pot to Sauté. Place in teriyaki sauce and simmer for 1 minute. Stir in chicken stock, salt, and pepper and seal the lid. Select Manual and cook for 12 minutes on High pressure. Once over, allow a natural release for 10 minutes and unlock the lid. Transfer the chicken to a plate and shred it. Remove 1/2 cup of cooking liquid. Put chicken back in the pot and stir in green onions. Top with sesame seeds and serve.

Za'atar Chicken with Baby Potatoes

Serving Size: 4 | **Total Time:** 30 minutes
1 lb chicken thighs
½ lb baby potatoes, halved
2 tbsp olive oil
1 tbsp za'atar seasoning
1 garlic clove, minced
1 large onion, sliced
Salt and pepper to taste

Warm the olive oil in your Instant Pot on Sauté. Place in onion and garlic and cook for 2 minutes. Add in chicken thighs and cook for 4-6 minutes on both sides. Scatter with za'atar seasoning, salt, pepper, potatoes, and pour in 1 cup of water. Seal the lid, select Manual, and cook for 15 minutes on High pressure.
Once ready, perform a quick pressure release and unlock the lid. Remove the chicken and shred it. Put chicken back to the pot and toss to coat. Serve right away.

Indian-Style Chicken

Serving Size: 6 | **Total Time:** 37 minutes + marinating time
6 chicken thighs, bone-in
½ cup Greek yogurt
1 tbsp curry paste
1 tbsp lemon juice
Salt and pepper to taste
1 tbsp fresh ginger, grated
2 tbsp cilantro, chopped

Combine yogurt, lemon juice, curry paste, salt, and pepper in a bowl. Add in chicken thighs and toss to coat. Let marinate in the fridge for 2 hours. Place the chicken, marinade, ginger, and 1 cup of water in your Instant Pot. Seal the lid, select Manual, and cook for 12 minutes on High pressure. When over, allow a natural release for 10 minutes and unlock the lid. Transfer to a baking tray and put under the broiler 3-5 minutes. Top with cilantro.

Chicken with Chili & Lime

Serving Size: 4 | **Total Time:** 25 minutes
1 lb chicken breasts
¾ cup chicken broth
Juice and zest of 1 lime
1 red chili, chopped
1 tsp cumin
1 tsp onion powder
2 garlic cloves, minced
1 tsp mustard powder
1 bay leaf
Salt and pepper to taste

Place the chicken breasts, chicken broth, lime juice, lime zest, red chili, cumin, onion powder, garlic cloves, mustard powder, bay leaf, salt, and pepper in your Instant Pot. Seal the lid, select Manual, and cook for 10 minutes on High. When ready, allow a natural release. Remove chicken and shred it. Discard the bay leaf. Top the chicken with cooking juices and serve.

Cuban Mojo Chicken Tortillas

Serving Size: 4 | **Total Time:** 80 minutes + marinating time
4 chicken breasts
2 tbsp olive oil
1 lime, juiced
1 grapefruit, juiced
4 garlic cloves, minced
1 tsp ground cumin
Salt and pepper to taste
2 tbsp chopped cilantro
4 tortillas
1 avocado, sliced
2 tbsp hot sauce

Combine olive oil, lime juice, grapefruit juice, garlic, cumin, cilantro, salt, and pepper in a bowl. Add in chicken breasts and let marinate covered for 30 minutes. Transfer chicken and marinade to your Instant Pot and pour in 1 cup of water. Seal the lid and cook for 20 minutes on Manual. Once done, allow a natural release for 10 minutes and unlock the lid. Remove the chicken and shred it, then add it back to the pot; stir. Divide the chicken between the tortillas and top with avocado slices and hot sauce. Serve right away.

Creole Chicken with Rice

Serving Size: 4 | **Total Time:** 45 minutes
2 tbsp olive oil
1 onion, diced
3 garlic cloves, minced
1 lb chicken breasts, sliced
1 cup chicken broth
1 (14.5-oz) can tomato sauce
1 cup white rice, rinsed
1 bell pepper, chopped
2 tsp creole seasoning
1 tbsp hot sauce

Warm the olive oil in your Instant Pot on Sauté. Place in onion and garlic and cook until fragrant, about 3 minutes. Stir in chicken breasts, bell pepper, hot sauce, and creole seasoning. Cook for 3 more minutes. Mix in chicken broth, tomato sauce, and rice and seal the lid. Select Manual and cook for 20 minutes on High pressure. When ready, allow a natural release for 10 minutes and unlock the lid. Serve warm.

Moroccan-Style Chicken

Serving Size: 4 | **Total Time:** 30 minutes
1 lb chicken thighs, skinless
2 tbsp vegetable oil

Salt and pepper to taste
3 garlic cloves, minced
1 large onion, chopped
¼ tsp cumin
½ cup chicken broth
12 dried apricots, sliced
1 lb canned tomatoes, diced
1 tbsp fresh ginger, grated
½ tsp cinnamon, ground
2 tbsp cilantro, chopped
2 tbsp flaked almonds

Warm the vegetable oil in your Instant Pot on Sauté. Sprinkle chicken thighs with salt and pepper and place in the pot along with garlic and onion. Cook for 5 minutes. Stir in chicken broth, apricots, tomatoes, fresh ginger, cumin, and cinnamon. Seal the lid, select Manual, and cook for 12 minutes on High pressure. Once ready, perform a quick pressure release and unlock the lid. Serve topped with cilantro and almonds.

Chicken in Creamy Mushroom Sauce

Serving Size: 4 | **Total Time:** 50 minutes
1 lb chicken breasts
1 tbsp olive oil
1 cup mushrooms, sliced
1 large onion, chopped
2 garlic cloves, minced
1 cup chicken stock
Salt and pepper to taste
1 cup heavy cream
2 green onions, chopped

Warm the olive oil in your Instant Pot on Sauté. Place in mushrooms, onion, and garlic and cook for 4-5 minutes. Sprinkle chicken breasts with salt and pepper and place in the pot. Cook for 6-8 minutes on all sides. Add in chicken stock and stir. Seal the lid, select Manual, and cook for 12 minutes on High pressure.
Once done, allow a natural release for 10 minutes. Remove the chicken. Add the heavy cream to the cooker and stir for 3 minutes on Sauté. Pour the sauce over the chicken, top with green onions, and serve warm.

Peppered Chicken with Chunky Salsa

Serving Size: 4 | **Total Time:** 30 minutes
3 mixed-color peppers, cut into strips
1 lb chicken breasts
2 tbsp olive oil
2 jalapeño peppers, sliced
1 onion, sliced
Salt and pepper to taste
½ tsp oregano
½ tsp cumin
2 cups chunky salsa

Warm the olive oil in your Instant Pot on Sauté. Place in onion, peppers, and jalapeño peppers and sauté for 5 minutes. Sprinkle chicken breasts with salt and pepper and place them in the pot along with oregano, cumin, chunky salsa, and ½ cup of water. Seal the lid and cook for 15 minutes on Manual on High. When ready, perform a quick pressure release. Shred chicken before serving.

Chicken & Bacon Cacciatore

Serving Size: 4 | **Total Time:** 45 minutes
2 cups canned tomatoes and juice, crushed
1 lb chicken drumsticks
4 oz bacon, chopped
1 red onion, chopped
1 cup chicken stock
1 garlic clove, minced
1 tsp oregano, dried
1 bay leaf
Salt to taste
1 roasted pepper, chopped
12 Kalamata olives, sliced

Set your Instant Pot to Sauté. Add in the bacon and cook for 5 minutes. Stir in onion and garlic and cook for 3 minutes. Pour in chicken stock, tomatoes, oregano, bay leaf, salt, and chicken. Seal the lid, select Manual, and cook for 15 minutes on High pressure. Once over, allow a natural release for 10 minutes and unlock the lid. Discard the bay leaf and mix in roasted pepper. Serve topped with olives.

Lemon & Thyme Chicken

Serving Size: 6 | **Total Time:** 40 minutes
3 lb red potatoes, peeled and quartered
2 lb chicken thighs
2 tbsp olive oil
1 onion, chopped
2 garlic cloves, minced
2 tbsp thyme, chopped
¾ cup chicken broth
1 lemon, juiced and zested
Salt and pepper to taste

Warm the olive oil in your Instant Pot on Sauté. Place in the chicken thighs and brown for 2-3 minutes, stirring occasionally. Add in onion and garlic and cook for 3 minutes. Stir in chicken broth, lemon zest, lemon juice, potatoes, half of the thyme, salt, and pepper. Seal the lid and cook for 15 minutes on Poultry. Once ready, allow a natural release for 10 minutes and unlock the lid. Top with thyme and serve.

Cumin Chicken with Capers

Serving Size: 4 | **Total Time:** 30 minutes
4 chicken breasts
½ cup butter
½ tsp cumin
Salt and pepper to taste
Juice of 1 lemon
1 cup chicken broth
½ cup capers

Melt butter in your Instant Pot on Sauté. Sprinkle chicken breasts with cumin, salt, and pepper and place in the pot. Cook for 7-8 minutes on all sides. Stir in lemon juice, chicken broth, and capers and seal the lid. Select Manual and cook for 10 minutes on High pressure. Once ready, allow a natural release for 5 minutes and unlock the lid.

Feta Cheese Turkey Balls

Serving Size: 6 | **Total Time:** 35 minutes
1 onion, minced
½ cup plain bread crumbs
1/3 cup feta, crumbled
Salt and pepper to taste
½ tsp dried oregano
1 lb ground turkey
1 egg, lightly beaten
1 tbsp olive oil
1 carrot, minced
½ celery stalk, minced
3 cups tomato puree
2 cups water

In a mixing bowl, combine half the onion, oregano, turkey, salt, crumbs, pepper, and egg, and stir until everything is well incorporated. Heat oil on Sauté in your Instant Pot. Cook celery, remaining onion, and carrot for 5 minutes until soft. Pour in water and tomato puree. Adjust the seasonings. Roll the mixture into meatballs, and drop into the sauce. Seal the lid. Press Meat/Stew and cook on High Pressure for 5 minutes. Release the pressure naturally for 20 minutes. Serve topped with feta.

Chicken with Port Wine Sauce

Serving Size: 6 | **Total Time:** 41 minutes
1 (3 lb) chicken, cut into pieces
2 tbsp olive oil
1 large onion, finely diced
1 cup mushrooms
¼ cup Port wine
Salt and pepper to taste
2 tbsp parsley, chopped

Warm olive oil in your IP on Sauté. Add in the chicken pieces and cook until the chicken is light brown, about 6-7 minutes; set aside. Add onion and mushrooms to the pot and sauté for 3-4 minutes. Deglaze with Port wine and pour in 1 cup of water. Season with salt and pepper and return the chicken. Seal the lid, select Manual, and cook for 20 minutes on High. Once ready, release pressure naturally. Sprinkle with parsley and serve.

Turkey Cakes with Ginger Gravy

Serving Size: 4 | **Total Time:** 25 minutes
1 lb ground turkey
¼ cup breadcrumbs
¼ cup grated Parmesan
½ tsp garlic powder
2 green onions, chopped
Salt and pepper to taste
2 tbsp olive oil
2 cups tomatoes, diced
¼ cup chicken broth
GINGER SAUCE
4 tbsp soy sauce
2 tbsp canola oil
2 tbsp rice vinegar
1 garlic clove, minced
1 tsp ginger, grated
½ tbsp honey
¼ tsp black pepper
½ tbsp cornstarch

Combine turkey, breadcrumbs, green onions, garlic powder, salt, pepper, and Parmesan cheese in a bowl. Mix with your hands and shape meatballs out of the mixture. In another bowl, mix soy sauce, canola oil, rice vinegar, garlic clove, ginger, honey, pepper, and cornstarch. Warm the olive oil in your Instant Pot on Sauté.
Place in meatballs and cook for 4 minutes on all sides. Pour in ginger gravy, tomatoes, and chicken stock and seal the lid. Select Manual and cook for 10 minutes on High pressure. Once over, perform a quick pressure release and unlock the lid. Serve in individual bowls.

Delicious Turkey Burgers

Serving Size: 4 | **Total Time:** 35 minutes
1 lb ground turkey
2 egg
1 tbsp flour
1 onion, finely chopped
Salt and pepper to taste
1 tbsp sour cream

In a bowl, add ground turkey, egg, flour, onion, salt, pepper, and sour cream and mix well. Form the mixture into patties. Line parchment paper over a baking dish and arrange the patties. Pour 1 cup of water into your Instant Pot. Lay the trivet and place the baking dish on top.
Seal the lid. Cook on Manual for 15 minutes on High. Release the pressure naturally for 10 minutes. Unlock the lid. Serve with lettuce and tomatoes.

Rigatoni with Turkey & Tomato Sauce

Serving Size: 4 | **Total Time:** 30 minutes
2 tbsp canola oil
1 lb ground turkey
1 egg
¼ cup bread crumbs
2 cloves garlic, minced
1 tsp dried oregano
1 tsp cumin
1 tsp red pepper flakes
Salt and pepper to taste
3 cups tomato sauce
8 oz rigatoni
2 tbsp grated Grana Padano

In a bowl, combine turkey, crumbs, cumin, garlic, and egg. Season with oregano, salt, red pepper flakes, and pepper. Form the mixture into meatballs. Warm the oil on Sauté in your Instant Pot. Cook the meatballs for 3-4 minutes until browned on all sides; set aside. Add rigatoni to the cooker and pour the tomato sauce over. Cover with water. Stir well. Throw in the meatballs. Seal the lid and cook for 4 minutes on High Pressure. Release the pressure quickly. Serve topped with cheese.

Sunday Turkey Lettuce Wraps

Serving Size: 4 | **Total Time:** 35 minutes
¾ cup olive oil
4 cloves garlic, minced
3 tbsp maple syrup

2 tbsp pineapple juice
1 cup coconut milk
3 tbsp rice wine vinegar
3 tbsp soy sauce
1 tbsp Thai-style chili paste
1 lb turkey breast, boneless, cut into strips
1 lettuce, leaves separated
1/3 cup chopped peanuts
¼ cup chopped cilantro

In your Instant Pot, mix oil, garlic, rice wine vinegar, soy sauce, pineapple juice, maple syrup, coconut milk, and chili paste until smooth; add turkey strips and ensure they are submerged in the sauce. Seal the lid and cook on High Pressure for 12 minutes. Release the pressure quickly. Place the turkey at the center of each lettuce leaf. Top with cilantro and chopped peanuts.

Homemade Turkey Pepperoni Pizza

Serving Size: 4 | **Total Time**: 25 minutes
1 cup fire-roasted tomatoes, diced
1 cup turkey pepperoni, chopped
1 pizza crust
1 tsp oregano
7 oz gouda cheese, grated
2 tbsp olive oil

Grease a baking pan with oil. Line some parchment paper and place the pizza crust in it. Spread the fire-roasted tomatoes over the pizza crust and sprinkle with oregano. Make a layer with cheese and top with pepperoni. Add a trivet to your Instant Pot and pour in 1 cup water. Seal the lid and cook for 15 minutes on High Pressure. Do a quick release. Remove the pizza and serve.

Turkish-Style Roasted Turkey

Serving Size: 6 | **Total Time**: 70 minutes
2 lb boneless turkey breast, halved
2 garlic cloves, crushed
1 tsp dried basil
Salt and pepper to taste
3 whole cloves
½ cup soy sauce
½ cup lemon juice
¼ cup oil
3 cups chicken broth

Place the turkey in a Ziploc bag and add basil, cloves, soy sauce, oil, salt, pepper, and lemon juice. Pour in 1 cup of broth and seal. Shake and refrigerate for 30 minutes. Heat oil on Sauté in your Instant Pot. Cook the garlic for 2 minutes. Add in turkey and 2 tbsp of the marinade and the remaining broth. Seal the lid. Cook on Manual for 25 minutes on High. Release the pressure naturally. Serve.

Spicy Turkey Casserole with Tomatoes

Serving Size: 4 | **Total Time**: 30 minutes
2 (14-oz) cans fire-roasted tomatoes
2 bell peppers, cut into thick strips
2 tbsp olive oil
½ sweet onion, diced
3 cloves garlic, minced
1 jalapeño pepper, minced
1 lb turkey breast, cubed
1 cup salsa
2 tsp chili powder
1 tsp ground cumin
Salt to taste
1 tbsp oregano, chopped

Warm oil on Sauté. Add in garlic, onion, and jalapeño and cook for 5 minutes until fragrant. Stir in turkey and cook for 5-6 minutes until browned. Add in salsa, tomatoes, bell peppers, and 1 ½ cups water. Season with salt, cumin, and chili powder. Seal the lid, press Manual, and cook for 10 minutes on High. Release the pressure quickly. Top with oregano and serve.

Cranberry Turkey with Hazelnuts

Serving Size: 4 | **Total Time**: 40 minutes
1 lb turkey breasts, sliced
3 tbsp butter, softened
2 cups fresh cranberries
1 cup hazelnuts, chopped
1 cup red wine
1 tbsp rosemary, chopped
2 tbsp olive oil
2 tbsp orange zest
Salt and pepper to taste

Rub the turkey with oil and sprinkle with orange zest, salt, pepper, and rosemary. Melt butter in your Instant Pot on Sauté and brown turkey breast for 5-6 minutes. Pour in the wine, cranberries, and 1 cup of water. Seal the lid. Cook on High Pressure for 25 minutes. Do a quick release. Serve with chopped hazelnuts.

Parsley & Lemon Turkey Risotto

Serving Size: 4 | **Total Time**: 40 minutes
2 boneless turkey breasts, cut into strips
2 lemons, zested and juiced
1 tbsp dried oregano
2 garlic cloves, minced
1 ½ tbsp olive oil
1 onion, diced
2 cups chicken broth
1 cup arborio rice, rinsed
Salt and pepper to taste
¼ cup chopped parsley
8 lemon slices

In a Ziploc bag, mix turkey, oregano, salt, garlic, juice and zest of two lemons. Marinate for 10 minutes. Warm oil on Sauté in your Instant Pot. Add onion and cook for 3 minutes. Stir in the rice and chicken broth and season with pepper and salt.
Empty the Ziploc having the chicken and marinade into the pot. Seal the lid and cook on High Pressure for 12 minutes. Release the pressure quickly. Garnish with lemon slices and parsley to serve.

Sage Turkey & Red Wine Casserole

Serving Size: 4 | **Total Time**: 50 minutes
1 lb boneless turkey breast, cubed
1 onion, sliced
1 celery stalk, sliced
2 tbsp olive oil
1 carrot, diced

½ cup red wine
Salt and pepper to taste
1 cup chicken broth
1 tbsp tomato puree
2 tbsp sage, chopped

Warm olive oil in your IP on Sauté. Add in the turkey cubes and brown for 4-5 minutes, stirring occasionally; set aside. Add onion, celery, and carrot to the pot and sauté for 3-4 minutes. Stir in tomato puree, red wine, salt, and pepper and pour in chicken broth. Stir and return the turkey. Seal the lid, select Manual, and cook for 20 minutes on High. Once ready, release pressure naturally for 10 minutes. Unlock the lid, top with sage and serve.

Spicy Ground Turkey Chili with Vegetables

Serving Size: 6 | **Total Time:** 60 minutes
1 tbsp olive oil
1 small onion, diced
2 garlic cloves, minced
1 lb ground turkey
2 bell peppers, chopped
6 potatoes, chopped
1 cup carrots, chopped
1 cup corn kernels, roasted
1 cup tomato puree
1 cup diced tomatoes
1 cup chicken broth
1 tbsp ground cumin
1 tbsp chili powder
Salt and pepper to taste

Warm oil on Sauté in your Instant Pot and stir-fry onion and garlic until soft for about 3 minutes. Stir in turkey and cook until thoroughly browned, about 5-6 minutes. Add the bell peppers, potatoes, carrots, corn, tomato puree, tomatoes, broth, cumin, chili powder, salt, and pepper, and stir to combine. Seal the lid and cook for 25 minutes on High Pressure. Do a quick release. Set to Sauté and cook uncovered for 15 more minutes. Serve.

Turkey & Black Bean Chili

Serving Size: 6 | **Total Time:** 30 minutes
2 lb chopped turkey breast
1 ½ cups vegetable stock
2 (14-oz) cans black beans
2 garlic cloves, peeled
1 onion, diced
1 yellow bell pepper, diced
1 (7 oz) green chiles, diced
1 (14 oz) can diced tomatoes
1 tbsp hot sauce
½ tsp cumin
½ tbsp chili powder
1 cup cheddar, shredded

Place turkey, vegetable stock, black beans, garlic, onion, bell pepper, tomatoes, chiles, cumin, hot sauce, and chili powder in your Instant Pot and stir. Seal the lid, select Manual, and cook for 20 minutes on High pressure. Once done, allow a natural release for 10 minutes, then a quick pressure release, and unlock the lid. Top with cheddar and serve.

Turkey Stew with Salsa Verde

Serving Size: 4 | **Total Time:** 52 minutes
1 lb turkey thighs, boneless and diced
2 tbsp olive oil
1 cup pearl onions
1 carrot, julienned
1 cup green peas
1 cup salsa verde
Salt and pepper to taste
¼ tsp turmeric
¼ tsp cumin

Warm olive oil in your IP on Sauté. Add in the turkey pieces and brown for 4-5 minutes, stirring occasionally; set aside. Add pearl onions and carrot to the pot and sauté for 3-4 minutes. Stir in the turmeric, cumin, salt, and pepper and pour in 1 cup of water. Return the turkey.
Seal the lid, select Manual, and cook for 20 minutes on High. Once ready, allow a natural pressure release for 10 minutes. Unlock the lid, add in the green peas and salsa verde, and stir. Press Sauté and cook for 3 minutes.

Potato Skins with Shredded Turkey

Serving Size: 4 | **Total Time:** 30 minutes
2 cups vegetable broth
1 tsp chili powder
1 tsp ground cumin
½ tsp onion powder
½ tsp garlic powder
1 lb turkey breast
4 potatoes
1 Fresno chili, minced
Salt and pepper to taste

In the pot, combine broth, cumin, garlic powder, onion powder, and chili powder. Toss in turkey to coat. Place a steamer rack over the turkey. On top of the rack, set the steamer basket. Use a fork to pierce the potatoes and transfer to the steamer basket. Seal the lid and cook for 20 minutes on High. Release the pressure quickly.
Remove rack and steamer basket from the cooker. Shred the turkey in a bowl. Place the potatoes on a plate. Cut in half each potato lengthwise and scoop out the insides. Season with salt and pepper. Stuff with shredded turkey. Top with chili pepper.

Turkey Soup with Noodle

Serving Size: 6 | **Total Time:** 40 minutes
1 tbsp olive oil
1 onion, minced
3 cloves garlic, minced
1 turnip, chopped
1 cup celery rib, chopped
1 tbsp dry basil
1 bay leaf
6 cups vegetable broth
1 lb turkey breasts, cubed
8 oz dry egg noodles
Salt and pepper to taste

Warm olive oil on Sauté. Stir-fry in garlic and onion for 3 minutes. Mix in celery, bay leaf, basil, and turnip. Pour in 3 cups of broth. Scrape any brown bits from the pan's bottom and add turkey. Seal the lid and cook on High Pressure for 10 minutes. Naturally release the pressure. Transfer turkey breasts to another bowl.

Do away with the skin and bones. Using two forks, shred the meat. Set the cooker on Sauté. Transfer the turkey to the pot; add noodles and the remaining broth. Simmer for 10 minutes until noodles are done. Season and serve.

Caribbean Turkey Wings

Serving Size: 4 | **Total Time**: 55 minutes
2 lb turkey wings
2 tbsp vegetable oil
2 tbsp butter
Salt and pepper to taste
1 yellow onion, sliced
½ cup brown sugar
1 tbsp bonnet pepper sauce
¼ cup chives, chopped
1 cup pineapple juice
1 tbsp cornstarch

Warm the vegetable oil and butter in your Instant Pot on Sauté. Sprinkle turkey wings with salt and pepper and place them in the pot. Sear for 5-6 minutes on all sides; set aside. Place onion in the pot and cook for 2 minutes. Stir in pineapple juice, bonnet pepper sauce, brown sugar, and 1/2 cup of water. Put in turkey wings and seal the lid. Select Manual and cook for 20 minutes on High.

When done, allow a natural release for 10 minutes and unlock the lid. Remove wings to a plate. Mix cornstarch and some cooking liquid in a bowl and pour into the pot. Simmer for 5 minutes on Sauté until the sauce thickens. Top with chives and serve with sauce.

Turkey Meatball Soup with Rice

Serving Size: 4 | **Total Time**: 30 minutes
1 green bell pepper, chopped
1 habanero pepper, seeded and minced
2 tbsp olive oil
1 onion, chopped
2 garlic cloves, minced
½ lb ground turkey
1 carrot, chopped
1 (14-oz) can diced tomatoes
½ tsp cumin
½ tsp oregano
½ cup white rice, rinsed
Salt and pepper to taste
1 egg, beaten
1 cup yogurt

Mix ground turkey with cumin, oregano, salt, and pepper in a bowl. Shape the mixture into 1-inch balls. Warm olive oil in your Instant Pot on Sauté. Add in onion, bell pepper, habanero pepper, carrot, and garlic. Cook for 3-4 minutes. Add in meatballs, tomatoes, 3 cups water, and rice. Seal the lid, select Manual and cook for 15 minutes.

Once ready, perform a quick pressure release and unlock the lid. Mix the egg and yogurt in a bowl, and temper with one cup of the soup liquid, adding it slowly and whisking constantly to prevent the egg from cooking. Stir this mixture into the pot. Ladle the soup into bowls and serve immediately.

Hungarian-Style Turkey Stew

Serving Size: 4 | **Total Time**: 40 minutes
1 lb chopped turkey pieces
2 tbsp butter
1 tsp paprika
1 can (15 oz) diced tomatoes
1 red onion, sliced
2 garlic cloves, chopped
1 red bell pepper, chopped
1 green bell pepper, chopped
1 cup chicken stock
Salt and pepper to taste
6 tbsp sour cream
2 tbsp parsley, chopped

Melt butter in your Instant Pot on Sauté and cook the turkey for 5 minutes, stirring occasionally. Add in onion, garlic, and bell peppers and sauté for another 3 minutes. Stir in paprika, tomatoes, and stock and seal the lid. Select Manual and cook for 20 minutes on High pressure. Once over, perform a quick pressure release and unlock the lid. Adjust the seasoning. Top with sour cream and parsley.

Buffalo Turkey Chili

Serving Size: 4 | **Total Time**: 40 minutes
1 lb ground turkey
2 tbsp olive oil
1 onion, diced
½ habanero pepper, diced
½ cup red bell pepper, diced
1 (14 oz) can pinto beans
½ cup hot Buffalo sauce
2 ½ cups chicken stock
1 tsp oregano
1 tbsp chili powder
Salt and pepper to taste
2 tbsp cilantro, chopped

Warm the olive oil in your Instant Pot on Sauté and cook the onion, habanero pepper, and bell pepper until tender, about 3-4 minutes. Stir in ground turkey, beans, chicken stock, buffalo sauce, oregano, chili powder, salt, and pepper. Seal the lid and cook for 15 minutes on Bean/Chili on High pressure. When over, allow a natural release for 10 minutes, then perform a quick pressure release and unlock the lid. Serve topped with cilantro.

Turkey Sausage with Brussels Sprouts

Serving Size: 4 | **Total Time**: 40 minutes
1 lb turkey sausage, sliced
2 tbsp olive oil
1 yellow onion, chopped
2 garlic cloves, minced
½ lb Brussels sprouts, sliced
¼ cup chicken broth
1 tsp yellow mustard
1 tsp balsamic vinegar
Salt and pepper to taste

Warm the olive oil in your Instant Pot on Sauté. Place in onion and garlic and cook for 2 minutes. Add in turkey sausage and cook for 5 more minutes. Stir in Brussels sprouts, mustard, vinegar, salt, and pepper for 3 minutes. Pour in chicken broth. Seal the lid, select Manual, and cook for 15 minutes on High pressure. When ready, allow a natural release for 5 minutes, then a quick pressure release, and unlock the lid. Serve right away.

Potato & Cauliflower Turkey Soup

Serving Size: 4 | Total Time: 35 minutes
1 tbsp olive oil
1 lb ground turkey
2 garlic cloves, minced
1 leek, chopped
1 cup cauliflower florets
1 carrot, chopped
1 celery stalk, chopped
1 cup tomato sauce
½ tsp dried sage
½ tsp dried thyme
4 cups chicken broth
3 potatoes, chopped
Salt and pepper to taste

Warm the olive oil in your Instant Pot on Sauté. Place the ground turkey and garlic and cook for 5-6 minutes. Remove to a bowl. Add the leek, carrot, celery, cauliflower, tomato sauce, chicken broth, potatoes, sage, and thyme to the pot and return the turkey. Seal the lid, select Manual, and cook for 8 minutes on High. When over, allow a natural release for 10 minutes and unlock the lid. Sprinkle with salt and pepper. Serve right away.

North African Turkey Stew

Serving Size: 4 | Total Time: 60 minutes
1 lb turkey breast, cubed
2 tbsp butter
1 onion, diced
½ tsp garlic powder
2 tsp ras el hanout
1 carrot, sliced
2 celery stalks, chopped
15.5 oz chickpeas, drained
2 oz green olives, pitted
3 ½ cups chicken broth
Salt and pepper to taste
2 tbsp cilantro, chopped

Melt butter in your Instant Pot on Sauté and cook the onion, carrot, and celery for 3-4 minutes. Stir in turkey breast and cook until browned, about 4-5 minutes. Mix in garlic powder, ras el hanout, salt, pepper, chickpeas, and chicken broth. Seal the lid, select Manual, and cook for 25 minutes on High pressure. When done, allow a natural release for 10 minutes and unlock the lid. Serve topped with green olives and cilantro.

Weekend Turkey with Vegetables

Serving Size: 4 | Total Time: 35 minutes
1 lb turkey breast, chopped
1 tsp red pepper flakes
2 cups canned tomatoes
3 cups chicken broth
1 tsp honey
2 cups zucchini, cubed
3 garlic cloves, chopped
1 onion, finely chopped
2 tbsp tomato paste
1 cup baby carrots, chopped
Salt and pepper to taste
2 tbsp olive oil

Mix turkey, red pepper flakes, tomatoes, broth, honey, zucchini, garlic, onion, tomato paste, carrots, salt, pepper, and olive oil in your Instant Pot. Seal the lid and cook on Meat/Stew for 25 minutes on High Pressure. When ready, do a quick release and open the lid. Serve.

Turkey with Rice & Peas

Serving Size: 6 | Total Time: 45 minutes
1 ½ lb turkey breasts, sliced
1 tbsp olive oil
1 small onion, sliced
1 cup brown rice
1 cup green peas
2 cups chicken broth
Salt and pepper to taste

Warm the olive oil in your Instant Pot on Sauté. Add in the onion and turkey and cook for 3 minutes, stirring occasionally. Stir in rice for 1 minute and pour in the broth; season with salt and pepper. Seal the lid, select Manual, and cook for 20 minutes on High.
Once ready, allow a natural release for 10 minutes, then perform a quick pressure release and unlock the lid. Mix in green peas and cook for 3-4 minutes on Sauté. Serve.

Mediterranean Duck with Olives

Serving Size: 4 | Total Time: 20 minutes
½ cup sun-dried tomatoes, chopped
1 lb duck breasts, halved
2 tbsp olive oil
½ tbsp Italian seasoning
Salt and pepper to taste
2 garlic cloves, minced
½ cup chicken stock
¾ cup heavy cream
1 cup kale, chopped
½ cup Parmesan, grated
10 Kalamata olives, pitted

Combine olive oil, Italian seasoning, pepper, salt, and garlic in a bowl. Add in the duck breasts and toss to coat. Set your Instant Pot to Sauté. Place in duck breasts and cook for 5-6 minutes on both sides. Pour in chicken stock and seal the lid. Select Manual and cook for 4 minutes.
When done, perform a quick pressure release and unlock the lid. Mix in heavy cream, tomatoes, Kalamata olives, and kale and cook for 5 minutes on Sauté. Serve topped with Parmesan cheese.

Honey-Glazed Turkey

Serving Size: 4 | Total Time: 60 minutes

1 large turkey breast
½ cup honey
½ tsp cumin
½ tsp turmeric
Salt and pepper to taste
2 cups chicken stock
1 onion, diced
2 garlic cloves, minced
1 tbsp dry sherry

Combine honey, cumin, turmeric, salt, and pepper in a bowl. Rub the mixture onto the turkey and let sit for 10 minutes. Place onion, garlic, and turkey in your Instant Pot. Add in chicken stock and sherry. Seal the lid and cook for 30 minutes on Manual. When ready, allow a natural release for 10 minutes. Slice turkey before serving.

Roast Goose with White Wine

Serving Size: 4 | **Total Time:** 40 minutes
1 lb goose fillets, sliced
1 onion, chopped
4 tbsp butter, softened
2 garlic cloves, crushed
1 cup white wine
2 tbsp fresh celery, chopped
1 tsp dried thyme
Salt and pepper to taste

Season the goose with salt and white pepper. Melt butter on Sauté in your Instant Pot and stir-fry onions, celery, and garlic for 3-4 minutes. Add the goose fillets and brown on both sides for 6-8 minutes. Add in the white wine and thyme. Pour in 1 cup of water, seal the lid, and set to Meat/Stew. Cook for 25 minutes on High Pressure. When ready, do a quick release and set aside. Serve.

Duck Breasts with Honey-Mustard Glaze

Serving Size: 4 | **Total Time:** 50 minutes
1 lb duck breast
1 tbsp oil
1 tsp onion powder
1 cup honey
¼ cup soy sauce
¼ cup dry sherry
1 tbsp Dijon mustard
3 cups chicken broth
Salt and pepper to taste

Rub the duck with onion powder, salt, and pepper. Place it in the Instant Pot. Pour the broth, seal the lid and cook on Meat/Stew for 35 minutes on High Pressure.

Do a quick release. Remove the duck. Heat oil on Sauté, add soy sauce, honey, sherry, and mustard. Stir well and cook for 3-4 minutes. Add the meat and coat well. Serve the meat topped with the sauce.

PORK

Christmas Ham with Honey-Mustard Glaze
Serving Size: 10 | **Total Time:** 35 minutes
- ½ cup apple cider
- ¼ cup honey
- 1 tbsp Dijon mustard
- ¼ cup brown sugar
- 2 tbsp orange juice
- 2 tbsp pineapple juice
- ½ tsp ground cinnamon
- ¼ tsp grated nutmeg
- 1 (5-pound) ham, bone-in

Set to Sauté. Mix in apple cider, mustard, pineapple juice, cinnamon, sugar, honey, orange juice, and nutmeg. Cook until the sauce becomes warm, and the sugar and spices are completely dissolved. Lay ham into the sauce. Seal the lid and cook on High Pressure for 10 minutes. Release the pressure quickly. Transfer the ham to a baking sheet.
On Sauté, cook the remaining liquid for 4 to 6 minutes until you have a thick and syrupy glaze. Preheat the oven's broiler. Brush the glaze onto ham. Set the glazed ham in the preheated broiler and bake for 3 to 5 minutes until the glaze is caramelized. Place the ham on a cutting board and slice. Transfer to a serving bowl and drizzle glaze over the ham.

Saucy Baby Back Ribs
Serving Size: 4 | **Total Time:** 60 minutes
- 2 lb baby back pork ribs
- 4 cups orange juice
- Juice from 1 lemon

FOR BBQ SAUCE
- 2 tbsp honey
- ½ cup ketchup
- Juice from ½ lemon
- 1 tbsp Worcestershire sauce
- 1 tsp mustard
- 2 tsp paprika
- ½ tsp cayenne pepper
- Salt to taste

Mix honey, ketchup, lemon juice, Worcestershire sauce, mustard paprika, cayenne pepper, and salt in a bowl until well incorporated. Place the ribs into your Instant Pot and add in the lemon and orange juices. Seal the lid, press Meat/Stew, and cook on High Pressure for 30 minutes. Release pressure naturally for 10 minutes. Carefully unlock the lid.
Meanwhile, preheat oven to 400°F. Line the sheet pan with aluminum foil. Transfer the ribs to the prepared sheet. Do away with the cooking liquid. Onto both sides of ribs, brush barbecue sauce. Bake ribs in the oven for 10 minutes until sauce is browned and caramelized; set the ribs aside and cut into individual bones to serve.

Steamed Red Cabbage with Crispy Bacon
Serving Size: 8 | **Total Time:** 35 minutes
- 1 lb red cabbage, chopped
- 8 bacon slices, chopped
- 1 ½ cups beef broth
- 2 tbsp butter
- Salt and pepper to taste

Add the bacon slices to your Instant Pot and cook for 5 minutes until crispy on Sauté. Stir in the cabbage, broth, salt, pepper, and butter. Seal the lid and cook on Steam for 10 minutes. Release the pressure naturally for 10 minutes. Serve.

Rice Chowder with Bacon & Green Peas
Serving Size: 4 | **Total Time:** 30 minutes
- 1 cup basmati rice
- 1 cup bacon, chopped
- 1 medium onion, chopped
- ½ cup green peas
- 3 tbsp olive oil
- 2 garlic cloves, chopped
- 1 tsp dried thyme
- 1 tsp salt
- 2 cups beef broth

Heat oil on Sauté in your Instant Pot. Stir-fry the onion and garlic for 3 minutes until translucent. Add in rice, bacon, green peas, thyme, salt, and broth and stir. Seal the lid. Cook on High Pressure for 5 minutes. Release the pressure naturally for 10 minutes. Plate and serve.

Caribbean-Style Pork with Mango Sauce
Serving Size: 6 | **Total Time:** 70 minutes
- 1 ½ tsp onion powder
- 1 tsp dried thyme
- Salt and pepper to taste
- 1 tsp cayenne pepper
- 1 tsp ground allspice
- ½ tsp ground nutmeg
- ½ tsp ground cinnamon
- 2 lb pork shoulder
- 1 mango, cut into chunks
- 1 tbsp olive oil
- ½ cup water
- 2 tbsp cilantro, minced

In a bowl, combine onion, thyme, allspice, cinnamon, pepper, sea salt, cayenne, and nutmeg. Coat the pork with olive oil. Season with seasoning mixture. Warm oil on Sauté in your Instant Pot. Add in the pork and cook for 5 minutes until browned completely. To the pot, add water and mango chunks. Seal the lid, press Meat/Stew, and cook on High Pressure for 45 minutes.
Release the pressure naturally for 10 minutes. Transfer the pork to a cutting board to cool. To make the sauce, pour the cooking liquid into a food processor and pulse until smooth. Shred the pork and arrange it on a serving platter. Serve topped with mango salsa and cilantro.

Pork Chops with Brussels Sprouts
Serving Size: 4 | **Total Time:** 35 minutes
- 1 lb pork chops
- 1 cup onions, sliced
- 1 cup carrots, sliced
- 1 tbsp butter

2 cups Brussels sprouts
1 tbsp arrowroot
1 garlic clove, minced
1 cup vegetable stock
Salt and pepper to taste

Melt butter on Sauté. Add the pork chops, and cook on all sides until golden in color. Transfer to a plate. Add the onions, and cook for 3 minutes, then add the garlic. Saute for one more minute. Return the pork chops to the pot and pour the stock over. Season with salt and pepper. Seal the lid and cook on High Pressure for 15 minutes.

When the timer goes off, do a quick pressure release. Stir in carrots and Brussel sprouts. Seal the lid again and cook for 3 minutes on High Pressure. Do a quick pressure release. Transfer the chops and veggies to a serving platter. Whisk the arrowroot into the pot and cook on Sauté until it thickens. Pour the sauce over the chops and veggies. Serve immediately.

Pork Tenderloin with Balsamic & Butter

Serving Size: 4 | **Total Time:** 50 minutes
2 lb pork tenderloin
2 tbsp butter, unsalted
2 tbsp brown sugar
2 tbsp balsamic vinegar
2 garlic cloves, crushed
1 cup beef broth
Salt and pepper to taste
1 tbsp cornstarch

Melt butter on Sauté in your Instant Pot. Stir-fry garlic for 1 minute. Add in sugar and vinegar and cook for 1 more minute. Rub the meat with salt and pepper. Place it in the pot and pour in the broth. Seal the lid. Cook on High Pressure for 35 minutes. Do a quick release and unlock the lid. Set the meat aside. Stir in cornstarch in the remaining liquid and cook for 1 minute on Sauté to thicken the sauce. Drizzle over meat and serve.

Spiced Pork with Orange & Cinnamon

Serving Size: 4 | **Total Time:** 70 minutes
2 tbsp olive oil
2 lb pork shoulder
1 cinnamon stick
1 cup orange juice
1 tbsp cumin
½ tsp garlic powder
¼ tsp onion powder
1 onion, chopped
1 jalapeño pepper, diced
2 tsp thyme
½ tsp oregano
Salt and pepper to taste

Place half of the oil in a small bowl. Add cumin, garlic powder, onion powder, thyme, oregano, salt, and pepper and stir well to combine the mixture. Rub it all over the meat, making sure that the pork is well-coated. Heat the remaining oil on Sauté. Add the pork and sear it on all sides until browned. Transfer to a plate. Pour the orange juice into the pan and deglaze the bottom with a spatula.

Add cinnamon stick, onion, and jalapeño and stir to combine well. Return the pork to the pot. Seal the lid, select Pressure Cook, and cook for 40 minutes. When ready, allow for a natural pressure release for about 10 minutes. Grab two forks and shred the pork inside the pot. Stir to combine with the juices and serve.

Pork Loin with Apples & Rutabaga

Serving Size: 4 | **Total Time:** 30 minutes
1 tbsp olive oil
1 lb pork loin, cubed
2 apples, peeled, chopped
1 large rutabaga, chopped
1 onion, diced
1 celery stalk, diced
1 tbsp parsley, chopped
½ cup leeks, sliced
1 ½ cups beef broth
½ tsp cumin
½ tsp thyme
Salt and pepper to taste

Heat half of the olive oil on Sauté in your Instant Pot. Add the pork and cook until it browned on all sides. Remove to a plate. Add leeks, onion, celery, and drizzle with the remaining oil. Stir to combine and cook for 3 minutes. Add the pork back to the cooker, pour the broth over, and stir in parsley, cumin, thyme, salt, and pepper. Seal the lid, and cook on High Pressure for 10 minutes. After the beep, do a quick pressure release. Stir in the rutabaga and apples. Seal the lid again and cook for 5 minutes on High. Do a quick pressure release. Serve.

Pork Loin with Pineapple Sauce

Serving Size: 6 | **Total Time:** 35 minutes
2 lb pork loin, cut into 6 equal pieces
16 oz canned pineapples
1 cup vegetable broth
1 tbsp brown sugar
3 tbsp olive oil
½ cup tomato paste
1 cup sliced onions
½ tsp ginger, grated
Salt and pepper to taste
¼ cup tamari
¼ cup rice wine vinegar
½ tbsp cornstarch

Heat the 2 tbsp oil on Sauté. Cook the onions for 3 minutes until translucent. Add the pork and stir in pineapples, sugar, broth, tomato paste, ginger, salt, pepper, tamari, and rice vinegar. Seal the lid and cook for 20 minutes on Soup/Broth on High. Release the pressure quickly. Mix cornstarch and 1 tbsp water and stir it in the pot. Cook for 2 minutes or until thickened on Sauté. Serve hot.

Pork Carnitas Wraps with Lime & Cilantro

Serving Size: 4 | **Total Time:** 65 minutes
1 (2-pound) boneless pork shoulder
2 tsp grapeseed oil
1 onion, chopped
2 garlic cloves, minced
1 grapefruit, juiced

1 lime, juiced
1 tsp sweet smoked paprika
1 tsp dried oregano
1 jalapeño pepper, chopped
1 avocado, sliced
2 tbsp cilantro, chopped
4 corn tortillas, warmed

Warm oil on Sauté in your Instant Pot. Add in pork and cook for 5 minutes until golden brown. Transfer the pork to a plate. Add garlic and onion to the pot and cook for 3 minutes until soft. Add lime and grapefruit juices into the pan and scrape the bottom to eliminate any browned bits of food. Stir in paprika, oregano, and 1 cup water. Return the pork to pot and stir to coat.

Seal the lid and cook for 35 minutes on High Pressure. Release the pressure quickly. Press Sauté. When the liquid starts to simmer, use two forks to shred the pork. Cook for 10 more minutes until liquid is reduced by half. Serve in warmed tortillas topped with jalapeños, avocado slices, and cilantro. Enjoy!

Pork Shoulder with Honey & Ginger

Serving Size: 6 | **Total Time:** 1 hour
2 lb pork shoulder, boneless
Salt and pepper to taste
½ tsp red pepper flakes
1 tbsp butter, unsalted
2 tsp fresh ginger, grated
1 tbsp apple cider vinegar
1 tbsp honey
3 tbsp soy sauce
1 tsp garlic powder

In a bowl, combine apple cider, honey, soy sauce, garlic powder, and ginger. Brush the meat with the mixture. Brown it for 5 minutes on all sides on Sauté. Stir in 2 cups water, salt, pepper, and red pepper flakes. Seal the lid and cook on High Pressure for 35 minutes on High. Do a quick release. Press Sauté and add the butter. Cook until the liquid evaporates, 10 minutes. Serve warm.

Pork Chops on Puréed Butternut Squash

Serving Size: 4 | **Total Time:** 35 minutes
3 tbsp olive oil
2 sprigs thyme, chopped
2 sprigs rosemary, chopped
4 pork chops
1 cup mushrooms, chopped
4 cloves garlic, minced
1 cup vegetable broth
1 tbsp soy sauce
1 lb butternut squash, cubed
1 tsp cornstarch

Set to Sauté and heat 2 tbsp of oil in your Instant Pot. Add the pork chops, rosemary, and thyme and sear for 1 minute for each side until lightly browned. Sauté garlic and mushrooms in the Instant Pot for 5-6 minutes until mushrooms are tender. Add soy sauce and broth. Over the chops, place a cake pan. Add in the butternut squash in the pan and drizzle with olive oil. Seal the lid.

Cook on High Pressure for 10 minutes. Release the pressure quickly. Remove the pan and trivet from the pot. Stir cornstarch into the mushroom mixture for 3 minutes until the sauce thickens. Transfer the mushroom sauce to a food processor. Blend until you attain the desired consistency. Scoop the sauce into a cup with a pour spout. Smash the squash into a purée and spoon into a serving platter. Top with the pork chops and drizzle with the gravy. Serve and enjoy!

Pulled Pork with Homemade BBQ Sauce

Serving Size: 6 | **Total Time:** 70 minutes
2 lb pork shoulder
1 tbsp onion powder
1 tbsp garlic powder
Salt and pepper to taste
1 tbsp chili powder
2 cups vegetable stock
6 dates, soaked
¼ cup tomato paste
½ cup coconut aminos

In a small bowl, combine onion powder, garlic powder, salt, black pepper, and chili powder. Rub the mixture onto the pork. Place the pork inside your pressure cooker. Pour the stock around the meat, not over it, and then seal the lid. Select Pressure Cook and set the timer to 60 minutes. Place the dates, tomato paste, and coconut aminos in a food processor; pulse until smooth. Release the pressure quickly. Grab two forks and shred the meat inside the pot. Pour the sauce over and stir to combine.

Spicy Garlic Pork

Serving Size: 4 | **Total Time:** 45 minutes
1 lb pork shoulder
2 tbsp olive oil
3 Jalapeño peppers, minced
1 tsp ground cumin
1 large onion, chopped
2 garlic cloves, crushed
3 cups beef broth
Salt and pepper to taste

Heat oil on Sauté in your Instant Pot and cook the jalapeño peppers for 3 minutes. Add in cumin, salt, pepper, garlic, and onion and stir-fry for another 2 minutes until soft. Add in the pork shoulder, and beef broth. Seal the lid, and cook on Meat/Stew for 30 minutes on High. Release the pressure quickly and serve hot.

Spring Onion & Pork Egg Casserole

Serving Size: 4 | **Total Time:** 35 minutes
1 tbsp butter, melted
4 spring onions, chopped
1 lb ground pork, chopped
6 eggs
Salt and pepper to taste
1 cup water

In a bowl, break the eggs and whisk until frothy. Mix in the onions and ground meat and season with salt and pepper. Grease a casserole dish with melted butter. Pour the egg mixture into the dish. Place a trivet in the pressure cooker and add water. Select

Manual and cook for 25 minutes on High. Do a quick pressure release.

Maple Pork Carnitas

Serving Size: 6 | **Total Time:** 50 minutes
10 sundried tomatoes, diced
2 lb pork butt roast
¼ cup maple syrup
2 cups beef stock
1 tbsp mustard powder
1 tsp onion powder
Salt to taste
3 tbsp cilantro, chopped
1 jalapeno, chopped
6 warm tortillas

Rub the meat with salt, mustard powder, and onion powder and place it in the Instant Pot. Mix the stock and maple syrup in bowl; stir in the tomatoes and jalapeño. Pour the mixture over the pork. Seal the lid and cook on High Pressure for 30 minutes. Allow the pressure to release naturally for 10 minutes. Shred the pork with two forks. Add it to the tortillas. Top with cilantro to serve.

Tasty Buckwheat & Pork Stew

Serving Size: 4 | **Total Time:** 57 minutes
1 cup buckwheat
1 lb pork tenderloin
1 carrot, chopped
1 onion, finely chopped
2 garlic cloves, minced
3 tbsp vegetable oil
1 tsp dry marjoram
Salt and pepper to taste
½ cup white wine
2 cups vegetable broth

Heat oil on Sauté. Add onion and garlic and stir-fry for 2 minutes until fragrant and translucent. Add carrot and pork. Cook for 5 minutes until lightly browned. Add buckwheat, marjoram, salt, pepper, wine, and broth. Seal the lid and cook on High Pressure for 35 minutes. Do a quick release. Stir and spoon onto bowls. Serve hot.

Sweet & Spicy Pulled Pork

Serving Size: 4 | **Total Time:** 60 minutes
1 lb pork shoulder
1 onion, finely chopped
2 tbsp butter, unsalted
1 tbsp cayenne pepper
1 tsp salt
1 cup beef broth
1 tsp maple syrup
2 tbsp soy sauce
¼ cup Worcestershire sauce

Warm butter on Sauté and stir-fry onions, cayenne pepper, and salt for 4 minutes. Add in maple syrup, soy sauce, and Worcestershire sauce and stir. Cook for 5 minutes. Add pork and pour in the broth. Seal the lid and cook on High Pressure for 40 minutes. When done, do a quick release. Divide between plates and serve hot.

Garlic Pork Meatloaf with Ketchup Glaze

Serving Size: 6 | **Total Time:** 70 minutes
1 lb pork sausages
1 lb ground pork
1 cup cooked rice
1 cup milk
½ tsp marjoram
2 eggs, beaten
2 garlic cloves, minced
1 onion, diced
Salt and pepper to taste
2 tbsp brown sugar
1 cup ketchup

In a bowl, crack the eggs and whisk them with milk. Stir in the meat, marjoram, rice, onion, salt, black pepper, and garlic. With hands, mix in the ingredients to combine and form a meatloaf. Add it to a greased baking dish. Whisk together the ketchup and sugar and pour over the meatloaf. Place a trivet inside your Instant Pot and pour 1 cup of water. Lay the dish on top, seal the lid and cook on Manual for 50 minutes on High. Do a quick release. Unlock the lid. Serve the meatloaf sliced.

Wine Pork Butt with Fennel & Mushrooms

Serving Size: 4 | **Total Time:** 30 minutes
3 tbsp olive oil
1 lb pork butt, sliced
2 cups mushrooms, sliced
1 fennel bulb, chopped
½ cup white wine
1 tsp garlic, minced
½ cup vegetable broth

Heat the olive oil on Sauté. Brown the pork slices and for a few minutes. Stir in mushrooms, fennel, wine, garlic, and broth. Seal the lid and cook for 20 minutes on Manual on High. When done, do a quick release. Serve.

Short Ribs with Wine Mushroom Sauce

Serving Size: 4 | **Total Time:** 75 minutes
2 lb boneless pork short ribs, cut into 3-inch pieces
Salt and pepper to taste
½ onion, chopped
½ cup red wine
3 tbsp olive oil
½ tbsp tomato paste
2 carrots, sliced
2 cups mushrooms, sliced
1 tbsp cornstarch
Minced parsley to garnish

Rub the ribs on all sides with salt and pepper. Heat the oil on Sauté in your Instant Pot and brown short ribs on all sides, about 6-7 minutes. Remove to a plate. Add onion to the pot and cook for 3-5 minutes. Pour in wine and tomato paste to deglaze by scraping any browned bits from the bottom of the cooker. Cook for 2 minutes until the wine has reduced slightly. Return ribs to the pot and cover with carrots. Pour 1 cup of water over.
Seal the lid, and select Manual on High Pressure for 35 minutes. When ready, let the pressure release

naturally for 10 minutes. Carefully unlock the lid. Transfer ribs and carrots to a plate. To the pot, add mushrooms. Press Sauté and cook them for 2-4 minutes. In a bowl, add 2 tbsp of water and cornstarch and mix until smooth. Pour this slurry into the pot, stirring constantly until it thickens slightly, 2 minutes. Season the gravy with salt and pepper. Pour over the ribs and garnish with parsley.

Pork Chops in Cinnamon Apple Sauce
Serving Size: 4 | **Total Time:** 55 minutes
- 4 pork loin chops
- 2 tbsp oil
- 1 tbsp butter
- 3 apples, peeled, chopped
- ¼ cup soy sauce
- 1 cup beef broth
- 2 tbsp honey
- ¼ tsp cinnamon
- Salt and pepper to taste

Heat oil on Sauté and briefly brown the chops for 3 minutes on each side. Remove and melt the butter. Add apples, soy sauce, broth, honey, and cinnamon. Cook until apples are slightly tender. Add the chops back, seal the lid and cook on Meat/Stew for 40 minutes on High. Do a quick release. Adjust the seasoning and serve.

White Peas with Jalapeño & Bacon
Serving Size: 4 | **Total Time:** 40 minutes
- 1 lb white peas
- 4 slices bacon
- 1 onion, chopped
- 1 jalapeño pepper, chopped
- 2 tbsp flour
- 2 tbsp butter
- 1 tbsp cayenne pepper
- 3 bay leaves, dried
- Salt and pepper to taste

Melt butter on Sauté, and stir-fry the onion for 2-3 minutes until translucent. Add bacon, peas, jalapeño pepper, bay leaves, salt, cayenne, and pepper. Stir in 2 tbsp of flour and add 3 cups of water. Seal the lid and cook on High Pressure for 15 minutes. Release the steam naturally for 10 minutes.

Homemade Braised Pork Belly
Serving Size: 4 | **Total Time:** 30 minutes
- 1 lb pork belly, sliced
- 2 tbsp oil
- ½ tsp cinnamon, ground
- ¼ tsp nutmeg, ground
- ¼ cup honey
- ¼ cup red wine
- 2 cups orange juice
- 1 cup water

Heat oil on Sauté, and brown the pork for 3 minutes. Add cinnamon, nutmeg, honey, wine, orange juice and water, seal the lid, and cook on High Pressure for 20 minutes. Do a quick release. Press Sauté and bring it to a boil. Let simmer until the excess liquid evaporates. Serve.

Pancetta Kale with Chickpeas
Serving Size: 4 | **Total Time:** 35 minutes
- 2 oz onion soup mix
- ¼ cup olive oil
- 1 tbsp garlic, minced
- 1 cup canned chickpeas
- 2 tsp mustard
- ½ lb pancetta slices, chopped
- 1 onion, chopped
- 1 cup kale, chopped
- Salt and pepper to taste

Heat the oil and cook the onion, garlic, and pancetta for 5 minutes on Sauté. Add 1 cup of water, soup mix, salt, and pepper, and cook for 5 more minutes. Then, add the chickpeas and 2 cups of water. Add in the kale and mustard. Seal the lid and cook for 15 minutes on Pressure Cook on High Pressure. Once done, perform a quick pressure release. Serve immediately.

Easy Pork Balls with Apple Sauce
Serving Size: 4 | **Total Time:** 40 minutes
- 1 lb ground pork
- ¼ cup tamari sauce
- 3 garlic cloves, minced
- ½ tbsp dried thyme
- ½ cup diced onions
- 2 tsp honey
- ¼ cup apple juice
- 1 cup breadcrumbs
- Salt and pepper to taste

Whisk together honey, tamari, apple juice, 1 ½ cups water, and thyme in the pressure cooker. Season with salt and pepper. Set to Sauté and cook for 15 minutes. Combine pork, garlic, onions, and breadcrumbs in a bowl. Shape meatballs out of the mixture and pour them into the sauce. Seal the lid and cook on Pressure Cook for 15 minutes. Release the pressure quickly. Serve.

Pork Meatloaf with Chili Tomato Sauce
Serving Size: 4 | **Total Time:** 45 minutes
- 2 lb ground pork
- 2 garlic cloves, minced
- 1 cup bread crumbs
- 1 large-sized egg
- ½ cup milk
- 2 onions, finely chopped
- Salt and pepper to taste
- ½ tsp turmeric powder
- ½ tsp dried oregano
- 2 tsp brown sugar
- 2 tbsp olive oil
- 1 shallot, finely chopped
- 28 oz canned tomatoes
- ½ red chili, finely chopped
- 2 tbsp Worcestershire sauce
- 1 tbsp lemon juice

Place a trivet in your pressure cooker and pour in 1 cup of water. Combine ground pork, bread crumbs, milk, onions, egg, garlic, salt, pepper, oregano, and turmeric powder in a bowl. Shape into a loaf and place onto a greased sheet pan. Lower the sheet pan

onto the trivet. Seal the lid, select Pressure Cook and cook for 20 minutes. Do a quick pressure release. Remove the meatloaf and set aside covered. Clean the pot and place the olive oil.
Select Sauté and add in the shallot and chili pepper. Stir-fry for 3 minutes until tender. Pour in tomatoes, brown sugar, Worcestershire sauce, and lemon juice and cook for 10 minutes. Blitz the mixture with an immersion blender. Adjust the seasoning with salt and pepper. Slice the meatloaf and spoon the sauce over to serve.

Pork with Onions & Cream Sauce

Serving Size: 6 | **Total Time**: 52 minutes
1 ½ lb pork shoulder, cut into pieces
2 onions, chopped
1 ½ cups sour cream
1 cup tomato puree
½ tbsp cilantro
¼ tsp cumin
¼ tsp cayenne pepper
1 garlic clove, minced
Salt and pepper to taste

Coat with cooking spray the inner pot and add the pork. Cook for 3-4 minutes on Sauté until lightly browned. Add onions and garlic and cook for 3 minutes until fragrant. Press Cancel. Stir in sour cream, tomato puree, cilantro, cumin, cayenne pepper, salt, and pepper and seal the lid. Select Soup/Broth and cook for 30 minutes on High. Let sit for 5 minutes before quickly release the pressure.

Thyme Pork Loin with Apples & Daikon

Serving Size: 4 | **Total Time**: 40 minutes
1 lb pork loin, cubed
1 onion, diced
1 daikon, chopped
1 cup vegetable broth
½ cup white wine
2 apples, peeled and diced
½ cup sliced leeks
1 tbsp vegetable oil
1 celery stalk, diced
2 tbsp dried parsley
¼ tsp thyme
½ tsp cumin
¼ tsp lemon zest
Salt and pepper to taste

Heat oil on Sauté. Add pork and cook for 6 minutes until browned. Add the onion and cook for 2 more minutes. Stir in daikon, broth, wine, leeks, celery, parsley, thyme, cumin, lemon zest, salt, and pepper. Seal the lid and cook for 15 minutes on Pressure Cook. Release the pressure quickly. Stir in apples, seal the lid again, and cook on High for another 5 minutes. Do a quick release. Carefully unlock the lid. Serve warm.

Apple Pork Chops

Serving Size: 4 | **Total Time**: 42 minutes
2 leeks, white part only, cut into rings
1 lb pork fillets
½ lb apples, cut into wedges
2 tbsp olive oil
¼ cup apple cider vinegar
1 tsp chili pepper
Salt and pepper to taste
1 tsp dry rosemary
1 tsp dry thyme

Heat 1 tbsp of olive oil on Sauté. Season the pork with salt, black and chili pepper. Brown the fillets for about 4 minutes per side. Set aside. Heat the remaining oil in the pressure cooker. Add in leeks and Sauté until soft, about 4 minutes. Add in apples, rosemary, and thyme and pour in the vinegar and 1 cup of water. Place the pork loin along with the apples and leeks. Seal the lid.
Cook for 20 minutes on Meat/Stew on High. Once cooking is complete, perform a quick pressure release and remove the lid. To serve, arrange the pork on a plate and pour the apple leeks mixture over the pork.

Fennel Pork Butt with Mushrooms

Serving Size: 8 | **Total Time**: 30 minutes
1 lb pork butt, sliced
2 cups mushrooms, sliced
1 fennel bulb, chopped
½ cup white wine
½ cup vegetable broth
Salt and pepper to taste

Grease with cooking spray and heat on Sauté. Brown the pork slices and for a few minutes. Stir in mushrooms, fennel, wine, broth, salt, and pepper. Seal the lid and cook for 20 minutes on Meat/Stew on High. When done, do a quick release.

Vegetable Casserole with Smoked Bacon

Serving Size: 4 | **Total Time**: 30 minutes
½ lb smoked bacon, chopped
½ cup carrots, sliced
1 cup vegetable stock
¾ cup half and half
4 golden potatoes, peeled and chopped
4 endives, chopped
Salt and pepper to taste

Set to Sauté and add the bacon. Cook for 2 minutes until slightly crispy. Add the potatoes, carrots, 2 cups water, and vegetable stock. Seal the lid and cook for 10 minutes on High Pressure. Release the pressure quickly. Add the endives and cook for 5 more minutes on Sauté. Stir in the half and half and season with salt and pepper. Cook for 3 more minutes. Serve.

Easy Pork Fillets with Peachy Sauce

Serving Size: 6 | **Total Time**: 30 minutes
1 lb pork loin fillets
16 oz canned peach
½ tsp ground coriander
½ tsp ginger, chopped
½ cup Worcestershire sauce
¼ cup apple cider vinegar
½ tsp garlic, minced
Salt and pepper to taste
1 cup onions, sliced
2 tbsp olive oil

1 cup tomato sauce
1 tbsp arrowroot slurry

On Sauté, heat oil. Cook onions until tender, about 4 minutes. Stir in pork, peaches, coriander, ginger, Worcestershire sauce, apple vinegar, garlic, salt, pepper, and tomato sauce. Seal the lid, Select Meat/Stew, and cook for 20 minutes. Do a quick pressure release. Stir in the slurry and cook on Sauté until the sauce thickens.

Garlic Mashed Potatoes with Sausages

Serving Size: 6 | **Total Time:** 30 minutes
4 potatoes, peeled and cut into chunks
6 Italian sausages
1 tbsp olive oil
2 garlic cloves, smashed
⅓ cup butter, melted
¼ cup milk
Salt and pepper to taste
1 tbsp chopped chives

Select Sauté and heat olive oil. Cook sausages for 8-10 minutes, turning often until browned. Set aside. Wipe the pot with paper towels. Add in 1 cup of water and set steamer rack over water and steamer basket onto the rack. Add in the potatoes. Seal the lid and cook on High Pressure for 12 minutes. Release the pressure quickly. Remove basket and rack from the pot.

Drain water from the pot. Return potatoes to the pot. Add in salt, butter, pepper, garlic, and milk and use a hand masher to mash until no large lumps remain. Using an immersion blender, blend potatoes on Low for 1 minute until fluffy and light. Transfer the mash to a serving plate. Top with sausages and chives to serve.

Party Apple-Glazed Pork Ribs

Serving Size: 4 | **Total Time:** 45 minutes
½ cup apple cider vinegar
2 lb pork ribs
3 ½ cups apple juice
Salt and pepper to taste

Pour apple juice and apple cider vinegar into the pressure cooker and lower the trivet. Season the pork ribs with salt and pepper, and place on top of the trivet and seal the lid. Cook on High Pressure for 30 minutes. Once it goes off, let the valve drop on its own for a natural release for about 10 minutes. Serve.

Oregano Pork with Pears & Dijon Mustard

Serving Size: 6 | **Total Time:** 60 minutes
3 lb pork roast
2 pears, peeled and sliced
3 tbsp Dijon mustard
1 tbsp dried oregano
½ cup white wine
1 tbsp garlic, minced
1 tbsp olive oil
Salt and pepper to taste

Brush the pork with mustard. Heat oil on Sauté and sear the pork on all sides for 6minutes. Stir in pears, oregano, wine, 1 cup of water, garlic, salt, and pepper. Seal the lid and cook for 40 minutes on Meat/Stew on High Pressure. Release the pressure naturally for 10 minutes.

Pork Tenderloin with Cherries & Apples

Serving Size: 4 | **Total Time:** 55 minutes
1 ¼ lb pork tenderloin
1 chopped celery stalk
2 apples, peeled, chopped
1 cup cherries, pitted
½ cup apple juice
½ cup water
¼ cup onions, chopped
Salt and pepper to taste
2 tbsp olive oil

Heat oil on Sauté and cook the onions and celery for 5 minutes until softened. Season the pork with salt and pepper, and add to the cooker. Brown for 2-3 minutes per side. Top with apples and cherries, and pour the water and apple juice. Seal the lid. Cook on Meat/Stew for 40 minutes on High pressure. Once ready, do a quick pressure release. Slice the pork tenderloin and arrange it on a serving platter. Spoon the apple-cheery sauce over the pork slices to serve.

Tasty Cajun Pork Chops

Serving Size: 4 | **Total Time:** 80 minutes
2 lb pork chops
1 cup beef broth
1 onion, diced
2 tbsp potato starch
1 carrot, chopped
MARINADE
2 tbsp fish sauce
½ tsp Cajun seasoning
2 tsp garlic, minced
½ cup soy sauce
1 tbsp sesame oil

Combine fish sauce, Cajun seasoning, garlic, soy sauce, and sesame oil in a bowl. Add in the pork chops and let marinate for 30 minutes. Coat the pressure cooker with cooking spray. Add onion and carrot and cook until soft on Sauté. Add the pork chops along with the marinade. Whisk in the broth and starch. Seal the lid and cook for 40 minutes on Meat/Stew. Do a quick release and serve.

Pork Belly with Tamari Sauce

Serving Size: 6 | **Total Time:** 35 minutes
4 garlic cloves, sliced
½ tsp ground cloves
1 tsp grated fresh ginger
1 ½ lb pork belly, sliced
2 ¼ cups water
¼ cup white wine
½ cup onions, chopped
¼ cup tamari sauce
1 tsp sugar maple syrup
4 cups white rice, cooked
Salt and pepper to taste

Brown pork belly for about 6 minutes per side on Sauté. Add garlic, cloves, ginger, water, wine, onions, tamari sauce, maple syrup, rice, salt, and pepper. Seal the lid and cook for 25 minutes on Pressure Cook. When ready, do a quick pressure release. Serve immediately.

Saucy Barbecue Baby Back Ribs

Serving Size: 4 | **Total Time**: 55 minutes
2 lb rack pork baby back ribs
2 tbsp olive oil
½ tsp garlic powder
½ tsp onion powder
1 tbsp Worcestershire sauce
1 tsp cayenne pepper
Salt and pepper to taste
2 cups barbecue sauce

Discard the membrane from the back of ribs and slice into individual bones. Mix the cayenne pepper, salt, pepper, garlic powder, and onion powder in a bowl. Sprinkle each rib with this mixture. Warm the olive oil in your Instant Pot on Sauté. Place in ribs and sear for 4-5 minutes on all sides. Add in Worcestershire sauce and barbecue sauce and seal the lid. Select Manual and cook for 20 minutes on High. Once over, allow a natural release for 10 minutes, then perform a quick pressure release, and unlock the lid. Transfer ribs to a plate. Cook the sauce for 5-6 minutes on Sauté until it thickens. Serve the ribs topped with sauce.

Savory Pork Chops with Brussel Sprouts

Serving Size: 4 | **Total Time**: 30 minutes
4 pork chops
½ lb Brussel sprouts
¼ cup sparkling wine
1 ½ cups beef stock
2 shallots, chopped
1 tbsp olive oil
1 cup celery stalk, chopped
1 tbsp coriander
Salt and pepper to taste

Heat olive oil on Sauté. Add the pork chops and cook until browned on all sides. Stir in sprouts, wine, stock, shallots, celery, coriander, salt, and pepper. Seal the lid and cook for 20 minutes on Meat/Stew on High. Release the pressure quickly. Serve.

Italian Sausage & Lentil Pot

Serving Size: 4 | **Total Time**: 40 minutes
1 cup canned tomatoes, diced
1 red bell pepper, cut into strips
1 lb Italian sausages, sliced
2 tbsp olive oil
1 cup lentils, rinsed
1 onion, chopped
1 tsp paprika
4 garlic cloves, minced
1 tbsp basil, chopped
Salt and pepper to taste
1 tbsp Italian seasoning

Warm the olive oil in your Instant Pot on Sauté. Place in sausages and cook for 3-4 minutes. Add in onion, bell pepper, garlic, and and cook for another 4 minutes. Stir in paprika, Italian seasoning, salt, pepper, lentils, tomatoes, and 3 cups of water. Seal the lid, select Manual, and cook for 15 minutes on High. Once over, allow a natural release for 10 minutes. Top with basil and serve.

Merlot Pork Chops

Serving Size: 4 | **Total Time**: 50 minutes
4 pork chops
3 carrots, chopped
1 tomato, chopped
1 onion, chopped
2 garlic cloves, minced
¼ cup merlot red wine
½ cup beef broth
1 tsp dried oregano
2 tbsp olive oil
2 tbsp flour
2 tbsp water
2 tbsp tomato paste
1 beef bouillon cube
Salt and pepper to taste

Heat the oil on Sauté. In a bowl, mix in flour, pepper, and salt. Coat the pork chops. Place them in the pressure cooker and cook for a few minutes until browned on all sides. Add the carrots, onion, garlic, and oregano.
Cook for 2 more minutes. Stir in tomato, wine, broth, water, tomato paste, and bouillon cube and seal the lid. Cook on Soup/Broth and cook for 25 minutes on High. When ready, do a natural pressure release for 10 minutes, and serve immediately.

Broccoli & Cauliflower Pork Sausages

Serving Size: 6 | **Total Time**: 20 minutes
1 lb pork sausage, sliced
½ lb broccoli florets
½ lb cauliflower florets
14 oz can mushroom soup
10 oz evaporated milk
Salt and pepper to taste

Place ¼ of the sausage slices in your pressure cooker. In a bowl, whisk the soup, salt, pepper, and milk. Pour some of the mixtures over the sausages. Top the sausage slices with ¼ of the cauliflower and broccoli florets. Pour some of the soup mixtures again. Repeat the layers until you use up all ingredients. Seal the lid and cook on Pressure Cook for 10 minutes on High. When ready, do a quick release. Serve.

Friday Night BBQ Pork Butt

Serving Size: 6 | **Total Time**: 55 minutes
2 lb pork butt
Salt and pepper to taste
1 cup barbecue sauce
¼ tsp cumin powder
½ tsp onion powder
1 ½ cups beef broth

In a bowl, combine the barbecue sauce, cumin, onion powder, salt, and pepper. Brush the pork with the mixture. On Sauté, coat with cooking oil. Add the pork and sear on all sides for 6 minutes. Pour the beef broth around the meat. Seal the lid and cook for 40 minutes on Meat/Stew on High. Do the pressure quickly. Serve.

Cajun Pork Carnitas

Serving Size: 4 | **Total Time:** 65 minutes
1 lb pork shoulder, trimmed of excess fat
3 tbsp olive oil
1 onion, chopped
1 cup chicken stock
½ cup sour cream
2 tbsp tomato paste
1 tbsp lemon juice
Salt and pepper to taste
1 tsp cayenne pepper
1 tsp garlic powder
1 tbsp Cajun seasoning
4 tortillas, warm

Warm the olive oil in your Instant Pot on Sauté. Place in the pork and cook for 7-8 minutes on all sides. Stir in onion and cook for 1-2 more minutes. Pour in chicken stock, sour cream, tomato paste, lemon juice, salt, pepper, cayenne pepper, Cajun seasoning, and garlic powder. Seal the lid, select Manual, and cook for 25 minutes on High.

When ready, allow a natural release for 10 minutes and unlock the lid. Remove pork and shred it. Put shredded pork back to the pot and cook for 6-8 minutes on Sauté. Serve with warm tortillas.

Pork Chops & Mushrooms with Tomato Sauce

Serving Size: 4 | **Total Time:** 35 minutes
1 cup white button mushrooms, sliced
4 large bone-in pork chops
1 cup tomato sauce
1 onion, chopped
1 tsp garlic, minced
½ cup water
1 tbsp oil

Heat oil on Sauté. Add garlic and onion and cook for 2 minutes until soft. Add pork and cook until browned, 6 minutes. Stir in mushrooms, tomato sauce, and water and seal the lid. Cook for 20 minutes on Meat/Stew. Do a quick pressure release. Carefully unlock the lid. Serve.

Garlic-Spicy Ground Pork with Peas

Serving Size: 6 | **Total Time:** 55 minutes
2 lb ground pork
1 onion, diced
1 can diced tomatoes
1 can peas
5 garlic cloves, minced
3 tbsp butter
1 serrano pepper, chopped
1 cup beef broth
1 tsp ground ginger
2 tsp ground coriander
Salt and pepper to taste
¾ tsp cumin
¼ tsp cayenne pepper
½ tsp turmeric

Melt butter on Sauté. Add onion and cook for 3 minutes until soft. Stir in ginger, coriander, salt, pepper, cumin, cayenne pepper, turmeric and garlic and cook for 2 more minutes. Add pork and cook until browned. Pour broth and add serrano pepper, peas, and tomatoes. Seal the lid and cook for 30 minutes on Meat/Stew on High. When ready, release the pressure naturally for 10 minutes. Carefully unlock the lid. Serve immediately.

Sweet Mustard Pork Chops with Piccalilli

Serving Size: 4 | **Total Time:** 30 minutes
1 lb pork chops, boneless
2 tbsp olive oil
2 tbsp Dijon mustard
½ tbsp brown sugar
1 tbsp honey
2 garlic cloves, minced
2 tbsp piccalilli
Salt and pepper to taste

Sprinkle pork chops with salt and pepper. Warm the olive oil in your Instant Pot on Sauté. Place the pork chops in the pot and brown for 6-8 minutes on both sides. Mix Dijon mustard, brown sugar, honey, garlic, and 1 cup of water in a bowl. Pour it into the pot and seal the lid. Select Manual and cook for 15 minutes on High pressure. Once done, perform a quick pressure release and unlock the lid. Top with piccalilli and serve.

Chili-Braised Pork Chops with Tomatoes

Serving Size: 4 | **Total Time:** 30 minutes
14 oz canned tomatoes with green chilies
4 pork chops
1 onion, chopped
2 tbsp chili powder
1 garlic clove, minced
½ cup beer
½ cup vegetable stock
1 tsp olive oil
Salt and pepper to taste

Heat oil on Sauté. Add onion, garlic, and chili powder and cook for 2 minutes. Add the pork chops and cook until browned on all sides. Stir in the tomatoes, stock, and beer. Season with salt and pepper. Seal the lid and cook for 20 minutes on Meat/Stew on High. When ready, quick Release the pressure and serve hot.

Chorizo with Macaroni & Cheddar Cheese

Serving Size: 6 | **Total Time:** 20 minutes
1 lb macaroni
3 oz chorizo, chopped
3 cups water
1 tbsp garlic powder
2 tbsp minced garlic
2 cups milk
2 cups cheddar, shredded
Salt to taste

On Sauté and stir-fry chorizo until crispy for about 6 minutes. Set aside. Wipe the pot with kitchen paper. Add in water, macaroni, garlic, and salt. Seal lid and cook for 5 minutes on High Pressure. Release the pressure quickly. Stir in cheese, garlic powder, and milk until the cheese melts. Top with chorizo and serve.

Baby Carrot & Onion Pork Chops
Serving Size: 4 | **Total Time:** 30 minutes
1 ½ lb pork chops
½ lb baby carrots
1 onion, sliced
2 tbsp butter
1 cup vegetable broth
Salt and pepper to taste

Season the pork with salt and pepper. Melt butter on Sauté and brown the pork on all sides. Stir in carrots and onion and cook for 2 more minutes until soft. Pour in the broth. Seal the lid and cook for 20 minutes on Meat/Stew on High. When ready, release the pressure quickly.

Thai-Style Chili Pork
Serving Size: 4 | **Total Time:** 29 minutes
2 red Thai chili peppers, chopped
½ lb sugar snap peas, trimmed
1 lb ground pork
2 tbsp olive oil
2 garlic cloves, minced
1-inch piece ginger, grated
2 shallots, thinly sliced
1 ½ cups coconut milk
1 tbsp soy sauce
2 tbsp cilantro, chopped

Warm the olive oil in your Instant Pot on Sauté. Place in ground pork and brown for 5-6 minutes. Add in garlic, Thai chili, ginger, and shallots and cook for another 2-3 minutes. Stir in coconut milk, sugar snap peas, and soy sauce and seal the lid. Select Manual and cook for 10 minutes on High. When ready, perform a quick pressure release and unlock the lid. Top with cilantro and serve.

Sweet & Spicy Pork Ribs
Serving Size: 4 | **Total Time:** 50 minutes
3 lb pork baby back ribs
2 tbsp olive oil
¼ tsp ground coriander
1 tsp garlic powder
2 tsp cayenne pepper
½ cup orange marmalade
2 tbsp ketchup
2 tbsp soy sauce
Salt and pepper to taste

Trim the ribs of excess fat and cut them into individual bones. In a bowl, combine olive oil, ground coriander, garlic powder, cayenne pepper, salt, and pepper and mix well. Add in the ribs and toss to coat. Transfer them to the Instant Pot and pour in 1 cup of water. Seal the lid, select Manual, and cook for 20 minutes on High.

When done, release the pressure naturally for 10 minutes. In a bowl, whisk together the ketchup, orange marmalade, and soy sauce until well combined. Transfer the ribs to a baking tray. Select Sauté and pour the marmalade mixture into the pot. Cook until the sauce has thickened to obtain a glaze texture, about 4-5 minutes. Brush the ribs with some glaze and place under a preheated broiler for 5 minutes or until charred and sticky. Serve the ribs with the remaining glaze.

BBQ Pork Lettuce Cups
Serving Size: 6 | **Total Time:** 60 minutes
1-2 little gem lettuces, leaves separated
3 lb pork roast, cut into chunks
2 tbsp olive oil
Salt and pepper to taste
1 cup chicken broth
½ cup BBQ sauce
1 red onion, thinly sliced
2 tbsp cilantro, chopped

Sprinkle pork roast with salt and pepper. Place the roast, olive oil, chicken broth, and BBQ sauce in your Instant Pot and stir. Seal the lid, select Manual, and cook for 40 minutes on High. When ready, allow a natural release for 10 minutes, then perform a quick pressure release, and unlock the lid. Remove roast and shred it using two forks. Divide shredded pork between lettuce leaves. Scatter with onion and cilantro. Serve with the gravy.

Beer-Braised Pork
Serving Size: 4 | **Total Time:** 53 minutes
2 lb pork loin roast
2 tbsp butter
1 onion, chopped
2 garlic cloves, minced
1 tsp thyme
1 bay leaf
2 cups beer
Salt and pepper to taste

Melt butter in your Instant Pot on Sauté. Place the pork roast fatty-side down and cook on both sides. Add in onion and garlic and cook for 3 minutes. Put in thyme, salt, pepper, beer, bay leaf, and ½ cup of water and seal the lid. Select Manual and cook for 30 minutes on High.

When over, allow a natural release for 10 minutes and unlock the lid. Transfer roast to a bowl and cover it. Press Sauté and cook until the sauce thickens. Cut the roast and top with the sauce.

Hoisin Spare Pork Ribs
Serving Size: 4 | **Total Time:** 75 minutes
2 lb pork spare ribs
3 garlic cloves, minced
2 green onions, chopped
3 ginger slices
2 tbsp sesame oil
¼ cup Mirin rice wine
½ cup hoisin sauce
2 red chilies, sliced
1 tbsp honey
2 tbsp cilantro, chopped

Warm sesame oil in your Instant Pot on Sauté. Place in garlic, green onions, chilies, and ginger and cook for 2-3 minutes. Slice spare ribs into individual ribs, place it in the pot, and sauté for 4-5 minutes. Stir in rice wine, honey, 1 cup of water, and hoisin sauce and cook for 3-4 minutes. Seal the lid, select Manual, and cook for 40 minutes.

Once done, allow a natural release for 10 minutes, then perform a quick pressure release, and unlock the lid. Top the ribs with sauce and cilantro and serve.

Cinnamon BBQ Pork Ribs

Serving Size: 6 | **Total Time:** 60 minutes
3 lb pork ribs
½ cup apple jelly
1 cup barbecue sauce
1 onion, diced
2 tbsp ground cloves
1 tbsp brown sugar
1 tsp Worcestershire sauce
1 tsp ground cinnamon
Salt and pepper to taste

Whisk together apple jelly, barbecue sauce, onion, cloves, sugar, Worcestershire sauce, cinnamon, salt, and pepper in your pressure cooker. Place the ribs inside and pour in ½ cup water. Seal the lid. Set the cooker to Meat/Stew and cook for 50 minutes. Release the pressure naturally.

Fruity Pork Steaks

Serving Size: 4 | **Total Time:** 30 minutes
4 pork steaks
¼ cup milk
8 prunes, pitted
½ cup white wine
2 apples, peeled, sliced
¼ cup heavy cream
1 tbsp fruit jelly
½ tsp ground ginger
Salt and pepper to taste

Place pork, milk, prunes, wine, apples, heavy cream, and ginger in your pressure cooker. Stir and season with salt and pepper. Seal the lid and cook on High Pressure for 15 minutes. Once done, wait 5 minutes and do a quick pressure release. Stir in the jelly and serve.

Pork Sirloin Chili

Serving Size: 6 | **Total Time:** 45 minutes
3 lb sirloin pork roast
1 tbsp honey
1 tsp chili powder
1 tbsp rosemary
1 tbsp olive oil
Salt and pepper to taste

Combine chili powder, rosemary, salt, and pepper in a bowl and rub them onto the pork. Heat oil on Sauté and sear the pork on all sides. Stir in honey and seal the lid. Cook for 30 minutes on Meat/Stew. Do a natural pressure release for 10 minutes. Carefully unlock the lid.

Awesome Herby Pork Butt with Yams

Serving Size: 4 | **Total Time:** 35 minutes
1 lb pork butt, cut into 4 equal pieces
1 lb yams, diced
2 tsp butter
¼ tsp thyme
¼ tsp oregano
1 ½ tsp sage
1 ½ cups beef broth
Salt and pepper to taste

Season the pork with thyme, sage, oregano, salt, and pepper. Melt butter on Sauté. Add pork and cook until brown, about 5 minutes. Add the yams and pour the broth. Seal the lid and cook for 20 minutes on Meat/Stew. Do a quick release. Serve hot.

Best Pork Chops with BBQ Sauce & Veggies

Serving Size: 4 | **Total Time:** 25 minutes
4 pork rib chops
1 cup carrots, thinly sliced
1 cup turnips, thinly sliced
1 cup onions, slice into rings
1 ½ cups BBQ sauce
2 cups water

Add the pork chops to your cooker. Pour in ½ cup of BBQ sauce and 2 cups of water. Select Meat/Stew. Stir in the onions, turnips, and carrots. Lock the lid and cook for 20 minutes on High. Once ready, Release the pressure quickly. Open the lid, drizzle with the remaining BBQ sauce and serve warm.

Chorizo & Tomato Pork Chops

Serving Size: 4 | **Total Time:** 40 minutes
4 pork chops, boneless
2 oz chorizo sausage, sliced
1 tsp paprika
2 garlic cloves, minced
2 tbsp olive oil
1 yellow onion, sliced
2 cups chopped tomatoes

Place the pork chops in your Instant Pot and sear for 5 minutes on Sauté. Add in onion and garlic and cook for 3 more minutes. Stir in chorizo, paprika, tomatoes, and ½ cup of water. Seal the lid, select Manual, and cook for 15 minutes on High pressure. When done, allow a natural release for 10 minutes, then perform a quick pressure release, and unlock the lid. Serve right away.

Tarragon Apple Pork Chops

Serving Size: 4 | **Total Time:** 25 minutes
2 tbsp olive oil
1 tsp nutmeg
1 tsp Dijon mustard
4 tbsp brown sugar
2 Granny Smith apples, sliced
4 pork chops
Salt and pepper to taste
2 tbsp tarragon, chopped

Combine nutmeg, mustard, and brown sugar in a bowl. Add in apples and toss to coat. Warm oil in your Instant Pot on Sauté. Place the apples in the pot and cook for 2 minutes. Sprinkle pork chops with salt and pepper and put it over the apples. Seal the lid, select Manual, and cook for 15 minutes on High. Once done, perform a quick pressure release. Top with tarragon and serve.

Paprika Pulled Pork Fajitas

Serving Size: 4 | **Total Time:** 65 minutes
2 lb pork shoulder, cut into chunks

½ tsp garlic powder
½ tsp dried chili flakes
½ tsp brown sugar
½ tsp cumin
1 yellow onion, sliced
1 ½ cups beef broth
1 tsp smoked paprika
Salt and pepper to taste
4 tortillas

Combine garlic powder, smoked paprika, brown sugar, cumin, salt, and pepper in a bowl. Sprinkle pork shoulder with the spice mixture. Place onion slices in your Instant Pot and top with the pork shoulder. Pour in beef broth and seal the lid. Select Manual and cook for 40 on High.

Once done, allow a natural release for 10 minutes, then perform a quick pressure release, and unlock the lid. Remove pork and shred it. Warm each tortilla in a skillet over medium heat for 1 minute. To assemble, divide shredded pork between tortillas and top with chili flakes.

Mexican Pork Chili Verde

Serving Size: 4 | **Total Time:** 45 minutes
2 lb pork shoulder, cubed
½ lb tomatillos, quartered
2 serrano peppers, chopped
2 jalapeño peppers, minced
1 onion, chopped
4 garlic cloves, minced
1 tsp cayenne pepper
½ tsp oregano
½ tsp ground coriander
1 tsp cumin
1 cup chicken stock
2 tbsp cilantro, chopped
Salt and pepper to taste

Place pork shoulder, tomatillos, serrano peppers, jalapeño peppers, onion, garlic cloves, cayenne pepper, oregano, ground coriander, cumin, chicken stock, salt, and pepper in your Instant Pot and stir. Seal the lid, select Manual, and cook for 35 minutes on High pressure. Once done, perform a quick pressure release and unlock the lid. Transfer the pork to a plate. Put the cilantro in the pot and blend sauce using an immersion blender. Put the pork back in the pot and toss to coat. Serve immediately.

Pear & Cider Pork Tenderloin

Serving Size: 4 | **Total Time:** 55 minutes
1 lb pork loin
1 tbsp garlic powder
2 tbsp olive oil
1 yellow onion, chopped
2 pears, cored and chopped
1 cup apple cider
1 tbsp fennel seeds
Salt and pepper to taste

Sprinkle pork loin with salt, pepper, and garlic powder. Warm the olive oil in your Instant Pot on Sauté. Place the loin and sear for 8 minutes on all sides. Set aside. Add onion to the pot and cook for 3 minutes. Put in pears and apple cider and scrape any brown bits from the bottom. Put loin back to the pot along with fennel seeds.
Seal the lid. Select Manual and cook for 20 minutes on High pressure. When ready, allow a natural release for 10 minutes and unlock the lid. Slice the pork loin before serving and top with sauce.

Hot Pork Chops with Cheddar Cheese

Serving Size: 4 | **Total Time:** 30 minutes
4 boneless pork chops
2 tbsp olive oil
1 cup water
4 tbsp habanero pepper sauce
2 tbsp butter
1 cup cheddar, grated
Salt and pepper to taste
2 tbsp parsley, chopped

Warm the olive oil in your Instant Pot on Sauté. Sprinkle pork chops with salt and pepper. Place the chops in the pot and brown for 3 minutes on all sides. Add in 1 cup of water and habanero pepper sauce. Top each pork chop with butter and seal the lid. Select Manual and cook for 15 minutes on High pressure.

When done, perform a quick pressure release and unlock the lid. Scatter pork chops with cheddar cheese and broil in the oven for a few minutes. Top with parsley and serve.

Juicy Pork Butt Steaks

Serving Size: 4 | **Total Time:** 57 minutes
2 lb pork butt steaks
2 tbsp olive oil
1 tsp garlic powder
1 onion, chopped
1 cup chicken broth
1 cup tomato sauce
1 tsp ground bay leaf
1 tsp oregano
½ cup red wine
1 tbsp paprika
Salt and pepper to taste

Warm the olive oil in your Instant Pot on Sauté. Place in pork steaks, salt, pepper, and garlic powder and cook for 4-5 minutes. Set aside. Put the onion in the pot and cook for 2 minutes. Pour in red wine and scrape any brown bits from the bottom. Put pork steaks back to the pot along with chicken stock, tomato sauce, bay leaf, oregano, and paprika. Seal the lid, select Manual, and cook for 30 minutes on High pressure. When ready, allow a natural release for 10 minutes, then perform a quick pressure release, and unlock the lid. Serve right away.

Japanese-Style Pork Tenderloin

Serving Size: 4 | **Total Time:** 30 minutes
2 lb pork tenderloins
2 tbsp peanut butter
1 cup teriyaki sauce
¼ cup coconut milk
1 tbsp sesame seeds
1 tbsp light soy sauce
Salt and pepper to taste

4 green onions, chopped
1 lime, zested

Melt peanut butter in your Instant Pot on Sauté. Sprinkle pork tenderloins with salt and pepper, place it in the pot and brown for a few minutes on all sides. Put in teriyaki sauce, soy sauce, lime zest, coconut milk, and 1/2 cup of water and seal the lid. Select Manual. Cook for 15 minutes on High.

Once done, allow a natural release for 10 minutes, then perform a quick pressure release, and unlock the lid. Slice the tenderloin and garnish with toasted sesame seeds, green onions, and cooking juice. Serve immediately.

Pork Medallions with Porcini Sauce

Serving Size: 4 | Total Time: 60 minutes
1 oz dried porcini mushrooms
4 boneless pork loin chops
½ cup dry Marsala wine
1 garlic clove, minced
1 tbsp paprika
½ tsp rosemary
1 onion, sliced
2 tbsp butter
Salt and pepper to taste
2 tbsp chopped parsley

Cover the porcini mushrooms with 1 cup of boiling water in a bowl and let soak for 10-15 minutes. Sprinkle pork chops with paprika, salt, and pepper. Melt butter in your Instant Pot on Sauté. Place the pork chops in the pot and sear for 6 minutes on all sides. Set aside.

Add onion and garlic to the pot and cook for 3 minutes. Put pork on top along with Marsala wine, rosemary, and porcini mushrooms with the water. Seal the lid, select Manual, and cook for 15 minutes on High pressure. When over, allow a natural release for 10 minutes and unlock the lid. Garnish with parsley and serve.

Fennel & Rosemary Pork Belly

Serving Size: 2 | Total Time: 60 minutes
1 lb pork belly
2 tbsp olive oil
¼ tsp ground cinnamon
¼ tsp chili flakes
1 tsp fennel seeds
1 rosemary sprig
1 clove garlic, minced
1 cup red wine
Salt and pepper to taste
2 tbsp chopped chives

Warm the olive oil in your Instant Pot on Sauté. Place the pork belly and cook 4 minutes on both sides. Add in salt, pepper, garlic, fennel seeds, cinnamon, rosemary sprig, chili flakes, red wine, and 1 cup of water. Seal the lid, select Manual, and cook for 35 minutes on High.

Once over, allow a natural release for 10 minutes, then perform a quick pressure release, and unlock the lid. Cut the pork and scatter with chives. Serve warm.

Spicy Pork Sausage Ragu

Serving Size: 4 | Total Time: 25 minutes
1 lb pork sausage, casings removed
2 tbsp olive oil
2 garlic cloves, minced
1 onion, chopped
1 cup chopped tomatoes
½ tsp oregano
1 tsp red chili flakes
1 cup chicken stock
Salt and pepper to taste
2 tbsp parsley, chopped

Warm the olive oil in your Instant Pot on Sauté. Place in garlic and onion and cook until fragrant. Add and brown the sausage for 8 minutes. Stir constantly, breaking the meat with a wooden spatula. Stir in chicken stock, red chili flakes, oregano, and chopped tomatoes and seal the lid. Select Manual and cook for 10 minutes on High.

When over, perform a quick pressure release and unlock the lid. Adjust seasoning to taste. Cook on Sauté until the sauce thickens. Top with parsley and serve.

German Pork with Sauerkraut

Serving Size: 4 | Total Time: 40 minutes
2 lb pork belly, cut into 2-inch pieces
3 tbsp lard
2 garlic cloves, minced
1 onion, chopped
1 cup chicken broth
5 cups sauerkraut
1 tsp paprika
1 cup canned diced tomatoes
1 tsp cumin
2 tbsp parsley, chopped
Salt and pepper to taste

Sprinkle the pork with salt and pepper. Melt lard in your Instant Pot on Sauté. Place the pork, onion, and garlic and cook for 5-6 minutes. Stir in paprika and cumin. Put in sauerkraut, chicken broth, tomatoes, and 1/2 cup of water and seal the lid. Select Manual and cook for 30 minutes on High pressure. Once over, perform a quick pressure release and unlock the lid. Serve with parsley.

Tandoori Pork Butt

Serving Size: 4 | Total Time: 61 minutes
2 lb pork butt, boneless, trimmed of excess fat
1 tsp ground cumin
1 tsp ground coriander
1 tsp paprika
1 green chili, minced
1 tsp garam masala
2 tbsp ghee
1 onion, chopped
2 garlic cloves, minced
1-inch piece ginger, grated
1 can (14 oz) coconut milk
Salt and pepper to taste
Lime wedges for garnish

Mix the salt, pepper, ground coriander, paprika, cumin, and garam masala in a bowl. Sprinkle pork butt with this mixture. Melt ghee in your Instant Pot on Sauté. Place in green chili, ginger, onion, and garlic and cook for 2 minutes. Add in pork butt and cook for 3-4 minutes.

Pour in coconut milk and ½ cup of water and seal the lid. Select Manual and cook for 35 minutes on High pressure. Once ready, allow a natural release for 10 minutes, then perform a quick pressure release, and unlock the lid. Cut the butt into slices and serve with lemon wedges.

Prune & Shallot Pork Tenderloin

Serving Size: 6 | **Total Time**: 45 minutes
3 lb pork tenderloins, cut into large chunks
2 tbsp olive oil
2 shallots, chopped
Salt and pepper to taste
½ cup vegetable broth
½ cup balsamic vinegar
½ cup dried pitted prunes
1 carrot, sliced diagonally
2 garlic cloves, minced
2 tbsp rosemary, chopped

Warm the olive oil in your Instant Pot on Sauté. Sprinkle pork tenderloins with salt and pepper, place them in the pot, and brown for 2-3 minutes. Add in shallots, garlic, and carrots and cook for 3 minutes. Stir in vegetable broth, balsamic vinegar, prunes, and rosemary. Seal the lid, select Manual, and cook for 20 minutes on High pressure. When done, allow a natural release for 10 minutes, then perform a quick pressure release, and unlock the lid.

Quick Pork & Vegetable Rice

Serving Size: 4 | **Total Time**: 40 minutes
4 pork chops
2 tbsp olive oil
1 onion, finely chopped
2 tbsp garlic cloves, minced
1 cup white rice, rinsed
1 ½ cups chicken broth
1 carrot, chopped
1 cup mushrooms, sliced
1 red bell pepper, sliced
Salt and pepper to taste
2 spring onions, sliced

Warm the olive oil in your Instant Pot on Sauté. Place in onion, garlic, carrot, bell pepper, and mushrooms and cook for 5 minutes. Add in rice, salt, and pepper. Put pork chops over the rice and pour in chicken broth. Seal the lid, select Manual, and cook for 15 minutes on High pressure. Once done, allow a natural release for 10 minutes. Garnish with spring onions and serve.

Mushroom & Pork Stroganoff

Serving Size: 4 | **Total Time**: 35 minutes
1 cup button mushrooms, sliced
1 lb pork loin, cut into strips
2 tbsp olive oil
1 leek, chopped
1 celery stalk, chopped
2 cups vegetable broth
2 tsp Dijon mustard
½ cup sour cream
½ cup white wine
Salt and pepper to taste
2 tbsp parsley, chopped

Warm the oil in your Instant Pot on Sauté. Sprinkle pork loin with salt and pepper, place it in the pot and brown on all sides. Set aside. Add leek, mushrooms, and celery to the pot and cook for 3 minutes. Pour in wine and scrape any brown bits from the bottom. Stir in vegetable broth and Dijon mustard. Put pork loin back to the pot.

Seal the lid. Select Manual and cook for 12 minutes on High. Once ready, allow a natural release for 10 minutes and unlock the lid. Mix in sour cream and simmer for 1 minute on Sauté. Top with parsley and serve.

Cilantro Pork with Avocado

Serving Size: 4 | **Total Time**: 45 minutes + marinating time
1 lb pork tenderloin, cut into strips
3 garlic cloves, chopped
½ tsp oregano
½ tsp ground cumin
1 tbsp Hungarian paprika
2 tbsp olive oil
2 cups chicken stock
Salt and pepper to taste
1 avocado, sliced
2 tbsp cilantro, chopped

Mix garlic, oregano, cumin, paprika, salt, and pepper in a bowl. Add in pork strips and toss to coat. Let marinate for 30 minutes in the fridge. Warm the olive oil in your Instant Pot on Sauté. Place the strips in the pot and sauté for 10 minutes. Stir in chicken stock and seal the lid. Select Manual and cook for 15 minutes on High pressure.

When done, allow a natural release for 10 minutes, then perform a quick pressure release, and unlock the lid. Scatter with cilantro. Serve topped with avocado slices.

Parsley Pork with Savoy Cabbage

Serving Size: 6 | **Total Time**: 35 minutes
2 lb pork roast, cut into chunks
1 head Savoy cabbage, shredded
3 tbsp canola oil
2 garlic cloves, minced
1 onion, chopped
1 tsp cumin
1 tsp mustard powder
1 cup chopped tomatoes
Salt and pepper to taste
2 tbsp parsley, chopped

Warm the canola oil in your Instant Pot on Sauté. Place in garlic and onion and cook for 3 minutes. Add in pork chunks and cook for 5 minutes on all sides. Stir in cumin, mustard powder, salt, pepper, tomatoes, cabbage, and 1 cup of water. Seal the lid, select Manual, and cook for 20 minutes on High pressure. Once ready, perform a quick pressure release. Top with parsley and serve.

Spiced Pork with Garbanzo Beans

Serving Size: 4 | **Total Time:** 60 minutes

1 ½ tbsp vegetable oil
1 ½ lb pork shoulder, diced
1 red onion, sliced
1 cup garbanzo beans, soaked
3 cups chicken broth
1 cup tomatoes, chopped
2 garlic cloves, minced
2 tbsp fresh dill, chopped
½ tsp ground mustard
½ tsp paprika
½ tsp dried thyme
½ tsp cayenne pepper
½ tsp garlic powder
Salt and pepper to taste

Mix the paprika, thyme, cayenne pepper, garlic powder, salt, and pepper in a bowl. Sprinkle pork with this mixture. Warm the vegetable oil in your Instant Pot on Sauté. Place in pork and brown for 4-5 minutes.
Remove to a bowl. Add red onion and garlic to the pot and cook for 2 minutes. Pour in chicken broth and scrape any brown bits from the bottom. Add in garbanzo beans, tomatoes, and mustard and seal the lid. Select Manual and cook for 30 minutes on High pressure. When over, allow a natural release for 10 minutes and unlock the lid. Garnish with dill and serve.

Smoky Shredded Pork with White Beans

Serving Size: 4 | **Total Time:** 65 minutes

2 lb pork shoulder, halved
2 tbsp vegetable oil
1 onion, chopped
1 cup vegetable broth
2 tbsp liquid smoke
Salt and pepper to taste
1 cup cooked white beans
2 tbsp parsley, chopped

Warm the vegetable oil in your Instant Pot on Sauté. Place in onion and cook for 3 minutes. Sprinkle pork shoulder with salt and pepper, add it to the pot and brown for 5 minutes on all sides. Pour in vegetable broth and liquid smoke and scrape any brown bits from the bottom. Seal the lid, select Manual, and cook for 35 minutes on High.
When ready, allow a natural release for 10 minutes, then perform a quick pressure release, and unlock the lid. Remove pork and shred it. Stir white beans in the pot and put shredded pork back. Top with parsley and serve.

Pulled Pork Tacos

Serving Size: 6 | **Total Time:** 55 minutes + marinating time

2 lb pork shoulder, trimmed of excess fat
3 garlic cloves, minced
1 cup onions, sliced
1 tsp ground cinnamon
1 tbsp cumin
1 tsp oregano
¼ tsp red chili flakes
½ cup pineapple juice
1 ½ cups tomatoes, diced
1 Iceberg lettuce, torn
1 red onion, thinly sliced
2 tbsp cilantro, chopped
Salt and pepper to taste
6 tortillas

Slice pork shoulder into 2-inch pieces. Place the garlic, onions, cinnamon, cumin, oregano, chili flakes, salt, and pepper in a bowl. Add in the pork pieces and toss to coat. Cover with cling film and let marinate for 30 minutes.
Transfer to your Instant Pot and pour in pineapple juice and tomatoes. Seal the lid, select Manual and cook for 30 minutes on High pressure. Once done, allow a natural release for 10 minutes and unlock the lid.
Shred the pork and simmer for 5 minutes on Sauté. To assemble, divide shredded pork between tortillas and top with lettuce, red onion, and cilantro. Serve right away.

Bacon & Potato Brussels Sprouts

Serving Size: 4 | **Total Time:** 20 minutes

4 bacon slices, chopped
1 lb Brussels sprouts, halved
1 cup potatoes, cubed
½ cup chicken stock
Salt and pepper to taste

Set to Sauté your Instant Pot and add the bacon. Cook for 5-6 minutes until crispy; remove to a paper-lined plate. Add potatoes, Brussels sprouts, chicken stock, salt, and pepper to the pot. Seal the lid, select Manual, and cook for 5 minutes on High. When done, perform a quick pressure release. Top with bacon. Serve warm.

Spiced Mexican Pork

Serving Size: 4 | **Total Time:** 55 minutes + marinating time

2 lb pork shoulder, cut into chunks
1 chipotle pepper in adobo sauce, chopped
3 garlic cloves, minced
1 red onion, chopped
½ tsp ground coriander
1 tsp ground cumin
1 tbsp lime juice
¼ cup chile enchilada sauce
1 tsp Mexican oregano
Salt and pepper to taste

Place garlic, onion, ground coriander, cumin, lime juice, Mexican oregano, chipotle pepper, enchilada sauce, salt, pepper, and ½ cup of water in a blender and pulse until smooth. Place the mixture in a large bowl and add in pork chunks; toss to coat. Cover with cling foil and let marinate in the fridge for 30 minutes. Next, remove from the fridge and transfer to your Instant Pot. Pour in ½ cup of water and seal the lid. Select Manual and cook for 25 minutes on High pressure. When ready, allow a natural release for 15 minutes and unlock the lid. Cook for 5 minutes on Sauté until the sauce thickens. Serve warm.

Asian Pork & Noodle Soup

Serving Size: 4 | **Total Time:** 60 minutes
1 lb pork tenderloin, cut into strips
1 (1-inch) piece fresh ginger, halved lengthwise
2 tbsp olive oil
1 yellow onion, halved
2 tsp fennel seeds
1 tsp red pepper flakes
½ tsp coriander seeds
2-star anise
Salt and pepper to taste
8 oz rice noodles
1 lime, cut into wedges
2 tbsp cilantro, chopped

Warm oil on Sauté. Cook ginger and onion for 4 minutes. Add in flakes, fennel seeds, anise, and coriander seeds and cook for 1 minute as you stir. Add in 4 cups of water, salt, pepper, and pork. Seal the lid and cook on High Pressure for 30 minutes. Soak the rice noodles in hot water for 8 minutes until softened and pliable. Stop the cooking process by draining and rinsing with cold water. Separate the noodles into 4 soup bowls.

Release the pressure naturally for 10 minutes. Remove the pork from the cooker and ladle among the bowls. Strain the broth to get rid of solids. Pour it over the pork and noodles. Season with red pepper flakes. Garnish with lime wedges and cilantro leaves and serve.

Awesome Pork & Celery Soup

Serving Size: 4 | **Total Time:** 45 minutes
1 ¼ lb pork ribs
1 leek, chopped
1 onion, chopped
1 cup celery root, diced
½ cup parsley, chopped
4 cups beef broth
1 tsp salt
1 tsp red chili flakes
2 bay leaves
A handful of basil, torn
2 tbsp olive oil

Heat oil on Sauté. Add the ribs in batches and brown on all sides for 5-6 minutes. Add leek, onion, celery, parsley, broth, salt, red chili flakes, bay leaves, and basil.
Seal the lid and cook on Meat/Stew on High for 30 minutes. Do a quick release. Serve.

Delicious Pork & Vegetables Soup

Serving Size: 4 | **Total Time:** 50 minutes
2 (8-oz) pork chops
1 tbsp cayenne pepper
1 tsp chili powder
½ tsp garlic powder
4 cups beef broth
2 tbsp olive oil
2 large carrots, chopped
2 celery stalks, diced
1 onion, diced
2 tbsp soy sauce

Warm the olive oil in your Instant Pot on Sauté and stir-fry the onion until translucent, 3 minutes. Add celery stalks, carrots, cayenne, and chili pepper. Give it a good stir and continue to cook for 6-7 minutes. Add in pork chops, garlic, and soy sauce.
Pour in the broth and seal the lid. Cook on Manual for 25 minutes on High. Do a quick release. Let chill for 5 minutes. Serve.

Cajun Orange Pork Shoulder

Serving Size: 6 | **Total Time:** 60 minutes + marinating time
3 lb pork shoulder, trimmed of excess fat
2 garlic cloves, sliced
1 tsp cumin
1 tsp Cajun seasoning
1 large onion, sliced
¼ cup lime juice
¼ cup orange juice
Salt and pepper to taste
2 tbsp olive oil
2 tbsp cilantro, chopped

Mix the cumin, Cajun seasoning, garlic, onion, lime juice, orange juice, salt, and pepper in a bowl. Place in the pork shoulder and toss to coat. Let sit covered in the fridge for 30 minutes. Warm the olive oil in your Instant Pot on Sauté. Place in pork shoulder and cook for 10 minutes on all sides. Set aside.
Pour the remaining marinade into the pot and scrape any brown bits from the bottom. Pour in 1 cup of water and fit in a trivet. Place the pork inside the trivet and seal the lid. Select Manual and cook for 30 minutes on High.
When over, allow a natural release for 10 minutes, then perform a quick pressure release, and unlock the lid. Remove and slice the pork. Top with cilantro. Serve.

Garlic & Thyme Pork

Serving Size: 4 | **Total Time:** 58 minutes
1 lb pork brisket
2 garlic cloves, minced
2 tsp paprika
1 tsp ground cumin
1 tsp onion powder
2 tbsp flour
2 tbsp olive oil
1 ½ cups chicken broth
½ cup red wine
6 garlic cloves, minced
1 tbsp thyme, chopped
1 tbsp butter
1 cup mushrooms, sliced
Salt and pepper to taste

Mix the onion powder, paprika, cumin, salt, pepper, and garlic in a bowl. Sprinkle pork brisket with this mixture. Cover all brisket with flour. Warm the oil in your Instant Pot on Sauté. Place in brisket and cook for 8 minutes on all sides. Pour in red wine and scrape any brown bits from the bottom. Add in garlic, thyme, and broth and seal the lid. Select Manual and cook for 30 minutes.
When ready, allow a natural release for 10 minutes, then perform a quick pressure release, and unlock the lid. Remove brisket to a plate and cooking liquid

in a bowl. Melt butter in your Instant Pot on Sauté. Place in mushrooms and cook until they are soft. Pour in reserved liquid and cook for another minute. Cut brisket in slices and top with mushroom sauce. Serve warm.

German-Style Red Cabbage with Apples

Serving Size: 4 | **Total Time:** 20 minutes
1 cup Granny Smith apples, cubed
1 head red cabbage, shredded
2 tbsp olive oil
4 oz bacon, chopped
1 sweet onion, chopped
2 garlic cloves, chopped
1 tbsp red wine vinegar
1 tsp ground cumin
Salt and pepper to taste

Warm olive oil in your Instant Pot on Sauté. Place the bacon, onion, and garlic and cook for 5 minutes. Put in cabbage, vinegar, apples, cumin, salt, pepper, and 1 cup of water and seal the lid. Select Manual and cook for 10 minutes on High pressure. When done, perform a quick pressure release. Carefully unlock the lid. Adjust the taste with salt and pepper and serve.

Gruyere Mushroom & Mortadella Cups

Serving Size: 4 | **Total Time:** 20 minutes
4 eggs, beaten
1 tsp olive oil
½ tsp paprika
½ cup mushrooms, chopped
1 cup mortadella, chopped
1 tbsp parsley, minced
Salt and pepper to taste
2 tbsp Gruyere, grated

Mix the eggs, olive oil, 1 tbsp of water, and paprika in a bowl. Add in mushrooms, parsley, salt, pepper, and mortadella. Divide the mixture between ramekins and top with Gruyere cheese.
Pour 1 cup of water into your Instant Pot and fit in a trivet. Place the ramekins on the trivet and seal the lid. Select Manual and cook for 12 minutes on High pressure. Once ready, perform a quick pressure release. Carefully unlock the lid. Serve warm.

Asparagus Wrapped in Parma Ham

Serving Size: 4 | **Total Time:** 15 minutes
1 lb asparagus, trimmed
½ lb Parma ham, sliced
2 tbsp Parmesan, grated

Pour 1 cup of water into your Instant Pot and fit in a trivet. Wrap each asparagus spear with a ham slice and place on the trivet. Seal the lid, select Manual, and cook for 3 minutes on High pressure.
When over, allow a natural release for 5 minutes, then perform a quick pressure release, and unlock the lid. Transfer the wraps to a greased baking dish and sprinkle with the Parmesan cheese. Place under preheated broiler for about 4 minutes until the cheese is melted. Serve.

Ranch Potatoes with Ham

Serving Size: 4 | **Total Time:** 20 minutes
1 lb Yukon gold potatoes, quartered
4 oz cooked ham, chopped
1 tsp garlic powder
2 tsp chives, chopped
Salt to taste
1/3 cup Ranch dressing

Cover potatoes with salted water in your Instant Pot and seal the lid. Select Manual and cook for 7 minutes on High pressure.
When done, perform a quick pressure release and unlock the lid. Drain the potatoes and transfer to a bowl. Stir in ranch dressing, garlic powder, and ham. Sprinkle with chives and serve.

BEEF & LAMB

Beef & Jasmine Rice Porridge
Serving Size: 6 | **Total Time**: 50 minutes
1 cup jasmine rice
2 cloves garlic, minced
1-inch piece ginger, minced
6 cups beef stock
1 cup kale, chopped
1 cup water
2 lb ground beef
Salt and pepper to taste
Fresh cilantro, chopped

Run cold water and rinse rice. Add garlic, rice, and ginger into the pot. Pour water and stock into the pot and Spread the beef on top of rice. Seal the lid and cook on High Pressure for 30 minutes. Release pressure naturally for 10 minutes. Stir in kale to obtain the desired consistency. Season with pepper and salt. Top with cilantro to serve.

Butternut Squash & Beef Stew
Serving Size: 6 | **Total Time**: 40 minutes
2 lb stew beef, cut into 1-inch chunks
½ butternut pumpkin, chopped
2 tbsp canola oil
1 cup red wine
1 onion, chopped
1 tsp garlic powder
1 tsp salt
3 whole cloves
1 bay leaf
3 carrots, chopped
2 tbsp cornstarch
3 tbsp water

Warm oil on Sauté. Brown the beef for 5 minutes on each side. Deglaze the pot with wine, scrape the bottom to get rid of any browned beef bits. Add in onion, salt, bay leaf, cloves, and garlic powder. Seal the lid, press Meat/Stew, and cook on High for 15 minutes. Release the pressure quickly. Add in pumpkin and carrots without stirring. Seal the lid. Cook on High Pressure for 5 minutes. Release the pressure quickly. In a bowl, mix water and cornstarch until cornstarch dissolves completely and mix into the stew. Allow to simmer on Sauté for 5 minutes until you attain the desired thickness.

Beef Fillets with Onions
Serving Size: 6 | **Total Time**: 50 minutes
2 lb beef fillets, cut into bite-sized pieces
4 onions, chopped
3 tbsp tomato paste
2 tbsp oil
1 tbsp butter, melted
Salt and pepper to taste

Grease your Instant Pot with 2 tbsp of oil. Make the first layer of meat. Add onions, tomato paste, salt, and pepper. Stir and Pour 2 cups of water. Seal the lid and cook on Meat/Stew for 30 minutes on High. Release the steam naturally for about 10 minutes. Stir in 1 tbsp of butter and serve warm.

Beef Gyros with Yogurt & Dill
Serving Size: 4 | **Total Time**: 55 minutes
1 lb beef sirloin, cut into thin strips
1 onion, chopped
1/3 cup beef broth
2 tbsp fresh lemon juice
2 tbsp olive oil
2 tsp dry oregano
1 clove garlic, minced
Salt and pepper to taste
4 slices pita bread
1 cup Greek yogurt
2 tbsp fresh dill, chopped

In your Instant Pot, mix beef, beef broth, oregano, garlic, lemon juice, pepper, onion, olive oil, and salt. Seal the lid and cook on High Pressure for 30 minutes. Release pressure naturally for 15 minutes. Carefully unlock the lid. Divide the beef mixture between the pita bread. Top with yogurt and dill and roll up to serve.

Ground Beef & Eggplant Casserole
Serving Size: 2 | **Total Time**: 40 minutes
2 eggplants, peeled, cut lengthwise
Salt and pepper to taste
1 cup lean ground beef
1 onion, chopped
1 tsp olive oil
2 tomatoes

Place eggplants in a bowl and season with salt. Let sit for 10 minutes. Rinse well and drain. Grease the inner pot with oil. Stir-fry onion for 2 minutes until soft. Add ground beef, tomatoes, and cook for 5 minutes. Remove to a deep bowl.
Make a layer with eggplant slices in the pot. Spread the ground beef mixture over and sprinkle with black pepper and salt. Make another layer with eggplants and repeat until you've used up all ingredients. Seal the lid and cook on High Pressure for 12 minutes. Do a quick release. Serve.

Sirloin Steaks with Red Wine
Serving Size: 4 | **Total Time**: 1 hour 25 minutes
2 lb beef sirloin
1 cup red wine
2 cups beef consomme
2 bay leaves
2 tbsp olive oil
Salt and pepper to taste
1 large onion, chopped
1 stalk celery, diced
1 tbsp tomato puree
2 cloves garlic, minced
2 sprigs fresh parsley

Rub the meat with salt and pepper on all sides. Heat oil on Sauté and sear the beef for 4-5 minutes. Set aside. In the same oil, add onion, celery, garlic, and tomato puree. Cook for 4-5 minutes until soft. Pour in wine to deglaze.

Bring the meat back to the pot, add consomme, parsley, and bay leaf. Seal the lid and cook on High Pressure for 50 minutes. Do a natural pressure release. Slice the sirloin and spoon over the cooking sauce to serve.

Chili Beef & Turnip Stew

Serving Size: 6 | Total Time: 30 minutes
3 tbsp olive oil
1 onion, chopped
Salt to taste
4 garlic cloves, minced
2 tbsp tomato puree
1 tbsp chili powder
2 tsp ground cumin
1 tsp dried oregano
½ tsp ground turmeric
1 lb ground beef meat
28-oz can whole tomatoes
2 cups beef stock
1 lb turnips, cubed
2 tomatoes, chopped
1 bell pepper, chopped

Warm oil on Sauté. Add in onion and salt and cook for 3 minutes until softened. Stir in garlic, chili powder, turmeric, cumin, tomato paste, and oregano. Cook for 2-3 minutes as you stir until very soft and sticks to the pot's bottom. Add beef and cook for 5 minutes until completely browned. Stir in tomatoes, turnips, bell pepper, and stock. Seal the lid and cook on High Pressure for 15 minutes. Release the pressure quickly. Serve.

Penne with Beef & Tomato Sauce

Serving Size: 5 | Total Time: 30 minutes
6 oz beef, braising steak cut into chunks
16 oz penne
1 onion, chopped
1 tomato peeled, diced
1 tbsp tomato paste
3 tbsp butter, unsalted
Salt and pepper to taste
1 tsp cayenne pepper
1 tbsp vegetable oil

Heat oil on Sauté and stir-fry the onion until translucent. Add tomato, tomato paste, butter, salt, black pepper, and cayenne pepper. Cook until tomato softens. Add beef chunks and 1 cup of water. Give it a good stir.
Seal the lid. Cook for 14 minutes on High Pressure. Do a quick release and set the meat aside. Add in penne and 2 cups of water. Seal the lid and cook on High Pressure for 4 minutes. Do a quick release. Transfer macaroni to a bowl, stir in beef sauce, and serve.

Moroccan Beef & Cherry Stew

Serving Size: 4 | Total Time: 1 hour 20 minutes
1 ½ lb stewing beef, trimmed
¼ cup toasted almonds, slivered
2 tbsp olive oil
1 onion, chopped
1 tsp ground cinnamon
½ tsp paprika
½ tsp turmeric
½ tsp salt
¼ tsp ground ginger
¼ tsp ground allspice
1-star anise
1 cup water
1 tbsp honey
1 cup dried cherries, halved

Set the Instant Pot to Sauté and warm olive oil. Add in onion and cook for 3 minutes. Mix in beef and cook for 2 minutes each side until browned. Stir in anise, cinnamon, turmeric, allspice, salt, paprika, and ginger; cook for 2 minutes until aromatic. Add in honey and water. Seal the lid, press Meat/Stew, and cook on High for 50 minutes.
In a bowl, soak dried cherries in hot water until softened. Once ready, release pressure naturally for 15 minutes. Drain cherries and stir into the tagine. Top with toasted almonds before serving.

Traditional Turkish Dolma (Stuffed Peppers)

Serving Size: 4 | Total Time: 35 minutes
2 lb red bell peppers
1 onion, finely chopped
1 lb lean ground beef
¼ cup rice
½ cup tomatoes, chopped
1 tomato, sliced
½ tsp salt
1 tsp cayenne pepper
1 tbsp olive oil

In a bowl, combine meat, onion, rice, tomatoes, salt, and cayenne. Stir well to combine. Remove the stems and seeds from the peppers. Fill each pepper with 2 tbsp of the meat mixture. Make sure to leave at least ½ inch of headspace. Grease the bottom of your Instant Pot with olive oil. Make the first layer with tomato slices and arrange the peppers on top of them. Add 2 cups of water. Seal the lid and cook on High Pressure for 15 minutes. Do a natural pressure release for 10 minutes.

Easy Wax Beans with Ground Beef

Serving Size: 4 | Total Time: 20 minutes
1 lb ground beef
1 lb wax beans
1 small onion, chopped
1 tbsp tomato paste
2 cups beef broth
2 garlic cloves, crushed
2 tbsp olive oil
2 tbsp parsley, chopped
1 tsp salt
½ tsp paprika
1 tbsp Parmesan, grated

Grease the pot with olive oil. Stir-fry the onion and garlic for a few minutes until translucent on Sauté. Add beef, tomato paste, parsley, salt, and paprika. Cook for 5 more minutes, stirring constantly. Add wax beans and beef broth. Press Cancel and seal the lid. Cook on High Pressure for 4 minutes. Do a natural release. Carefully unlock the lid. Top with Parmesan and serve hot.

Pesto Beef Sandwiches with Pepperoncini
Serving Size: 4 | **Total Time**: 50 minutes
1 ½ lb beef steak, cut into strips
½ cup pepperoncini peppers, chopped
Salt and pepper to taste
1 tbsp olive oil
¼ cup dry red wine
1 cup beef broth
1 tbsp oregano
1 tsp onion powder
1 tsp garlic powder
4 hoagie rolls, halved
8 slices mozzarella cheese
4 tbsp pesto

Season the beef strips with salt and pepper. Warm oil on Sauté and sear the beef for 2-3 minutes for each side until browned. Add wine into the pot to deglaze and scrape the bottom to eliminate any browned beef bits. Stir garlic powder, beef broth, onion powder, and oregano into the pot. Seal the lid, press Meat/Stew, and cook for 25 minutes on High. Release pressure naturally for 10 minutes. Spread each bread half with pesto, put beef on top, place pepperoncini over, add mozzarella cheese slices, and cover with the second half of bread.

Creamy Beef & Cauliflower Chili
Serving Size: 6 | **Total Time**: 20 minutes
1 lb beef stew meat
4 oz cauliflower, chopped
1 onion, chopped
2 cups beef broth
2 cups heavy cream
1 tsp Italian seasoning
1 tsp salt
½ tsp chili pepper

Add beef, cauliflower, onion, broth, heavy cream, Italian seasoning, salt, and chili pepper to your Instant Pot. Pour in 1 cup water. Seal the lid and cook on High Pressure for 15 minutes. When ready, do a quick release and serve.

Gingered Beef Pot Roast
Serving Size: 6 | **Total Time**: 45 minutes
2 lb beef chuck roast, cubed
2 tbsp olive oil
Salt and pepper to taste
1 cup beef broth
½ cup soy sauce
3 minced garlic cloves
1 tbsp grated ginger
2-star anise
1 jalapeño pepper, minced

Warm the olive oil in your Instant Pot on Sauté. Sprinkle beef with salt and pepper and place it in the pot and garlic, ginger, and jalapeño pepper and cook until browned. Remove to a plate.
Pour beef broth in the pot and scrape any brown bits from the bottom. Stir in soy sauce and star anise. Put the beef back in the pot and seal the lid. Select Manual and cook for 35 minutes on High pressure. Once ready, perform a quick pressure release and unlock the lid.

Beef Lasagna with Eggplant & Almonds
Serving Size: 4 | **Total Time**: 25 minutes
2 lb stewed beef, boneless, sliced
3 oz toasted almonds, chopped
3 eggplants, halved
2 tomatoes, chopped
2 red bell peppers, sliced
¼ tbsp tomato paste
2 tbsp parsley, chopped
2 tbsp capers
¼ cup olive oil

Grease the Instant Pot with 2 tbsp of olive oil. Make the first layer with halved eggplants tucking the ends gently to fit in. Make the second layer with beef slices, tomatoes, and red bell peppers. Spread the tomato paste evenly over, sprinkle with almonds and capers. Add in the remaining olive oil. Pour 1 ½ cups of water and seal the lid. Cook on High Pressure for 13 minutes. Do a quick release. Serve with fresh parsley.

T-Bone Steaks with Basil & Mustard
Serving Size: 4 | **Total Time**: 40 minutes + marinating time
1 lb T-bone steak
Salt and pepper to taste
2 tbsp Dijon mustard
¼ cup oil
½ tsp dried basil, crushed

Whisk together oil, mustard, salt, pepper, and basil. Brush each steak and Refrigerate for 1 hour. Then, insert a steamer tray in the Instant Pot. Pour in 1 cup of water and arrange the steaks on the tray. Seal the lid and cook on Manual for 25 minutes on High. Do a quick release. Discard the liquid, remove the tray, and hit Sauté. Brown the steaks for 5 minutes, turning once.

Stewed Beef with Potatoes
Serving Size: 4 | **Total Time**: 60 minutes
1 lb russet potatoes, cut into chunks
1 lb beef shoulder
2 carrots, chopped
1 onion, finely chopped
4 tbsp olive oil
2 tbsp tomato paste
1 tbsp flour
4 cups beef broth
1 celery stalk, chopped
1 tbsp parsley, chopped
1 cayenne pepper, chopped
Salt and pepper to taste

Warm oil on Sauté. Stir-fry onion, carrots, and potatoes for 7-8 minutes. Stir in flour and press Cancel. Add beef, tomato paste, broth, celery, parsley, cayenne pepper, salt, and pepper Seal the lid and cook on High Pressure for 40 minutes. Do a quick release.

Carrot Casserole with Beef & Potato

Serving Size: 3 | **Total Time**: 20 minutes
1 lb lean beef, with bones
2 carrots
1 potato, sliced
3 tbsp olive oil
½ tsp salt

Mix beef, carrots, potato, olive oil, and salt in the Instant Pot. Pour enough water to cover and seal the lid. Cook on High Pressure for 15 minutes. Do a quick release and serve hot.

Beef Goulash with Cabbage & Potatoes

Serving Size: 6 | **Total Time**: 45 minutes
1 cup sun-dried tomatoes, diced
2 lb beef stew meat
3 potatoes, cut into chunks
1 onion, chopped
1 carrot, chopped
1 cabbage head, shredded
4 cups beef broth
3 tbsp tomato paste
1 tsp tabasco sauce
Salt and pepper to taste
3 tbsp butter

Melt the butter oil in your Instant Pot on Sauté and cook the onion until translucent for 2 minutes. Add the tomato paste and stir. Add the beef, tomatoes, potatoes, carrot, cabbage, broth, tabasco sauce, salt, and pepper and seal the lid. Cook on High Pressure for 35 minutes. Do a quick release.

Beef Arancini with Potatoes

Serving Size: 4 | **Total Time**: 40 minutes
1 lb lean ground beef
6 oz rice
2 onions, peeled, chopped
2 garlic cloves, crushed
1 egg, beaten
1 potato peeled, chopped
3 tbsp olive oil
1 tsp salt

In a bowl, combine beef, rice, onions, garlic, egg, and salt. Shape the mixture into 15-16 meatballs. Grease the inner pot with 1 tbsp of olive oil. Press Sauté and cook the meatballs for 3-4 minutes, or until slightly brown.

Remove the meatballs. Add the remaining oil and make a layer of potato. Top with meatballs, cover with water, and seal the lid. Adjust the release steam handle. Cook on Meat/Stew for 15 minutes on High. Do a quick release.

Green Pea & Beef Ragout

Serving Size: 4 | **Total Time**: 25 minutes
2 lb beef, tender cuts, cut into bits
2 cups green peas
1 onion, diced
1 tomato, diced
3 cups beef broth
½ cup tomato paste
1 tsp cayenne pepper
1 tbsp flour
1 tsp salt
½ tsp dried thyme
½ tsp red pepper flakes

Add beef, green peas, onion, tomato, broth, tomato paste, cayenne pepper, flour, salt, thyme, and red pepper flakes to the Instant Pot. Seal the lid, press Manual/Pressure Cook and cook for 10 minutes on High Pressure. When done, release the steam naturally for 10 minutes. Serve.

Classic Mushroom Beef Stroganoff

Serving Size: 6 | **Total Time**: 45 minutes
1 lb beef steak, cut into bite-sized pieces
1 cup button mushrooms, chopped
1 cup sour cream
2 cups beef broth
3 tbsp Worcestershire sauce
3 tbsp olive oil
1 tbsp flour
1 onion, chopped
Salt and pepper to taste

In a bowl, mix flour, salt, and pepper. Coat steaks with the mixture. Place the meat and broth in the inner pot. Seal the lid and cook for 10 minutes on High Pressure. Do a quick release. Add mushrooms, onion, and Worcestershire sauce. Seal the lid and cook on High Pressure for 15 minutes. Do a quick release. Stir in sour cream. Let simmer for 10 minutes and serve.

Eggplant & Beef Stew with Parmesan

Serving Size: 6 | **Total Time**: 70 minutes
9 oz beef neck, cut into bite-sized pieces
2 cups fire-roasted tomatoes
1 eggplant, chopped
½ tbsp fresh green peas
1 tbsp cayenne pepper
1 tbsp beef broth
4 tbsp olive oil
2 tbsp tomato paste
1 tbsp ground chili pepper
½ tsp salt
Parmesan, for garnish

Rub the meat with salt, cayenne, and chili pepper. Grease the Instant Pot with oil and brown the meat for 5-7 minutes or until golden on Sauté. Add tomatoes, eggplant, green peas, broth, and tomato paste and seal the lid. Cook on Meat/Stew for 40 minutes on High. Do a natural release for 10 minutes. Carefully unlock the lid. Serve warm sprinkled with grated Parmesan cheese.

Tasty Spicy Beef

Serving Size: 6 | **Total Time**: 33 minutes
2 lb lean beef, cut into bite-sized pieces
5 onions, chopped
5 garlic cloves, minced
1 jalapeño pepper, chopped
Salt and pepper to taste
1 tsp cayenne pepper
2 tbsp tomato sauce
2 tbsp vegetable oil

Heat oil on Sauté. Stir-fry onions and garlic for 3 minutes. Add in the meat, salt, pepper, cayenne pepper, jalapeño pepper, and tomato sauce. Mix and cover with water. Seal the lid. Cook for 20 minutes on High Pressure. Do a quick pressure release. Carefully unlock the lid. Serve.

Red Wine Beef & Vegetable Hotpot

Serving Size: 6 | **Total Time**: 40 minutes
2 sweet potatoes, cut into chunks
2 lb stewing beef meat
¾ cup red wine
1 tbsp ghee
6 oz tomato paste
6 oz baby carrots, chopped
1 onion, finely chopped
½ tsp salt
4 cups beef broth
½ cup green peas
1 tsp dried thyme
3 garlic cloves, crushed

Heat ghee on Sauté. Add beef and brown for 5-6 minutes. Add onion and garlic, and keep stirring for 3 more minutes. Add the sweet potatoes, wine, tomato paste, carrots, salt, broth, green peas, and thyme and seal the lid. Cook on Meat/Stew for 20 minutes on High Pressure. Do a quick release. Serve.

Beef Bones with Beans & Chili Pepper

Serving Size: 4 | **Total Time**: 30 minutes
14.5 oz canned beans
12 oz beef bones
1 onion, chopped
3 garlic cloves
1 carrot, chopped
1 tbsp parsley, chopped
1 bay leaf
Salt and pepper to taste
1 chili pepper, minced
3 tbsp vegetable oil

Place beans, beef bones, onion, garlic, carrot, parsley, bay leaf, salt, pepper, chili pepper, and oil in the Instant Pot. Pour water enough to cover. Seal the lid. Cook on High Pressure for 15 minutes. Release the steam naturally for 10 minutes. Let it chill for a while before serving.

Beef & Potatoes Moussaka

Serving Size: 4 | **Total Time**: 35 minutes
2 lb potatoes, chopped
1 lb lean ground beef
1 onion, chopped
Salt and pepper to taste
½ cup milk
2 eggs, beaten
1 tbsp vegetable oil
Sour cream for serving

Grease the pot with vegetable oil. Make 1 layer of potatoes and brush with milk. Spread the beef on top and make another layer of potatoes. Brush with the remaining milk. Seal the lid and cook for 15 minutes on High Pressure. Do a quick release. Sprinkle with salt and pepper and top with the eggs and onion. Seal the lid and let it stand for about 10 minutes. Top with sour cream.

Beef with Potatoes & Mushrooms

Serving Size: 6 | **Total Time**: 40 minutes
2 lb round roast
2 tbsp olive oil
2 cups vegetable broth
2 garlic cloves, minced
1 celery stalk, chopped
Salt and pepper to taste
1 tsp oregano
2 cups sliced mushrooms
1 large white onion, diced
1 lb potatoes, quartered

Place the olive oil, vegetable broth, garlic, salt, pepper, and oregano in your Instant Pot and stir. Mix in the round roast, mushrooms, potatoes, celery, and onion. Seal the lid, select Manual, and cook for 25 minutes on High pressure. When done, perform a quick pressure release and unlock the lid. Serve immediately.

Chinese Beef with Bok Choy

Serving Size: 4 | **Total Time**: 45 minutes
1 lb stew beef meat, cubed
1 onion, quartered
1 garlic clove, minced
2 tbsp sesame oil
1 carrot, thinly chopped
1 tbsp rice wine
1 (12 oz) bok choy, sliced
12 oz broccoli florets
1 red chili, sliced
1 tsp ground ginger
1 cup beef broth
¼ cup soy sauce
2 tbsp fish sauce

Warm the sesame oil in your Instant Pot on Sauté. Add in beef meat, onion, garlic, carrot, ginger, and red chili and cook for 5-6 minutes. Stir in beef broth, rice wine, soy sauce, and fish sauce and seal the lid. Select Manual and cook for 30 minutes on High pressure. When done, perform a quick pressure release. Put in broccoli and bok choy and cook for 4-5 minutes on Sauté. Serve.

Simple Beef with Rice & Cheese

Serving Size: 4 | **Total Time**: 65 minutes
2 lb beef shoulder
1 cup rice
2 cups beef broth
3 tbsp butter
¼ cup Parmesan, grated
Salt and pepper to taste

Rub the beef with salt and pepper. Place it in the pot and pour in broth. Seal the lid and cook on Meat/Stew for 25 minutes on High. Do a quick release. Unlock the lid and remove the meat but keep the broth. Add rice and stir in 1 tbsp butter. Season with pepper and salt. Seal the lid. Cook on Manual for 20 minutes on High. Do a quick release. Remove the rice and wipe the pot clean. Melt 2 tbsp of butter on Sauté. Add meat and lightly brown for 10 minutes. Serve with rice topped with Parmesan.

Fall Beef Steak with Vegetables

Serving Size: 4 | Total Time: 51 minutes
1 lb beef chuck roast, cut into chunks
2 tbsp olive oil
1 leek, sliced
2 garlic cloves, minced
1 tsp thyme
1 tsp steak seasoning
2 green bell peppers, sliced
1 cup mushrooms, sliced
1 carrot, chopped
1 celery stalk, chopped
1 cup beef stock
Salt and pepper to taste

Warm the olive oil in your Instant Pot on Sauté. Place in garlic and leek and cook for 3-4 minutes. Stir in beef chunks and brown for 6-7 minutes, stirring occasionally. Mix in steak seasoning, bell peppers, celery, carrot, mushrooms, beef stock, thyme, salt, and pepper. Seal the lid, select Manual, and cook for 30 minutes on High pressure. When done, perform a quick pressure release and unlock the lid. Serve right away.

Calf's Liver Venetian-Style

Serving Size: 2 | Total Time: 55 minutes
1 lb calf's liver, rinsed
3 tbsp olive oil
2 garlic cloves, crushed
1 tbsp mint, chopped
½ tsp cayenne pepper
½ tsp Italian seasoning

In a bowl, mix oil, garlic, mint, cayenne, and Italian seasoning. Brush the liver and chill for 30 minutes. Remove from the fridge and pat dry with paper. Place the liver into the inner pot. Seal the lid and cook on High Pressure for 5 minutes. When ready, release the steam naturally for about 10 minutes.

Thyme Ground Beef Roll

Serving Size: 6 | Total Time: 50 minutes
2 lb ground beef
2 large eggs
½ tsp minced garlic
1 cup all-purpose flour
1 tsp dried thyme
3 tbsp olive oil
½ tsp salt

In a bowl, combine the meat, garlic, flour, and eggs. Sprinkle with thyme and salt. Mix with hands and set aside. Grease a baking dish with olive oil. Form the meatloaf at the bottom. Add 1 cup water and place a trivet in your cooker. Lay the baking dish on the trivet. Seal the lid, press Meat/Stew, and cook for 40 minutes on High. Do a quick release. Carefully transfer the meatloaf to a serving dish. Garnish with salad and serve.

Pino Noir Beef Pot Roast

Serving Size: 6 | Total Time: 61 minutes
3 lb beef chuck roast
2 tbsp olive oil
1 cup beef broth
4 carrots, julienned
1 lb potatoes, chopped
2 celery stalks, chopped
3 garlic cloves, peeled
1 cup Pino Noir red wine
1 onion, sliced
2 sprigs rosemary
2 tbsp tomato puree
Salt and pepper to taste

Warm the olive oil in your Instant Pot on Sauté. Add in the beef roast and brown for 5-6 minutes on all sides. Remove to a plate. Pour in the red wine and scrape any brown bits from the bottom. Stir in onion, garlic, carrots, potatoes, celery, tomato puree, rosemary sprigs, salt, and pepper. Put the beef back on the vegetables and add in the beef broth. Seal the lid. Select Manual and cook for 35 minutes on High. When over, allow a natural release for 10 minutes and unlock the lid. Discard rosemary sprigs and remove beef to a plate. Serve with gravy and vegetables.

Beer-Braised Beef Short Ribs

Serving Size: 6 | Total Time: 70 minutes
3 lb beef short ribs
Salt and pepper to taste
2 tbsp olive oil
3 garlic cloves, minced
4 carrots, chopped
1 onion, diced
1 tsp dried thyme
1 ½ cups beef broth
1 cup pilsner beer

Sprinkle beef ribs with salt and pepper. Warm the olive oil in your Instant Pot on Sauté. Add in the ribs and cook for 10 minutes on all sides until browned; set aside. Add carrot, onion, garlic, and thyme to the pot and cook for 5 more minutes. Pour in beef broth and scrape any brown bits from the bottom. Mix in beer and return the ribs.

Maple Beef Teriyaki

Serving Size: 4 | Total Time: 50 minutes
2 lb flank steak, cut into strips
2 garlic cloves, minced
¼ cup soy sauce
¼ cup maple syrup
¼ cup tamari sauce
1-inch piece grated ginger

Place the soy sauce, garlic, maple syrup, tamari sauce, ginger, and ½ cup of water in your Instant Pot and cook for 5 minutes on Sauté. Stir in steak strips. Seal the lid. Select Manual and cook for 25 minutes on High pressure. Once over, allow a natural release for 10 minutes, then perform a quick pressure release. Carefully unlock the lid. Serve immediately.

Beef with Snow Peas

Serving Size: 4 | Total Time: 46 minutes
1 lb beef brisket, cubed
Salt and pepper to taste
2 tbsp olive oil
1 onion, chopped

2 garlic cloves, minced
2 bay leaves
8 oz bag snow peas, trimmed
1 carrot, chopped
1 turnip, chopped
1 lb potatoes, cut into quarters
Bearnaise sauce for serving

Warm the olive oil in your Instant Pot on Sauté. Place in beef brisket, onion, garlic, carrot, and turnip and cook for 5 minutes. Add in 2 cups of water, potatoes, bay leaves, salt, and pepper and seal the lid. Select Manual and cook for 25 minutes on High pressure. When ready, perform a quick pressure release and unlock the lid. Discard bay leaves and put in snow peas, and cook for 6 minutes on Sauté. Serve with bearnaise sauce.

Italian Roast Beef

Serving Size: 4 | **Total Time:** 75 minutes
1 lb boneless beef chuck roast
2 oz dried porcini mushrooms
4 oz pancetta, diced
1 onion, chopped
2 garlic cloves, minced
1 cup chicken broth
1 tsp tomato paste
14 oz can crushed tomatoes
½ cup Chianti red wine
1 tsp dried oregano
2 bay leaves
½ tsp Italian seasonings
Salt and pepper to taste
2 tbsp parsley, chopped

In a bowl, place porcini mushrooms and pour in ½ cup of boiling water to cover. Let sit for 10 minutes. Set your Instant Pot to Sauté. Place in pancetta and cook for 5 minutes until crispy; set aside. Add in onion and garlic and cook for 3 minutes until fragrant. Stir in the beef roast, pancetta, soaked mushrooms with their water, chicken broth, tomato paste, tomatoes, red wine, oregano, bay leaves, Italian seasonings, salt, and pepper.
Seal the lid, select Meat/Stew, and cook for 35 minutes on High pressure. Once over, allow a natural release for 10 minutes, then perform a quick pressure release, and unlock the lid. Serve topped with parsley.

Classic Beef Stroganoff

Serving Size: 6 | **Total Time:** 45 minutes
2 lb chuck roast, thin slices
2 tbsp butter
1 tbsp olive oil
1 onion, sliced
Salt and pepper to taste
1 cup mushrooms, sliced
2 garlic cloves, minced
1 ¼ cups beef broth
½ cup crème fraiche
2 cup cooked rice

Warm the olive oil and butter in your Instant Pot on Sauté. Place in onion and cook for 3 minutes. Sprinkle chuck roast with salt and pepper and place it in the pot and brown for 2 minutes on all sides. Add in mushrooms and garlic and cook for another 3 minutes. Stir in beef broth and seal the lid. Select Manual and cook for 20 minutes on High pressure. Once ready, perform a quick pressure release and unlock the lid. Mix in créme fraiche and lock the lid. Let sit for 5 minutes. Serve with rice.

Sambal Beef Noodles

Serving Size: 4 | **Total Time:** 65 minutes
1 lb beef chuck roast, cubed
2 tbsp sesame oil
Salt and pepper to taste
1 chopped onion
2 minced garlic cloves
3 tbsp sambal oelek chili paste
2 cups water
8 oz egg noodles

Warm the sesame oil in your Instant Pot on Sauté. Place in the beef roast and cook for 6-7 minutes, stirring often. Add in salt, pepper, onion, sambal oelek chili paste, garlic, and 1 cup of water. Seal the lid, select Manual, and cook for 30 minutes on High pressure.
Once done, allow a natural release for 10 minutes, then perform a quick pressure release. Transfer beef roast to a plate. Pour in 1 cup of water in the pot and bring to a boil on Sauté. Add in noodles and cook for 4-5 minutes. Put the beef back to the pot and stir. Serve warm.

Beef Tikka Masala

Serving Size: 4 | **Total Time:** 50 minutes
2 tbsp tikka masala powder
1 lb beef chuck steak, cubed
2 tbsp olive oil
1 green chili, chopped
2 tsp ginger purée
2 tsp garlic purée
1 onion, chopped
1 cup beef broth
1 (14 oz) diced tomatoes
½ cup coconut cream
Salt and pepper to taste
3 tbsp chopped cilantro

Warm the olive oil in your Instant Pot on Sauté. Sprinkle beef steak with salt and pepper. Place it in the pot and sauté for 4-5 minutes, stirring periodically; set aside. Add onion, ginger puree, garlic puree, green chili, tikka masala powder, salt, and pepper in the pot.
Cook for 3 minutes. Pour in beef broth and scrape any brown bits from the bottom. Put back beef to the pot and diced tomatoes and seal the lid. Select Manual and cook for 25 minutes on High pressure. Once done, perform a quick pressure release and unlock the lid. Mix in coconut cream for 4-5 minutes. Scatter cilantro on top and serve.

Traditional American Beef Meatloaf

Serving Size: 6 | **Total Time:** 45 minutes
2 lb ground beef
½ cup milk

½ cup breadcrumbs
1 onion, grated
1 egg, beaten
1 tsp allspice
Salt and pepper to taste
¼ cup ketchup
½ garlic powder
½ tsp brown sugar
2 tbsp tomato paste

I a bowl, add ground beef, beaten egg, onion, milk, breadcrumbs, allspice, salt, and pepper and stir with your hands. Pour 1 cup of water into your Instant Pot and fit in a trivet. Place the meatloaf on an aluminum sheet and shape a loaf. Combine ketchup, garlic powder, brown sugar, and tomato paste in a bowl. Spread the ketchup mixture on top of the meatloaf and place it on the trivet. Seal the lid, select Manual, and cook for 25 minutes on High pressure. Once over, allow a natural release for 10 minutes and unlock the lid. Cut into slices and serve with rice or cooked potatoes.

Savory Herb Meatloaf

Serving Size: 4 | **Total Time:** 45 minutes
1 lb ground beef
1 egg, beaten
1 tsp garlic powder
1 tsp onion powder
1 shredded potato
½ tsp rosemary
½ tsp thyme
1 ½ tsp parsley
Salt and pepper to taste
Dill pickles, to serve

Add the ground beef, egg, onion powder, garlic powder, shredded potato, rosemary, thyme, parsley, salt, and pepper to a bowl and combine them until everything is well mixed. Press the meatloaf mixture to a greased cooking pan. Pour 1 cup of water into your Instant Pot and fit in a trivet. Place the pan on the trivet and seal the lid. Select Manual and cook for 25 minutes on High.
When ready, allow a natural release for 10 minutes, then perform a quick pressure release, and unlock the lid. Remove the meatloaf to a plate and let cool before slicing. Serve with dill pickles.

Beef Steak with Mustard Sauce

Serving Size: 4 | **Total Time:** 55 minutes
1 lb flank steak, sliced
2 tbsp olive oil
Salt and pepper to taste
½ cup beef broth
¼ cup apple cider vinegar
1 tbsp onion powder
1 tbsp Worcestershire sauce
1 cup heavy cream
1 tbsp yellow mustard

Warm 1 tbsp of olive oil in your Instant Pot on Sauté. Season the flank steak with onion powder, salt, and pepper and place in the pot; brown for 4-5 minutes on both sides. Stir in beef broth, vinegar, and Worcestershire sauce and seal the lid. Cook on Meat/Stew for 30 minutes.
Once ready, allow a natural release for 10 minutes, then perform a quick pressure release, and unlock the lid. Mix in heavy cream and mustard. Serve immediately.
Seal the lid, select Manual, and cook for 35 minutes on High pressure. Once done, allow a natural release for 10 minutes, then perform a quick pressure release, and unlock the lid. Serve with vegetables or potatoes.

Thai Beef Short Ribs

Serving Size: 6 | **Total Time:** 55 minutes
3 tbsp Thai yellow curry paste
12 beef short ribs
2 tbsp olive oil
Salt to taste
½ cup soy sauce
2 tbsp tomato paste
2 tbsp apple cider vinegar
4 garlic cloves, minced
1 tbsp ginger root, grated
2 tbsp sriracha sauce
¼ cup raw honey

Warm the olive oil in your Instant Pot on Sauté. Sprinkle beef ribs with salt and place them in the pot. Sear until browned on all sides; set aside. Place the soy sauce, curry paste, tomato paste, vinegar, garlic, ginger, sriracha, and honey in the pot. Stir well and scrape any bits from the bottom. Put ribs back to the pot. Pour in 1 cup of water.
Seal the lid, select Manual, and cook for 35 minutes on High pressure. When over, allow a natural release for 10 minutes and unlock the lid. Serve with gravy.

Mediterranean Beef Stew with Olives

Serving Size: 6 | **Total Time:** 50 minutes
2 cups canned spicy diced tomatoes with juice
2 lb beef stew meat, cubed
3 tbsp olive oil
1 onion, sliced
2 garlic cloves, minced
½ cup dry white wine
1 red pepper, sliced
20 kalamata olives, pitted
Salt and pepper to taste

Warm the oil in your Instant Pot on Sauté. Place in the beef cubes and cook for 4-5 minutes or until no longer pink, stirring often. Add in onion, garlic, red pepper, salt, and pepper and cook for another 3 minutes. Pour in white wine and scrape any brown bits from the bottom. Stir in tomatoes, kalamata olives, and 1 cup of water.
Seal the lid. Select Manual and cook for 30 minutes on High pressure. Once done, perform a quick pressure release and unlock the lid. Adjust the seasoning with salt and pepper. Serve with potatoes or cooked rice.

Smoky Chipotle Beef Brisket

Serving Size: 4 | **Total Time:** 60 minutes + marinating time

1 tsp seasoned meat tenderizer
2 lb beef brisket, flat cut
¼ tsp garlic salt
1 tbsp smoked paprika
1 tbsp Worcestershire sauce
1 cup smoky chipotle sauce

Combine garlic salt, smoked paprika, Worcestershire sauce, and seasoned meat tenderizer in a bowl. Rub the brisket with the mixture. Cover with cling film and allow to marinate for 30 minutes in the fridge. Place 1 cup of water, smoky chipotle, and brisket with its marinate in your Instant Pot and seal the lid. Select Manual and cook for 40 minutes on High pressure.

Once done, allow a natural release for 10 minutes, then perform a quick pressure release, and unlock the lid. Remove brisket to a plate. Slice before serving with sauce.

Beef Ragù Bolognese

Serving Size: 4 | **Total Time:** 40 minutes
½ cup Pecorino Romano cheese, shredded
1 lb ground beef
2 tbsp butter
1 onion, chopped
1 carrot, chopped
1 celery stalk, chopped
Salt and pepper to taste
2 tbsp basil, chopped
1 tbsp red wine
16 oz tomato sauce
2 tbsp passata
16 oz fettuccine pasta

In the Instant Pot, add the pasta and cover with salted water. Seal the lid, press Manual, and cook for 4 minutes on High. Once ready, do a quick pressure release. Drain the pasta and remove to a bowl; cover with foil to keep warm.

Melt the butter on Sauté. Add in onion, carrot, and celery. Cook for 3-4 minutes. Mix in the ground beef and brown for 8-10 minutes, stirring occasionally. Pour in red wine, tomato sauce, and passata, and season with salt and black pepper. Seal the lid and select Manual.

Cook for 10 minutes on High. When ready, do a quick pressure release. Carefully unlock the lid. Pour the Bolognese sauce over the pasta, sprinkle with Pecorino Romano cheese, and top with basil to serve.

Leftover Beef Sandwiches

Serving Size: 4 | **Total Time:** 30 minutes
1 lb leftover roast beef
4 ciabatta rolls
Salt and pepper to taste
1 tsp brown sugar
½ tsp garlic powder
1 tsp mustard powder
1 tsp paprika
2 tsp onion flakes
2 cups beef stock
2 tbsp Worcestershire sauce
1 tbsp balsamic vinegar
4 tsp butter, softened
4 cheddar cheese slices

In a bowl, mix salt, pepper, sugar, garlic powder, mustard powder, paprika, and onion flakes and rub the beef roast with the mixture. Transfer to your Instant Pot and add beef stock, Worcestershire sauce, and balsamic vinegar.

Seal the lid, select Manual, and cook for 10 minutes on High pressure. When over, allow a natural release for 10 minutes, then perform a quick pressure release, and unlock the lid. Remove beef roast and shred it.

Discard sauce and reserve 1 cup for serving. Brush ciabatta rolls with butter and top with cheddar cheese. Stuff the rolls with some shredded beef. Serve sandwiches with sauce.

Rich Beef & Vegetable Casserole

Serving Size: 4 | **Total Time:** 40 minutes
1 cup mixed mushrooms, sliced
1 lb stewing steak, cubed
2 tbsp olive oil
1 onion, chopped
2 garlic cloves, minced
1 celery stalk, chopped
Salt and pepper to taste
1 red bell pepper, chopped
2 tbsp tomato paste
1 lb tomatoes, chopped
½ cup red wine
½ cup green olives
2 tbsp oregano, chopped

Warm the olive oil in your Instant Pot on Sauté. Add in the steak and cook for 5 minutes until browned, stirring often. Add in onion, bell pepper, garlic, celery, mushrooms, salt, and pepper and sauté for 3-4 minutes. Stir in tomato paste, tomatoes, red wine, 1 cup of water, and green olives and seal the lid. Select Manual and cook for 20 minutes on High pressure. Once ready, perform a quick pressure release and unlock the lid. Serve topped with fresh oregano.

Rosemary Braised Beef in Red Wine

Serving Size: 6 | **Total Time:** 75 minutes
3 lb diced braising steak
3 tbsp olive oil
Salt and pepper to taste
10 pearl onions, peeled
1 tsp Worcestershire sauce
4 baby carrot, chopped
1 celery stalk, diced
1 tbsp tomato paste
2 garlic cloves, minced
1 cup beef broth
1 cup red wine
2 sprigs fresh rosemary
1 bay leaf
1 tbsp cornstarch

Warm the olive oil in your Instant Pot on Sauté. Sprinkle beef with salt and pepper and place it in the pot. Cook for 8-10 minutes on all sides; reserve. Add pearl onions, garlic, baby carrot, celery, and tomato paste to the pot and cook for 4-5 minutes. Pour in red wine and scrape any brown bits from the bottom. Put meat back to the pot and thyme, Worcestershire sauce, beef broth, rosemary sprigs, and bay leaf. Seal the lid, select Manual, and cook for 40 minutes on High pressure. When over, allow a natural release for 10 minutes, then perform a quick pressure release, and unlock the lid. Remove meat to a plate and let cool before slicing. Discard the rosemary and bay leaf. Combine cornstarch with 1 cup of cooking liquid and pour in the pot, and simmer on Sauté until the sauce thickens. Serve brisket with the sauce.

Beef & Bean Chili

Serving Size: 4 | **Total Time**: 70 minutes
1 lb ground beef
2 tbsp olive oil
½ lb white beans, soaked
14 oz can diced tomatoes
1 tbsp tomato paste
1 white onion, diced
2 garlic cloves, chopped
1 green bell pepper, diced
1 cup beef broth
Salt and pepper to taste
½ tsp oregano
1 jalapeño pepper, minced
1 tsp ground cumin

Heat olive oil on Sauté. Add onion, garlic, green pepper, and jalapeño pepper, and sauté for 3-5 minutes until tender. Stir in beef and cook for another 6 minutes. Season with oregano, cumin, salt, and pepper, and pour in tomato paste, tomatoes, beef broth, and white beans.
Seal the lid, select the Bean/Chili and cook for 25 minutes on High. When the timer is over, let the pressure release naturally for 10 minutes. Unlock the lid. Select Sauté to cook for another 8-10 minutes until the desired texture and thickness is reached. Ladle into bowls and serve.

Garlicky Herb-Rubbed Beef Brisket

Serving Size: 4 | **Total Time**: 60 minutes + marinating time
2 lb beef brisket, flat cut
2 garlic cloves, minced
Salt and pepper to taste
½ tsp oregano
½ tsp marjoram
½ tsp ground cumin
½ tsp dried rosemary
1 ½ cups beef stock

Combine garlic, salt, pepper, marjoram, oregano, cumin, and rosemary in a bowl. Add in the brisket, toss to coat, and marinate for 30 minutes in the fridge. Place the brisket and beef stock in your Instant Pot and seal the lid. Select Manual and cook for 40 minutes on High pressure. When done, allow a natural release for 10 minutes, then perform a quick pressure release, and unlock the lid. Slice before serving.

Beef & Lentil Stew

Serving Size: 4 | **Total Time**: 45 minutes
2 lb beef shoulder, cut into chunks
2 tbsp olive oil
Salt and pepper to taste
1 cup lentils
1 cup beef broth
½ cup sun-dried tomatoes
1 onion, sliced
2 garlic cloves, minced
½ tsp oregano
½ tsp marjoram

Combine the beef shoulder, olive oil, salt, pepper, lentils, beef broth, sun-dried tomatoes, onion, garlic cloves, oregano, and marjoram in your Instant Pot and stir. Seal the lid, select Manual, and cook for 25 minutes on High pressure. Once ready, allow a natural release for 10 minute and unlock the lid. Serve.

Beef & Vegetable Stew

Serving Size: 6 | **Total Time**: 55 minutes
2 lb beef stew meat, cubed
Salt and pepper to taste
½ tsp onion powder
1/3 cup flour
1 tsp Italian seasoning
2 tbsp olive oil
1 onion, chopped
3 garlic cloves, minced
1 tbsp red wine
1 tbsp tomato paste
4 potatoes, peeled, chopped
1 cup green beans, trimmed
1 tsp paprika
1 cup tomatoes, chopped
1 celery rib, chopped
2 carrots, sliced
3 cups beef broth
1 bay leaf
2 tbsp parsley, chopped

Combine salt, pepper, onion powder, flour, and Italian seasoning in a bowl. Add in beef meat and toss to coat. Warm the olive oil in your Instant Pot on Sauté. Place the meat in the pot and cook for 5-6 minutes, stirring occasionally; set aside. Place the onion, garlic, celery, carrot, and paprika in the pot and cook for 3-4 minutes.
Pour in wine and scrape any brown bits from the bottom. Put the meat back to the pot and tomato paste, tomatoes, potatoes, green beans, broth, bay leaf, salt, and pepper and stir. Seal the lid, select Manual, and cook for 25 minutes on High. When ready, allow a natural release for 10 minutes. Serve topped with parsley.

Beef & Root Vegetable Pot

Serving Size: 4 | **Total Time**: 65 minutes
1 lb beef stew meat, cubed
2 tbsp olive oil
Salt and pepper to taste
1 leek, chopped
2 garlic cloves, minced
1 tsp dried thyme
2 tbsp flour
1 cup dry red wine

2 cups chopped tomatoes
1 turnip, chopped
1 lb sweet potatoes, sliced
2 carrots, chopped
2 cups beef broth
¼ cup parsley, chopped

Warm the olive oil in your Instant Pot on Sauté. Sprinkle beef meat with salt and pepper and place it in the pot. Sauté for 6-7 minutes on all sides until browned; set aside. Add leek and garlic to the pot and cook for 3 minutes. Stir in thyme and flour and cook for 1 minute. Pour in red wine and scrape any brown bits from the bottom.

Add in turnip, carrots, sweet potatoes, tomatoes, and beef broth. Put the meat back to the pot and seal the lid. Select Manual and cook for 30 minutes on High pressure. Once over, allow a natural release for 10 minutes and unlock the lid. Serve topped with parsley.

Beef & Butternut Squash Chili

Serving Size: 4 | **Total Time:** 65 minutes
2 tbsp olive oil
1 lb stewed beef meat, cubed
1 lb butternut squash, cubed
1 cup canned tomatoes, diced
1 onion, diced
2 garlic cloves
2 cups beef broth
Salt and pepper to taste
2 tbsp tomato paste
1 tsp chili powder
1 tsp ground cumin
1 tsp oregano
1 tsp cayenne pepper

Warm the olive oil in your Instant Pot on Sauté. Place in beef meat and cook for 7-8 minutes on all sides; reserve. Add onion, garlic, chili powder, cumin, oregano, cayenne pepper, salt, and pepper to the pot and cook for 5 minutes. Put in butternut squash, tomato paste, tomatoes, and beef broth and return the beef.

Seal the lid, select Manual, and cook for 30 minutes on High pressure. When ready, allow a natural release for 10 minutes, then perform a quick pressure release, and unlock the lid. Serve warm.

Beef Neapolitan Ragù

Serving Size: 4 | **Total Time:** 53 minutes
1 ½ lb beef steak, cut into strips
2 tbsp lard
1 onion, chopped
2 cups crushed tomatoes
1 carrot, chopped
1 celery stalk, chopped
1 cup beef broth
½ cup red wine
1 tbsp passata
Salt and pepper to taste

Melt lard in your Instant Pot on Sauté. Place in onion, carrot, and celery and sauté until fragrant. Add in beef steak and cook for 3 minutes, stirring often. Pour in tomatoes, beef broth, red wine, passata, salt, and pepper and seal the lid. Select Meat/Stew. Cook for 30 minutes on High pressure. When over, allow a natural release for 10 minutes, then perform a quick pressure release, and unlock the lid. Serve immediately.

Boeuf Bourguignon

Serving Size: 4 | **Total Time:** 63 minutes
1 lb flank steak
2 tbsp olive oil
1 cup pearl onions
2 garlic cloves, minced
1 cups crimini mushrooms
1 carrot, sliced
4 oz bacon, chopped
1 cup beef broth
1 cup Burgundy red wine
Salt and pepper to taste
1 bay leaf
2 tbsp thyme, chopped

Warm the oil in your Instant Pot on Sauté. Place in the steak and cook for 6-8 minutes in total. Set aside. Add onions, garlic, mushrooms, carrots, and bacon to the pot and cook for 4-5 minutes. Stir in beef broth and wine.

Put the meat back to the pot and salt, pepper, and bay leaf and seal the lid. Select Manual and cook for 30 minutes on High. When over, allow a natural release for 10 minutes, then perform a quick pressure release, and unlock the lid. Discard bay leaf. Top with thyme.

Pulled BBQ Beef

Serving Size: 6 | **Total Time:** 65 minutes
3 lb beef chuck roast
2 tbsp olive oil
1 cup BBQ sauce
1 tbsp Dijon mustard
1 tsp smoked paprika
Salt and pepper to taste
2 cups beef broth
3 tbsp cilantro, chopped

Warm the olive oil in your Instant Pot on Sauté. Sprinkle beef with salt and pepper and place it in the pot and cook for 8-10 minutes on all sides. Add in BBQ sauce, Dijon mustard, smoked paprika, salt, pepper, and beef broth and seal the lid. Select Manual and cook for 35 minutes on High pressure. Once ready, allow a natural release for 10 minutes, then perform a quick pressure release, and unlock the lid. Remove beef and shred it using 2 forks. Put it back to the pot and mix with the remaining liquid. Top with cilantro and serve.

Beef Meatballs with Tomato-Basil Sauce

Serving Size: 4 | **Total Time:** 30 minutes
2 cups tomato and basil pasta sauce
1 ¼ lb ground beef
1 tsp garlic powder
1 tsp onion powder
1 tsp oregano
2 tbsp breadcrumbs

Salt and pepper to taste
2 tbsp olive oil

Combine ground beef, garlic powder, onion powder, oregano, breadcrumbs, salt, and pepper in a bowl. Make 2-inch meatballs of the mixture. Warm the olive oil in your Instant Pot on Sauté. Add in the meatballs and cook for 4-5 minutes on all sides until browned. Stir in tomato and basil pasta sauce and ¼ cup of water.

Seal the lid, select Manual, and cook for 10 minutes on High pressure. When done, allow a natural release for 10 minutes, then perform a quick pressure release, and unlock the lid. Serve immediately.

Vietnamese Beef

Serving Size: 6 | **Total Time:** 60 minutes
2 lb beef steak, sliced
3 tbsp olive oil
Salt and pepper to taste
4 garlic cloves, minced
1 tsp minced ginger
3 white onions, chopped
3 tbsp fish sauce
1 tbsp brown sugar
2 tbsp cornflour
2 tbsp mint leaves, chopped
1 red chili pepper, minced

Sprinkle beef steak with salt and pepper. Warm the olive oil in your Instant Pot on Sauté. Place in the steak and sauté for 10-12 minutes on all sides. Set aside.

Add garlic, ginger, red chili pepper, and onions to the pot and cook for 2-3 minutes. Stir in fish sauce, brown sugar, and 1 ¼ cups of water. Put the steak back to the pot.

Seal the lid. Select Manual and cook for 25 minutes on High pressure. When done, allow a natural release for 10 minutes, then perform a quick pressure release, and unlock the lid. Combine ½ cup of water and cornflour in a bowl and pour it into the pot. Simmer on Sauté until the liquid thickens. Serve topped with mint leaves.

Greek-Style Stuffed Peppers

Serving Size: 4 | **Total Time:** 39 minutes
¼ cup Halloumi cheese, grated
2 tbsp olive oil
1 lb ground beef
2 onions, chopped
Salt and pepper to taste
4 bell peppers, tops removed
1 tsp oregano
1 tsp paprika
½ tsp ground cinnamon
1 cup canned tomato sauce
1 tbsp flour

Mix the cheese, ground beef, onions, paprika, cinnamon, salt, and pepper in a bowl. Stuff each bell pepper with the mixture. Pour the tomato sauce and ½ of water in your Instant Pot and fit in a trivet. Place the peppers on the trivet and seal the lid. Select Manual and cook for 15 minutes on High pressure.

When over, allow a natural release for 10 minutes and unlock the lid. Remove peppers to a plate. Whisk the flour and oregano with some cooking sauce in a bowl. Pour it in the pot and select Sauté; cook until the sauce thickens, about 3-4 minutes. Adjust the seasoning before pouring it over the peppers.

Chipotle Shredded Beef

Serving Size: 4 | **Total Time:** 45 minutes
2 lb beef shoulder roast
2 tbsp vegetable oil
1 onion, chopped
3 garlic cloves, minced
3 cups beef broth
2 tbsp tomato salsa
1 tsp chipotle chili pepper
Salt and pepper to taste
4 tbsp sour cream
2 tbsp cilantro, chopped

Rub the beef roast with chipotle chili pepper, salt, and pepper on all sides. Warm the vegetable oil in your Instant Pot on Sauté. Place the onion and garlic and cook for 2-3 minutes. Add in the beef roast and beef broth and seal the lid.

Select Manual and cook for 30 minutes on High pressure. Once ready, perform a quick pressure release and unlock the lid. Remove meat and shred it. Pour tomato salsa in the pot and cook until the sauce thickens on Sauté. Stir in shredded beef. Top with cilantro and serve with a dollop of sour cream on the side.

Veal Chops with Greek Yogurt

Serving Size: 4 | **Total Time:** 60 minutes
2 lb boneless veal shoulder, cubed
3 tomatoes, chopped
2 tbsp flour
3 tbsp butter
1 tbsp cayenne pepper
1 tsp salt
1 tbsp parsley, chopped
1 cup Greek yogurt
1 pide bread

Grease the bottom of the inner pot with 1 tbsp of butter. Make a layer with veal pieces and Pour water to cover. Season with salt and seal the lid. Cook on High Pressure for 45 minutes. Do a quick release. Melt the remaining butter in a skillet. Add the cayenne pepper and flour and briefly stir-fry, about 2 minutes. Slice pide bread and arrange on a serving plate. Place the meat and tomatoes on top. Drizzle with cayenne pepper, Top with yogurt and sprinkle with parsley to serve.

Easy Lamb & Spinach Soup

Serving Size: 5 | **Total Time:** 45 minutes
1 lb lamb shoulder, cubed
10 oz spinach, chopped
3 eggs, beaten
5 cups vegetable broth
3 tbsp olive oil
1 tsp salt

Place in your Instant Pot the lamb, spinach, eggs, broth, olive oil, and salt. Seal the lid, press Soup/Broth, and cook for 30 minutes on High Pressure. Do a natural pressure release for about 10 minutes. Serve warm.

Roast Lamb Leg with Potatoes

Serving Size: 6 | **Total Time:** 35 minutes
2 lb lamb leg
2 garlic cloves
1 tbsp thyme, chopped
1 lb potatoes
1 lemon, chopped
3 tbsp oil
¼ cup red wine vinegar
1 tsp brown sugar
1 tsp salt

Place the potatoes in the pot, and pour enough water to cover. Season with salt, add garlic, and seal the lid. Set to Meat/Stew. Cook for 20 minutes on High Pressure. Do a quick release and remove potatoes; reserve the liquid.
Rub the meat with oil and thyme. Place in the pot. Pour in red wine vinegar, sugar, and add lemon. Add 1 cup of the reserved liquid and seal the lid. Cook on High Pressure for 7 minutes. Do a quick release.

Lamb Shanks with Garlic & Thyme

Serving Size: 4 | **Total Time:** 65 minutes
2 ½ lb lamb shanks, trimmed of excess fat
Salt and pepper to taste
10 whole garlic cloves, peeled
1 cup vegetable broth
1 (14-oz) can diced tomatoes
1 onion, sliced
2 tbsp tomato paste
½ cup red wine
2 tbsp fresh thyme, chopped
2 tbsp butter
2 tsp balsamic vinegar

Sprinkle lamb shanks with salt and pepper. Warm the butter in your Instant Pot on Sauté. Place in lamb shanks and cook for 4-5 minutes on all sides until browned. Add in onion and garlic and sauté for 2 more minutes. Stir in vegetable broth, tomato paste, red wine, tomatoes, and thyme and seal the lid. Select Manual and cook for 35 minutes on High.
Once done, allow a natural release for 10 minutes and unlock the lid. Remove lamb to a plate. Stir the butter and balsamic vinegar in the pot and select Sauté; cook until the sauce thickens. Serve the lamb with sauce.

Lamb with Tomato & Green Peas

Serving Size: 4 | **Total Time:** 65 minutes
1 cup green peas
1 lb lamb, cubed
1 tomato, roughly chopped
1 onion, peeled, chopped
2 carrots, peeled, chopped
1 celery stalk, chopped
2 tbsp parsley, chopped
2 garlic cloves, crushed
4 tbsp tomato sauce
2 tbsp olive oil
4 cups vegetable stock
Salt and pepper to taste

Warm the olive oil in your Instant Pot on Sauté. Cook the onion, carrots, celery, and garlic for 8 minutes until tender. Add in the lamb and sauté for another 5-6 minutes. Season with salt and black pepper. Add in green peas, tomato, tomato sauce, and stock and seal the lid. Cook on High Pressure for 30 minutes. Do a natural pressure release for about 10 minutes. Carefully fully unlock the lid. Top with parsley to serve.

Minty Lamb

Serving Size: 6 | **Total Time:** 55 minutes
3 lb lamb, boneless and cubed
2 tbsp butter
4 garlic cloves, minced
4 green onions, chopped
1 tsp cumin seeds
1 tsp coriander seeds
3 tbsp flour
1 ½ cups vegetable stock
1 cup carrots, sliced
4 mint sprigs
Salt and pepper to taste

Sprinkle the lamb with salt and pepper and coat in flour. Melt butter in your Instant Pot on Sauté. Add in onion and garlic and cook for 3 minutes. Put in lamb and cook for 5-6 minutes until browned. Stir in stock, carrots, cumin and coriander seeds, and mint sprigs and seal the lid. Select Manual and cook for 25 minutes on High.
When ready, allow a natural release for 10 minutes. Carefully unlock the lid. Discard the mint sprigs. Top the lamb with sauce and serve warm.

Hot Paprika & Oregano Lamb

Serving Size: 4 | **Total Time:** 70 minutes + marinating time
1 lb lamb shoulder
1 tsp hot paprika
1 tsp oregano
1 tsp cumin
¼ tsp ground cinnamon
2 tbsp tomato puree
¼ cup red wine
¼ cup chicken stock
1 tbsp olive oil
½ cup water
2 tbsp butter
Salt and pepper to taste

Mix the oregano, hot paprika, salt, black pepper, cumin, and cinnamon in a bowl. Add in lamb and toss to coat. Cover and let marinate for 20-30 minutes. Warm the olive oil in your Instant Pot on Sauté. Place in lamb shoulder and brown for 5 minutes on all sides. Pour in red wine, chicken stock, tomato puree, butter, and ½ cup of water.
Seal the lid, select Manual, and cook for 45 minutes on High pressure. Once over, allow a natural release for 10 minutes, then perform a quick pressure

release, and unlock the lid. Remove the lamb to a cutting board shred it. Return to the pot and stir. Serve warm.

Mediterranean Lamb

Serving Size: 4 | Total Time: 55 minutes
1 lb lamb meat, cut into strips
1 tsp vegetable oil
4 tomatoes, chopped
2 tbsp tomato paste
1 red bell pepper, sliced
2 garlic cloves, minced
1 yellow onion, chopped
1 carrot, sliced
2 thyme sprigs
½ cup dry white wine
10 black olives, sliced
Salt and pepper to taste
2 tbsp parsley, chopped

Warm oil in your Instant Pot on Sauté. Add in lamb and cook for 8 minutes on all sides. Stir in tomatoes, tomato paste, bell pepper, garlic, onion, carrots, salt, pepper and sauté for 5 more minutes. Pour in wine and enough water to cover everything. Add in thyme sprigs and olives. Seal the lid, select Manual, and cook for 30 minutes on High.

Once done, perform a quick pressure release and unlock the lid. Remove the lamb to a plate, discard bones and shred it. Put the shredded lamb back to the pot and stir parsley. Serve immediately.

Quick French-Style Lamb with Sesame

Serving Size: 4 | Total Time: 45 minutes
12 oz lamb, tender cuts, ½-inch thick
1 cup rice
1 cup green peas
3 tbsp sesame seeds
4 cups beef broth
1 tsp salt
½ tsp dried thyme
3 tbsp butter

Mix the meat in the pot with broth. Seal the lid and cook on High Pressure for 15 minutes. Do a quick release. Remove the meat but keep the liquid. Add rice and green peas. Season with salt and thyme. Stir well and top with the meat. Seal the lid and cook on Manual for 18 minutes on High. Do a quick release. Carefully unlock the lid. Stir in butter and sesame seeds. Serve immediately.

Lamb Stew with Lemon & Parsley

Serving Size: 4 | Total Time: 60 minutes
2 potatoes, cut into bite-sized pieces
1 lb lamb neck, boneless
2 large carrots, chopped
1 tomato, diced
1 red bell pepper, chopped
1 garlic head, whole
2 tbsp parsley, chopped
¼ cup lemon juice
Salt and pepper to taste

Add the meat and season with salt. Add in potatoes, carrots, tomato, bell pepper, lemon juice, and pepper, tuck in one garlic head in the middle of the pot and add 2 cups water. Add parsley and seal the lid. Cook on High Pressure for 45 minutes. When ready, do a quick release. Carefully unlock the lid. Serve.

Simple Roast Lamb

Serving Size: 4 | Total Time: 40 minutes
2 lb lamb leg
1 tbsp garlic powder
3 tbsp extra virgin olive oil
Salt and pepper to taste
4 rosemary sprigs, chopped

Grease the inner pot with oil. Rub the meat with salt, pepper, and garlic powder, and place in the Instant Pot. Pour enough water to cover and seal the lid. Cook on Meat/Stew for 30 minutes on High. Do a quick release. Make sure the meat is tender and falls off the bones. Top with cooking juices and rosemary. Serve.

Traditional Lamb with Vegetables

Serving Size: 6 | Total Time: 30 minutes
1 lb lamb chops, 1-inch thick
1 cup green peas, rinsed
3 carrots, chopped
3 onions, chopped
1 potato, chopped
1 tomato, chopped
3 tbsp olive oil
1 tbsp paprika
Salt and pepper to taste

Grease the Instant Pot with olive oil. Rub salt onto the lamb and make a bottom layer. Add peas, carrots, onions, potato, and tomato. Season with paprika. Add olive oil, 1 cup of water, salt, and pepper. Give it a good stir and seal the lid. Cook on Meat/Stew for 20 minutes on High Pressure. When ready, do a natural pressure release. Carefully unlock the lid. Serve hot.

Garlic Lamb with Thyme

Serving Size: 4 | Total Time: 60 minutes
2 lb lamb, cubed
2 garlic cloves, minced
1 cup onions, chopped
1 cup red wine
2 cups beef stock
2 tbsp butter, softened
2 celery stalks, chopped
1 tbsp fresh thyme
2 tbsp flour
Salt and pepper to taste

Rub the lamb with salt and pepper. Melt butter on Sauté and cook onions, celery, and garlic for 5 minutes. Add lamb and fry until browned for about 5-6 minutes. Dust the flour and stir. Pour in the stock and red wine. Seal the lid, and cook on High Pressure for 30 minutes. Do a natural release for 10 minutes. Serve with thyme.

Leg of Lamb with Garlic and Pancetta

Serving Size: 6 | Total Time: 40 minutes
2 lb lamb leg
6 garlic cloves

1 large onion, chopped
6 pancetta slices
1 tsp rosemary
Salt and pepper to taste
2 tbsp oil
3 cups beef broth

Heat the oil in your Instant Pot on Sauté. Add the pancetta and onion, making two layers. Season with salt and pepper and cook for 3 minutes until lightly browned.

Place the lamb on a separate dish. Using a sharp knife, make 6 incisions into the meat and place a garlic clove in each. Rub the meat with rosemary and transfer to the pot. Press Cancel and pour in the beef broth. Seal the lid and cook on High Pressure for 25 minutes. When done, do a natural pressure release. Serve.

Savory Irish Lamb Stew

Serving Size: 4 | **Total Time**: 36 minutes
1 lb lamb, cut into pieces
1 ½ tbsp canola oil
1 onion, sliced
2 tbsp cornstarch
2 potatoes, cubed
2 carrots, chopped
2 ½ cups beef broth
½ tsp dried oregano
Salt and pepper to taste

Season the lamb with salt and pepper. Heat the canola oil in your Instant Pot on Sauté. Sear the lamb until browned on all sides, about 4-5 minutes. Add onion, potatoes, carrots, broth, and oregano, and stir. Seal the lid and cook on High Pressure for 18 minutes. When ready, do a quick pressure release. Whisk the cornstarch with a little bit of water and stir it into the stew. Cook on Sauté for 3 more minutes. Serve hot.

Asian-Style Lamb Curry

Serving Size: 4 | **Total Time**: 55 minutes + marinating time
1 ½ lb lamb stew meat, cubed
½ cup coconut milk
4 garlic cloves, minced
Juice of ½ lime
1-inch piece ginger, grated
Salt and pepper to taste
2 tbsp yellow curry paste
½ tsp turmeric
2 tbsp butter
1 tbsp soy sauce
14 oz canned tomatoes, diced
3 carrots, sliced
1 onion, diced
1 eggplant, diced
2 tbsp cilantro, chopped
2 cups basmati rice, cooked

Mix coconut milk, garlic, lime juice, ginger, salt, and pepper in a bowl. Add in lamb cubes and toss to coat. Let marinate for 30 minutes. Set your Instant Pot to Sauté. Melt butter and add onion, curry paste, turmeric, eggplant, and carrots and cook for 3-4 minutes. Stir in tomatoes, soy sauce, and 1 cup water.

Add in the marinated lamb with their juice and seal the lid. Select Manual and cook for 30 minutes on High pressure. Once ready, allow a natural release for 10 minutes, then perform a quick pressure release, and unlock the lid. Serve with the rice topped with cilantro.

Spicy Lamb & Bean Chili

Serving Size: 4 | **Total Time**: 53 minutes
1 cup chopped green chilies
1 cup cannellini beans, soaked
1 lb ground lamb
2 tbsp olive oil
1 onion, chopped
½ tbsp chili powder
½ tsp cayenne pepper
1 tsp cumin
1 tsp fennel seeds
1 (14-oz) can diced tomatoes
1 tbsp tomato paste
3 cups chicken broth
Salt and pepper to taste

Warm the olive oil in your Instant Pot on Sauté. Add in ground lamb and cook for 5 minutes until mostly brown. Stir in onion, chili powder, cayenne pepper, cumin, fennel seeds, salt, and pepper and sauté for 3 minutes.

Pour in tomatoes, tomato paste, green chilies, cannellini beans, and chicken broth and seal the lid. Select Manual and cook for 25 minutes on High. When ready, allow a natural release for 10 minutes and unlock the lid. Serve with sour cream.

Fennel Lamb Ribs

Serving Size: 4 | **Total Time**: 47 minutes
3 lb lamb ribs
2 tbsp olive oil
4 garlic cloves, chopped
3 tbsp all-purpose flour
1 ½ cups vegetable stock
½ tsp cumin
½ fennel bulb, sliced
2 carrots, chopped
4 rosemary sprigs
Salt and pepper to taste

Warm olive oil in your Instant Pot on Sauté. Sprinkle lamb ribs with salt and pepper and add them to the pot. Cook for 6-7 minutes on all sides. Add in garlic, cumin and fennel and cook for 3 more minutes. Stir in flour, stock, rosemary, and carrots and seal the lid. Select Manual and cook for 22 minutes on High. When ready, allow a natural release for 5 minutes and unlock the lid. Remove rosemary sprigs. Serve the ribs with sauce.

Lamb Chops with Mashed Potatoes

Serving Size: 6 | **Total Time**: 20 minutes
8 lamb chops
Salt to taste
3 sprigs rosemary, chopped
3 tbsp butter, softened
2 tbsp olive oil
1 tbsp tomato puree

1 green onion, chopped
1 cup beef stock
5 potatoes, peeled, chopped
1/3 cup milk
2 tbsp cilantro, chopped

Rub rosemary leaves and salt to the lamb chops. Warm oil and 2 tbsp of butter on Sauté. Brown lamb chops for 1 minute per each side; set aside. In the pot, mix tomato puree and green onion and cook for 2-3 minutes. Add the stock into the pot to deglaze and scrape the bottom to get rid of any browned food bits. Return the lamb chops to the pot. Set a steamer rack on lamb chops. Place the steamer basket on the rack. Pour in the potatoes.

Seal the lid and cook on High Pressure for 4 minutes. Release the pressure quickly. Remove trivet and steamer basket.

In a blender, add potatoes, milk, salt, and remaining butter. Blend well until you obtain a smooth consistency. Place the potato mash on a serving dish. Lay lamb chops on the mash. Drizzle with cooking liquid and top with cilantro.

Vegetable & Lamb Casserole

Serving Size: 4 | **Total Time:** 50 minutes
1 lb lamb stew meat, cubed
2 tbsp olive oil
1 onion, chopped
3 garlic cloves, minced
2 tomatoes, chopped
½ lb baby potatoes
½ lb green beans, chopped
1 carrot, chopped
1 onion, chopped
1 celery stalk, chopped
2 tbsp white wine
2 cups lamb stock
1 tsp Hungarian paprika
1 tsp cumin, ground
¼ tsp oregano, dried
¼ tsp rosemary, dried
Salt and pepper to taste

Warm the olive oil in your Instant Pot on Sauté. Add in lamb cubes and cook for 5-6 minutes until no longer pink. Stir in onion and garlic and sauté for another 3 minutes. Pour in tomatoes, potatoes, green beans, carrot, onion, celery, white wine, lamb stock, paprika, cumin, oregano, rosemary, salt, and pepper and seal the lid. Select Manual and cook for 20 minutes on High pressure. When over, allow a natural release for 10 minutes and unlock the lid.

Balsamic Lamb

Serving Size: 4 | **Total Time:** 45 minutes
2 lb lamb shanks
2 tbsp sesame oil
2 garlic cloves, peeled
1 onion, chopped
1 cup vegetable broth
1 tbsp tomato paste
½ tsp thyme
¼ tsp dried dill weed
1 tbsp balsamic vinegar
1 tbsp butter

Warm sesame oil in your Instant Pot on Sauté. Place in onion and garlic and sauté for 3 minutes. Stir in broth, tomato paste, dill, and thyme. Add in the lamb and seal the lid. Select Manual and cook for 25 minutes on High.

When ready, allow a natural release for 5 minutes and unlock the lid. Remove the lamb to a bowl. Stir the balsamic vinegar and butter in the pot for 1-2 minutes until the butter melts. Serve the lamb with sauce.

Lamb Chorba

Serving Size: 4 | **Total Time:** 35 minutes
2 lb lamb shanks
2 tbsp olive oil
2 garlic cloves, peeled
1 onion, chopped
1 celery stalk, chopped
1 tomato, chopped
1 carrot, chopped
2 tbsp oregano, chopped
Salt and pepper to taste
4 cups vegetable broth
1 tbsp white wine vinegar

Warm the olive oil in your Instant Pot on Sauté. Place in the lamb, celery, onion, carrot, and garlic and sauté for 6 minutes. Stir in vegetable broth, tomato, salt, and pepper. Seal the lid. Select Manual and cook for 20 minutes. Release the pressure quickly. Drizzle with vinegar and sprinkle with oregano to serve.

FISH & SEAFOOD

Pizza with Tuna & Goat Cheese
Serving Size: 4 | **Total Time:** 25 minutes
1 cup canned tuna, oil-free
½ cup mozzarella, shredded
¼ cup goat's cheese
3 tbsp olive oil
1 tbsp tomato paste
½ tsp dried rosemary
14 oz pizza crust
1 cup olives

Grease the bottom of a baking dish with some olive oil. Line with parchment paper. Flour the working surface and roll out the pizza dough to the approximate size of your Instant Pot. Gently fit the dough in the previously prepared baking dish.
In a bowl, combine olive oil, tomato paste, and rosemary. Whisk together and Spread the mixture over the crust. Sprinkle with goat cheese, mozzarella, olives, and tuna.
Place a trivet inside the pot and pour in 1 cup of water. Seal the lid, and cook for 15 minutes on High Pressure. Do a quick release. Cut and serve.

Tuna & Pasta Bake
Serving Size: 4 | **Total Time:** 25 minutes
28 oz canned cream of mushroom soup
14 oz canned tuna, drained
16 oz penne pasta
1 cup green beans, frozen
Salt and pepper to taste
4 oz colby cheese, grated
¼ cup breadcrumbs

Mix 3 cups of water with mushroom soup in your Instant Pot. Add in penne and seal the lid. Select Manual and cook for 4 minutes on High pressure. When ready, perform a quick pressure release and unlock the lid. Press Sauté and stir in tuna, green beans, salt, and pepper. Cook an additional 3 minutes or until everything is heated through and transfer to a baking dish.
Sprinkle with colby cheese and breadcrumbs on top and place under the broiler for 5 minutes until the cheese melts. Plate and serve immediately.

Cheesy Tuna
Serving Size: 4 | **Total Time:** 20 minutes
1 lb tuna fillets
2 tbsp butter
1 tbsp flour
Salt and pepper to taste
½ cup milk
1 cup mozzarella, grated

Melt the butter in your Instant Pot on Sauté. Place in flour, salt, and pepper and cook for 1 minute. Pour in milk and cook for 3-5 minutes, stirring often.
Stir in mozzarella cheese. Place the tuna fillets in a greased baking pan and pour the cheese sauce over the fish. Cover with aluminium foil.
Clean the pot and add 1 cup of water. Fit in a trivet. Place the pan on the trivet and seal the lid. Select Manual and cook for 5 minutes on High pressure. When ready, perform a quick pressure release and unlock the lid.

Spicy Haddock with Beer & Potatoes
Serving Size: 4 | **Total Time:** 25 minutes
4 potatoes, cut into matchsticks
8 oz beer
2 eggs
1 cup flour
½ tbsp cayenne powder
1 tbsp cumin powder
Salt and pepper to taste
4 haddock fillets
2 tbsp olive oil

In a bowl, whisk beer and eggs. In another bowl, combine flour, cayenne, cumin, pepper, and salt. Coat each fish piece in the egg mixture, then dredge in the flour mixture, coating all sides. Grease a baking dish with cooking spray.
Place in the fish fillets, pour ¼ cup of water, and grease with cooking spray. Place the potatoes in the pot and cover with water and place a trivet over the potatoes. Lay the baking dish on top and seal the lid. Cook on High Pressure for 15 minutes. Do a quick release. Drain and crush the potatoes with olive oil and serve with the fish.

Haddock with Edamame Soybeans
Serving Size: 4 | **Total Time:** 25 minutes
1 pack (12-oz) edamame soybeans
1 lb haddock fillets
1 clove garlic, minced
2 tsp grated ginger
¼ red chili, sliced
1 tbsp honey
2 tbsp soy sauce
Salt and pepper to taste

Pour 1 cup of water into your Instant Pot and fit in a trivet. Mix garlic, ginger, red chili, honey, soy sauce, salt, and pepper in a bowl. Add in the haddock fillets and toss to coat. Spread the fillets on a greased baking pan; scatter edamame soybeans around. Place the pan on the trivet.
Seal the lid. Cook on Steam for 6 minutes on High pressure. When done, allow a natural release for 10 minutes, then perform a quick pressure release. Serve.

Italian Steamed Sea Bream with Lemon
Serving Size: 4 | **Total Time:** 50 minutes
2 pieces sea bream (2 lb), cleaned
¼ cup olive oil
¼ cup lemon juice
1 tbsp fresh thyme sprigs
1 tbsp Italian seasoning
½ tsp sea salt
1 tsp garlic powder
4 cups fish stock

In a bowl, mix oil, lemon juice, thyme, Italian seasoning, sea salt, and garlic powder. Brush onto fish and wrap tightly with a plastic foil. Refrigerate for 30 minutes. Pour fish stock into the pot. Set the steamer rack and place the fish on top. Seal the lid. Cook on Steam for 8 minutes on High. Do a quick release. Unwrap the fish. Serve immediately with steam vegetables.

Tilapia with Basil Pesto & Rice
Serving Size: 2 | **Total Time**: 15 minutes
2 tilapia fillets
2 tbsp basil pesto
½ cup basmati rice
Salt and pepper to taste

Place the rice and 1 cup of water in your Instant Pot and season with salt and pepper; fit in a trivet. Place tilapia fillets in the middle of a parchment paper sheet. Top each fillet with pesto and roll all the edges to form a packet. Place it on the trivet and seal the lid. Select Manual and cook for 6 minutes on Low pressure. Once ready, perform a quick pressure release. Carefully unlock the lid. Fluff the rice with a fork and transfer to a plate. Top with tilapia and serve.

Tilapia Fillets with Hazelnut Crust
Serving Size: 4 | **Total Time**: 15 minutes
4 tilapia fillets
2 tsp olive oil
¼ tsp lemon pepper
2 tbsp Dijon mustard
½ cup chopped hazelnuts
2 tbsp parsley, chopped
Salt and pepper to taste

Pour 1 cup of water into your Instant Pot and fit in a trivet. Mix the olive oil, lemon pepper, and Dijon mustard in a bowl. Rub each fillet with mustard mixture, then roll them in the hazelnuts to coat. Place the fillets on the trivet, sprinkle with salt and pepper, and seal the lid. Select Manual, and cook for 5 minutes on High. When done, perform a quick pressure release. Unlock the lid. Serve scattered with parsley.

Lemon & Leek Tilapia
Serving Size: 2 | **Total Time**: 15 minutes
2 tilapia fillets
¼ tsp garlic powder
2 sprigs fresh dill
4 slices lemon
1 leek, white part, sliced
1 tbsp cold butter, sliced
Salt and pepper to taste

Pour 1 cup of water into your Instant Pot and fit in a trivet. Season the tilapia fillets with salt, pepper, and garlic and place on the trivet. Top each fillet with 1 sprig of dill, 2 lemon slices, leek slices, and butter and seal the lid. Select Manual and cook for 5 minutes on High pressure. When done, perform a quick pressure release.

Thyme Sea Bass with Turnips
Serving Size: 4 | **Total Time**: 15 minutes
1 white onion, chopped into thin rings
1 lemon, chopped
4 sea bass fillets
4 sprigs thyme
2 turnips, sliced
Salt and pepper to taste
2 tsp olive oil

Add 1 cup water and set a rack into the pot. Line a parchment paper to the bottom of the steamer basket. Place lemon slices in a single layer on the basket. Arrange fillets on the top of the lemons, cover with onion and thyme sprigs. Top with turnips. Sprinkle pepper, salt, and oil over the mixture. Put a steamer basket onto the rack.
Seal lid and cook on High Pressure for 8 minutes. Release the pressure quickly. Carefully unlock the lid. Serve over the delicate onion rings and thinly turnips.

Stuffed Tench with Herbs & Lemon
Serving Size: 2 | **Total Time**: 20 minutes
1 tench, cleaned, gutted
1 lemon, quartered
2 tbsp olive oil
1 tsp rosemary, chopped
¼ tsp dried thyme
2 garlic cloves, crushed

In a bowl, mix olive oil, garlic, rosemary, and thyme. Stir to combine. Brush the fish with the previously prepared mixture and stuff with lemon. Pour 4 cups of water into the Instant Pot, set the steamer tray, and place the fish on top. Seal the lid and cook on Steam for 15 minutes on High Pressure. Do a quick release. Unlock the lid. For a crispier taste, briefly brown the fish in a grill pan.

Pollock & Tomato Stew
Serving Size: 4 | **Total Time**: 30 minutes
1 lb pollock fillets
4 cloves, crushed
1 lb tomatoes, chopped
2 bay leaves, whole
2 cups fish stock
Salt and pepper to taste
1 onion, finely chopped
½ cup olive oil

Heat 2 tbsp olive oil on Sauté. Add onion and sauté for 3 minutes. Add tomatoes and cook until soft. Press Cancel. Add pollock fillets, cloves, bay leaves, stock, salt, and pepper and seal the lid. Cook on High pressure for 15 minutes. When ready, do a quick release. Serve warm.

Dijon Catfish Fillets with White Wine
Serving Size: 3 | **Total Time**: 15 minutes + cooling time
1 lb catfish fillets
1 lemon, juiced
½ cup parsley, chopped
2 garlic cloves, crushed
1 onion, finely chopped
1 tbsp dill, chopped
1 tbsp rosemary, chopped
2 cups white wine
2 tbsp Dijon mustard

1 cup extra virgin olive oil

In a bowl, mix lemon juice, parsley, garlic, onion, dill, rosemary, wine, mustard, and oil. Stir well. Submerge the fillets and cover with a tight lid. Refrigerate for 1 hour. Insert a trivet in the Instant Pot. Remove the fish from the fridge and place it on the rack. Pour in 1 cup of water and marinade. Seal the lid. Cook on Steam for 8 minutes on High. Release the pressure quickly. Serve immediately.

Chili Steamed Catfish

Serving Size: 4 | **Total Time:** 70 minutes
1 lb flathead catfish
1 cup orange juice
¼ cup lemon juice
½ cup olive oil
1 tbsp dried thyme
1 tbsp dried rosemary
1 tsp chili flakes
1 tsp sea salt

In a bowl, mix orange juice, lemon juice, olive oil, thyme, rosemary, chili flakes, and salt. Brush the fish with the mixture and refrigerate for 30 minutes. Remove from the fridge, drain, and reserve the marinade. Insert a trivet in the pot. Pour in 1 cup of water and marinade. Place the fish onto the top. Seal the lid and cook on High Pressure for 10 minutes. Do a quick release. Serve immediately.

Mackerel with Potatoes & Spinach

Serving Size: 4 | **Total Time:** 20 minutes
4 mackerels, skin on
1 lb spinach, torn
5 potatoes, peeled, chopped
3 tbsp olive oil
2 garlic cloves, crushed
2 tbsp mint leaves, chopped
1 lemon, juiced
Sea salt to taste

Heat 2 tbsp of the olive oil on Sauté. Stir-fry garlic for 1 minute. Stir in spinach and salt and cook for 4-5 minutes until wilted; set aside. Make a layer of potatoes in the pot. Top with fish and drizzle with lemon juice, remaining olive oil, and salt. Pour in 1 cup of water, seal the lid, and cook on Steam for 7 minutes on High. When ready, do a quick release. Carefully unlock the lid. Plate the fish and potatoes with spinach and serve topped with mint leaves.

Corn & Mackerel Chowder

Serving Size: 4 | **Total Time:** 45 minutes
6 oz mackerel fillets
½ cup wheat groats, soaked
½ cup kidney beans, soaked
¼ cup sweet corn
1 lb tomatoes, chopped
4 cups fish stock
4 tbsp olive oil
2 garlic cloves, crushed

Heat olive oil on Sauté. Stir-fry tomatoes and garlic for 5 minutes. Add in stock, corn, kidney beans, and wheat groats. Seal the lid and cook on High Pressure for 25 minutes. Do a quick release. Add mackerel fillets. Seal the lid and cook on Steam for 8 minutes on High. Do a quick release. Serve.

Steamed Halibut Packets

Serving Size: 4 | **Total Time:** 20 minutes
4 halibut fillets
1 lb cherry tomatoes, halved
1 cup olives, chopped
2 tbsp olive oil
1 garlic clove, minced
½ tsp thyme
Salt and pepper to taste
Arugula for garnish

Pour 1 cup of water into your Instant Pot and insert a trivet. Divide the halibut fillets, cherry tomatoes, and olives between 4 sheets of aluminum foil. Drizzle with olive oil and season with salt, pepper, garlic, and thyme. Close the packets and seal the edges. Place them on the trivet. Secure the lid, select Steam, and cook for 4 minutes on Low. When done, allow a natural release for 10 minutes. Serve scattered with arugula.

Seafood & Fish Stew

Serving Size: 6 | **Total Time:** 25 minutes
2 lb different fish and seafood
3 tbsp olive oil
2 onions, peeled, chopped
2 carrots, grated
2 tbsp parsley, chopped
2 garlic cloves, crushed
3 cups water
1 tsp sea salt

Heat olive oil on Sauté. Stir-fry onions and garlic for 3-4 minutes, or until translucent. Add carrots, fish and seafood, parsley, water, and salt. Seal the lid, and cook on High Pressure for 10 minutes. Do a quick release. Serve.

Vietnamese Fish & Noodle Soup

Serving Size: 6 | **Total Time:** 32 minutes
2 tbsp sesame oil
1 lb snapper fillets, chopped
12 oz squid
5 oz rice noodles
¼ cup soy sauce
¼ tsp thyme
½ tbsp cilantro, chopped
1 tsp chili flakes
1 garlic clove, sliced
1 onion, thinly sliced
Salt and pepper to taste

Heat the sesame oil in your Instant Pot on Sauté. Add in onion, garlic, salt, and pepper and cook for 2 minutes. Stir in fish, squid, chili flakes, and thyme and sauté for 5-6 minutes. Pour in soy sauce and 5 cups of water and seal the lid. Select Manual and cook for 10 minutes.

Once ready, perform a quick pressure release. Press Sauté and add in the rice noodles. Cook for 3-4 minutes until just tender. Ladle into bowls and serve scattered cilantro.

Seafood Medley with Rosemary Rice

Serving Size: 4 | **Total Time:** 45 minutes
- 1 lb frozen seafood mix
- 1 cup brown rice
- 1 tbsp calamari ink
- 2 tbsp extra virgin olive oil
- 2 garlic cloves, crushed
- 1 tbsp chopped rosemary
- ½ tsp salt
- 3 cups fish stock
- ½ lemon

Add in seafood mix, rice, calamari ink, olive oil, garlic, rosemary, salt, stock, and lemon, seal the lid and cook on Manual for 25 minutes on High. Release the pressure naturally for 10 minutes. Squeeze lemon juice and serve.

Seafood Chowder with Oyster Crackers

Serving Size: 4 | **Total Time:** 40 minutes
- 20 oz canned mussels, drained, liquid reserved
- ¼ cup grated Pecorino Romano cheese
- 1 lb potatoes, peeled and cut chunks
- 2 cups oyster crackers
- 2 tbsp olive oil
- ½ tsp garlic powder
- Salt and pepper to taste
- 2 pancetta slices, chopped
- 2 celery stalks, chopped
- 1 medium onion, chopped
- 1 tbsp flour
- ¼ cup white wine
- 1 tsp dried rosemary
- 1 bay leaf
- 1 ½ cups heavy cream
- 2 tbsp chopped fresh chervil

Fry pancetta on Sauté for 5 minutes until crispy. Remove to a paper towel-lined plate and set aside. Sauté the celery and onion in the same fat for 1 minute, stirring until the vegetables soften. Mix in the flour to coat the vegetables. Pour in the wine simmer. Cook for about 1 minute or until reduced by about one-third.
Pour in 1 cup water, the reserved mussel liquid, potatoes, salt, rosemary, and bay leaf. Seal the lid and cook on High Pressure for 4 minutes. Do a natural pressure release for 10 minutes. Stir in mussels and heavy cream.
Press Sauté and bring the soup to a simmer to heat the mussels through. Discard the bay leaf. Top with pancetta, chervil, cheese, and crackers and serve.

Seafood Traditional Spanish Paella

Serving Size: 4 | **Total Time:** 30 minutes
- 2 tbsp olive oil
- 1 onion, chopped
- 4 garlic cloves, minced
- ½ cup dry white wine
- 1 cup rice
- 1 ½ cups chicken stock
- 1 ½ tsp sweet paprika
- 1 tsp turmeric powder
- 1 lb small clams, scrubbed
- 1 lb prawns, deveined
- 1 red bell pepper, diced
- 1 lemon, cut into wedges

Cook onion and garlic in 1 tbsp of oil on Sauté for 3 minutes. Pour in wine to deglaze, scraping the bottom of the pot of any brown. Cook for 2 minutes until the wine is reduced by half. Add in rice and broth. Stir in paprika, turmeric, and bell pepper. Seal the lid and cook on High Pressure for 10 minutes. Do a quick release. Remove to a plate and wipe the pot clean. Heat the remaining oil on Sauté. Cook clams and prawns for 6 minutes until the shrimp are pink. Discard unopened clams. Arrange seafood and lemon wedges over paella to serve.

Easy Seafood Paella

Serving Size: 4 | **Total Time:** 20 minutes
- 1 cup tiger prawns, peeled and deveined
- 1 lb mussels, cleaned and debearded
- ½ tsp guindilla (cayenne pepper)
- ½ lb clams
- 2 tbsp olive oil
- 1 onion, chopped
- 2 garlic cloves, minced
- 1 red bell pepper, chopped
- 1 cup rice
- 2 cups clam juice
- ¾ cup green peas, frozen
- 1 tbsp parsley, chopped
- 1 tbsp turmeric
- 1 whole lemon, quartered

Warm the olive oil in your Instant Pot on Sauté. Add in prawns, red pepper, onion, and garlic and cook for 3 minutes. Stir in rice for 1 minute and pour in clam juice, turmeric, mussels, and clams. Seal the lid, select Manual, and cook for 5 minutes on High pressure. When ready, perform a quick pressure release and unlock the lid. Stir in green peas and guindilla for 3-4 minutes. Top with lemon quarters and parsley. Serve immediately.

Seafood Pilaf

Serving Size: 6 | **Total Time:** 35 minutes
- 1 lb chopped catfish fillets
- 2 cups mussels and shrimp
- 4 tbsp olive oil
- 1 onion, diced
- 2 garlic cloves, minced
- ½ tsp cayenne pepper
- ½ tsp basil
- ½ tsp oregano
- 1 red bell pepper, diced
- 1 green bell pepper, diced
- 2 cups Jasmine rice
- A few saffron threads
- 3 cups fish stock
- Salt and pepper to taste

Warm the olive oil in your Instant Pot on Sauté. Add in onion, garlic, and bell peppers and cook for 4 minutes. Add in catfish, rice, and saffron and cook for another 2 minutes. Add mussels, shrimps, cayenne pepper, basil, oregano, stock, salt, and pepper, stir, and seal the lid. Select Manual and cook for 6 minutes.

When done, allow a natural release for 10 minutes. Serve.

Seafood Hot Pot with Rice

Serving Size: 4 | **Total Time:** 20 minutes
½ lb shrimp, deveined
½ lb scallops
2 tbsp butter
1 onion, chopped
1 bell pepper, sliced
1 carrot, shredded
1 cup basmati rice
Salt and pepper to taste
2 cups fish broth
1 lemon, sliced

Melt the butter in your Instant Pot on Sauté. Add in onion, bell pepper, and carrot and cook for 3-4 minutes. Stir in rice, shrimp, scallops, salt, pepper, and fish broth and seal the lid. Press Manual and cook for 6 minutes on High pressure. Once done, use a quick pressure release and unlock the lid. Top with lemon slices and serve.

Spicy Pasta with Seafood

Serving Size: 4 | **Total Time:** 20 minutes
2 tbsp olive oil
1 onion, diced
16 oz penne
24 oz arrabbiata sauce
3 cups chicken broth
Salt and pepper to taste
16 oz scallops
¼ cup Parmesan, grated
Basil leaves for garnish

Heat oil on Sauté. Stir-fry onion for 3 minutes. Stir in penne, arrabbiata sauce, salt, pepper, and 2 cups of broth. Seal the lid and cook for 6 minutes on High Pressure. Do a quick release. Remove to a plate. Pour the remaining broth and add scallops. Press Sauté and cook for 4 minutes. Mix in the pasta and serve topped with Parmesan cheese and basil leaves.

Creole Seafood Gumbo

Serving Size: 4 | **Total Time:** 20 minutes
12 oz pollock filets, cut into chunks
1 lb medium raw shrimp, deveined
Salt and pepper to taste
1 tbsp creole seasoning
1 olive oil
1 yellow onion, diced
2 celery ribs, diced
1 cup chicken broth
14 oz diced tomatoes
¼ cup tomato paste
2 bay leaves
6 oz okra, trimmed

Sprinkle the pollock with salt, pepper, and creole seasoning. Warm the olive oil in your Instant Pot on Sauté. Add in the fish and cook for 4 minutes. Set aside. Add onions and celery to the pot and cook for 2 minutes.
Put in chicken broth, tomatoes, tomato paste, bay leaves, okra, shrimp, and cooked fish and seal the lid.

Select Manual and cook for 5 minutes on High pressure. When ready, perform a quick pressure release. Serve.

Shrimp with Chickpeas & Olives

Serving Size: 6 | **Total Time:** 25 minutes
2 lb shrimp, deveined
2 garlic cloves, minced
1 carrot, chopped
1 cup chickpeas, soaked
3 cups fish broth
½ cup olives, pitted
Salt and pepper to taste
1 cup tomatoes, chopped
2 tbsp olive oil
1 onion, chopped

Warm the olive oil in your Instant Pot on Sauté. Add in onion, garlic, carrot, salt, and pepper and cook for 4 minutes until soft. Add tomatoes, chickpeas, olives and broth. Simmer for 5 minutes. Add the shrimp and toss to coat in the sauce. Seal the lid and cook on High Pressure for 4 minutes. Release the pressure naturally. Serve warm.

Shrimp Boil with Chorizo Sausages

Serving Size: 4 | **Total Time:** 15 minutes
3 red potatoes
3 ears corn, cut into rounds
1 cup white wine
4 chorizo sausages, chopped
1 lb shrimp, deveined
2 tbsp of seafood seasoning
Salt to taste
1 lemon, cut into wedges
¼ cup butter, melted

Add potatoes, corn, wine, chorizo, shrimp, seafood seasoning, and salt. Do not stir. Add in 2 cups of water. Seal the lid and cook for 2 minutes on High Pressure. Release the pressure quickly. Drain the mixture through a colander. Transfer to a plate. Serve with melted butter and lemon wedges.

Party Shrimp with & Rice Veggies

Serving Size: 4 | **Total Time:** 36 minutes
¼ cup olive oil
1 onion, chopped
1 red bell pepper, diced
2 garlic cloves, minced
1 tsp turmeric
Salt and pepper to taste
1 cup rice
¼ cup green peas
2 cups fish broth
1 lb shrimp, deveined
Chopped fresh parsley
1 lemon, cut into wedges

Warm oil on Sauté. Add in bell pepper and onion and garlic and cook for 5 minutes until fragrant. Season with pepper, salt, and turmeric and cook for 1 minute. Stir in fish broth and rice. Seal the lid and cook on High Pressure for 15 minutes. Release the pressure quickly. Stir in green peas and shrimp and cook for 5 minutes on Sauté. Serve with parsley and lemon.

Quick Shrimp Gumbo with Sausage

Serving Size: 4 | Total Time: 30 minutes
1 lb jumbo shrimp
2 tbsp olive oil
1/3 cup flour
1 ½ tsp Cajun seasoning
1 onion, chopped
1 red bell pepper, chopped
2 celery stalks, chopped
2 garlic cloves, minced
1 serrano pepper, minced
2 ½ cups chicken broth
6 oz andouille sausage, sliced
2 green onions, finely sliced
Salt and pepper to taste

Heat olive oil on Sauté. Whisk in the flour with a wooden spoon and cook 3 minutes, stirring constantly. Stir in Cajun seasoning, onion, bell pepper, celery, garlic, and serrano pepper for about 5 minutes. Pour in the chicken broth, ¾ cup water, and andouille sausage. Seal and cook for 6 minutes on High Pressure. Do a natural pressure for 5 minutes. Stir the shrimp into the gumbo to eat it up for 3 minutes. Adjust the seasoning. Ladle the gumbo into bowls and garnish with the green onions.

Hot Shrimp & Potato Chowder

Serving Size: 4 | Total Time: 35 minutes
4 slices pancetta, chopped
4 tbsp minced garlic
1 onion, chopped
2 potatoes, chopped
16 oz canned corn kernels
4 cups vegetable stock
1 tsp dried rosemary
Salt and pepper to taste
1 lb jumbo shrimp, deveined
1 tbsp olive oil
½ tsp red chili flakes
¾ cup heavy cream

Fry pancetta for 5 minutes until crispy on Sauté and set aside. Add in onion and stir-fry for 3 minutes. Pour in the potatoes, corn, stock, rosemary, salt, and pepper. Seal the lid and cook on High Pressure for 10 minutes. Do a quick pressure release. Carefully unlock the lid.
In a bowl, toss the shrimp in the garlic, salt, olive oil, and flakes. Remove the chowder from the pot to a serving bowl. Wipe the pot clean and fry shrimp for 3-4 minutes until pink. Mix in the heavy cream and cook for 2 minutes. Add shrimp to chowder and garnish with the reserved pancetta. Ladle into bowls and serve.

Shrimp with Okra & Brussels Sprouts

Serving Size: 4 | Total Time: 40 minutes
1 lb large shrimp, cleaned, rinsed
6 oz Brussels sprouts
4 oz okra, whole
2 carrots, chopped
2 cups vegetable broth
2 tomatoes, diced
2 tbsp tomato paste
½ tsp cayenne pepper
Salt and pepper to taste
2 tbsp olive oil
¼ cup balsamic vinegar
1 tbsp rosemary, chopped
2 tbsp sour cream

Mix olive oil, vinegar, rosemary, salt, and pepper in a large bowl. Stir the shrimp into the mixture. Toss well to coat. Mix tomatoes, tomato paste, and cayenne pepper in the pressure cooker. Cook on Sauté for 5 minutes, stirring constantly. Set aside. Pour broth, Brussels sprouts, carrots, and okra into the pot. Cook on High pressure for 15 minutes. Do a quick release.
Remove the vegetables and add the shrimp to the remaining broth in the pot. Press Sauté and cook for 5 minutes. Add in the cooked vegetables. Cook for 2-3 minutes, stirring constantly. Stir in sour cream and serve.

Spinach & Shrimp Fusilli

Serving Size: 4 | Total Time: 15 minutes
1 ¼ lb shrimp, deveined
2 tbsp melted butter
2 garlic cloves, minced
¼ cup white wine
10 oz fusilli pasta
1/3 cup tomato puree
½ tsp red chili flakes
1 tsp lemon zest
1 tbsp lemon juice
6 cups spinach

On Sauté, pour the white wine and bring to simmer for 2 minutes to reduce the liquid by half. Stir in the fusilli pasta, 2 ½ cups water, garlic, puréed tomato, shrimp, melted butter, and chili flakes. Seal the lid. Cook for 5 minutes on High pressure. Do a quick release. Stir in lemon zest, juice, and spinach until wilted and soft. Serve.

Jalapeño Shrimp with Herbs & Lemon

Serving Size: 4 | Total Time: 25 minutes
1 lb shrimp, deveined
½ cup olive oil
1 tsp garlic powder
1 tsp rosemary, chopped
1 tsp thyme, chopped
½ tsp basil, chopped
½ tsp sage, chopped
½ tsp salt
1 tsp jalapeño pepper

Pour 1 cup of water into the inner pot. In a bowl, mix oil, garlic, rosemary, thyme, basil, sage, salt, and jalapeño pepper. Brush the marinade over the shrimp. Insert a steamer rack in the pot and arrange the shrimp on top.
Seal the lid and cook on Steam for 3 minutes on High. Release the steam naturally for 10 minutes. Press Sauté and stir-fry for 2 more minutes or until golden brown.

Creole Shrimp with Okra

Serving Size: 2 | Total Time: 10 minutes

1 lb shrimp, deveined
6 oz okra, trimmed
2 tbsp olive oil
1 tsp garlic powder
½ tsp cayenne pepper
½ tbsp Creole seasoning
Salt and pepper to taste

Pour 1 cup water into your Instant Pot and fit in a trivet. In a baking dish, combine shrimp, okra, olive oil, garlic powder, cayenne pepper, Creole seasoning, salt, and pepper and mix to combine. Place the dish on the trivet. Seal the lid and cook for 2 minutes on Steam on High. When ready, perform a quick pressure release. Serve.

Rich Shrimp Risotto

Serving Size: 4 | Total Time: 30 minutes
¾ cup Pecorino Romano cheese, grated
1 lb shrimp, deveined
4 tbsp butter
2 garlic cloves, minced
1 yellow onion, chopped
1 ½ cups Arborio rice
2 tbsp dry white wine
4 cups fish broth
½ tsp Italian seasoning
2 tbsp heavy cream
Salt and pepper to taste

Melt half of the butter in your Instant Pot. Add in garlic and onion and cook for 4 minutes. Stir in rice and cook for another minute. Mix in white wine and cook for 3 minutes until the wine evaporates. Pour in 3 cups of fish broth and Italian seasoning and seal the lid. Select Manual and cook for 10 minutes on High pressure.

When ready, perform a quick pressure release and unlock the lid. Add in shrimp and the remaining broth and cook for 4-5 minutes on Sauté. Stir in Pecorino Romano cheese, heavy cream, and the remaining butter.

Tangy Shrimp Curry

Serving Size: 4 | Total Time: 15 minutes
1 lb shrimp, deveined
2 tbsp sesame oil
1 onion, chopped
½ tsp fresh ginger, grated
1 garlic clove, minced
1 tsp cayenne pepper
1 tbsp lime juice
1 cup coconut milk
1 tbsp curry powder
Salt and pepper to taste

Heat the sesame oil in your Instant Pot on Sauté and cook the onion, garlic, and ginger for 3-4 minutes. Stir in curry powder, cayenne pepper, salt, and pepper and cook for 3 minutes. Pour in coconut milk, shrimp, and 1 cup of water and seal the lid. Select Manual and cook for 4 minutes on Low pressure. Once done, perform a quick pressure release. Drizzle with lime juice and serve.

Chinese Shrimp with Green Beans

Serving Size: 2 | Total Time: 20 minutes
1 tbsp sesame oil
1 lb shrimp, deveined
½ cup diced onion
2 cloves garlic, minced
1 carrot, cut into strips
½ lb green beans, chopped
2 cups vegetable stock
3 tbsp soy sauce
2 tbsp rice wine vinegar
10 oz lo mein egg noodles
½ tsp toasted sesame seeds
Sea Salt and pepper to taste

Warm oil on Sauté. Stir-fry the shrimp for 5 minutes; set aside. Add in garlic and onion and cook for 3 minutes until fragrant. Mix in soy sauce, carrot, stock, beans, and rice wine vinegar. Add in noodles and ensure they are covered. Season with pepper and salt. Seal the lid and cook on High Pressure for 5 minutes. Release the pressure quickly. Place the main in 2 plates. Add the reserved shrimp, sprinkle with sesame seeds, and serve.

Cheesy Shrimp Scampi

Serving Size: 4 | Total Time: 10 minutes
1 lb shrimp, deveined
2 tbsp olive oil
1 clove garlic, minced
1 tbsp tomato paste
10 oz canned tomatoes, diced
½ cup dry white wine
1 tsp red chili pepper
1 tbsp parsley, chopped
Salt and pepper to taste
1 cup Grana Padano, grated

Warm the olive oil in your Instant Pot on Sauté. Add in garlic and cook for 1 minute. Stir in shrimp, tomato paste, tomatoes, white wine, chili pepper, parsley, salt, pepper, and ¼ cup of water and seal the lid. Select Manual and cook for 3 minutes on High pressure. Once done, perform a quick pressure release and unlock the lid. Serve garnished with Grana Padano cheese.

Indian Prawn Curry

Serving Size: 4 | Total Time: 30 minutes
1 ½ lb prawns, deveined
2 tbsp ghee
2 garlic cloves, minced
1 onion, chopped
1 tsp ginger, grated
½ tsp ground turmeric
1 tsp red chili powder
2 tsp ground cumin
2 tsp ground coriander
2 tbsp curry paste
2 cups coconut milk
1 cup tomatoes, chopped
2 habanero peppers, minced
Salt and pepper to taste
1 tbsp fresh lemon juice

Melt the ghee in your Instant Pot on Sauté. Add in garlic, onion, and ginger and cook for 4 minutes. Stir

in the turmeric, chili powder, cumin, coriander, and curry paste and cook for 1 more minute. Stir in coconut milk, prawns, tomatoes, habanero peppers, salt, and pepper.
Seal the lid. Select Manual and cook for 5 minutes on Low. Once ready, allow a natural release for 10 minutes, then perform a quick pressure release, and unlock the lid. Top with lemon juice and serve.

Butter & Wine Lobster Tails
Serving Size: 4 | **Total Time**: 10 minutes
1 lb lobster tails, cut in half
½ cup white wine
½ cup butter, melted
1 tsp red pepper flakes
Pour ½ cup of water and white wine in your Instant Pot and fit in a trivet. Place lobster tails on the trivet and seal the lid. Select Steam and cook for 5 minutes on Low. When ready, perform a quick pressure release. Drizzle with butter and top with red pepper flakes to serve.

Ginger & Garlic Crab
Serving Size: 4 | **Total Time**: 15 minutes
1 lb crabs, halved
2 tbsp butter
1 shallot, chopped
1 garlic cloves, minced
1 cup coconut milk
1-inch ginger, sliced
1 lemongrass stalk
Salt and pepper to taste
1 lemon, sliced
Melt the butter in your Instant Pot on Sauté. Place in shallot, garlic, and ginger and cook for 3 minutes. Pour in coconut milk, crabs, lemongrass, salt, and pepper and seal the lid. Select Manual and cook for 6 minutes on High pressure. Once ready, perform a quick pressure release and unlock the lid. Serve with lemon slices.

Herby Crab Legs with Lemon
Serving Size: 4 | **Total Time**: 10 minutes
3 lb king crab legs, broken in half
1 tsp rosemary
1 tsp thyme
1 tsp dill
¼ cup butter, melted
Salt and pepper to taste
1 lemon, cut into wedges
Pour 1 cup of water into your Instant Pot and fit in a trivet. Season the crab legs with rosemary, thyme, dill, salt, and pepper; place on the trivet. Seal the lid, select Manual, and cook for 3 minutes. When ready, perform a quick pressure release. Remove crab legs to a bowl and drizzle with melted butter. Serve with lemon wedges.

Black Squid Ink Tagliatelle
Serving Size: 4 | **Total Time**: 25 minutes
18 oz squid ink tagliatelle, cooked
1 lb fresh seafood mix
¼ cup olive oil
4 garlic cloves, crushed
1 tbsp parsley, chopped
1 tsp rosemary, chopped
½ tbsp white wine
Heat 3 tbsp olive oil on Sauté and stir-fry the garlic for 1-2 minutes until fragrant. Add seafood, parsley, and rosemary and stir. Add the remaining oil, wine, and ½ cup of water. Seal the lid and cook on High Pressure for 4 minutes. Do a quick release and set aside. Open the lid, add the pasta, and stir. Serve hot.

Crab Pilaf with Broccoli & Asparagus
Serving Size: 4 | **Total Time**: 30 minutes
½ lb asparagus, trimmed and cut into 1-inch pieces
½ lb broccoli florets
Salt to taste
2 tbsp olive oil
1 small onion, chopped
1 cup rice
1/3 cup white wine
2 cups vegetable stock
8 oz lump crabmeat
Heat oil on Sauté and cook the onion for 3 minutes until soft. Stir in rice and cook for 1 minute. Pour in the wine. Cook for 2 to 3 minutes, stirring until the liquid has almost evaporated. Add vegetable stock and salt; stir.
Place a trivet on top. Arrange the broccoli and asparagus on the trivet. Seal the lid and cook on High Pressure for 8 minutes. Do a quick release. Remove the vegetables to a bowl. Fluff the rice with a fork and add in the crabmeat, heat for a minute. Taste and adjust the seasoning. Serve immediately topped with broccoli and asparagus.

Red Wine Squid
Serving Size: 4 | **Total Time**: 25 minutes
2 lb squid, chopped
2 tbsp olive oil
Salt and pepper to taste
½ cup red wine
½ fennel bulb, sliced
28 oz can crushed tomatoes
1 red onion, sliced
2 garlic cloves, minced
1 tsp Italian seasoning
½ cup parsley, chopped
Mix the olive oil, squid, salt, and pepper in a bowl. Pour the red wine, tomatoes, onion, garlic, Italian seasoning, and fennel in your Instant Pot and fit in a steamer basket. Put in the squid and seal the lid. Select Manual and cook for 4 minutes on High pressure. When ready, allow a natural release for 10 minutes, then perform a quick pressure release. Serve scattered with parsley.

White Wine Marinated Squid Rings
Serving Size: 3 | **Total Time**: 25 minutes + cooling time
1 lb fresh squid rings
1 cup dry white wine
1 cup olive oil

2 garlic cloves, crushed
1 lemon, juiced
2 cups fish stock
¼ tsp red pepper flakes
¼ tsp dried oregano
1 tbsp rosemary, chopped
1 tsp sea salt

In a bowl, mix wine, olive oil, lemon juice, garlic, flakes, oregano, rosemary, and salt. Submerge squid rings in this mixture and cover with a lid. Refrigerate for 1 hour. Remove the squid from the fridge and place it in the pot along with stock and half of the marinade. Seal the lid. Cook on High Pressure for 6 minutes. Release the pressure naturally for 10 minutes. Transfer the rings to a plate and drizzle with some marinade to serve.

Mussels With Lemon & White Wine
Serving Size: 5 | **Total Time:** 10 minutes
2 lb mussels, cleaned and debearded
1 cup white wine
½ cup water
1 tsp garlic powder
Juice from 1 lemon

In the pot, mix garlic powder, water, and wine. Put the mussels into the steamer basket; rounded-side should be placed facing upwards to fit as many as possible.
Insert a rack into the cooker and lower the steamer basket onto the rack. Seal the lid and cook on Low Pressure for 1 minute. Release the pressure quickly. Remove unopened mussels. Coat the mussels with the wine mixture and lemon juice and serve.

Chili Squid
Serving Size: 4 | **Total Time:** 35 minutes
1 lb squid, sliced into rings
1 tsp onion powder
2 tbsp flour
1 garlic clove, minced
1 tbsp chives
¼ tsp chili pepper, chopped
¼ tsp smoked paprika
1 tbsp lemon juice
1 cup vegetable broth
2 tbsp butter
Salt and pepper to taste
2 tbsp parsley, chopped

Mix the onion powder, smoked paprika, flour, garlic, chives, chili pepper, salt, and pepper in a bowl. Add in the squid slices and toss to coat. Let sit for 10 minutes.
Melt the butter in your Instant Pot on Sauté. Place in the squid mixture and cook for 3-4 minutes. Pour in the vegetable broth and seal the lid. Cook on Manual for 12 minutes on High. Once done, perform a quick pressure release and unlock the lid. Serve sprinkled with parsley.

Spicy Mussels & Anchovies with Rice
Serving Size: 4 | **Total Time:** 40 minutes
1 cup rice
6 oz mussels
1 onion, finely chopped
1 garlic clove, crushed
1 tbsp dried rosemary
¼ cup capers
Salt and chili pepper to taste
3 tbsp olive oil
4 salted anchovies

Add rice to the pot and pour 2 cups of water. Seal the lid and cook on Manual for 18 minutes on High. Do a quick release. Remove the rice and set aside. Grease the pot with oil, and stir-fry garlic and onion for 2 minutes on Sauté. Add mussels and rosemary. Cook for 10 more minutes. Stir in rice and season with salt and chili pepper. Serve with anchovies and capers.

Beer-Steamed Mussels
Serving Size: 4 | **Total Time:** 15 minutes
3 lb mussels, debearded
4 tbsp butter
1 shallot, chopped
2 garlic cloves, minced
2 tbsp parsley, chopped
1 cup beer
1 cup chicken stock

Melt butter in your Instant Pot on Sauté. Add in shallot and garlic and cook for 2 minutes. Stir in beer and cook for 1 minute. Mix in stock and mussels and seal the lid.
Select Manual and cook for 3 minutes on High pressure. Once ready, perform a quick pressure release. Discard unopened mussels. Serve sprinkled with parsley.

Basil Clams with Garlic & White Wine
Serving Size: 4 | **Total Time:** 15 minutes
1 lb clams, scrubbed
2 tbsp butter
4 green garlic, chopped
1 tbsp lemon juice
½ cup white wine
½ cup chicken stock
Salt and pepper to taste
2 tbsp basil, chopped

Melt the butter in your Instant Pot on Sauté. Add in the garlic and clams and cook for 3-4 minutes. Stir in lemon juice and chicken stock, white wine, salt, and pepper and seal the lid. Select Manual and cook for 3 minutes on High pressure. Once done, perform a quick pressure release and unlock the lid. Discard unopened clams. Serve topped with basil.

Saucy Clams with Herbs
Serving Size: 4 | **Total Time:** 15 minutes
1 lb clams, scrubbed
2 tsp olive oil
2 garlic cloves, minced
1 onion, chopped
2 celery stalks, diced
1 bell pepper, diced
1 tbsp tomato paste
28 oz can crushed tomatoes
½ tsp basil
1 tsp rosemary

½ tsp oregano
Salt and pepper to taste
¼ tsp chili pepper

Warm the olive oil in your Instant Pot on Sauté. Place in garlic, onion, celery, and bell pepper and cook for 3-4 minutes. Add in tomato paste and cook for another 1 minute. Stir in clams, tomatoes, basil, rosemary, oregano, salt, pepper, and chili pepper and seal the lid. Select Manual and cook for 2 minutes on High pressure. Once done, perform a quick pressure release and unlock the lid. Discard unopened clams. Serve with cooked rice.

Clam & Corn Chowder

Serving Size: 4 | **Total Time:** 30 minutes
2 tbsp olive oil
1 onion, chopped
3 potatoes, cubed
4 cups corn kernels
12 oz canned clams, chopped
1 green bell pepper, diced
1 red bell pepper, diced
Salt and pepper to taste
4 cups chicken broth
1 cup milk
1 tbsp flour
3 tbsp butter

Warm the olive oil in your Instant Pot on Sauté. Add in onion and bell peppers and cook for 3-4 minutes until tender. Stir in potatoes, corn kernels, clams with their juice, and chicken broth.
Seal the lid, select Manual, and cook for 12 minutes on High. Once ready, perform a quick pressure release. Combine milk with flour and pour it into the pot. Press Sauté and stir in butter. Let simmer for 3-4 minutes.

Lime & Honey Scallops

Serving Size: 2 | **Total Time:** 15 minutes
1 lb sea scallops, shells removed
1 cup water
1 tbsp olive oil
3 tbsp honey
1 lime, juiced and zested
½ cup soy sauce
½ tsp ground ginger
½ tsp garlic powder
Salt to taste

Pour 1 cup of water into your Instant Pot and fit in a trivet. Place scallops, olive oil, honey, soy sauce, ginger, garlic powder, lime zest, and salt in a small pan and put it on the trivet. Seal the lid and cook for 6 minutes on Steam. Once ready, perform a quick pressure release and unlock the lid. Serve drizzled with lime juice.

Octopus & Shrimp with Collard Greens

Serving Size: 4 | **Total Time:** 30 minutes
6 oz octopus, cut into bite-sized pieces
1 lb collard greens, chopped
1 lb shrimp, whole
1 tomato, chopped
3 cups fish stock
4 tbsp olive oil
3 garlic cloves
2 tbsp parsley, chopped
1 tsp sea salt

Place shrimp and octopus in the pot. Add tomato and fish stock. Seal the lid and cook on High Pressure for 15 minutes. Do a quick release. Remove shrimp and octopus. Drain the liquid. Heat olive oil on Sauté and add garlic and parsley and cook for 1 minute. Add in collard greens, season with salt, and simmer for 5 minutes. Serve with shrimp and octopus.

Galician-Style Octopus

Serving Size: 6 | **Total Time:** 30 minutes
1 lb potatoes, sliced into rounds
2 lb whole octopus, cleaned and sliced
1 tbsp Spanish paprika
3 tbsp olive oil
Salt and pepper to taste

Place the potatoes in your Instant Pot and cover them with water. Place a trivet over the potatoes. Season the octopus with salt and pepper and place it onto the trivet. Seal the lid, select Manual, and cook for 15 minutes.
Once done, perform a quick pressure release and unlock the lid. Remove the octopus and let cool, then slice it into slices about half-inch thick. Transfer the sliced potatoes to a baking sheet and arrange octopus slices over the potatoes. Drizzle with olive oil and place under the broiler for 5 minutes. Sprinkle with paprika and serve.

White Wine Oysters

Serving Size: 4 | **Total Time:** 10 minutes
2 lb in-shell oysters, cleaned
1 cup vegetable broth
4 tbsp white wine
2 tbsp thyme, chopped
1 garlic clove, minced
Salt and pepper to taste
4 tbsp butter, melted

Place the vegetable broth, oysters, white wine, garlic, salt, and pepper in your Instant Pot and seal the lid. Select Manual and cook for 3 minutes on High pressure. Once done, perform a quick pressure release and unlock the lid. Drain the oysters, drizzle with the melted butter, and top with thyme to serve.

PASTA & RICE

Spinach & Anchovy Fusilli

Serving Size: 4 | **Total Time:** 15 minutes
- 1 lb fusilli pasta
- 4 cups spinach, chopped
- 4 anchovy fillets, chopped
- ½ cup Parmesan, shredded
- 2 tbsp butter
- ½ tsp grated nutmeg
- 3 tbsp pine nuts, toasted
- Salt and pepper to taste

Place fusilli pasta and 4 cups of salted water in your Instant Pot and seal the lid. Select Manual and cook for 4 minutes on High. When done, perform a quick pressure release and unlock the lid. Drain the pasta, reserving 1 cup of the liquid and set aside. Melt butter on Sauté

Add in spinach. Stir for 2 minutes and pour in the pasta liquid. Return the pasta, stir in anchovies, nutmeg, and pine nuts. Adjust the taste. Top with Parmesan and serve.

Bean Pasta with Vegetables

Serving Size: 4 | **Total Time:** 30 minutes
- 1 cup butternut squash, shredded
- 1 lb penne pasta
- 1 cup pasta sauce
- 1 cup canned white beans
- ½ cup frozen lima beans
- ½ cup black olives, sliced
- 1 cup baby spinach
- ½ zucchini, sliced
- ½ tsp garlic powder
- ½ tsp onion powder
- ½ tsp ground nutmeg
- ½ tsp oregano
- ½ tbsp Italian seasoning

Place pasta, 3 cups of water, butternut squash, and pasta sauce in your Instant Pot. Seal the lid, select Manual, and cook for 4 minutes on High. When done, allow a natural release for 10 minutes and unlock the lid. Stir in white beans, lima beans, olives, spinach, zucchini, garlic powder, onion powder, nutmeg, oregano, and Italian seasoning and press Sauté. Cook for 5-6 minutes and adjust the seasoning. Serve right away.

Tomato & Mushroom Rotini

Serving Size: 4 | **Total Time:** 35 minutes
- 1 lb rotini pasta
- 2 tbsp olive oil
- ½ yellow onion, diced
- 2 garlic cloves, minced
- 16 oz crushed tomatoes
- 1 cup Mushrooms, sliced
- ½ tbsp grated nutmeg
- ¼ cup basil, chopped
- Salt and pepper to taste

Cover rotini pasta with salted water in your Instant Pot and seal the lid. Select Manual and cook for 4 minutes on High. When done, allow a natural release for 10 minutes, then perform a quick pressure release, and unlock the lid. Drain the pasta and transfer to a bowl.

Heat the olive oil on Sauté and cook the onion, mushrooms, and garlic for 3-4 minutes. Stir in tomatoes and nutmeg and simmer for 5-6 minutes. Stir in basil and cooked pasta; adjust the seasoning. Serve.

Sicilian Seafood Linguine

Serving Size: 4 | **Total Time:** 25 minutes
- 2 tbsp olive oil
- 1 onion, chopped
- 2 garlic cloves, minced
- 2 tomatoes, chopped
- 1 red bell pepper, chopped
- ½ cup dried white wine
- 3 cups vegetable stock
- 16 oz linguine
- ½ lb prawns, peeled
- 4 sardines, chopped
- 2 tbsp parsley, chopped
- 1 tbsp tomato purée
- Salt and pepper to taste
- ½ cup Parmesan, grated

Warm the olive oil in your Instant Pot on Sauté. Add in the onion and garlic and cook for 3 minutes. Pour in tomatoes and bell pepper and cook for another 3-4 minutes. Stir in white wine and simmer for 3 minutes. Mix in vegetable stock, linguine, prawns, tomato purée, salt, and pepper and seal the lid. Select Manual on High.

Cook for 4 minutes on High. When ready, perform a quick pressure release and unlock the lid. Stir in sardines and parsley. Scatter with Parmesan cheese and serve.

Spicy Rice Noodles with Tofu & Chives

Serving Size: 6 | **Total Time:** 15 minutes
- ½ cup soy sauce
- 2 tbsp brown sugar
- 2 tbsp rice vinegar
- 1 tbsp sweet chili sauce
- 1 tbsp sesame oil
- 1 tsp fresh minced garlic
- 20 oz tofu, cubed
- 8 oz rice noodles
- ¼ cup chopped chives

Heat the oil on Sauté. Fry the tofu for 5 minutes until golden brown; reserve. To the pot, add 2 cups water, garlic, vinegar, sugar, soy sauce, and chili sauce and mix until smooth. Stir in rice noodles. Seal the lid and cook on High Pressure for 3 minutes. Divide noodles between bowls. Top with tofu and sprinkle with chives and serve.

Beef Garam Masala with Rice

Serving Size: 4 | **Total Time:** 30 minutes
- ¼ cup yogurt
- 2 cloves garlic, smashed
- 1 tbsp olive oil

1 lime, juiced
Salt and pepper to taste
2 lb beef stew meat, cubed
1 tbsp garam masala
1 tbsp fresh ginger, grated
1 ½ tbsp smoked paprika
1 tsp ground cumin
¼ tbsp cayenne pepper
3 tbsp butter
1 onion, chopped
14-oz can puréed tomatoes
1 cup beef broth
1 cup basmati rice, rinsed
½ cup heavy cream
2 tbsp cilantro, chopped

In a bowl, mix garlic, lime juice, olive oil, pepper, salt, and yogurt. Add in the beef and toss to coat. In another bowl, mix paprika, garam masala, cumin, ginger, and cayenne pepper. Melt butter on Sauté and stir-fry the onion for 3 minutes. Sprinkle spice mixture over onion and cook for about 30 seconds. Add in the beef-yogurt mixture. Sauté for 3 to 4 minutes until the meat is slightly cooked. Mix in broth and puréed tomatoes.

Set trivet over beef in the Pressure cooker's inner pot. In an oven-proof bowl, mix 2 cups of water and rice. Set the bowl onto the trivet. Seal the lid and cook on High Pressure for 10 minutes. Release pressure quickly. Remove the bowl with rice and trivet. Add pepper, salt, and heavy cream into beef and stir. Use a fork to fluff rice and divide into serving plates; apply a topping of beef. Garnish with cilantro and serve.

Spinach, Garlic & Mushroom Pilaf

Serving Size: 6 | Total Time: 45 minutes
2 cups button mushrooms, sliced
1 tbsp olive oil
2 cloves garlic, minced
1 onion, chopped
1 cup spinach, chopped
4 cups vegetable stock
2 cups white rice
1 tsp salt
2 sprigs parsley, chopped

Select Sauté and heat oil. Add mushrooms, onion, and garlic, and stir-fry for 5 minutes until tender. Mix in rice, stock, spinach, and salt. Seal the lid and cook on High Pressure for 20 minutes. Release pressure naturally for 10 minutes. Fluff the rice and top with parsley. Serve.

Salmon & Tomato Farfalle

Serving Size: 4 | Total Time: 15 minutes
16 oz farfalle pasta
2 tbsp olive oil
2 garlic cloves, sliced
2 cups tomatoes, diced
¼ tsp chili pepper
¼ tsp oregano
¾ cup red wine
4 oz smoked salmon, flaked
10 green olives, sliced
½ cup Parmesan, grated

Warm olive oil in your Instant Pot on Sauté. Add in garlic and cook for 1 minute. Stir in tomatoes, farfalle, chili pepper, 4 cups water, red wine, and oregano. Seal the lid.
Select Manual, and cook for 5 minutes on High. Once ready, perform a quick pressure release. Mix in salmon and green olives. Serve sprinkled with Parmesan cheese.

Vegetarian Wild Rice with Carrots

Serving Size: 6 | Total Time: 32 minutes
4 cups vegetable broth
2 carrots, chopped
2 cups wild rice
3 tbsp butter
Zest and juice from 1 lemon
Salt and pepper to taste

Add rice, carrots, lemon zest, butter, and broth. Stir, seal the lid, and cook on High Pressure for 12 minutes. Release pressure naturally for 10 minutes. Carefully unlock the lid. Sprinkle salt, lemon juice, and pepper over the rice and use a fork to gently fluff. Serve warm.

Risotto with Spring Vegetables & Shrimp

Serving Size: 4 | Total Time: 40 minutes
1 tbsp avocado oil
1 lb asparagus, chopped
1 cup spinach, chopped
1 cup mushrooms, sliced
1 cup rice
1 ¼ cups chicken broth
¾ cup coconut milk
1 tbsp coconut oil
1 lb shrimp, deveined
Salt and pepper to taste
¾ cup Parmesan, shredded

Warm the avocado oil on Sauté. Add spinach, mushrooms, and asparagus and sauté for 5 minutes until cooked through. Add in rice, coconut milk, and chicken broth as you stir. Seal the lid, press Manual, and cook for 20 minutes on High Pressure.
Do a quick release. Place the rice on a serving plate. Press Sauté. Heat the coconut oil. Add shrimp and cook for 6 minutes until it turns pink. Set the shrimp over rice and season with pepper and salt. Serve topped with Parmesan cheese.

Stuffed Mushrooms with Rice & Cheese

Serving Size: 4 | Total Time: 25 minutes
4 portobello mushrooms, stems and gills removed
2 tbsp melted butter
½ cup brown rice, cooked
1 tomato, chopped
¼ cup black olives, chopped
1 green bell pepper, diced
½ cup feta, crumbled
Salt and pepper to taste
2 tbsp cilantro, chopped
1 cup vegetable broth

Brush the mushrooms with butter. Arrange them in a single layer on a greased baking pan. In a bowl, mix the rice, tomato, olives, bell pepper, feta cheese, salt, and black pepper. Spoon the rice mixture into the mushrooms. Pour in the broth.

Pour 1 cup of water into the Instant Pot and insert a trivet. Place the baking dish on the trivet. Seal the lid and cook on High Pressure for 10 minutes. Do a quick release. Garnish with fresh cilantro and serve immediately.

Risotto with Broccoli & Grana Padano

Serving Size: 6 | **Total Time:** 35 minutes
2 tbsp Grana Padano cheese flakes
10 oz broccoli florets
1 onion, chopped
3 tbsp butter
2 cups carnaroli rice, rinsed
¼ cup dry white wine
4 cups chicken stock
Salt and pepper to taste
2 tbsp Grana Padano, grated

Warm butter on Sauté. Stir-fry onion for 3 minutes until translucent. Add in broccoli and rice and cook for 5 minutes, stirring occasionally. Pour wine into the pot and scrape away any browned bits of food from the pan.

Stir in stock, pepper, and salt. Seal the lid, press Manual and cook on High for 15 minutes. Release the pressure quickly. Sprinkle with grated Grana Padano cheese and stir well. Top with flaked Grana Padano cheese to serve.

Arugula & Wild Mushroom Risotto

Serving Size: 4 | **Total Time:** 30 minutes
½ cup wild mushrooms, chopped
4 tbsp pumpkin seeds, toasted
1/3 cup grated Pecorino Romano cheese
2 tbsp olive oil
1 onion, chopped
2 cups arugula, chopped
1 cup arborio rice
1/3 cup white wine
3 cups vegetable stock

Heat oil on Sauté and cook onion and mushrooms for 5 minutes until tender. Add the rice and cook for a minute. Stir in white wine and cook for 2-3 minutes until almost evaporated. Pour in the stock. Seal the lid and cook on High Pressure for 10 minutes. Do a quick release. Stir in arugula and Pecorino Romano cheese to melt and serve scattered with pumpkin seeds.

Yummy Mexican-Style Rice & Pinto Beans

Serving Size: 4 | **Total Time:** 30 minutes
3 tbsp olive oil
1 small onion, chopped
2 garlic cloves, minced
1 serrano pepper, chopped
1 cup rice
1/3 cup red salsa
¼ cup tomato sauce
½ cup vegetable broth
1 tsp Mexican seasoning
16 oz canned pinto beans
1 tsp salt
1 tbsp chopped parsley

Warm oil on Sauté and cook onion, garlic, and serrano pepper for 2 minutes, stirring occasionally until fragrant. Stir in rice, salsa, tomato sauce, vegetable broth, Mexican seasoning, beans, and salt. Seal the lid and cook on High Pressure for 10 minutes. Do a natural pressure release for 10 minutes. Sprinkle with fresh parsley and serve.

Butternut Squash with Rice & Feta

Serving Size: 4 | **Total Time:** 30 minutes
2 cups vegetable broth
1 lb butternut squash, sliced
2 tbsp melted butter
Salt and pepper to taste
1 cup feta cheese, cubed
1 tbsp coconut aminos
2 tsp arrowroot starch
1 cup jasmine rice, cooked

Pour the rice and broth into the pot and stir to combine. In a bowl, toss butternut squash with 1 tbsp of melted butter and season with salt and black pepper. Mix in the pot with the rice. In another bowl, mix the remaining butter, water, and coconut aminos. Toss feta in the mixture, add the arrowroot starch, and toss again to combine well. Transfer to a greased baking dish.

Lay a trivet over the rice butternut squash and place the baking dish on the trivet. Seal the lid and cook on High for 15 minutes. Do a quick pressure release. Fluff the rice with a fork and serve with feta cheese.

Avocado & Cherry Tomato Jasmine Rice

Serving Size: 6 | **Total Time:** 25 minutes
2 avocados, chopped
½ lb cherry tomatoes, halved
2 cups jasmine rice
2 tsp olive oil
½ tsp salt
2 tbsp cilantro, chopped

Place the rice, 2 cups water, olive oil, and salt in your Instant Pot and stir. Seal the lid, select Manual, and cook for 4 minutes on High pressure. Once done, allow a natural release for 10 minutes and unlock the lid. Using a fork, fluff the rice and add in avocados and cherry tomatoes. Top with cilantro and serve.

Date & Apple Risotto

Serving Size: 4 | **Total Time:** 30 minutes
1 tbsp butter
1 ½ cups Arborio rice
1/3 cup brown sugar
2 apples, cored and sliced
1 cup apple juice
2 cups milk
1 ½ tsp cinnamon powder
½ cup dates, pitted

Melt butter in your Instant Pot on Sauté and place in rice; cook for 1-2 minutes. Stir in brown sugar, apples, apple juice, milk, and cinnamon. Seal the lid, select Manual, and cook for 6 minutes on High pressure. Once done, allow a natural release for 6 minutes and unlock the lid. Mix in dates and cover with the lid. Let sit for 5 minutes.

Butternut Squash & Cheese Risotto

Serving Size: 4 | **Total Time:** 45 minutes
½ lb butternut squash, cubed
3 tbsp olive oil
2 cloves garlic, minced
1 yellow onion, chopped
2 cups arborio rice
4 cups chicken stock
½ cup pumpkin puree
1 tsp thyme, chopped
½ tsp nutmeg
½ tsp ginger, grated
½ tsp cinnamon
½ cup heavy cream
Salt and pepper to taste
¼ cup shaved Parmesan

Preheat the oven to 360°F. Spread the squash cubes on a baking tray and drizzle with olive oil. Roast for 20 minutes until tender. Warm oil in your Instant Pot on Sauté and add garlic and onion; cook for 3 minutes.
Stir in rice, stock, pumpkin puree, thyme, nutmeg, ginger, and cinnamon. Seal the lid, select Manual, and cook for 10 minutes on High. When done, perform a quick pressure release. Mix in heavy cream, salt, and pepper. Top with pumpkin cubes and Parmesan shaves and serve.

Spring Risotto

Serving Size: 6 | **Total Time:** 40 minutes
3 tbsp Pecorino Romano cheese, shredded
½ cup green peas
1 cup baby spinach
2 tbsp olive oil
2 spring onions, chopped
1 ½ cups arborio rice
3 ½ cups chicken stock
Salt and pepper to taste

Warm olive oil in your Instant Pot on Sauté. Add spring onions and cook for 3 minutes. Pour in rice and stock. Seal the lid and cook for 15 minutes on Manual.
Once done, allow a natural release for 10 minutes and unlock the lid. Adjust the seasoning with salt and pepper. Mix in green peas and spinach and cover with the lid. Let sit for 5 minutes until everything is heated through. Top with Pecorino Romano cheese and serve.

Arroz con Pollo

Serving Size: 4 | **Total Time:** 40 minutes
2 tbsp olive oil
1 sweet onion, diced
2 garlic cloves, minced
1 lb boneless chicken thighs
Salt and pepper to taste
½ tsp chili powder
2 carrots, diced
1 cup white jasmine rice
1 ½ cups chicken stock
½ tsp Mexican oregano

Warm olive oil in your Instant Pot on Sauté. Add in onion and garlic and cook until fragrant, about 3 minutes. Stir in chicken, salt, and pepper and cook for 5 minutes more. Mix in carrots, rice, chili powder, chicken stock, and oregano. Seal the lid, select Manual, and cook for 10 minutes on High pressure. Once done, allow a natural release for 10 minutes and unlock the lid. Fluff the rice.

Chicken & Broccoli Rice

Serving Size: 4 | **Total Time:** 40 minutes
1 red chili, finely chopped
2 tbsp butter
1 lb chicken breasts, sliced
1 onion, chopped
2 cloves garlic, minced
Salt and pepper to taste
1 cup long-grain rice
2 cups chicken broth
10 oz broccoli florets
2 tbsp cilantro, chopped

Melt butter in your Instant Pot on Sauté and add chicken, onion, red chili, garlic, salt, and pepper; cook for 5 minutes, stirring often. Stir in rice, chicken broth, milk, and broccoli. Seal the lid, select Manual, and cook for 15 minutes on High. When ready, allow a natural release for 10 minutes. Sprinkle with cilantro and serve.

Hawaiian Rice

Serving Size: 4 | **Total Time:** 30 minutes
2 tsp olive oil
1 ½ cups coconut water
1 cup jasmine rice
2 green onions, sliced
½ pineapple, and chopped
Salt to taste
¼ tsp red pepper flakes

Stir olive oil, water, rice, pineapple, and salt in your Instant Pot. Seal the lid, select Manual, and cook for 10 minutes on low pressure. Once over, allow a natural release for 10 minutes, then a quick pressure release. Carefully unlock the lid. Using a fork, fluff the rice. Scatter with green onions and red pepper flakes and serve.

Lime Brown Rice

Serving Size: 6 | **Total Time:** 45 minutes
½ bunch spring onions, chopped diagonally
2 cups brown rice, rinsed
2 small bay leaves
2 tbsp olive oil
1 lime, juiced
Salt to taste

Place the rice, 2 ¾ cups of water, salt, and bay leaves in your Instant Pot. Seal the lid and cook on Manual for 22 minutes on High. When done, allow a natural release for 10 minutes and unlock the lid. Drizzle with olive oil and lime juice and top with spring onions to serve.

South American Pot

Serving Size: 4 | **Total Time:** 30 minutes
- 1 cups brown rice
- ½ cup soaked black beans
- 1 tbsp tomato paste
- 1 garlic clove, minced
- 2 tsp onion powder
- 2 tsp chili powder
- Salt to taste
- ¼ tsp cumin
- 1 tsp hot paprika
- 3 cups corn kernels

Place rice, beans, 4 cups water, tomato paste, garlic, onion powder, chili powder, salt, cumin, paprika, and corn in your Instant Pot and stir. Seal the lid, select Manual, and cook for 20 minutes on High pressure. Once ready, perform a quick pressure release and unlock the lid. Adjust the seasoning. Serve immediately.

Honey Coconut Rice

Serving Size: 4 | **Total Time:** 30 minutes
- 1 cup Thai sweet rice
- 1 cup coconut milk
- 2 tbsp honey

Place rice and 1 ½ cups of water in your Instant Pot. Seal the lid, select Manual, and cook for 3 minutes on High pressure. When over, allow a natural release for 10 minutes. Warm coconut milk, and honey in a pot over medium heat until the honey has dissolved. Unlock the lid of the pressure cooker and stir in coconut mix. Cover with the lid and let sit for 5-10 minutes. Serve.

Beef & Brussels Sprout Rice

Serving Size: 6 | **Total Time:** 35 minutes
- 1 ½ cups basmati rice
- 1 lb ground beef, cooked
- 3 cups beef broth
- ½ lb Brussels sprouts, halved
- 2 tbsp olive oil
- 3 cloves garlic, minced
- 1 onion, chopped
- 1 tbsp shawarma spice
- Salt to taste
- ¼ cup cilantro, chopped

Place the rice, ground beef, broth, Brussels sprouts, olive oil, garlic, onion, shawarma spice, and salt in your Instant Pot and stir. Seal the lid, select Manual, and cook for 15 minutes on High pressure. Once ready, allow a natural release for 10 minutes and unlock the lid. Serve topped with cilantro.

Pork Rice Porridge

Serving Size: 4 | **Total Time:** 35 minutes
- 2 tbsp olive oil
- 2 cloves garlic, minced
- 1 onion, diced
- 1 lb ground pork
- 1 cup basmati rice, rinsed
- 1 ½ cups vegetable stock
- Salt and pepper to taste
- 2 tbsp parsley, chopped

Warm olive oil in your Instant Pot on Sauté. Add in onion and garlic and sauté for 2 minutes. Stir in ground pork and cook until get browned, about 5-6 minutes.
Pour in rice, stock, salt, and pepper. Seal the lid, select Manual, and cook for 6 minutes on High pressure. Once ready, allow a natural release for 10 minutes. Carefully unlock the lid. Serve sprinkled with parsley.

Broccoli & Ham Risotto

Serving Size: 4 | **Total Time:** 25 minutes
- 2 cups broccoli florets
- 4 oz ham, cut into strips
- 1 tbsp olive oil
- 2 tbsp butter
- 1 onion, chopped
- 1 ½ cups arborio rice
- 3 ½ cups chicken stock
- 2 tbsp Parmesan cheese, finely grated
- 2 tbsp parsley, chopped
- 1 tsp lemon zest, grated
- Salt and pepper to taste

Warm olive oil and 1 tbsp of butter in your Instant Pot on Sauté. Add onion and cook for 3 minutes. Stir in rice and cook for 1 minute. Mix in 3 cups of chicken stock. Seal the lid, select Manual, and cook for 5 minutes.
When over, perform a quick pressure release. Stir in broccoli and remaining stock and cook for 5-6 minutes on Sauté. Mix in Parmesan cheese, ham, parsley, remaining butter, lemon zest, salt, and pepper. Serve.

Button Mushroom Risotto

Serving Size: 4 | **Total Time:** 25 minutes
- 1 cup button mushrooms, sliced
- 2 oz olive oil
- 2 cloves garlic, crushed
- 1 red onion, chopped
- 1 cup arborio rice
- 2 cups chicken stock
- ¼ cup white wine
- ½ cup heavy cream
- 2 tbsp Parmesan, grated
- 2 tbsp basil, finely chopped
- Salt to taste

Warm olive oil in your Instant Pot on Sauté and add garlic, onion, and mushrooms; cook for 3 minutes. Stir in rice, stock, and wine. Seal the lid, select Manual, and cook for 10 minutes on High. Once ready, perform a quick pressure release and unlock the lid. Mix in heavy cream, Parmesan cheese, and salt. Top with basil to serve.

Provençal Rice

Serving Size: 6 | **Total Time:** 45 minutes
- 2 tbsp butter
- 1 onion, diced
- 2 garlic cloves, minced
- 2 cups brown rice
- 3 cups vegetable stock
- 1 tsp herbs de Provence

3 anchovy fillets, finely chopped
6 pitted Kalamata olives

Melt butter in your Instant Pot on Sauté and add in onion and garlic; cook for 3 minutes. Stir in rice and herbs for 1 minute and pour in the stock. Seal the lid, select Manual, and cook for 22 minutes on High. When ready, allow a natural release for 10 minutes and unlock the lid. Stir in anchovy fillets. Serve topped with Kalamata olives.

Vegetable Paella

Serving Size: 4 | **Total Time:** 37 minutes
2 tbsp butter
1 cup long-grain rice
1 ½ cups vegetable stock
A pinch of saffron
1 red bell pepper, chopped
½ cup green peas
1 cup tomato sauce
1 tsp cumin
1 tsp chili powder
½ tsp garlic powder
½ tsp onion powder
1 lemon, cut into wedges

Melt butter in your Instant Pot to Sauté. Add in rice and bell pepper and cook for 2 minutes. Mix in vegetable stock, tomato sauce, cumin, saffron, chili powder, garlic powder, and onion powder. Seal the lid, select Manual, and cook for 10 minutes on High pressure. Once ready, allow a natural release for 10 minutes and unlock the lid. Stir in green peas and cook for 4-5 minutes more on Sauté. Serve with lemon wedges.

Coconut Rice Breakfast

Serving Size: 4 | **Total Time:** 25 minutes
1 cup brown rice
1 cup water
1 cup coconut milk
½ cup coconut chips
¼ cup walnuts, chopped
¼ cup raisins
¼ tsp cinnamon powder
½ cup maple syrup

Place the rice and water in your Instant Pot. Seal the lid, select Manual, and cook for 15 minutes on High. When ready, perform a quick pressure release and unlock the lid. Stir in coconut milk, coconut chips, raisins, cinnamon, and maple syrup. Seal the lid, select Manual, and cook for another 5 minutes on High pressure. When over, perform a quick pressure release. Top with walnuts.

Prawn Basmati Rice

Serving Size: 4 | **Total Time:** 32 minutes
½ lb cooked prawns
¼ frozen peas
2 tbsp butter
1 cup basmati rice
1 ¼ cups water
Salt and pepper to taste

Place the rice, water, butter, and salt in your Instant Pot and stir. Seal the lid, select Manual, and cook for 6 minutes on High pressure. When ready, allow a natural release for 10 minutes and unlock the lid. Using a fork, fluff the rice and mix in prawns, peas, salt, and pepper. Let sit for 5-6 minutes until heated through. Serve.

Pomegranate Rice with Vegetables

Serving Size: 4 | **Total Time:** 15 minutes
¼ cup pomegranate seeds
2 tbsp olive oil
1 onion, finely chopped
2 cloves garlic, minced
1 cup basmati rice
1 cup sweet corn, frozen
1 cup garden peas, frozen
¼ tsp salt
1 tsp turmeric powder
1 ¼ cups vegetable stock

Warm oil your Instant Pot on Sauté and add onion and garlic; cook for 3 minutes until fragrant. Stir in rice, corn, peas, salt, turmeric, and stock. Seal the lid, select Manual, and cook for 4 minutes on High pressure. When ready, perform a quick pressure release and unlock the lid. With a fork, fluff the rice. Top with pomegranate and serve.

Hazelnut Brown Rice Pilaf

Serving Size: 4 | **Total Time:** 45 minutes
¼ cup hazelnuts, toasted and chopped
2 tbsp olive oil
1 cup brown rice
2 cups vegetable broth
Salt and pepper to taste

Place the rice, vegetable broth, olive oil, pepper, and salt in your Instant Pot and stir. Seal the lid, select Manual, and cook for 25 minutes on High. Once ready, allow a natural release for 10 minutes and unlock the lid. Using a fork, fluff the rice. Top with hazelnuts and serve.

Vegetable Green Biryani

Serving Size: 6 | **Total Time:** 15 minutes
1 tbsp olive oil
2 cups basmati rice
3 tbsp butter
2 garlic cloves, minced
1 lb spinach, chopped
1 cup broccoli florets, chopped
Salt and pepper to taste
4 tbsp cilantro, chopped
4 cups vegetable broth

Warm olive oil in your Instant Pot on Sauté. Add in the rice, butter, and garlic and cook for 1-2 minutes. In a food processor, blend the spinach, broccoli, and cilantro. Pour vegetable broth and mixed greens in the pot and stir. Season with salt and pepper. Seal the lid and cook on Manual for 6 minutes on High. Once ready, perform a quick pressure release and unlock the lid. Divide between four serving bowls and serve.

Wild Rice Pilaf

Serving Size: 4 | **Total Time:** 20 minutes
1 cup wild rice

2 tbsp butter
Salt and pepper to taste
2 tbsp chives, chopped

Stir the rice, butter, 2 cups of water, salt, and pepper in your Instant Pot. Seal the lid, select Manual, and cook for 5 minutes on High pressure. When ready, allow a natural release for 10 minutes and unlock the lid. Using a fork, fluff the rice. Top with chives and serve.

Spicy Indian Rice

Serving Size: 4 | Total Time: 40 minutes
2 tbsp olive oil
2 garlic cloves, minced
2 shallots, chopped
1 cup basmati rice
½ cup carrots, chopped
2 tsp masala curry paste
1 tsp ginger paste
1 ½ cups chicken broth
1 cup frozen green beans
Salt and pepper to taste
2 tbsp cilantro, chopped

Warm olive oil in your Instant Pot to Sauté. Add in shallots, ginger, and garlic and cook until fragrant, about 3 minutes. Stir in rice, carrots, masala curry paste, chicken broth, green beans, salt, and pepper. Seal the lid and cook on Manual for 20 minutes on High. Once ready, allow a natural release for 10 minutes and unlock the lid. With a fork, fluff the rice. Scatter with cilantro and serve.

Pilau Brown Rice

Serving Size: 4 | Total Time: 20 minutes
2 tbsp olive oil
1 bay leaf
1 tsp cumin
1 cup basmati brown rice
Sea salt to taste
1 ¼ cups vegetable broth
½ tbsp turmeric
2 tbsp cilantro, chopped

Place the olive oil, bay leaf, cumin, rice, salt, vegetable broth, and turmeric in your Instant Pot and stir. Seal the lid and cook for 6 minutes on Multigrain. When done, allow a natural release for 10 minutes and unlock the lid. Using a fork, fluff the rice. Transfer to a serving plate. Top with cilantro and serve.

Rice & Red Bean Pot

Serving Size: 4 | Total Time: 55 minutes
1 cup red beans, soaked
2 tbsp vegetable oil
½ cup rice
½ tbsp cayenne pepper
1 ½ cups vegetable broth
1 onion, diced
1 garlic clove, minced
1 red bell pepper, diced
1 stalk celery, diced
Salt and pepper to taste

Place beans in your Instant Pot with enough water to cover them by a couple of fingers. Seal the lid and cook for 25 minutes on High Pressure. Release the pressure quickly. Drain the beans and set aside. Rinse and pat dry the inner pot. Add in oil and press Sauté. Add in onion and garlic and sauté for 3 minutes until soft. Add celery and bell pepper and cook for 2 minutes.

Add in the rice, reserved beans, vegetable broth. Stir in pepper, cayenne pepper, and salt. Seal the lid and cook for 15 minutes on High Pressure. Release the pressure quickly. Carefully unlock the lid. Serve warm.

Rice & Chicken Soup

Serving Size: 4 | Total Time: 35 minutes
1 lb chicken breasts, cubed
1 carrot, chopped
1 onion, chopped
¼ cup rice
1 potato, finely chopped
1 tsp cayenne pepper
2 tbsp olive oil
4 cups chicken broth

Heat the olive oil in your Instant Pot on Sauté. Cook the onion, carrot, and chicken for 5 minutes, stirring often. Add in rice, potato, cayenne pepper, and broth and stir. Seal the lid. Cook on Soup/Broth for 20 minutes. Do a quick pressure release. Carefully unlock the lid. Serve.

One-Pot Mexican Rice

Serving Size: 4 | Total Time: 35 minutes
2 tbsp olive oil
1 onion, diced
2 garlic cloves, sliced
1 cup long-grain white rice
2 cups chicken stock
1 tbsp chipotle chili paste
2 mixed peppers, sliced
1 cup salsa
Salt and pepper to taste
2 tbsp cilantro, chopped

Warm olive oil in your Instant Pot on Sauté and add in onion, garlic, and mixed peppers; cook for 2-3 minutes.

Add in rice and cook for another 1-2 minutes. Mix in stock, salsa, salt, and pepper. Seal the lid, select Manual, and cook for 10 minutes on High pressure. When over, allow a natural release for 10 minutes and unlock the lid. Stir in the chipotle paste. Serve topped with cilantro. Enjoy!

BEANS & GRAINS

Sausage & Red Bean Stew
Serving Size: 4 | **Total Time:** 50 minutes
- 1 cup red beans, soaked
- 4 sausages, sliced
- 6 cups water
- 2 carrots, chopped
- Salt and pepper to taste
- 2 tbsp vegetable oil
- 1 yellow onion, diced
- 1 tomato, chopped
- 2 green onions, chopped
- 2 tbsp cilantro, chopped

Place red beans and water in your Instant Pot. Seal the lid, select Manual, and cook for 10 minutes on High pressure. Once ready, allow a natural release for 10 minutes and unlock the lid. Drain the beans and set aside. Warm the vegetable oil in the pot on Sauté. Add in sausage, carrots, yellow onion, salt, and pepper and cook for 5 minutes. Stir in tomatoes, green onions, cooked beans, and 1 cup of water. Seal the lid, select Manual, and cook for 15 minutes on High pressure. Once done, perform a quick pressure release and unlock the lid. Scatter with cilantro and serve.

Spinach & Kidney Beans
Serving Size: 4 | **Total Time:** 55 minutes
- 1 cup kidney beans, soaked
- 2 tomatoes, chopped
- Salt and pepper to taste
- 2 tbsp olive oil
- 1 carrot, diced
- 1 celery stick, chopped
- 1 onion, finely chopped
- 3 cups chicken stock
- 1 cup baby spinach
- 2 tbsp parsley, chopped

Heat olive oil on Sauté and stir-fry onion, carrot, celery, salt, and black pepper for 3 minutes. Pour in tomatoes, chicken stock, and beans. Seal the lid, select Manual, and cook for 25 minutes on High pressure.
Once ready, allow a naturally pressure release for 10 minutes. Stir in baby spinach, press Sauté and cook for 5 minutes until the spinach wilts. Top with parsley.

Navy & Pinto Bean Pot
Serving Size: 4 | **Total Time:** 40 minutes
- 2 tbsp olive oil
- 1 onion, chopped
- 2 cloves garlic, minced
- 5 cups vegetable broth
- ½ cup pinto beans, soaked
- ½ cup navy beans, soaked
- 3 carrots, chopped
- 1 large celery stalk, chopped
- 1 tsp dried thyme
- 16 oz zucchini noodles
- Salt and pepper to taste

Warm oil on Sauté. Stir in garlic and onion and cook for 5 minutes. Mix in pepper, broth, carrots, salt, celery, beans, and thyme. Seal the lid and cook for 15 minutes on High Pressure. Release the pressure naturally. Mix zucchini noodles into the soup and stir until wilted. Taste and adjust the seasoning.

Greek-Style Navy Beans
Serving Size: 4 | **Total Time:** 45 minutes
- 1 cup navy beans, soaked
- 2 spring onions, sliced
- 1 garlic clove, smashed
- 1 tbsp olive oil
- 1 tsp Greek seasoning
- Salt and pepper to taste

Place beans, 3 cups water, and garlic in your Instant Pot. Seal the lid, select Manual, and cook for 25 minutes on High pressure. Once done, allow a natural release for 10 minutes and unlock the lid. Drain the beans and combine with olive oil, Greek seasoning, salt, and pepper in a bowl. Serve sprinkled with green onions.

Simple Black Bean Soup
Serving Size: 6 | **Total Time:** 25 minutes
- 1 tsp olive oil
- 1 onion, chopped
- 2 celery stalks, chopped
- 1 carrot, chopped
- 2 serrano peppers, minced
- 5 cups vegetable broth
- 30 oz can diced tomatoes
- 1 (14 oz) can black beans
- ¼ cup chopped cilantro
- 2 tsp ground cumin
- Salt and pepper to taste

Warm oil on Sauté. Add in carrot, onion, serrano peppers, and celery. Cook for 6 to 7 minutes. Mix in broth, sea salt, black beans, cumin, tomatoes, cilantro, and pepper. Seal lid and cook for 8 minutes on High Pressure. Release pressure naturally.

Pancetta with Garbanzo Beans
Serving Size: 6 | **Total Time:** 60 minutes
- 3 strips pancetta
- 1 onion, diced
- 15 oz can garbanzo beans
- 1 cup apple cider
- 2 garlic cloves, minced
- ½ cup ketchup
- 1 tbsp mustard powder
- Salt and pepper to taste

Cook pancetta for 5 minutes until crispy on Sauté. Add onion and garlic, and cook for 3 minutes until soft. Mix in garbanzo beans, ketchup, salt, apple cider, mustard powder, 2 cups water, and black pepper. Seal the lid, press Bean/Chili, and cook on High Pressure for 30 minutes. Release pressure naturally for 10 minutes. Serve.

Chickpea & Jalapeño Chicken

Serving Size: 4 | **Total Time:** 40 minutes
1 lb boneless, skinless chicken legs
½ tsp ground cumin
½ tsp cayenne pepper
2 tbsp olive oil
1 onion, minced
2 jalapeño peppers, minced
3 garlic cloves, crushed
2 tbsp freshly grated ginger
¼ cup chicken stock
24 oz can crushed tomatoes
28 oz can chickpeas
Salt to taste
½ cup coconut milk
¼ cup parsley, chopped
2 cups cooked basmati rice

Season the chicken with salt, cayenne pepper, and cumin. Set your Instant Pot to Sauté and warm the oil. Add in jalapeño peppers and onion and cook for 5 minutes, stirring occasionally until soft. Mix in ginger and garlic, and cook for 3 minutes until tender. Add ¼ cup chicken stock into the cooker to ensure the pan is deglazed. From the pan's bottom, scrape any browned bits of food.

Mix the onion mixture with chickpeas, tomatoes, and salt. Stir in the chicken to coat. Seal the lid and cook on High Pressure for 20 minutes.

Release the pressure quickly. Remove the chicken and slice into chunks. Into the remaining sauce, mix coconut milk and simmer for 5 minutes on Sauté. Split rice into 4 bowls. Top with chicken, sauce, and parsley and serve.

Chickpea & Lentil Soup
Serving Size: 6 | **Total Time:** 40 minutes
2 tbsp olive oil
1 onion, chopped
3 garlic cloves, minced
2 carrots, sliced
1 cup canned chickpeas
1 sweet pepper, chopped
½ banana pepper, chopped
1 cup canned diced tomatoes
1 celery stalk, diced
1 tsp sweet paprika
1 tsp cumin
1 cup brown lentils, rinsed
2 cups spinach, chopped
Salt and pepper to taste

Warm the olive oil in your Instant Pot on Sauté. Add in onion, garlic, carrot, banana pepper, sweet pepper, celery, paprika, and cumin and cook for 5 minutes. Stir in lentils, chickpeas, tomatoes, salt, pepper, and 6 cups of water and seal the lid. Select Manual and cook for 10 minutes on High pressure. Once done, allow a natural release for 10 minutes and unlock the lid. Mix in the spinach and adjust the seasoning. Serve warm.

Quinoa Bowls with Broccoli & Pesto
Serving Size: 2 | **Total Time:** 15 minutes
1 bunch baby heirloom carrots, peeled
1 cup quinoa
2 cups vegetable broth
Salt and pepper to taste
1 potato, peeled, cubed
10 oz broccoli florets
¼ cabbage, chopped
2 eggs
1 avocado, sliced
¼ cup pesto sauce
Lemon wedges, for serving

In your Instant Pot, mix the vegetable broth, pepper, quinoa, and salt. Set a trivet on top of the quinoa and place a steamer basket on the trivet. Mix carrots, potato, eggs, and broccoli in the steamer basket. Seal the lid and cook for 1 minute on High Pressure. Quick-release the pressure. Remove the trivet and basket from the pot.

Set the eggs in a bowl of ice water. Then peel and halve them. Fluff the quinoa. In two bowls, equally divide avocado, quinoa, broccoli, eggs, carrots, potato, cabbage, and pesto dollop. Serve with lemon wedges.

Homemade Veggie Quinoa
Serving Size: 6 | **Total Time:** 30 minutes
1 cup quinoa, rinsed
2 carrots, cut into sticks
1 large onion, chopped
2 tbsp olive oil
Salt to taste
2 tbsp cilantro, chopped

Heat olive oil in the Instant Pot on Sauté. Add in onion and carrots and stir-fry for about 10 minutes until tender and crispy. Remove to a plate and set aside. Add 2 cups of water, salt, and quinoa to the pot. Seal the lid and cook on High Pressure for 10 minutes. Do a quick release. Transfer to a serving plate and top with the carrots and onion. Serve scattered with cilantro.

Colorful Quinoa with Red Salsa
Serving Size: 4 | **Total Time:** 30 minutes
2 tbsp olive oil
1 green bell pepper, diced
1 red onion, diced
1 tsp ground cumin
½ tsp salt
14 oz can pinto beans
1 cup tri-color quinoa
1 cup red salsa
1 cup vegetable broth

Warm oil on Sauté. Add red onion and green bell pepper as you stir. Add salt and cumin, and cook for 7-8 minutes until fragrant. To the vegetable mixture, add quinoa, broth, red salsa, and pinto beans. Seal the lid and cook on High Pressure for 12 minutes. Do a quick pressure release. Carefully unlock the lid. Use a fork to fluff quinoa and divide between serving bowls to serve.

Almond & Raisin Quinoa
Serving Size: 4 | **Total Time:** 15 minutes
1 cup quinoa
1 cup raisins, soaked
½ cup slivered almonds
¼ cup sunflower seeds

Place quinoa and 2 cups water in your Instant Pot. Seal the lid, select Manual, and cook for 10 minutes on High pressure. Once done, perform a quick pressure release. Stir in sunflower seeds, almonds, and raisins. Serve.

Saffron Quinoa Pilaf

Serving Size: 4 | Total Time: 30 minutes
1 shallot, chopped
2 tbsp olive oil
2 cloves garlic, minced
1 cup quinoa
Pinch of saffron
Salt to taste
2 tbsp parsley, chopped

Submerge saffron in ½ cup of hot water and let soak for 10 minutes. Set your Instant Pot to Sauté. Heat the olive oil and add the garlic and shallot; sauté for 3 minutes. Stir in quinoa, saffron with the liquid, salt, and 2 cups of water. Seal the lid, select Manual, and cook for 1 minute on High pressure. Once over, allow a natural release for 10 minutes. Using a fork, fluff the quinoa. Adjust the seasoning with salt. Serve topped with parsley.

Chorizo & Veggie Quinoa

Serving Size: 4 | Total Time: 20 minutes
1 lb chorizo sausages, casings removed
2 tbsp olive oil
1 sweet onion, chopped
1 tsp turmeric powder
½ tsp paprika
2 cups chicken stock
1 cup quinoa
1 red bell pepper, chopped
½ cup mushrooms, halved

Set your Instant Pot to Sauté. Heat the olive oil and add in chorizo sausages, onion, mushrooms, and bell pepper. Cook for 3-4 minutes until tender. Stir in turmeric and paprika, pour in chicken stock and quinoa. Seal the lid, select Manual, and cook for 1 minute on High pressure. When done, allow a natural release for 10 minutes. Using a fork, fluff the quinoa and serve.

Cilantro & Spring Onion Quinoa

Serving Size: 4 | Total Time: 15 minutes
1 cup quinoa
2 cups vegetable broth
Juice of 1 lemon
½ tsp salt
2 spring onions, sliced
2 tbsp cilantro, chopped

Place the quinoa, broth, and salt in your Instant Pot. Seal the lid, select Manual, and cook for 1 minute on High.
Once ready, allow a natural release for 10 minutes and unlock the lid. Using a fork, fluff the quinoa. Sprinkle lemon juice, cilantro, and spring onions and serve.

Chorizo & Lentil Stew

Serving Size: 4 | Total Time: 60 minutes
1 cups lentils
4 oz chorizo, chopped
1 onion, diced
2 garlic cloves, minced
2 cups tomato sauce
2 cups vegetable broth
½ cup mustard
½ cup cider vinegar
3 tbsp Worcestershire sauce
2 tbsp maple syrup
2 tbsp liquid smoke
1 tbsp lime juice
2 cups brown sugar
Salt and pepper to taste
1 tsp chili powder
1 tsp paprika
¼ tsp cayenne pepper

Set to Sauté the Instant Pot. Add in chorizo and cook for 3 minutes as you stir until crisp. Add garlic and onion and cook for 2 minutes. Mix in tomato sauce, cider vinegar, liquid smoke, Worcestershire sauce, lime juice, mustard, and maple syrup and cook for 2 minutes.
Stir in broth and scrape the bottom to do away with any browned bits of food. Add pepper, chili, sugar, paprika, salt, and cayenne into the sauce as you stir to mix.
Stir in lentils to coat. Seal the lid and cook on High Pressure for 30 minutes. Release pressure naturally for 10 minutes and unlock the lid. Serve warm.

Easy Red Lentil Dhal with Spinach

Serving Size: 6 | Total Time: 35 minutes
2 tbsp olive oil
1 jalapeño pepper, minced
1 cup spinach, chopped
4 cloves garlic, minced
1 tsp fresh ginger, grated
1 tbsp cumin seeds
1 tbsp coriander seeds
1 tsp ground turmeric
¼ tsp cayenne pepper
1 ½ cups red lentils
1 tomato, diced
¼ cup lemon juice
Salt to taste
2 tbsp cilantro, chopped
Natural yogurt for garnish

Heat oil on Sauté, add cayenne, red jalapeño, ginger, turmeric, cumin, garlic, and coriander, and cook for 3 minutes until seeds become fragrant and begin to pop.
Pour in 3 cups water, tomato, and lentils and stir. Seal the lid and cook on High Pressure for 10 minutes. Release pressure naturally for 10 minutes. Stir in spinach.
Cook until wilted, 5 minutes. Add lemon juice and season to taste. Garnish with yogurt and cilantro and serve.

Traditional Indian Lentil Soup

Serving Size: 6 | Total Time: 30 minutes
1 tbsp ghee

2 tsp cumin seeds
1 onion, chopped
4 garlic cloves, minced
1-inch ginger, minced
Salt to taste
1 tomato, chopped
1 cup split yellow lentils
2 tbsp garam masala
½ tsp ground turmeric
½ tsp cayenne pepper
1 tbsp cilantro, chopped

Warm ghee on Sauté. Add cumin seeds and cook for 10 seconds until they begin to pop. Stir in onion and cook for 2-3 minutes until softened. Mix in ginger, salt, and garlic and cook for 1 minute as you stir. Mix in tomato and cook for 3 to 5 minutes until the mixture breaks down. Stir in the turmeric, lentils, garam masala, and cayenne pepper. Cover with water. Seal the lid and cook for 8 minutes on High Pressure. Release the pressure quickly. Serve in bowls sprinkled with fresh cilantro.

Creamed Lentils

Serving Size: 4 | **Total Time:** 20 minutes
1 tbsp horseradish sauce
¼ cup crème fraiche
1 cup brown lentils
1 cup tomato sauce
½ tsp cumin
Salt to taste
1 tsp onion powder
1 tsp garlic powder
1 tsp chili powder
2 tbsp thyme, chopped

Place 3 cups of water, lentils, tomato sauce, chili powder, garlic powder, onion powder, cumin, and salt in your Instant Pot. Seal the lid, select Manual, and cook for 15 minutes on High pressure. Once ready, perform a quick pressure release and unlock the lid. Stir in horseradish sauce and crème fraiche. Scatter thyme and serve.

Lentil & Chorizo Chili

Serving Size: 4 | **Total Time:** 40 minutes
½ lb chorizo sausage, sliced
2 tbsp olive oil
1 onion, diced
1 cup canned diced tomatoes
1 cup lentils
3 cups vegetable broth

Warm the olive oil in your Instant Pot on Sauté. Place in onion and chorizo and sauté for 5 minutes. Add in tomatoes and cook for 1 more minute. Stir in lentils and vegetable broth. Seal the lid, select Manual, and cook for 15 minutes on High pressure. When ready, allow a natural release for 10 minutes and unlock the lid. Serve.

Lime Bulgur with Olives

Serving Size: 4 | **Total Time:** 30 minutes
1 tbsp olive oil
1 small onion, chopped
2 cloves garlic, minced
1 tbsp cilantro
1 cup bulgur
2 ½ cups vegetable broth
1 tbsp lime juice
10 black olives to garnish
Salt and pepper to taste

Heat oil on Sauté. Stir in garlic and onion and cook for 5 minutes. Add in cilantro, bulgur, pepper, and salt. Place 1 tbsp of lime juice and broth into the cooker.
Seal the lid and cook on High Pressure for 15 minutes. Do a quick release. Unlock the lid. Use a fork to fluff bulgur. Serve in bowls topped with olives.

Bulgur Pilaf with Roasted Bell Peppers

Serving Size: 4 | **Total Time:** 25 minutes
2 tbsp olive oil
1 garlic clove, minced
1 onion, chopped
2 cups vegetable stock
¼ cup lemon juice
1 tsp grated lemon zest
1 cup bulgur
Salt and pepper to taste
6 oz roasted bell peppers

In a bowl, toss bell peppers with some oil, salt, and pepper. Warm the remaining oil on Sauté and cook onion and garlic until soft, about 3 minutes. Stir in stock, lemon juice, lemon zest, and bulgur. Seal the lid and cook on High Pressure for 5 minutes. Do a natural pressure release for 10 minutes. Carefully unlock the lid. Fluff the rice with a fork. Top with roasted peppers to serve.

Kale & Parmesan Pearl Barley

Serving Size: 2 | **Total Time:** 30 minutes
1 tbsp butter
1 small onion, diced
1 cup pearl barley
2 garlic cloves, smashed
2 cups vegetable broth
½ cup grated Parmesan
1 cup kale, chopped
½ lemon, juiced

Warm butter on Sauté. Add in onion and cook for 3 minutes until soft. Stir in garlic and barley and continue cooking for 1 to 2 minutes. Mix in broth and season. Seal the lid and cook for 9 minutes on High Pressure. Release pressure naturally for 10 minutes. Add in Parmesan cheese and kale and stir until the cheese is fully melted. Drizzle with lemon juice and serve.

Pearl Barley Sloppy Joes

Serving Size: 6 | **Total Time:** 35 minutes
1 cup pearl barley, rinsed
1 cup green onion, chopped
1 clove garlic, minced
2 cups tomato sauce
2 tbsp brown sugar
2 tbsp Worcestershire sauce
1 tsp Dijon mustard
1 tsp smoked paprika

1 tsp chili powder
Salt and pepper to taste
6 brioche buns
Dill pickles for garnish

In the pot, mix Worcestershire sauce, 2 cups water, onion, garlic, brown sugar, barley, tomato sauce, mustard, paprika, and chili powder. Season with salt and pepper. Seal the lid and cook for 25 minutes on High Pressure. Release the pressure quickly. Carefully unlock the lid. Press Sauté and cook until the mixture becomes thick. Transfer the sloppy joe mixture to the brioche buns and top with dill pickles.

Barley & Smoked Salmon Salad

Serving Size: 4 | Total Time: 30 minutes
4 smoked salmon fillets, flaked
1 cup pearl barley
Salt and pepper to taste
1 cup arugula
1 green apple, chopped

Place the barley, 2 cups of water, salt, and pepper in your Instant Pot. Seal the lid, select Manual, and cook for 20 minutes on High pressure.
Once ready, perform a quick pressure release and unlock the lid. Remove barley to a serving bowl. Mix in apple and salmon. Top with arugula.

Tomato & Feta Pearl Barley

Serving Size: 4 | Total Time: 30 minutes
½ cup sundried tomatoes in oil, chopped
½ cup feta, crumbled
1 cup pearl barley
2 cups chicken broth
Salt to taste
2 tbsp butter, melted

Place barley, chicken broth, and salt in your Instant Pot. Seal the lid, select Manual, and cook for 25 minutes on High pressure. When done, allow a natural release for 15 minutes and unlock the lid. Mix in tomatoes and top with feta and butter to serve.

Cranberry Millet Pilaf

Serving Size: 4 | Total Time: 20 minutes
½ cup dried cranberries. chopped
2 tbsp olive oil
1 garlic clove, minced
1 shallot, chopped
1 cup long-grain white rice
1 cup millet
Salt and pepper to taste

Warm olive oil in your Instant Pot on Sauté. Add in shallot and garlic and cook for 3 minutes. Stir in rice, millet, 3 cups water, cranberries, salt, and pepper. Seal the lid and for 10 minutes on Rice. When ready, perform a quick pressure release and unlock the lid. Using a fork, fluff the pilaf. Serve immediately.

Rich Millet with Herbs & Cherry Tomatoes

Serving Size: 4 | Total Time: 20 minutes
1 cup millet
2 cups vegetable stock
1 sweet onion, chopped
1 cup cherry tomatoes, halved
1 tbsp fresh sage, chopped
1 tsp fresh thyme, chopped
1 tsp parsley, chopped
Salt and pepper to taste

Add millet, onion, and vegetable stock. Seal the lid and cook for 10 minutes on High Pressure. Release pressure quickly. Fluff the millet with a fork, add in sage, thyme, parsley, and tomatoes, and season with pepper and salt.

Feta & Vegetable Faro

Serving Size: 4 | Total Time: 30 minutes
1 cup faro, rinsed
2 cups chicken broth
1 celery stalk, chopped
4 cups spinach
1 bell pepper, chopped
½ cup feta, crumbled

Place faro, broth, celery, spinach, and bell pepper in your Instant Pot. Seal the lid, select Manual, and cook for 10 minutes on High. When ready, allow a natural release for 10 minutes. Top with feta cheese and serve.

Harissa Chicken with Fruity Farro

Serving Size: 4 | Total Time: 45 minutes
2 tbsp dried cherries, chopped
1 lb chicken breasts, sliced
1 tbsp harissa paste
1 cup whole-grain farro
Salt to taste
3 tbsp olive oil
1 tbsp apple cider vinegar
4 green onions, chopped
10 mint leaves, chopped

In a bowl, place chicken, apple cider vinegar, 1 tbsp of olive oil, and harissa paste and combine everything thoroughly. Allow marinating covered for 15 minutes.
Heat the remaining olive oil on Sauté and cook green onion for 3 minutes. Stir in farro and salt and pour 2 cups of water. Insert a trivet over the farro and place the chicken on the trivet. Seal the lid, select Manual, and cook for 20 minutes on High. When ready, do a quick pressure release. Open the lid, remove the chicken and the trivet. Add dried cherries and mint to the farro. Stir and transfer to a plate. Top with chicken and serve.

Gluten-Free Porridge

Serving Size: 4 | Total Time: 25 minutes
1 cup buckwheat groats
2 cups rice milk
1 banana, sliced
¼ cup raisins
1 tsp ground cardamom
½ tsp vanilla
2 tbsp pistachios, chopped

Place buckwheat, milk, raisins, cardamom, and vanilla in your Instant Pot. Seal the lid, select Manual, and cook for 6 minutes on High pressure. When done, allow a natural release for 10 minutes and unlock the lid. Serve topped with banana and pistachios.

Broccoli Couscous

Serving Size: 4 | **Total Time:** 15 minutes
- 10 oz broccoli florets
- 2 tbsp butter, melted
- 1 cup couscous
- Salt and pepper to taste
- 2 tbsp parsley, chopped

Pour 1 cup of water into the Instant Pot and add a steamer basket. Place the broccoli in the basket and seal the lid. Select Steam and cook for 3 minutes on High. Once pressure cooking is complete, use a quick release.

In a bowl cover couscous with salted boiled water. Let it stand for 2-3 minutes until the water has absorbed. Fluff with a fork and stir in broccoli and adjust the seasoning with salt and pepper. Top with parsley and serve.

Couscous with Lamb & Vegetables

Serving Size: 4 | **Total Time:** 40 minutes
- 2 tbsp olive oil
- 1 large onion, chopped
- 2 garlic cloves, minced
- 1 lb lamb stew meat, cubed
- 3 cups vegetable stock
- 1 carrot, grated
- 1 red bell pepper, chopped
- 1 cup Israeli couscous
- ½ tsp cumin
- Salt and pepper to taste
- 2 tbsp cilantro, chopped
- 4 lemon wedges

Heat olive oil on Sauté and cook onion, garlic, and lamb for 6-7 minutes. Stir in carrot, bell pepper, and cumin and sauté for another 3 minutes. Pour in vegetable stock and adjust the seasoning with salt and pepper. Close and secure the lid. Select Manual and cook for 10 minutes on High. Once cooking is complete, use a natural release.

Add the couscous and select Sauté on Low. Cover with the lid and simmer for 8-10 minutes until the couscous is tender. Select Cancel and let it sit for 2-3 minutes. Fluff and top with cilantro. Serve with lemon wedges.

Salmon & Spinach Couscous

Serving Size: 4 | **Total Time:** 20 minutes
- 4 salmon fillets
- 2 tbsp butter
- 1 cup couscous
- 1 ¼ cups vegetable broth
- 2 tomatoes, chopped
- 1 cup spinach, chopped
- 4 lemon wedges
- Salt and pepper to taste

Pour the vegetable broth into the Instant Pot and insert a trivet. Season the fillets with salt and pepper, and arrange them on the trivet. Seal the lid, select Steam and set to 5 minutes on high. Once ready, do a quick pressure release.

Open the lid and remove the fish and the trivet. Add butter and couscous to the broth and press Sauté. Bring to a boil, then stir in tomatoes, spinach, salt, and pepper. Cover with the lid. Let it rest for 5-7 minutes until all the liquid is absorbed and spinach is wilted. Fluff the couscous. Top with salmon and lemon wedges and serve.

Ham & Peas with Goat Cheese

Serving Size: 4 | **Total Time:** 40 minutes
- 4 goat cheese, crumbled
- 1 cup dried peas, rinsed
- 3 oz ham, diced
- 3 cups vegetable stock
- 1 tsp mustard powder
- Salt and pepper to taste

Place peas, ham, mustard powder, and vegetable stock in your Instant Pot. Seal the lid, select Manual, and cook for 20 minutes on High. Once done, allow a natural release for 10 minutes and unlock the lid. Sprinkle with salt and pepper to taste. Top with goat cheese slices and serve.

Mom's Black-Eyed Peas with Garlic & Kale

Serving Size: 6 | **Total Time:** 20 minutes
- 1 cup fire-roasted red peppers, diced
- 15 oz can fire-roasted tomatoes
- 1 tsp olive oil
- 1 onion, chopped
- 2 garlic cloves, minced
- ½ tsp ground allspice
- ½ tsp red pepper, crushed
- 1 ½ cups black-eyed peas
- 1 ½ cups vegetable broth
- 2 cups chopped kale

Warm oil on Sauté. Add onion and garlic and cook for 5 minutes. Season with crushed red pepper, and allspice. Add broth and black-eyed peas to the pot. Seal the lid and cook on High Pressure for 5 minutes. Do a quick pressure release. Mix the peas with kale, red peppers, and tomatoes. Seal the lid and cook on High for 1 minute. Release the pressure quickly. Serve.

Apricot Steel Cut Oats

Serving Size: 2 | **Total Time:** 25 minutes
- ¾ cup dry apricots, soaked and chopped
- 1 tbsp butter
- 1 cup steel oats
- A pinch of salt
- 2 tbsp white sugar
- 2 oz cream cheese, softened
- 1 tsp milk
- 1 tsp cinnamon
- ¼ cup brown sugar

Melt butter in your Instant Pot on Sauté. Stir in oats for 3 minutes. Add in salt and 3 ½ cups water. Seal the lid, select Manual, and cook for 10 minutes on High pressure.

When done, allow a natural release for 5 minutes and unlock the lid. Stir in apricots and set aside. In the meantime, combine white sugar with cream cheese and milk in a bowl. In a separate bowl, mix cinnamon and brown sugar. Divide oats between bowls. Top with cinnamon and cream cheese and serve.

Honey Oat & Pumpkin Granola

Serving Size: 4 | **Total Time:** 45 minutes

1 tbsp soft butter
1 cup steel-cut oats
1 cup pumpkin puree
3 cups water
2 tsp cinnamon
A pinch of salt
¼ cup clear honey
1 tsp pumpkin pie spice

Set your Instant Pot to Sauté and melt in the butter. Stir in oats and cook for 3 minutes. Add in pumpkin puree, water, cinnamon, salt, honey, and pumpkin spice and stir. Seal the lid, select Manual, and cook for 10 minutes on High. Once ready, allow a natural release for 10 minutes. Stir the granola and let sit for 10 minutes. Serve.

Kiwi Steel Cut Oatmeal

Serving Size: 4 | **Total Time:** 25 minutes

2 kiwi, mashed
2 cups steel cut oatmeal
¼ tsp nutmeg
1 tsp cinnamon
1 tsp vanilla
¼ tsp salt
½ cup hazelnuts, chopped
¼ cup honey

Place the kiwi, oats, 3 cups water, nutmeg, cinnamon, vanilla, and salt in your Instant Pot and stir to combine. Seal the lid and cook on Manual for 10 minutes on High. When done, allow a natural release for 10 minutes and unlock the lid. Mix in hazelnuts and honey and let chill.

Southern Cheese Grits

Serving Size: 6 | **Total Time:** 35 minutes

2 tbsp olive oil
1 cup stone-ground grits
2 cups vegetable broth
1 cup milk
4 oz cheddar, shredded
3 tbsp butter
Salt to taste

Set your Instant Pot to Sauté. Warm the olive oil, place in grits and cook for 3 minutes until fragrant. Stir in broth, milk, cheese, butter, and salt. Seal the lid, select Manual, and cook for 10 minutes on High. Once ready, allow a natural release for 15 minutes and unlock the lid. Serve.

Coconut Cherry Steel Cut Oats

Serving Size: 4 | **Total Time:** 20 minutes

1 cup cherries, pitted and halved
1 cup steel-cut oats
1 cup coconut milk
2 cups water
½ tsp vanilla extract

Place cherries, oats, milk, water, and vanilla extract in your Instant Pot. Seal the lid, select Manual, and cook for 3 minutes on High pressure. Once ready, allow a natural release for 10 minutes and unlock the lid. Serve.

Jamaican Cornmeal Porridge

Serving Size: 4 | **Total Time:** 25 minutes

1 cup cornmeal
1 cup coconut milk
½ tsp nutmeg, ground
1 tsp vanilla extract
½ cup condensed milk
1 mango, sliced

Combine 1 cup of water and cornmeal in a bowl and stir. Add 3 cups of water, coconut milk, vanilla, nutmeg, and cornmeal mixture in your Instant Pot. Seal the lid, select Manual, and cook for 6 minutes on High. Once over, allow a natural release for 10 minutes and unlock the lid. Stir in condensed milk. Top with mango and serve.

Cheesy Polenta with Sundried Tomatoes

Serving Size: 4 | **Total Time:** 25 minutes

1 cup sun-dried tomatoes, finely chopped
2 tbsp olive oil
1 cup onion, diced
2 cloves garlic, chopped
2 tsp fresh oregano, minced
2 tbsp fresh parsley, minced
1 tsp kosher salt
4 cups vegetable stock
¼ cup Parmesan, shredded
1 cup polenta

Warm olive oil in your Instant Pot on Sauté and add in onion and garlic. Cook for 3 minutes until fragrant. Stir in tomatoes, oregano, parsley, salt, and stock. Top with polenta. Seal the lid, select Manual, and cook for 5 minutes on High pressure. When done, allow a natural release for 10 minutes. Top with Parmesan and serve.

Garlic Mushroom Polenta

Serving Size: 4 | **Total Time:** 35 minutes

1 cup mixed mushrooms, sliced
2 tsp olive oil
4 green onions, chopped
2 garlic cloves, sliced
2 tbsp cilantro, minced
1 tbsp chili powder
½ tsp cumin
Salt and pepper to taste
¼ tsp cayenne pepper
2 cups veggie stock
1 cup polenta

Warm olive oil in your Instant Pot on Sauté and add mushrooms, garlic, and green onions. Cook for 4 minutes. Stir in chili powder, cumin, salt, pepper, cayenne, and stock. Combine polenta with 1 ½ cups of hot water in a bowl and transfer to the Instant Pot. Seal the lid, select Manual, and cook for 10 minutes on High pressure. Once done, allow a natural release for 10 minutes and unlock the lid. Top with cilantro and serve.

APPETIZERS & SIDE DISHES

Mediterranean Meatballs with Mint Sauce

Serving Size: 4 | **Total Time:** 35 minutes
- 1 lb lean ground beef
- ¼ cup flour
- 1 tbsp rosemary, chopped
- 1 cup tomato sauce
- 1 large egg, beaten
- ½ tsp salt
- 2 tbsp olive oil
- 1 cup Greek yogurt
- 2 tbsp fresh mint
- 1 garlic clove, crushed

In a bowl, mix ground beef, rosemary, egg, flour, and salt. Lightly dampen hands and shape into balls. Warm the olive oil in your Instant Pot on Sauté. Fry the balls for 5-6 minutes on all sides. Pour in the tomato sauce and ½ cup of water. Seal the lid and cook on High Pressure for 13 minutes. When ready, do a quick release. Press Sauté and cook until the sauce thickens, about 5 minutes. In a bowl, mix the Greek yogurt, mint, and garlic. Stir well and drizzle over the meatballs. Serve and enjoy!

Saucy Carrots with Crispy Bacon

Serving Size: 4 | **Total Time:** 20 minutes
- 3 slices bacon, crumbled
- 2 lb carrots, chopped
- ½ cup orange juice
- ¼ cup olive oil
- 1 tsp honey
- 1 tsp salt
- 2 tsp cornstarch
- 1 tbsp cold water

Fry the bacon on Sauté until crispy, about 5 minutes. Set aside. In a bowl, mix salt, olive oil, orange juice, and honey; add the mixture and carrots to the pot and mix well to coat. Seal the lid, and cook for 6 minutes on High Pressure. Release the pressure quickly. Transfer carrots to a serving dish. Press Cancel, then press Sauté. In a bowl, mix cold water and cornstarch until dissolved. Add to the liquid remaining in the cooker. Simmer sauce as you stir for 2 minutes to obtain a thick and smooth consistency. Spoon the sauce over the carrots and scatter over the bacon. Serve.

Scrambled Eggs with Cranberries & Mint

Serving Size: 2 | **Total Time:** 10 minutes
- 4 large eggs, beaten
- ¼ tsp cranberry extract
- 2 tbsp butter
- 1 tbsp skim milk
- 4-5 cranberries, to garnish
- 2 tbsp fresh mint, chopped

In a bowl, whisk eggs, cranberry extract, and milk. Melt butter in your Instant Pot on Sauté. Pour the egg mixture and pull the eggs across the pot with a spatula.
Do not stir constantly. Cook for 2 minutes or until thickened and no visible liquid egg lumps. When done, press Cancel and transfer to a serving plate. Top with cranberries and garnish with fresh mint. Serve and enjoy!

Four Cheeses Party Pizza

Serving Size: 4 | **Total Time:** 25 minutes
- 1 pizza crust
- ½ cup tomato paste
- 1 tsp dried oregano
- 1 oz cheddar, grated
- 5-6 mozzarella slices
- ¼ cup grated gouda cheese
- ¼ cup grated Parmesan
- 2 tbsp olive oil

Grease the bottom of a baking dish with 1 tbsp of olive oil. Line some parchment paper. Flour the working surface and roll out the pizza dough to the approximate size of your Instant Pot. Gently fit the dough in the previously prepared baking dish.
In a bowl, combine tomato paste with water and dried oregano. Spread the mixture over the dough and finish with cheeses. Add a trivet inside your the pot and Pour in 1 cup of water. Seal the lid, and cook for 15 minutes on High Pressure. Do a quick release. Remove the pizza from the pot using parchment paper. Cut and serve.

Dill Marinated Gherkins

Serving Size: 6 | **Total Time:** 15 minutes + chilling time
- 1 lb cucumbers, sliced
- 2 cups white vinegar
- 1 cup sugar
- 2 tbsp dill pickle seasoning
- 2 tsp salt
- 1 tsp cumin

Into the pot, add cucumbers, vinegar, 1 cup water, sugar, cumin, dill pickle seasoning, and salt. Stir well to dissolve the sugar. Seal the lid and cook for 4 minutes on High Pressure. Release the pressure quickly. Ladle cucumbers into a large storage container and pour cooking liquid over. Chill for 1 hour. Serve.

Steamed Leek with Parmesan Topping

Serving Size: 2 | **Total Time:** 10 minutes
- 3 leeks, cut into 2-inches long pieces
- 3 garlic cloves, crushed
- 1 tsp salt
- ¼ cup olive oil
- 3 tbsp lemon juice
- ½ cup Parmesan, grated

Pour 1 cup of water into your Instant Pot and insert a trivet. In a baking pan, combine leeks, oil, garlic, and salt. Lower the pan onto the trivet. Cook on High Pressure for 3 minutes. Do a quick pressure release. Transfer to a plate and sprinkle with lemon juice and Parmesan cheese.

Tomato & Mozzarella Egg Scramble

Serving Size: 2 | **Total Time:** 20 minutes

1 cup button mushrooms, sliced
½ cup fresh mozzarella cheese, crumbled
4 eggs
1 large tomato, chopped
2 spring onions, chopped
¼ cup milk
2 tbsp olive oil
½ tsp salt

Warm the olive oil in your Instant Pot on Sauté. Stir-fry the spring onions for 3 minutes. Add tomato and mushrooms. Cook until liquid evaporates, about 5-6 minutes. Whisk eggs, cheese, milk, and salt. Pour into the pot and stir. Cook for 5-6 minutes, stirring often. Serve.

Beef Layer Tart with Yogurt

Serving Size: 6 | **Total Time:** 30 minutes
2 lb lean ground beef
4 garlic cloves, minced
Salt and pepper to taste
1 (16 oz) pack pie dough
½ tbsp butter, melted
1 tbsp sour cream
3 cups liquid yogurt

In a bowl, mix beef, garlic, salt, and pepper until fully incorporated. Lay a sheet of dough on a flat surface and brush with melted butter. Line with the meat mixture and roll-up. Repeat the process until you have used all the ingredients. Grease a baking dish and carefully place the rolls inside. In your Instant Pot, pour in 1 ½ cups of water and place a trivet. Lay the baking dish on the trivet.

Seal the lid and cook on High Pressure for 15 minutes. When ready, do a quick pressure release. Transfer the pie to a serving plate. Mix sour cream and yogurt. Spread the mixture over the pie and serve cold.

Warm Spinach Salad With Eggs & Nuts

Serving Size: 4 | **Total Time:** 20 minutes
1 lb spinach, chopped
3 tbsp olive oil
1 tbsp butter
1 tbsp almonds, crushed
1 tbsp peanuts, crushed
4 eggs
½ tsp chili flakes
½ tsp salt

Pour 1 ½ cups of water into the inner pot and insert a steamer basket. Place the eggs onto the basket. Seal the lid and cook on High Pressure for 5 minutes. Do a quick release. Unlock the lid. Remove the eggs to an ice bath.

Wipe the pot clean, and heat oil on Sauté. Add spinach and cook for 2-3 minutes, stirring occasionally. Stir in 1 tbsp of butter and season with salt and chili flakes. Mix well and cook for 1 more minute. Sprinkle with nuts. Peel and slice each egg in half, lengthwise. Transfer to a serving plate and pour over spinach mixture. Enjoy!

Garlic & Herbed Potatoes

Serving Size: 4 | **Total Time:** 25 minutes
1 ½ lb potatoes
3 tbsp butter
3 cloves garlic, chopped
2 tbsp rosemary, chopped
½ tsp fresh thyme, chopped
½ tsp parsley, chopped
Salt and pepper to taste
½ cup vegetable broth

Use a small knife to pierce each potato to ensure there are no blowouts when placed under pressure. Melt butter on Sauté. Add in potatoes, rosemary, parsley, pepper, salt, thyme, and garlic, and cook for 10 minutes until potatoes are browned and the mixture is aromatic. Stir in the broth. Seal the lid and cook for 5 minutes on High Pressure. Release the pressure quickly. Serve and enjoy!

Chicken Drumsticks with Hot Sauce

Serving Size: 6 | **Total Time:** 30 minutes
2 lb chicken drumsticks, boneless and skinless
1 ½ cups hot tomato salsa
Salt to taste
1 onion, chopped
1 cup feta, crumbled

Sprinkle salt over the chicken and set in the Instant Pot. Stir in salsa, 1 cup water, and onion. Seal the lid and cook for 15 minutes on Pressure Cook. When ready, do a quick release. Unlock the lid. Press Sauté and cook for 8 minutes until excess liquid has evaporated. Top with feta.

Poached Eggs with Watercress

Serving Size: 1 | **Total Time:** 10 minutes
2 eggs
1 cup watercress, chopped
¼ tsp garlic powder
Salt and pepper to taste

In a bowl, whisk eggs and ½ cup water. Add watercress, garlic powder, salt, and pepper and stir well. Transfer the mixture to a heat-proof bowl. Add 1 cup of water to the pot. Set the steamer tray and place the bowl on top. Seal the lid and cook on High Pressure for 5 minutes. When ready, do a quick release. Carefully unlock the lid. Serve.

Chili Poached Eggs with Leeks

Serving Size: 4 | **Total Time:** 20 minutes
1 cup leeks, chopped into 1-inch pieces
8 eggs
2 tbsp olive oil
1 tbsp butter
1 tsp mustard seeds
1 tbsp dried rosemary
¼ tsp chili flakes

Heat the olive oil on Sauté and add mustard seeds. Stir-fry for 2-3 minutes. Add leeks and butter. Cook for 5 minutes, stirring occasionally. Crack eggs and season with dried rosemary, and chili flakes. Cook until set for about 4 minutes. Press Cancel and serve immediately.

Egg Pancake with Spinach & Herbs

Serving Size: 2 | **Total Time:** 15 minutes
6 oz spinach, chopped

2 eggs
3 tbsp oil
½ tsp garlic powder
¼ tsp dried oregano
¼ tsp dried rosemary
½ tsp salt
10 Kalamata olives

Heat the oil in your Instant Pot on Sauté and add chopped spinach. Season with salt and garlic powder. Give it a good stir and cook for 5 minutes until soft. Crack eggs and season with oregano, rosemary, and salt. Cook until completely set for about 5 more minutes. Transfer to a serving plate and top with kalamata olives to serve.

Old-Fashioned Apple Pie

Serving Size: 6 | Total Time: 30 minutes
2 lb apples, cubed
¼ cup sugar
¼ cup breadcrumbs
2 tsp cinnamon
¼ tbsp oil
1 egg, beaten
¼ cup flour
Pie dough

Combine breadcrumbs, sugar, apples, and cinnamon in a bowl. On a lightly floured surface, roll out the pie dough, making 2 circle-shaped crusts. Place one pie crust on a greased baking dish. Spoon the apple mixture on top, and cover with the remaining crust. Seal by crimping edges and brush with beaten egg. Pour 1 cup of water into the Instant Pot and lay a trivet. Lower the baking sheet onto the trivet. Seal the lid and cook on High Pressure for 20 minutes. When ready, do a quick release. Carefully unlock the lid. Serve chilled.

Easy Camembert Cakes

Serving Size: 4 | Total Time: 45 minutes
1 cup Camembert cheese, cubed
2 tbsp butter
1 white onion, sliced
2 cups spinach, chopped
Salt and pepper to taste
¼ cup dry white wine
1 pie pastry, thawed
3 thinly sliced green onions

Melt 1 tbsp of butter on Sauté and cook onion and spinach for 5 minutes until tender. Season with salt and pepper, then pour in white wine and cook until evaporated, about 2 minutes. Set aside. Unwrap the pie pastry and cut it into 4 squares. Prink the dough with a fork and brush both sides with the remaining butter. Share half of the cheese over the pie pastry squares. Cover with spinach and remaining cheese. Arrange the tarts in a buttered baking dish. Pour 1 cup of water into the pot. Insert a trivet and lower the baking dish on top. Seal the lid and cook on High Pressure for 30 minutes. Do a quick release. Serve topped with green onions.

Goat Cheese & Beef Steak Salad

Serving Size: 4 | Total Time: 55 minutes
1 lb rib-eye steak, boneless
4 oz fresh arugula
1 large tomato, sliced
¼ cup fresh goat's cheese
4 almonds, chopped
4 walnuts, chopped
4 hazelnuts
3 tbsp olive oil
2 cups beef broth
2 tbsp red wine vinegar
1 tbsp Italian seasoning

In a bowl, whisk the red wine vinegar, Italian seasoning, and olive oil. Brush each steak with the mixture and place it in your Instant Pot. Pour in the broth and seal the lid. Cook on Meat/Stew for 25 minutes on High. Release the pressure naturally for 10 minutes. Unlock the lid. Remove the steaks along with the broth. Grease the inner pot with oil and hit Sauté. Brown the steaks on both sides for 5-6 minutes. Remove from the pot and chill for 5 minutes before slicing. In a bowl, mix arugula, tomato, cheese, almonds, walnuts, and hazelnuts. Top with steaks and drizzle with red wine mixture. Serve.

Feta & Potato Salad

Serving Size: 4 | Total Time: 25 minutes + chilling time
3 lb potatoes, chopped
1 cup mayonnaise
¼ cup mustard
¼ cup pickles
1 white onion, chopped
1 cup feta, crumbled

Place the potatoes in your Instant Pot and cover them with water. Seal the lid and cook for 6 minutes on High Pressure. Once ready, do a natural release for 10 minutes. Drain the potatoes and allow to cool. Chop into small pieces. In a bowl, mix pickles, mayonnaise, potatoes, mustard, and onion. Top with feta cheese to serve.

Healthy Kale & Egg Muffins

Serving Size: 3 | Total Time: 10 minutes
6 eggs
1 cup kale, chopped
½ cup cheddar, grated
1 small onion, chopped
½ tsp Italian seasoning
Salt and pepper to taste
2 tbsp heavy cream

In a bowl, mix eggs, salt, pepper, and heavy cream. Whisk until well combined and add cheddar, onion, kale, and Italian seasoning. Divide the mixture between greased ramekins. Add 1 cup of water in the Instant Pot and lay a trivet inside. Lower the ramekins on the trivet and seal the lid. Cook on High Pressure for 6 minutes. When ready, do a quick release. Serve.

Potatoes & Tuna Salad with Pickles

Serving Size: 4 | Total Time: 15 minutes
½ cup pimento-stuffed green olives
½ cup chopped roasted red peppers

1 lb potatoes, quartered
2 eggs
3 tbsp melted butter
Salt and pepper to taste
6 pickles, chopped
2 tbsp red wine vinegar
10 oz canned tuna, drained

Pour 2 cups of water into the pot and add potatoes. Place a trivet over the potatoes. Lay the eggs on the trivet. Seal the lid and cook for 8 minutes on High Pressure. Do a quick release. Drain and remove potatoes to a bowl.
Fill a bowl with ice water. Add in the eggs to cool. Drizzle melted butter over the potatoes and season with salt and pepper. Peel and chop the chilled eggs. Add pickles, eggs, peppers, tuna, and red wine vinegar to the potatoes and mix to coat. Serve topped with olives. Enjoy!

Grandma's Egg Salad

Serving Size: 6 | **Total Time:** 15 minutes
6 eggs
¼ cup crème fraîche
2 spring onions, minced
1 tbsp dill, minced
1 tbsp curry paste
2 tsp mustard
Salt and pepper to taste

Grease a cake pan with cooking spray. Carefully crack in the eggs. To the inner pot, add 1 cup water and a trivet. Set the pan with the eggs on the trivet. Seal the lid and cook for 5 minutes on High Pressure. When ready, do a quick release. Drain any water from the eggs in the pan.
Loosen the eggs on the edges with a knife. Transfer to a cutting board and chop into smaller sizes. Transfer the chopped eggs to a bowl. Add in onions, mustard, salt, dill, crème fraîche, curry paste, and pepper. Serve.

Arugula Salad with Sweet Potatoes & Eggs

Serving Size: 4 | **Total Time:** 20 minutes
4 sweet potatoes, peeled and diced
2 large eggs
2 ½ cups mayonnaise
¼ cup dill, chopped
1/3 cup Greek yogurt
½ cup arugula

Pour 1 cup of water into the Instant Pot and insert a steamer basket. Place in the eggs and potatoes. Seal the lid. Cook for 4 minutes on High Pressure. When ready, do a quick release. Take out the eggs and place in a bowl of ice-cold water for purposes of cooling. In a bowl, mix yogurt, mayonnaise, and dill. In a separate bowl, mash potatoes using a potato masher. Coat them with the mayonnaise mixture. Skin and dice the eggs. Add them to the potato salad and mix. Serve with arugula.

Authentic German Salad with Bacon

Serving Size: 6 | **Total Time:** 20 minutes
6 smoked bacon slices, chopped
6 red potatoes, peeled and quartered
½ cup apple cider vinegar
2 tsp mustard
Salt and pepper to serve
2 red onions, chopped

Set your Instant Pot to Sauté. Briefly brown the bacon for 5 minutes until crispy. Set aside. In a bowl, mix mustard, vinegar, ½ cup water, salt, and pepper. In the pot, add potatoes, bacon, and onions and top with the vinegar mixture. Seal the lid and cook for 6 minutes on High Pressure. Release pressure naturally for 10 minutes. Transfer to a serving plate. Enjoy!

Delicious Broccoli & Cauliflower Salad

Serving Size: 4 | **Total Time:** 10 minutes
1 lb cauliflower florets
1 lb broccoli, into florets
3 garlic cloves, crushed
¼ tbsp olive oil
1 tsp salt
1 tbsp dry rosemary

Cut the veggies into bite-sized pieces and place them in the pot. Add olive oil and 1 cup of water. Season with salt, garlic, and rosemary. Seal the lid. Cook on High Pressure for 3 minutes. When ready, do a quick release.

Greek-Style Pasta Salad

Serving Size: 6 | **Total Time:** 15 minutes
1 lb rotini pasta
2 plum tomatoes, halved
1 cucumber, sliced
1 red bell pepper, diced
¼ cup extra-virgin olive oil
2 tbsp white wine vinegar
1 cup feta, crumbled
2 tbsp fresh dill, chopped

Cover the rotini pasta with salted water in your Instant Pot and seal the lid. Select Manual and cook for 4 minutes on High. When ready, perform a quick pressure release and unlock the lid. Drain the pasta and set aside. Mix the extra-virgin olive oil, white wine vinegar, and salt in a large serving bowl. Add in the cooked pasta, tomatoes, cucumber, and bell pepper and toss to combine. Top with feta cheese and dill and serve.

BROTHS & SAUCES

Authentic Neapolitan Sauce
Serving Size: 4 | **Total Time**: 50 minutes
1 lb mushrooms, sliced
14 oz can tomatoes, diced
1 carrot, chopped
1 onion, chopped
1 celery stick, chopped
1 tbsp olive oil
2 garlic cloves
½ tsp paprika
1 tsp fish sauce

Heat olive oil on Sauté. Stir-fry carrot, onion, celery, and paprika for 5 minutes. Add mushrooms, garlic, and fish sauce, and pour in 1 cup water. Cook for 5-6 more minutes until the meat is slightly browned. Seal the lid. Cook on High Pressure for 10 minutes. Release the steam naturally for 10 minutes. Hit Sauté, add in tomatoes and cook for 7-8 minutes to thicken the sauce.

Cranberry Orange Sauce
Serving Size: 4 | **Total Time**: 20 minutes
2 cups cranberries
1 tsp orange zest
½ cup orange juice
¼ cup brown sugar
1 cup water
2 tbsp maple syrup

Combine maple syrup, water, cranberries, and orange juice in the Instant Pot. Sprinkle with orange zest. Seal the lid, and cook on High Pressure for 5 minutes. When done, release the pressure naturally for about 10 minutes. Press Sauté, add brown sugar, and stir until a thick sauce mixture is formed. Turn off the heat and transfer the sauce to the serving dish.

Herbed Squash Sauce
Serving Size: 4 | **Total Time**: 30 minutes
2 cups butternut squash, peeled, cubed
3 beets, trimmed, peeled, cubed
3 carrots, peeled, cubed
1 cup red wine
1 tsp dried basil
1 tbsp dried parsley
1 tsp dried oregano, ground
½ tsp garlic powder
Salt and pepper to taste

Add squash, beets, and carrots to your Instant Pot. Pour in 2 cups of water and seal the lid. Press Manual and set the timer to 10 minutes n High. Do a quick pressure release. Carefully unlock the lid. Transfer to a food processor and pulse until smooth and creamy. Add wine, basil, parsley, oregano, garlic powder, salt, and pepper and blend for a minute. Return to the pot, press Sauté, and cook for 10 minutes, stirring occasionally. Serve.

Garlic Red Bell Pepper Sauce
Serving Size: 3 | **Total Time**: 15 minutes
3 red bell peppers, chopped
1 cup cherry tomatoes, diced
1 onion, chopped
1 tsp garlic powder
½ cup sour cream
2 cups vegetable broth
1 tbsp balsamic vinegar
1 tbsp cayenne pepper

Combine bell peppers, cherry tomatoes, onion, garlic powder, sour cream, broth, balsamic vinegar, and cayenne pepper in a mixing bowl. Add the mixture to the Instant Pot, seal the lid, and cook on High Pressure for 6 minutes. When ready, do a quick release. Carefully unlock the lid. Transfer to your food processor and purée until the mixture is smooth. Serve and enjoy!

Quick Zucchini Sauce with Greek Yogurt
Serving Size: 4 | **Total Time**: 10 minutes
1 zucchini, chopped
1 cup Greek yogurt
1 cup sour cream
1 tsp garlic powder
¼ cup shallots, minced
Salt and pepper to taste

In the pot, mix zucchini, sour cream, garlic, shallots, salt, and pepper and stir until combined. Seal the lid and cook on High Pressure for 3 minutes. Do a quick release. Remove the sauce to a bowl and stir in the yogurt. Serve.

Mediterranean Tomato Sauce
Serving Size: 4 | **Total Time**: 15 minutes
2 cups tomatoes, diced
½ cup tomato sauce
½ cup sun-dried tomatoes
1 medium onion, chopped
3 tbsp balsamic vinegar
3 garlic cloves, chopped
1 tsp dried oregano
1 tbsp olive oil
Salt and pepper to taste

Combine tomatoes, tomato sauce, sun-dried tomatoes, onion, balsamic vinegar, garlic, oregano, oil, salt, and pepper in a mixing bowl and give it a good stir. Transfer to the Instant Pot and seal the lid. Cook on High Pressure for 6 minutes. When done, remove to serving bowls and serve with pasta or rice.

Caprese Sauce with Goat Cheese
Serving Size: 4 | **Total Time**: 15 minutes
1 cup goat cheese, crumbled
1 cup tomatoes, diced
3 tbsp tomato paste
1 onion, finely chopped
3 tbsp apple cider vinegar
3 garlic cloves, chopped
¼ cup mozzarella cheese
2 cups vegetable broth
Salt and pepper to taste

Add goat cheese, tomatoes, tomato paste, onion, vinegar, garlic, mozzarella cheese, broth, salt, and pepper to your Instant Pot, seal the lid and cook on High Pressure for 6 minutes. When done, press Cancel and do a quick pressure release. Serve.

Homemade Honey Applesauce

Serving Size: 4 | **Total Time:** 25 minutes
4 apples, cored, chopped
1 tsp ground cinnamon
1 tsp honey

Add apples, cinnamon, ½ cup water, and honey. Seal the lid and cook on High Pressure for 4 minutes. Release Pressure naturally for 10 minutes. If you desire a chunky blend, stir vigorously. For smooth applesauce, puree the mixture in a blender. Allow to cool before transferring in containers for storage.

Spicy Green Sauce

Serving Size: 4 | **Total Time:** 10 minutes
4 oz green jalapeño peppers, chopped
1 green bell pepper, chopped
2 garlic cloves, crushed
½ cup white vinegar
1 tbsp apple cider vinegar
1 tsp salt

Add jalapeño peppers, bell pepper, garlic, white vinegar, apple vinegar, and salt to the Instant Pot. Pour in 4 tbsp water. Seal the lid and cook on High Pressure for 2 minutes. When done, release the steam naturally for about 5 minutes. Transfer to a blender, pulse until combined, and store in jars.

SOUPS

Black Bean & Corn Chicken Soup
Serving Size: 4 | **Total Time**: 25 minutes
½ lb boneless, skinless chicken thighs
5 cups chicken broth
Salt and pepper to taste
14 oz can tomatoes, diced
2 jalapeño peppers, minced
2 tbsp tomato puree
3 cloves garlic, minced
1 tbsp chili powder
1 tbsp ground cumin
½ tsp dried oregano
1 (14.5-oz) can black beans
2 cups corn kernels
Crushed tortilla chips
¼ cup cheddar, shredded
2 tbsp cilantro, chopped

Add the chicken, oregano, garlic, tomato puree, broth, cumin, tomatoes, chili, and jalapeño to your Instant Pot. Seal the lid and cook on High Pressure for 10 minutes.

Once cooking is done, release the pressure quickly. Unlock the lid. Transfer the chicken to a plate. Press Sauté and cook corn and black beans. Shred the chicken with a pair of forks, and return to the pot, stirring well.

Select Keep Warm and simmer the soup for 5 minutes until heated through. Adjust the seasoning and divide among serving plates. Garnish with cilantro, shredded cheese, and crushed tortilla chips to serve.

Traditional Italian Vegetable Soup
Serving Size: 6 | **Total Time**: 32 minutes
2 tbsp olive oil
1 onion, diced
1 cup celery, chopped
1 carrot, diced
1 green bell pepper, chopped
2 cloves garlic, minced
3 cups chicken broth
½ tsp dried parsley
½ tsp dried thyme
½ tsp dried oregano
Salt and pepper to taste
2 bay leaves
28 oz can diced tomatoes
1 tbsp tomato paste
2 cups kale
14 oz canned navy beans
½ cup rice
¼ cup Parmesan, shredded

Warm olive oil on Sauté. Stir in carrot, celery, and onion and cook for 5 minutes until soft. Add garlic and bell pepper and cook for 2 minutes as you stir until aromatic. Stir in pepper, thyme, broth, salt, parsley, oregano, tomatoes, bay leaves, and tomato paste. Mix in rice. Seal the lid and cook on High Pressure for 15 minutes. Do a quick release. Add kale and stir. Use residual heat to slightly wilting the greens. Discard bay leaves. Stir in navy beans and serve topped with Parmesan cheese.

Chipotle Pumpkin Soup
Serving Size: 4 | **Total Time**: 30 minutes
1 tbsp olive oil
1 onion, chopped
2 chipotle peppers, minced
1 tsp ground black pepper
¼ tsp grated nutmeg
¼ tsp ground cinnamon
1 butternut pumpkin, cubed
4 cups vegetable broth
1 tsp salt
1 cup half-and-half

Warm oil on Sauté and cook nutmeg, pepper, cinnamon, and onion for 3-5 minutes until translucent. Add pumpkin and cook for 5 minutes, stirring infrequently. Pour in broth and add chipotle peppers and any remaining pumpkin. Seal the lid and cook on High Pressure for 10 minutes. Release pressure quickly. Stir in half-and-half and transfer to a blender to purée until you obtain a smooth consistency. Season with salt and serve hot.

Spicy Tomato Soup with Rice
Serving Size: 4 | **Total Time**: 55 minutes
1 cup tomato puree
1 onion, chopped
1 garlic clove, minced
¼ cup rice
Salt and pepper to taste
2 tbsp olive oil
4 cups vegetable broth
¼ tsp cayenne pepper
1 tsp basil, chopped

Heat oil on Sauté and cook garlic and onion 3 minutes until soft. Add in tomato puree, rice, vegetable broth, and cayenne pepper. Season with salt and black pepper. Seal the lid and cook on Soup/Broth for 30 minutes on High Pressure. Release the pressure naturally for about 10 minutes. Serve in bowls sprinkled with basil.

Green Immune-Boosting Soup
Serving Size: 4 | **Total Time**: 35 minutes
1 lb Brussels sprouts, halved
6 oz baby spinach
1 tsp salt
1 tbsp whole milk
3 tbsp sour cream
¼ cup celery, chopped
3 cups water
1 tbsp butter

Add sprouts, spinach, salt, milk, sour cream, celery, water, and butter to the Instant Pot. Seal the lid and set the steam release. Press Soup/Broth and cook for 30 minutes on High. Do a quick release. Transfer to a food processor, and blend well to combine.

Chowder with Broccoli, Carrot & Tofu

Serving Size: 4 | **Total Time:** 35 minutes
1 head broccoli, chopped
1 carrot, chopped
2 tbsp sesame oil
1 onion, chopped
2 garlic cloves
1 cup soy milk
2 cups vegetable broth
¼ cup tofu, crumbled
A pinch of salt

Heat oil on Sauté. Add onion and garlic and stir-fry for 2 minutes, or until translucent. Pour in broth, a cup of water, broccoli, salt, and carrot. Seal the lid and cook on Manual/Pressure Cook for 5 minutes on High. Do a quick release. Stir in the soy milk and transfer to a food processor. Pulse until creamy. Serve with crumbled tofu.

Vegetarian Lentil Soup with Nachos

Serving Size: 6 | **Total Time:** 40 minutes
2 ½ cups vegetable broth
1 ½ cups tomato sauce
1 onion, chopped
1 cup dry red lentils
½ cup prepared salsa verde
2 garlic cloves, minced
1 tbsp smoked paprika
2 tsp ground cumin
1 tsp chili powder
¼ tsp cayenne pepper
Salt and pepper to taste
Crushed tortilla chips

Add in tomato sauce, broth, onion, salsa verde, cumin, cayenne pepper, chili powder, garlic, lentils, paprika, salt, and pepper. Seal the lid and cook for 20 minutes on High Pressure. Release pressure naturally for 10 minutes. Garnish with crushed tortilla chips and serve. Enjoy!

White Cabbage & Beetroot Borscht Soup

Serving Size: 4 | **Total Time:** 30 minutes
1 dried habanero pepper, crushed
2 tbsp olive oil
1 cup leeks, chopped
1 tsp garlic, smashed
2 beets, peeled and diced
1 tbsp cayenne pepper
4 cups beef stock
1 lb white cabbage, grated
2 tsp apple cider vinegar
¼ tsp paprika
Greek yogurt for garnish

Warm oil on Sauté. Stir in garlic and leeks and cook for 5 minutes until soft. Mix in the beef stock, paprika, cayenne pepper, vinegar, beets, white cabbage, and crushed habanero pepper. Seal the lid and cook on High Pressure for 20 minutes. Do a quick release. Place in serving bowls and top with Greek yogurt to serve.

Chorizo Soup with Roasted Tomatoes

Serving Size: 6 | **Total Time:** 25 minutes
28 oz fire-roasted diced tomatoes
3 tbsp olive oil
2 shallots, chopped
3 cloves garlic, minced
Salt and pepper to taste
4 cups beef broth
½ cup tomatoes, chopped
½ cup raw cashews
1 tbsp red wine vinegar
3 chorizo sausage, chopped
½ cup chopped basil

Warm oil on Sauté and cook chorizo until crispy. Remove to a plate lined with paper towels. Add in garlic and shallots and cook for 5 minutes until soft. Season with salt. Stir in red wine vinegar, broth, fire-roasted tomatoes, cashews, tomatoes, and pepper into the cooker. Seal the lid and cook on High Pressure for 8 minutes. Release the pressure quickly. Pour the soup into a blender and process until smooth. Divide into bowls. Top with chorizo and decorate with basil.

Mediterranean Carrot & Chickpea Soup

Serving Size: 6 | **Total Time:** 15 minutes
14 oz can chickpeas
2 carrots, chopped
2 onions, chopped
2 tomatoes, chopped
3 tbsp tomato paste
2 tbsp chopped parsley
2 cups vegetable broth
2 tbsp olive oil
1 tsp salt

Add in chickpeas, oil, onions, carrots, and tomatoes. Pour in the broth and sprinkle salt. Stir in the paste and seal the lid. Cook on High Pressure for 6 minutes. Do a quick release. Carefully unlock the lid. Remove the meal to a serving place. Sprinkle with parsley and serve.

Chili Cream of Acorn Squash Soup

Serving Size: 4 | **Total Time:** 25 minutes
4 cups vegetable broth
2 tbsp butter
1 onion, diced
1 lb acorn squash, chopped
2 carrots, diced
¼ tsp chili pepper
A pinch of salt
½ cup coconut milk
1/3 cup sour cream

Melt butter on Sauté. Add onion and cook for 3 minutes until soft. Add in carrots, squash, salt, and chili pepper and stir-fry for 2 minutes until fragrant. Add the broth to the vegetable mixture. Seal the lid and cook for 12 minutes on High Pressure. Quick-release the pressure.
Add soup to a food processor and puree to obtain a smooth consistency. Take the soup back to the cooker, stir in coconut milk until you get a consistent color. Serve hot with a dollop of sour cream.

Cauliflower & Potato Soup with Parsley

Serving Size: 4 | **Total Time:** 30 minutes

1 lb cauliflower florets
2 potatoes, chopped
4 cups chicken broth
2 tbsp parsley, chopped
Salt and pepper to taste
¼ cup heavy cream
¼ cup sour cream
1 cup milk

Add cauliflower, potatoes, broth, parsley, salt, pepper, heavy cream, sour cream, and milk to the pot. Seal the lid and set the steam release handle. Cook on High Pressure for 20 minutes. Do a quick release. Let chill and transfer to a blender. Pulse until well-combined. Serve.

Squash Soup with Yogurt & Cilantro

Serving Size: 6 | **Total Time**: 50 minutes
1 lb acorn squash, peeled diced
1 tbsp olive oil
1 onion, diced
1 stalk celery, diced
1 large carrot, diced
2 garlic cloves, minced
6 cups chicken stock
Juice from 1 lemon
1 cup coconut milk
Salt and pepper to taste
2 tbsp cilantro, chopped
Yogurt for garnish

Heat oil on Sauté and stir-fry carrot, celery, garlic, salt, and onion for 4 to 5 minutes until soft. Mix acorn squash with the vegetables; cook for 1 more minute until tender. Add stock and seal the lid and cook on High Pressure for 20 minutes. Release pressure naturally for 10 minutes. Add in lemon juice and coconut milk and stir. Transfer the soup to a blender and process until smooth. Divide soup into serving plates. Garnish with cilantro, black pepper, and yogurt.

Simple Carrot & Oregano Soup

Serving Size: 4 | **Total Time**: 30 minutes
2 carrots, chopped
4 cups vegetable broth
1 tbsp butter
½ tsp dried oregano
½ tsp salt

Add carrots, broth, butter, oregano, and salt to the pot. Seal the lid and cook on Manual/Pressure Cook for 12 minutes on High. Do a natural release for 10 minutes. Transfer to a food processor and pulse until creamy.

Garam Masala Parsnip & Red Onion Soup

Serving Size: 4 | **Total Time**: 20 minutes
2 tbsp vegetable oil
1 red onion, finely chopped
3 parsnips, chopped
2 garlic cloves, crushed
2 tsp garam masala
½ tsp chili powder
1 tbsp plain flour
4 cups vegetable stock
1 whole lemon, juiced
Salt and pepper to taste
Strips of lemon rind

Heat oil on Sauté, and stir-fry onion, parsnips, and garlic for 5 minutes, or until soft but not changed color. Stir in garam masala and chili powder and cook for 30 seconds. Stir in the flour for another 30 seconds. Pour in the stock, lemon rind, and lemon juice, and seal the lid. Cook on Manual for 5 minutes on High. Do a quick release. Remove a third of the vegetable pieces with a slotted spoon and reserve. Process the remaining soup and vegetables in a food processor until smooth. Return to the pot and stir in the reserved vegetables. Press Sauté and heat the soup until piping hot. Season with salt and pepper. Garnish with strips of lemon and serve.

Fall Vegetable Soup

Serving Size: 4 | **Total Time**: 35 minutes
2 tbsp olive oil
1 onion, chopped
2 carrots, chopped
1 cup celery, chopped
2 cloves garlic, minced
5 cups vegetable broth
2 turnips, chopped
28 oz canned tomatoes
15 oz can garbanzo beans
1 cup frozen green peas
2 bay leaves
1 sprig fresh sage
Salt and pepper to taste
¼ cup Parmesan, grated

On Sauté, warm oil, stir in celery, carrots, and onion, and cook for 4 minutes until soft. Add in garlic and cook for 30 seconds. Add in vegetable broth, turnips, garbanzo beans, bay leaves, tomatoes, pepper, salt, peas, and sage.
Seal the lid and cook on High Pressure for 12 minutes. Allow natural pressure release for 10 minutes. Carefully unlock the lid. Serve topped with Parmesan cheese.

Farro & Vegetable Chicken Soup

Serving Size: 6 | **Total Time**: 45 minutes
4 boneless, skinless chicken thighs
1 tbsp olive oil
¼ cup white wine
1 cup farro
1 large onion, chopped
2 celery stalks, chopped
3 large carrots, chopped
1 tsp garlic powder
1 tsp ground cumin
1 bay leaf
6 cups chicken broth
2 tsp parsley to garnish

Warm oil on Sauté. Brown the chicken on all sides for 6 minutes. Transfer the chicken to a bowl. Into the pot, add the wine to deglaze, scraping any brown bits present at the bottom of the cooker. Mix the wine with farro, cumin, broth, onion, carrots, celery, garlic powder, and bay leaf. Seal the lid, press Meat/Stew, and cook on High for 20 minutes. Release pressure naturally for about 10 minutes. Add parsley for garnish. Serve and enjoy!.

Chili Soup with Avocado & Corn

Serving Size: 4 | **Total Time:** 25 minutes
1 avocado, mashed
2 tbsp lemon juice
1 tbsp vegetable oil
4 oz canned sweet corn
2 tomatoes, chopped
1 garlic clove, crushed
1 leek, chopped
1 red chili, chopped
14 oz vegetable stock
4 oz soy milk
Chopped leeks to garnish

In a bowl, mix the avocado mash with lemon juice and reserve until required. Heat the oil on Sauté and add corn, tomatoes, garlic, leek, and chili. Stir-fry for 4-5 minutes until softened. Put half of the vegetable mixture in a food processor, add the mashed avocado and process until smooth. Transfer the contents to the Instant Pot.
Pour in the stock, soy milk, and reserved vegetables, and seal the lid. Cook on Manual/Pressure Cook for 4 minutes on High. Once ready, press Cancel and release the steam naturally for about 10 minutes. Carefully unlock the lid. Garnish with chopped leeks and serve.

Kimchi Ramen Noodle Soup

Serving Size: 4 | **Total Time:** 20 minutes
1 chicken breast, cubed
2 tbsp olive oil
½ tsp ground ginger
2 tbsp garlic, minced
4 cups chicken stock
2 tbsp soy sauce
½ tbsp kimchi paste
1 cup mushrooms, chopped
10 oz ramen noodles
1 lb collard greens, trimmed
2 tbsp cilantro, chopped
1 red chili, chopped to serve

Warm the olive oil on Sauté. Add in the chicken and cook for 5-6 minutes until slightly browned. Add in the mushrooms, garlic, kimchi paste, and ginger and sauté for 4-5 minutes. Mix in chicken stock and soy sauce. Seal the lid and cook on High Pressure for 10 minutes. Release pressure quickly. Press Sauté and stir in the ramen noodles and collard greens and simmer for 2 minutes. Top with red chili and cilantro to serve.

Quick Mushroom-Quinoa Soup

Serving Size: 4 | **Total Time:** 30 minutes
4 cups vegetable broth
1 carrot, chopped
1 stalk celery, diced
2 cups quinoa, rinsed
1 cup mushrooms, sliced
1 onion, chopped
2 garlic cloves, smashed
1 tsp salt
½ tsp dried thyme
3 tbsp butter
½ cup heavy cream

Melt the butter on Sauté. Add onion, garlic, celery, and carrot, and cook for 8 minutes until tender. Mix in broth, thyme, quinoa, mushrooms, and salt. Seal the lid and cook on High Pressure for 10 minutes. Release pressure quickly. Stir in heavy cream. Cook for 2 minutes to obtain a creamy consistency. Serve warm.

Garden Vegetable Soup

Serving Size: 4 | **Total Time:** 25 minutes
1 carrot, finely chopped
2 spring onions, chopped
1 red bell pepper, chopped
2 celery stalks, chopped
½ cup celery, chopped
½ tsp dried thyme
2 tbsp butter
1 tsp vegetable oil
4 cups vegetable broth
1 cup milk
Salt and pepper to taste

Melt butter on Sauté. Add carrot, onions, bell pepper, and celery. Cook for 5 minutes, stirring constantly. Pour in vegetable broth, seal the lid and cook on Manual/Pressure Cook for 5 minutes on High. Do a quick release. Carefully unlock the lid. Stir in celery stalks, thyme, milk, oil, salt, and pepper and cook for 2-3 minutes on Sauté.

Potato-Leek Soup with Tofu

Serving Size: 4 | **Total Time:** 25 minutes
3 large leeks
3 tbsp butter
1 onion, chopped
1 lb potatoes, chopped
5 cups vegetable stock
2 tsp lemon juice
¼ tsp nutmeg
¼ tsp ground coriander
1 bay leaf
5 oz silken tofu
Salt and pepper to taste
2 tbsp chopped chives

Remove most of the green parts of the leeks. Slice the white parts very finely. Melt butter on Sauté. Stir-fry leeks and onion for 5 minutes. Add potatoes, stock, lemon juice, nutmeg, ground coriander, and bay leaf. Season to taste with salt and white pepper, and seal the lid. Press Manual and set the timer to 10 minutes. Cook on High. Do a quick release and discard the bay leaf. Process the soup in a food processor until smooth. Season to taste and add silken tofu. Sprinkle with chives and serve.

Delicious Chicken & Potato Soup

Serving Size: 4 | **Total Time:** 35 minutes
1 lb chicken breasts, cubed
1 onion, chopped

1 carrot, chopped
2 potatoes, peeled, chopped
1 tsp cayenne pepper
2 egg yolks
1 tsp salt
3 tbsp lemon juice
3 tbsp olive oil

Add chicken, onion, carrot, potatoes, cayenne pepper, egg yolks, salt, lemon juice, oil, and 4 cups of water to the pot and seal the lid. Set the steam release handle and cook on Soup/Broth for 20 minutes on High. Release the pressure naturally for 10 minutes. Serve.

Homemade Winter Soup

Serving Size: 4 | **Total Time**: 40 minutes
3 sweet potatoes, chopped
1 tsp salt
2 fennel bulbs, chopped
16 oz pureed pumpkin
1 large onion, chopped
1 tbsp coconut oil
4 cups water
1 tbsp sour cream

Heat the oil on Sauté, and add onion and fennel bulbs. Cook for 3-5 minutes until tender. Add sweet potatoes, salt, pumpkin puree, and water, and seal the lid. Cook on High Pressure for 25 minutes. Do a quick release. Carefully unlock the lid. Transfer the soup to a food processor and blend for 20 seconds until creamy. Top with sour cream and serve.

Potato & Broccoli Soup with Rosemary

Serving Size: 4 | **Total Time**: 30 minutes
1 lb broccoli, cut into florets
2 potatoes, peeled, chopped
4 cups vegetable broth
½ tsp dried rosemary
½ tsp salt
½ cup sour cream

Place broccoli and potatoes in the pot. Pour the broth, rosemary, and seal the lid. Cook on Soup/Broth for 20 minutes on High. Do a quick release. Carefully unlock the lid and remove the soup to a blender. Pulse to combine. Stir in sour cream and add salt. Serve.

Traditional Cheesy Onion Soup

Serving Size: 4 | **Total Time**: 35 minutes
2 tbsp butter
1 thinly chopped onion
Salt and pepper to taste
½ cup dry white wine
4 cups beef stock
2 sprigs fresh thyme
2 bay leaves
4 baguette slices
1 cup Swiss cheese, grated

Melt butter on Sauté. Add in onions and cook for 3-5 minutes until soft. Add in beef stock, wine, bay leaves, thyme, salt, and pepper as you stir. Seal the lid, press Manual, and cook for 15 minutes. Do a quick release. Discard bay leaves and thyme. Preheat the oven's broiler. Divide into four soup bowls. Top with ¼ cup Swiss cheese and 1 baguette slice. Transfer the bowls to a baking sheet and cook for 2-4 minutes under broiler until golden brown. Serve.

Parsley Noodle Soup with Chicken

Serving Size: 4 | **Total Time**: 35 minutes
1 lb chicken breasts, cubed
½ cup egg noodles
4 cups chicken broth
2 tbsp parsley, chopped
Salt and pepper to taste

Season the fillets with salt and place them in the pot. Pour the broth and seal the lid. Cook on Soup/Broth for 20 minutes on High. Do a quick release. Add in the noodles and seal the lid again. Press Manual/Pressure Cook and cook for 5 minutes on High Pressure. Release the pressure quickly. Carefully unlock the lid. Sprinkle with black pepper and parsley. Serve warm.

Creamy Broccoli-Gorgonzola Soup

Serving Size: 4 | **Total Time**: 35 minutes
8 oz Gorgonzola cheese, crumbled
1 cup broccoli, chopped
2 tbsp olive oil
½ cup full-fat milk
1 tbsp parsley, chopped
Salt and pepper to taste

Add broccoli, oil, milk, salt, pepper, and gorgonzola cheese to the pot and 4 cups of water. Seal the lid and cook on Soup/Broth for 30 minutes on High Pressure. Do a quick release. Carefully unlock the lid. Remove the lid and sprinkle with fresh parsley. Serve.

Rustic Soup with Turkey Balls & Carrots

Serving Size: 4 | **Total Time**: 45 minutes
2 tbsp olive oil
6 oz turkey balls
4 cups chicken broth
1 onion, chopped
1 garlic clove, minced
3 large carrots, chopped
Salt and pepper to taste
1 tbsp cilantro, chopped

Heat olive oil on Sauté and stir-fry onion, carrots, and garlic for 5 minutes until soft. Add turkey balls, broth, salt, and pepper to the pot. Seal the lid and press Manual. Cook for 25 minutes on HIgh. Release the pressure naturally for 10 minutes and serve sprinkled with cilantro.

Vegetable Beef Soup

Serving Size: 4 | **Total Time**: 45 minutes
½ lb lean beef, cut into bite-sized pieces
1 onion, chopped
2 carrots, chopped
1 tsp cayenne pepper
Salt and pepper to taste
2 tbsp butter

Melt butter on Sauté. Add onion and stir-fry for 3 minutes. Add carrots, cayenne pepper, salt, and pepper. Cook for 2 more minutes. Add the meat and pour in 4 cups of water. Seal the lid and cook on

Manual for 35 minutes. Release the pressure quickly. Serve warm.

Modern Minestrone with Pancetta

Serving Size: 6 | **Total Time:** 30 minutes
2 tbsp olive oil
2 oz pancetta, chopped
1 onion, diced
1 parsnip, chopped
2 carrots, cut into rounds
2 celery stalks
2 garlic cloves, minced
1 tbsp dried basil
1 tbsp dried thyme
1 tbsp dried oregano
6 cups vegetable broth
1 lb green beans, chopped
1 (15-oz) can diced tomatoes
1 (15-oz) can chickpeas
2 cups small shaped pasta
Salt and pepper to taste
½ cup grated Parmesan

Heat oil on Sauté. Add onion, carrots, garlic, pancetta, celery, and parsnip and cook for 5 minutes until they become soft. Stir in basil, oregano, beans, broth, tomatoes, pepper, salt, thyme, chickpeas, and pasta. Seal the lid and cook for 6 minutes on High Pressure. Release pressure naturally for 10 minutes. Carefully unlock the lid. Garnished with Parmesan cheese and serve.

Piri Piri Chicken Soup

Serving Size: 4 | **Total Time:** 40 minutes
2 chicken breasts, cubed
1 garlic clove, minced
1 sweet onion, diced
½ cup celery, diced
2 tbsp butter
3 cups chicken bone broth
1/3 cup Piri Piri spicy sauce
1 tsp thyme
1 tbsp lemon juice
Salt and pepper to taste

Melt butter in your Instant Pot on Sauté and cook onion, celery, and garlic for 3 minutes. Add in the chicken and Sauté for another 4-5 minutes, stirring occasionally. Pour in chicken broth, thyme, and spicy sauce and seal the lid. Select Manual and cook for 12 minutes on High pressure.

When done, allow a natural release for 10 minutes, then perform a quick pressure release. Carefully unlock the lid. Adjust the taste and drizzle with the lemon juice. Ladle into bowls and serve warm. Enjoy!

Turmeric Butternut Squash Soup

Serving Size: 4 | **Total Time:** 40 minutes
1.5 lb butternut squash, peeled and chopped
1 onion, chopped
4 cups vegetable broth
1 tbsp ground turmeric
½ tbsp heavy cream
Salt and pepper to taste
2 tbsp parsley, chopped
3 tbsp olive oil

Heat oil on Sauté and stir-fry onion for 3 minutes. Add in butternut squash, turmeric, vegetable broth, salt, and pepper and stir well. Seal the lid. Press Soup/Broth and cook for 30 minutes on High. Do a quick release. With an immersion blender, blend until smooth. Stir in heavy cream and top with freshly chopped parsley. Serve warm.

Vegetarian Soup with White Beans

Serving Size: 4 | **Total Time:** 30 minutes
1 cup green peas
1 carrot, chopped
2 red bell peppers, chopped
½ cup white beans, soaked
1 tomato, roughly chopped
4 cups vegetable broth
1 onion, chopped
2 tbsp olive oil
Salt and pepper to taste
¼ tsp dried oregano

Heat the olive oil on Sauté and stir-fry onion, carrot, and bell peppers for 5 minutes until tender. Stir in green peas, white beans, tomato, broth, salt, pepper, and oregano. Seal the lid. Cook on High Pressure for 20 minutes. Do a quick release. Serve warm.

Yellow Beef Soup

Serving Size: 4 | **Total Time:** 35 minutes
1 bay leaf
2 garlic cloves
½ lb beef sirloin, cubed
2 shallots
2 candlenuts
½ tsp turmeric
2 tbsp beansprouts
1 lemongrass
1 tsp vegetable oil
Salt and pepper to taste

In a blender, combine the shallots, garlic, candlenuts, and turmeric until smooth. Warm vegetable oil in your Instant Pot on Sauté. Place the shallot mixture and cook for 3-4 minutes, stirring often until aromatic. Add in the beef and lemongrass and stir-fry until the lemongrass is wilted, about 5 minutes. Put in 4 cups water, bay leaf, salt, and pepper and seal the lid. Select Manual and cook for 15 minutes on High. When done, perform a quick pressure release. Discard bay leaf. Mix in beansprouts and cook for 2-3 minutes until wilted. Serve warm.

Spicy Red Kidney Bean Soup

Serving Size: 4 | **Total Time:** 45 minutes
14.5 oz can red kidney beans
14.5 oz canned tomatoes
2 tbsp oil
1 onion, chopped
2 cloves garlic, crushed
2 red chilies, chopped
1 green bell pepper, diced
½ cup tomato sauce

Heat oil on Sauté and stir-fry garlic, chilies, and onion for 3 minutes. Add tomatoes, beans, bell pepper, tomato sauce, and 4 cups of water. Seal the lid. Cook on Manual for 25 minutes on High Pressure. Release the steam naturally for 10 minutes. Carefully unlock the lid. Serve.

Creamy Celery & Green Pea Soup
Serving Size: 4 | **Total Time**: 25 minutes
3 oz carrots, finely chopped
3 oz celery root, chopped
1 cup green peas
2 tbsp butter
2 tbsp parsley, chopped
1 egg yolk
2 tbsp cream cheese
Salt and pepper to taste
4 cups beef broth

Add carrots, celery, green peas, butter parsley, egg yolk, cream cheese, salt, pepper, and broth to the Instant Pot and seal the lid. Cook on High Pressure for 10 minutes. When done, release the steam naturally for 10 minutes.

Creamy Bean & Potato Soup
Serving Size: 4 | **Total Time**: 35 minutes
½ cup canned beans
4 cups beef broth
1 potato, chopped
½ cup heavy cream
Salt and pepper to taste
1 tsp garlic powder

Add beans, broth, potato, heavy cream, salt, pepper, and garlic powder to the pot, seal the lid, and cook on Manual/Pressure for 10 minutes on High. Release the steam naturally for 10 minutes. Carefully unlock the lid. Transfer the ingredients to a blender. Pulse until smooth. Return the soup to the pot. Press Sauté and add a half cup of water. Cook for 5 more minutes, or until desired thickness. Let it chill for a while before serving.

Effortless Tomato-Lentil Soup
Serving Size: 4 | **Total Time**: 35 minutes
1 cup red lentils
1 carrot, cut into thin slices
1 tbsp tomato paste
3 garlic cloves, crushed
4 cups vegetable broth
2 tomatoes, chopped
1 onion, diced
½ tsp dried thyme
2 tbsp olive oil

Warm oil on Sauté. Cook onion, carrot, and garlic for 5 minutes. Add in tomato paste, tomatoes, lentils, broth, and thyme. Seal the lid and cook on Soup/Broth for 15 minutes on High Pressure. Release the pressure naturally for 10 minutes. Carefully unlock the lid. Serve.

Parsley Creamy Tomato Soup
Serving Size: 4 | **Total Time**: 50 minutes
2 lb tomatoes, diced
1 cup canned white beans
1 small onion, diced
2 garlic cloves, crushed
1 cup heavy cream
1 cup vegetable broth
½ tsp sugar
Salt and pepper to taste
2 tbsp olive oil
2 tbsp parsley, chopped

Warm oil on Sauté. Stir-fry onion and garlic for 2 minutes. Add tomatoes, beans, broth, 3 cups of water, parsley, salt, pepper, and a little bit of sugar to balance the bitterness. Seal the lid and cook on Soup/Broth for 30 minutes on High Pressure. Release the pressure naturally for 10 minutes. Carefully unlock the lid. Top with a dollop of heavy cream and serve.

Tasty Asparagus Soup
Serving Size: 4 | **Total Time**: 35 minutes
2 lb asparagus, chopped
2 onions, chopped
1 cup heavy cream
4 cups vegetable broth
2 tbsp butter
1 tbsp vegetable oil
½ tsp salt
½ tsp dried oregano
½ tsp paprika

Melt butter on Sauté, and add 1 tbsp of oil. Stir-fry the onions for 2 minutes until translucent. Add asparagus, oregano, salt, and paprika. Stir well and cook until asparagus soften for a few minutes. Pour the broth and mix well to combine. Seal the lid and cook on Soup/Broth for 20 minutes on High. Do a quick release and whisk in 1 cup of heavy cream. Unlock the lid. Serve.

Gingery Squash & Leek Soup
Serving Size: 4 | **Total Time**: 35 minutes
2 cups butternut squash, chopped
4 leeks, chopped
Salt and pepper to taste
1 tsp ginger, grated
4 cups vegetable broth
2 tbsp olive oil
1 tsp cumin
1 tsp ginger powder

Heat the oil on Sauté, add stir-fry leeks for about 5 minutes, on Sauté. Add ginger powder and cumin. Give it a good stir and continue to cook for 1 more minute. Pour in squash, ginger, salt, pepper, and broth and seal the lid. Cook on Soup/Broth for 10 minutes on High. Release the pressure naturally for about 10 minutes.

Lentil & Carrot Soup
Serving Size: 4 | **Total Time**: 40 minutes
1 cup red lentils, rinsed
1 red bell pepper, chopped
1 onion, chopped
½ cup carrot puree
Salt and pepper to taste
½ tsp cumin, ground
2 tbsp olive oil

2 tbsp parsley, chopped

Heat the oil on Sauté, add stir-fry the onion for 4 minutes. Add lentils, bell pepper, carrot puree, salt, pepper, and cumin and pour in 4 cups of water. Seal the lid and cook on Soup/Broth for 30 minutes on High. Do a quick pressure release. Sprinkle with fresh parsley and serve.

Cabbage & Pork Soup

Serving Size: 6 | Total Time: 20 minutes
1 lb ground pork
1 onion, diced
2 lb napa cabbage, chopped
1 potato, diced
6 button mushrooms, sliced
3 scallions, sliced
2 tbsp butter
4 cups vegetable broth
Salt and pepper to taste

Melt butter on Sauté and add the pork. Cook until it browned, breaking it with a spatula. Once browned, add onion and mushrooms and cook for another 4-5 minutes. Season with salt and pepper. Pour in vegetable broth and stir in cabbage, potato, and scallions. Seal the lid, cook on Pressure Cook for 6 minutes on High. Do a quick release. Carefully unlock the lid. Serve.

Millet & Beef Soup

Serving Size: 4 | Total Time: 35 minutes
½ lb beef stew meat, cubed
2 tbsp vegetable oil
1 celery rib, chopped
2 shallots, chopped
2 garlic cloves, minced
1 carrot, chopped
½ cup millet, rinsed
1 cup canned tomatoes, diced
12 oz spicy vegetable juice
4 cups beef bone broth
Salt and pepper to taste
½ cup frozen peas
½ tsp dried rosemary
½ tsp dried sage

Heat vegetable oil in your Instant Pot on Sauté and cook shallots, carrot, celery, and garlic for 3 minutes. Add in the beef and Sauté for another 4-5 minutes, stirring often. Pour in beef broth, tomatoes, spicy vegetable juice, millet, rosemary, and sage and seal the lid. Select Manual and cook for 15 minutes on High pressure. Once ready, perform a quick pressure release and unlock the lid. Mix in peas and let sit for 5 minutes; adjust the seasoning. Serve right away. Enjoy!

Jalapeño Chicken Soup with Tortilla Chips

Serving Size: 6 | Total Time: 50 minutes
¾ lb chicken thighs
1 onion, chopped
2 garlic cloves, minced
1 cup tomatoes, chopped
1 tbsp ginger, minced
2 cups collard greens
2 tbsp butter, softened
1 jalapeño pepper, minced
½ tsp dried basil
½ tsp dried oregano
Salt and pepper to taste
6 oz tortilla chips

Melt the butter in your Instant Pot on Sauté. Add in the onion, ginger, garlic, and jalapeño pepper and cook for 3 minutes. Add in the chicken thighs and brown for another 5 minutes, stirring occasionally. Mix in tomatoes, 6 cups of water, oregano, basil, salt, and pepper and seal the lid. Select Manual and cook for 15 minutes on High.

Once done, allow a natural release for 15 minutes. Shred the chicken and discard the bones; return it to the soup Stir in collard greens and simmer for 3 minutes on Sauté. Adjust the seasoning. Serve topped with tortilla chips.

Dilled Salmon Soup

Serving Size: 2 | Total Time: 20 minutes
¼ cup chopped green tomatoes
½ lb salmon fillet
1 cup fresh dill
2 tsp sliced shallots
1 tsp sliced garlic
¼ tsp ginger
¼ tsp tamarind
1 tbsp lemon juice
1 cup water
1 bay leaf
½ tsp salt

Slice salmon fillet into medium dices and place them in your Instant Pot. Add in water, green tomatoes, fresh dill, shallot, garlic, ginger, bay leaf, salt, tamarind, and lemon juice. Seal the lid, select Soup, and cook for 4 minutes on High. When done, allow a natural release for 10 minutes and unlock the lid. Serve warm and enjoy!

Spicy Sweet Potato Soup

Serving Size: 2 | Total Time: 30 minutes
2 sweet potatoes, chopped
1 carrot, chopped
1 onion, chopped
2 cups chicken broth
2 garlic cloves, chopped
Salt and pepper to taste
1 tbsp chili flakes
1 tbsp olive oil

Warm oil on Sauté, and stir-fry potatoes, onion, and garlic for 3-4 minutes. Stir in carrot, broth, salt, pepper, and chili flakes, seal the lid and cook on High Pressure for 7 minutes. Do a natural release for 10 minutes. Serve.

Quick Beef Soup

Serving Size: 4 | Total Time: 45 minutes
2 tbsp olive oil
½ lb beef sirloin, cubed
2 shallots, chopped
2 garlic cloves, minced
¼ tsp ginger

1 tsp celery seeds
1 carrot, chopped
½ tsp dry basil
Salt and pepper to taste
4 cups bone broth
2 russet potatoes, chopped
2 bay leaves
1 tbsp soy sauce
2 tbsp parsley, chopped

Warm the olive oil in your Instant Pot on Sauté. Add and cook the beef for 5-6 minutes, stirring occasionally until slightly brown on all sides. Add the shallots, garlic, ginger, celery seeds, and carrot and sauté for 4 minutes. Season with basil, salt, and pepper.

Add the broth to deglaze the pot. Stir the remaining ingredients. Seal the lid, select Manual, and cook for 20 minutes on High pressure. When done, allow a natural release for 10 minutes; open the lid. Discard the bay leaves. Divide between plates and serve topped with parsley.

Pork Soup with Cabbage & Beans

Serving Size: 4 | **Total Time:** 30 minutes
2 tbsp olive oil
1 onion, cubed
½ lb cubed pork meat
½ head cabbage, shredded
14 oz can cannellini beans
1 carrot, shredded
1 garlic clove, minced
½ tsp dried rosemary
4 cups chicken broth
Salt and pepper to taste

Warm the oil in your Instant Pot on Sauté. Place the onion, garlic, and pork and cook for 4-5 minutes. Add in cabbage, carrot, broth, rosemary, salt, pepper, and cannellini beans. Seal the lid and cook on Manual for 20 minutes on High. Perform a quick pressure release.

Chicken & Potato Soup

Serving Size: 4 | **Total Time:** 45 minutes
2 tbsp olive oil
½ lb chicken thighs
2 potatoes, cut into chunks
1 carrot, cut into chunks
1 yellow onion, diced
2 garlic cloves, minced
1 celery rib, chopped
4 cups chicken bone broth
Salt and pepper to taste
2 tbsp parsley, chopped

Heat oil in your Instant Pot on Sauté and cook onion, carrot, celery, and garlic for 3 minutes. Add in chicken and Sauté for 4-5 minutes. Pour in broth and potatoes and seal the lid. Select Manual and cook for 15 minutes on High. Once ready, allow a natural release for 10 minutes. Adjust the taste and top with parsley. Serve.

Smoked Ham & Potato Soup

Serving Size: 4 | **Total Time:** 20 minutes
1 lb russet potatoes, cut into small chunks
2 tbsp butter
2 garlic cloves, minced
1 onion, diced
½ tsp celery seeds
½ tsp chili powder
½ lb smoked ham, diced
4 cups chicken broth
2 tbsp parsley, chopped

Melt butter in your Instant Pot on Sauté. Add in garlic and onion and cook for 3 minutes. Stir in celery seeds, chili powder, and smoked ham for 1-2 minutes and pour in potatoes and broth. Seal the lid. Select Manual and cook for 10 minutes on High. Once done, perform a quick pressure release. Serve topped with parsley.

Hearty Beef Soup

Serving Size: 6 | **Total Time:** 65 minutes
2 tbsp olive oil
2 lb beef stew meat, cubed
1 leek, finely chopped
2 garlic cloves, minced
2 carrots, chopped
1 celery stalk, chopped
½ cup pearl barley
1 bay leaf
6 cups beef bone broth
½ tsp soy sauce sauce
Salt and pepper to taste
1 tbsp Parmesan, grated

Warm the olive oil in your Instant Pot on Sauté. Season beef with salt and pepper and cook in the pot for 10 minutes, stirring frequently; set aside. Add the leek, garlic, carrots, and celery to the pot and cook for 4 minutes. Put the beef back to the pot with pearl barley, bay leaf, beef broth, and soy sauce. Seal the lid and select Manual.

Cook for 30 minutes on High pressure. When done, allow a natural release for 10 minutes, then perform a quick pressure release and unlock the lid. Discard the bay leaf. Adjust the taste and top with Parmesan cheese.

Lentil & Pork Shank Soup

Serving Size: 6 | **Total Time:** 45 minutes
2 lb pork shank, trimmed of excess fat
2 carrots, cut into chunks
1 celery stalk, chopped
3 garlic cloves, sliced
2 tbsp olive oil
1 yellow onion, chopped
½ tsp paprika
½ tsp cayenne pepper
2 tomatoes, chopped
½ lb lentils, rinsed
Salt and pepper to taste

Warm the olive oil in your Instant Pot on Sauté. Place the onion, carrots, garlic, and celery and cook for 3 minutes, stirring often. Add in pork chank, paprika, cayenne pepper, tomatoes, lentils, salt, pepper, and 6 cups water.

Seal the lid, select Manual, and cook for 25 minutes on High pressure. When over, allow a natural release for 10 minutes and unlock the lid. Serve warm.

Ukrainian-Style Borscht

Serving Size: 4 | **Total Time:** 40 minutes
2 tbsp grapeseed oil
½ lb beets, peeled, diced
½ lb potatoes, peeled, diced
1 parsnip, diced
1 celery stalk, diced
1 red onion, diced
2 garlic cloves, diced
3 cups grated red cabbage
4 cups vegetable stock
½ tsp ground cumin
Salt and pepper to taste

Heat the grapeseed oil in your Instant Pot on Saué and cook celery, red onion, garlic, parsnip, and red cabbage for 4-5 minutes, stirring periodically. Pour in the vegetable stock, potatoes, beets, cumin, salt, and pepper.Seal the lid. Select Manual and cook for 15 minutes on High pressure. When over, allow a natural release for 10 minutes and unlock the lid. Serve immediately.

Chicken & Spinach Soup

Serving Size: 6 | **Total Time:** 35 minutes
3 tbsp butter
1 white onion, diced
3 celery stalks, diced
2 carrots, diced
3 garlic cloves, minced
½ tsp dried rosemary
2 chicken breasts, cubed
6 cups chicken broth
1 cup orzo pasta
2 cups spinach, chopped
Salt and pepper to taste
2 tbsp fresh dill, chopped

Melt butter in your Instant Pot on Sauté. Add in onion, celery, carrot, garlic, salt, and pepper and cook for 5 minutes. Stir in chicken breasts, and rosemary and Sauté for 5 minutes. Pour in chicken broth and orzo and seal the lid. Select Manual and cook for 12 minutes on High.Once ready, perform a quick pressure release and unlock the lid. Mix in spinach and let sit covered for 5 minutes until the spinach wilts. Scatter with dill to serve.

Mom's Meatball Soup

Serving Size: 4 | **Total Time:** 25 minutes
2 Yukon Gold potatoes, peeled and diced
2 tbsp canola oil
1 onion, diced
1 garlic clove, minced
½ lb ground pork
14 oz can diced tomatoes
4 cups vegetable broth
½ tsp dried oregano
½ tsp dried thyme
Salt and pepper to taste
2 tbsp parsley, chopped

Place the ground pork in a bowl and season with oregano, thyme, salt, and pepper. Mix well with your hands and form form the mixture into small balls. Warm the canola oil in your Instant Pot on Sauté. Add in the onion and garlic and cook for 3 minutes. Pour in vegetable broth, tomatoes, potatoes, and meatballs and seal the lid. Select Manual and cook for 10 minutes on High pressure. Once ready, perform a quick pressure release and unlock the lid. Sprinkle with par and serve warm.

Coconut Chicken Soup

Serving Size: 4 | **Total Time:** 30 minutes
2 green onions, sliced diagonally
2 tbsp ghee
1 sweet onion, chopped
1 cup celery, chopped
1 cup carrots, chopped
6 oz rice noodles
½ lb chicken breasts, cubed
1 tbsp parsley
3 cups chicken stock
1 tsp red pepper flakes
Salt and pepper to taste
1 cup coconut milk
1 cup green peas

Melt ghee in your Instant Pot on Sauté. Add in onion, celery, and carrots and cook for 3 minutes. Stir in chicken, parsley, stock, pepper flakes, salt, and pepper. Seal the lid and select Manual. Cook for 15 minutes on High. When done, perform a quick pressure release. Stir in coconut milk, green peas, and rice noodles and cook for 3 minutes on Sauté. Serve topped with green onions.

Cilantro & Coconut Chicken Soup

Serving Size: 4 | **Total Time:** 20 minutes
1 tsp ground nutmeg
2 cups diced tomatoes
4 chicken breasts, cubed
1 tbsp olive oil
1 onion, chopped
1 tsp garlic powder
1 tsp ginger powder
1 tsp turmeric
1 tsp paprika
1 tsp Cayenne Powder
2 tbsp Tomato Puree
1 cup Coconut Milk Whey
1 cup Coconut Cream
¼ cup Almonds, sliced
¼ cup Chopped Cilantro
Salt to taste

Warm olive oil in your Instant Pot on Sauté. Place the onions and salt and cook for 3 minutes. Add in nutmeg, garlic powder, ginger powder, turmeric, paprika, and cayenne pepper and cook for 2 minutes, stirring often.

Mix in diced tomatoes, coconut milk, and chicken breasts and seal the lid. Select Manual and cook for 10 minutes on High pressure. When done, perform a quick pressure release. Stir in tomato puree, coconut cream, and cilantro. Adjust seasoning to taste. Serve topped with almond.

Spring Chicken Vermicelli Soup

Serving Size: 6 | **Total Time:** 50 minutes
2 tbsp olive oil
½ cup vermicelli
¾ lb chicken breasts, cubed
2 carrots, diced
3 waxy potatoes, diced
3 green onions, sliced
1 green garlic stalk, sliced
1 celery stalk, chopped
4 cups chicken stock
½ tsp oregano
1 bay leaf
Salt and pepper to taste
2 tbsp cilantro, chopped

Warm the olive oil in your Instant Pot on Sauté. Add in the green onion, carrots, green garlic, and celery and cook for 3 minutes. Add in chicken and Sauté for 5 minutes, stirring often. Mix in potatoes, chicken stock, 2 cups of water, oregano, salt, pepper, and bay leaf and seal the lid. Select Manual, and cook for 20 minutes on High pressure. When over, allow a natural release for 10 minutes, then perform a quick pressure release. Discard the bay leaf, stir in vermicelli, and press Sauté. Cook for 5 minutes. Serve topped with cilantro.

Veggie & Elbow Pasta Soup

Serving Size: 2 | **Total Time:** 25 minutes
1 cup canned chickpeas
1 carrot, diced
14 oz can tomatoes, diced
½ cup elbow pasta
2 cups chicken broth
1 tsp dried basil
1 tbsp olive oil
1 tsp dried oregano
2 garlic cloves, minced
1 onion, diced
¼ cup fresh spinach
Salt and pepper to taste

Place the olive oil, carrot, onion, and garlic in your Instant Pot and cook until tender and soft on Sauté. Stir in oregano, basil, black pepper, salt, tomatoes, spinach, pasta, and chicken broth. Seal the lid, select Manual, and cook for 6 minutes on High. When done, allow a natural release for 10 minutes. Mix in chickpeas and serve.

Kale, Bean & Pancetta Soup

Serving Size: 6 | **Total Time:** 35 minutes
1 can (15-oz) pinto beans
1 tbsp olive oil
4 slices pancetta, chopped
1 onion, chopped
1 carrot, chopped
1 celery stalk, chopped
2 tbsp tomato paste
1 sprig fresh rosemary
2 bay leaves
4 cups chicken broth
3 cups baby kale
Salt and pepper to taste

Press the Sauté on your Instant Pot and heat the olive oil. Add in the pancetta and cook until it becomes crispy, about 4-5 minutes. Remove to a lined with paper towel plate. Put the onion, carrot, and celery in the pot and cook for 3 minutes. Stir in tomato paste, pinto beans, rosemary, bay leaves, and chicken broth. Seal the lid, select Manual, and cook for 10 minutes on High. When done, allow a natural release for 10 minutes, then perform a quick pressure release and unlock the lid. Discard rosemary and bay leaves. Mix in the kale and adjust the seasoning. Serve topped with pancetta. Enjoy!

Navy Bean & Zucchini Soup

Serving Size: 4 | **Total Time:** 25 minutes
2 tbsp olive oil
1 onion, chopped
2 garlic cloves, minced
1 zucchini, chopped
1 carrot, chopped
1 celery stalk, chopped
1 cup canned navy beans
1 tsp fresh thyme
1 bay leaf
4 cups vegetable stock
Salt and pepper to taste
2 tbsp parsley, chopped

Warm the olive oil in your Instant Pot on Sauté. Add in onion and garlic and sweat for 4-5 minutes. Add in zucchini, carrot, and celery and cook for 5 more minutes.
Stir in beans, thyme, bay leaf, stock, salt, and pepper and seal the lid. Select Manual and cook for 8 minutes on High. When over, perform a quick pressure release. Discard bay leaf. Top with parsley and serve. Enjoy!

Turkish-Inspired Lentil Soup

Serving Size: 6 | **Total Time:** 30 minutes
2 tbsp olive oil
1 white onion, chopped
1 celery stalk, diced
4 garlic cloves, minced
1 carrot, chopped
1 tsp paprika
½ tsp ground cumin
½ tsp ground coriander
1 tbsp red pepper paste
¼ cup bulgur
1 cup red lentils
14 oz can diced tomatoes
6 cups vegetable broth
Salt and pepper to taste
2 tbsp parsley, chopped

Warm the olive oil in your Instant Pot on Sauté. Add in onion, carrot, and celery and cook for 4-5 minutes. Stir in garlic, paprika, cumin, coriander, and red pepper paste and cook for another 1-2 minutes. Pour in vegetable broth, lentils, tomatoes, and bulgur and seal the lid. Select Manual and cook for 12 minutes on

High. Once ready, perform a quick pressure release. Unlock the lid and adjust the seasoning. Top with parsley and serve.

Mexican Bean Soup

Serving Size: 6 | Total Time: 40 minutes
2 tbsp olive oil
2 garlic cloves, minced
1 onion, chopped
1 red bell pepper, chopped
½ tsp dried oregano
1 tsp ground cumin
1 bay leaf
1 lb black beans, soaked
4 cups vegetable broth
14 oz can diced tomatoes
2 hot cherry peppers, sliced
Salt and pepper to taste
1 lime, cut into wedges
3 tbsp cilantro, chopped
Chili oil to serve

Warm the olive oil in your Instant Pot on Sauté. Add in garlic and onion and cook for 3 minutes. Stir in bell pepper, oregano, cumin, cherry peppers, and bay leaf and cook for another minute.
Pour in black beans, vegetable broth, tomatoes, salt, and pepper and seal the lid. Select Manual and cook for 30 minutes. Once done, perform a quick pressure release and unlock the lid. Discard the bay leaf. Drizzle with chili oil and sprinkle with cilantro. Serve with lime wedges.

Black-Eyed Pea Soup

Serving Size: 4 | Total Time: 40 minutes
2 tbsp canola oil
2 shallots, diced
2 garlic cloves, minced
1 celery stalk, sliced
1 carrot, chopped
1 lb dry black-eyed peas
¼ tsp cayenne pepper
¼ tsp dried dill
¼ tsp dried oregano
¼ tsp dried sage
1 cup spinach, torn
4 cups vegetable broth

Warm the canola oil in your Instant Pot on Sauté. Add in shallots, garlic, celery, and carrot and cook for 4 minutes. Add in black-eyed peas, cayenne pepper, dill, oregano, sage, and vegetable broth and stir well.
Seal the lid, select Manual, and cook for 10 minutes on High pressure. Once over, allow a natural release for 10 minutes, then perform a quick pressure release and unlock the lid. Stir in spinach, cover with the lid, and leave to sit in the residual heat for 5 minutes. Serve warm.

Greek-Style Fish Soup

Serving Size: 4 | Total Time: 20 minutes
1 lb codfish, cut into bite-sized pieces
2 tbsp olive oil
1 onion, chopped
1 carrot, chopped
2 garlic cloves, minced
2 tomatoes, chopped
½ tsp dill weed
½ tsp Greek oregano
½ tsp hot sauce
4 cups seafood stock
10 Kalamata olives, chopped

Warm olive oil in your Instant Pot on Sauté. Add in onion, garlic, and carrot and cook for 4 minutes. Stir in dill weed, oregano, hot sauce, and fish and cook for 3-4 minutes. Pour in stock and tomatoes and seal the lid. Select Manual and cook for 5 minutes on High. When ready, perform a quick pressure release. Carefully unlock the lid. Sprinkle with Kalamata olives and serve.

Chicken & Lima Bean Soup

Serving Size: 6 | Total Time: 45 minutes
2 tbsp sesame oil
1 cup lima beans, soaked
¾ lb chicken breasts, cubed
1 serrano pepper, minced
½ tsp cayenne pepper
1 sweet onion, sliced
2 garlic cloves, minced
2 tomatoes, chopped
2 tbsp rosemary, chopped
6 cups vegetable broth
4 tbsp salsa
1 tsp soy sauce
Salt and pepper to taste

Press Sauté and heat the sesame oil in your Instant Pot. Cook the onion and garlic until tender and fragrant. Add the chicken, serrano pepper, cayenne pepper, salt, and black pepper and sauté for 4-5 minutes. Pour in salsa, tomatoes, vegetable broth, soy sauce, and lima beans.
Seal the lid, select Manual, and cook for 30 minutes on High pressure. Once ready, perform a quick pressure release. Sprinkle with rosemary and serve warm. Enjoy!

Zuppa Toscana

Serving Size: 4 | Total Time: 40 minutes
2 tbsp olive oil
1 white onion, diced
2 garlic cloves, minced
1 lb Italian sausages, chopped
4 oz bacon, chopped
2 potatoes, sliced
14 oz can cannellini beans
1 red pepper, crushed
4 cups chicken broth
Salt and pepper to taste
1 tsp Italian seasoning
2 cups kale, chopped
½ cup grated Parmesan

Warm the olive oil in your Instant Pot on Sauté. Add in onion, garlic, bacon, and Italian sausages and cook for 4-5 minutes. Stir in potatoes, cannellini beans, Italian seasoning, chicken broth, and red pepper and seal the lid.

Select Manual and cook for 20 minutes on High pressure. Once done, perform a quick pressure release and unlock the lid. Stir in kale and simmer for 3-4 minutes on Sauté. Adjust the seasoning and top with Parmesan to serve.

Moroccan Lentil Soup

Serving Size: 4 | **Total Time:** 30 minutes
2 tsp olive oil
2 garlic cloves, minced
1 onion, chopped
1 cup red lentils
2 tbsp tomato purée
1 potato, chopped
1 carrot, chopped
½ cup celery
½ tsp ground coriander
½ tsp ground cumin
½ tsp cinnamon
1 red chili pepper, chopped
4 cups water
Salt and pepper to taste
2 tbsp fresh mint, chopped

Warm olive oil in your Instant Pot on Sauté. Add in garlic, celery, carrot, and onion and cook for 3 minutes. Stir in chili pepper, tomato puree, ground coriander, cumin, salt, pepper, and cinnamon and cook for 1 minute. Pour in lentils, potato, and 4 cups of water and stir.

Seal the lid, select Manual, and cook for 10 minutes on High pressure. When done, allow a natural release for 10 minutes and unlock the lid. Sprinkle with mint and serve.

Green Soup

Serving Size: 4 | **Total Time:** 20 minutes
2 tbsp olive oil
1 onion, chopped
1 celery rib, chopped
10 oz broccoli florets
2 cups kale
4 cups chicken broth
Salt and pepper to taste
2 tbsp peanut butter
¼ cup heavy cream

Warm the olive oil in your Instant Pot on Sauté. Place the onion and cook for 3 minutes until translucent. Add in celery and broccoli and cook for another 2 minutes.

Pour in chicken broth and kale and seal the lid. Select Manual and cook for 5 minutes on High pressure. Once done, perform a quick pressure release and unlock the lid. Let chill, then blend it. Stir in peanut butter and heavy cream and adjust the seasonings. Serve right away.

Harvest Vegetable Soup with Pesto

Serving Size: 6 | **Total Time:** 30 minutes
10 oz spinach
½ cup canned white beans
2 tbsp olive oil
1 onion, chopped
2 garlic cloves, minced
1 carrot, chopped
1 celery stalk, chopped
1 can crushed tomatoes
2 tbsp parsley
6 cups chicken bone broth
Salt and pepper to taste
2 tbsp pesto

Warm the olive oil in your Instant Pot on Sauté. Add in onion, garlic, carrot, and celery and cook for 3 minutes until tender. Pour in chicken broth, white beans, parsley, and tomatoes and seal the lid. Select Manual and cook for 10 minutes on High pressure. When done, allow a natural release for 10 minutes and unlock the lid. Stir in spinach, seal the lid, and let sit in the residual heat until the spinach wilts. Adjust the seasonings and top with pesto. Serve immediately.

Mediterranean Soup with Tortellini

Serving Size: 4 | **Total Time:** 40 minutes
1 cup cream of mushroom soup
½ cup mushrooms, chopped
9 oz refrigerated tortellini
1 cup green peas
2 carrots, chopped
2 tbsp olive oil
2 shallots, chopped
2 garlic cloves, minced
½ tsp oregano
3 cups vegetable broth
Salt and pepper to taste
2 tbsp Parmesan, shredded

Heat the olive oil in your Instant Pot on Sauté. Add in shallots and garlic and cook for 3 minutes until translucent. Add in the carrots and mushrooms and continue sautéing for 3-4 minutes. Pour in broth, mushroom soup, and oregano, and tomatoes and seal the lid. Select Manual and cook for 7 minutes on High. Once over, allow a natural release for 10 minutes, then perform a quick pressure release and unlock the lid. Stir in green peas and tortellini and cook for 3-5 minutes on Sauté. Sprinkle with Parmesan cheese and serve.

Creamed Butternut Squash Soup

Serving Size: 4 | **Total Time:** 30 minutes
1 lb butternut squash, cut into chunks
1 tbsp pumpkin seeds, toasted
2 tbsp grapeseed oil
1 onion, chopped
1 turnip, diced
½ tsp nutmeg
½ tsp ground cinnamon
4 cups vegetable stock
1 cup heavy cream
Salt and pepper to taste

Heat the grapeseed oil in your Instant Pot on Sauté. Add in onion and cook for 3 minutes until softened. Stir in vegetable stock, butternut squash, turnip, nutmeg, and cinnamon and seal the lid. Select Manual and cook for 10 minutes on High pressure. When over, allow a natural release for 10 minutes and unlock the lid. Blend the soup using an immersion blender and stir in heavy cream; adjust the seasonings. Sprinkle with pumpkin seeds and serve immediately.

French Onion Soup

Serving Size: 4 | **Total Time:** 45 minutes
1 cup cream of mushroom soup
2 tbsp olive oil
2 tbsp butter
2 lb onions, chopped
2 sprigs fresh thyme
½ cup Gruyere, grated
4 cups chicken stock
Salt and pepper to taste
1 baguette, sliced
1 tbsp chives, chopped

Heat butter and olive oil in your Instant Pot on Sauté. Add in onion and cook for 10 minutes, stirring occasionally until caramelized. Pour in the chicken stock, thyme, mushroom soup, salt, and pepper and seal the lid. Select Manual and cook for 10 minutes on High. When ready, allow a natural release for 10 minutes. Discard the thyme sprigs.
Divide the soup between four oven-safe bowls and top each one with bread slices and cheese. Cook under the broiler for 4-5 minutes until the cheese has melted and bubbly. Serve topped with chives.

Peasant Bean Soup

Serving Size: 6 | **Total Time:** 45 minutes
1 cup cipollini onions, chopped
2 tbsp olive oil
1 garlic clove, minced
1 chopped celery rib
1 cup chopped carrots
1 cup ham, chopped
1 cup great northern beans
1 potato, peeled, diced
1 cup stewed tomatoes, diced
5 cups vegetable broth
Salt and pepper to taste
2 tbsp parsley, chopped

Warm the olive oil in your Instant Pot on Sauté. Place the garlic, cipollini onions, celery, and carrots and cook for 5 minutes. Pour in vegetable broth, tomatoes, ham, great northern beans, and potato and stir. Seal the lid, select Manual, and cook for 20 minutes on High pressure. When ready, allow a natural release for 10 minutes. Adjust the seasoning. Serve topped with parsley.

Pea & Garbanzo Bean Soup

Serving Size: 4 | **Total Time:** 30 minutes
2 tbsp olive oil
½ cup shallots, sliced
14 oz can garbanzo beans
½ cup green peas
2 Roma chopped tomatoes
4 cups vegetable broth
Salt and pepper to taste
1 lemon, zested and juiced

Warm the olive oil in your Instant Pot on Sauté. Add in shallots and cook for 3 minutes until tender and fragrant. Pour in vegetable broth, tomatoes, lemon zest, and garbanzo beans and stir.
Seal the lid, select Manual, and cook for 10 minutes on High pressure. Once over, allow a natural release for 10 minutes, then perform a quick pressure release and unlock the lid. Stir in green peas and let it sit covered in the residual heat until warmed through. Season with salt and pepper and drizzle with lemon juice. Serve.

Cauliflower Cheese Soup

Serving Size: 4 | **Total Time:** 30 minutes
2 tbsp butter
1 onion, diced
2 garlic cloves, minced
2 russet potatoes, chopped
5 oz cauliflower florets
4 cups vegetable broth
1 cup heavy cream
1 tsp mustard powder
1 cup cheddar, shredded
1 green onion, chopped
Salt and pepper to taste

Melt the butter in your Instant Pot on Sauté. Add in onion and garlic and cook for 2-3 minutes until lightly golden. Add in potato, cauliflower, mustard powder, vegetable broth, and give it a good stir. Seal the lid, select Manual, and cook for 8 minutes on High. Once over, allow a natural release for 10 minutes and unlock the lid. Stir in heavy cream and half of the cheddar cheese and whizz until smooth, using a stick blender. Adjust the seasoning. Scatter the remaining cheddar on top and sprinkle with green onion to serve.

Minestrone with Fresh Herbs

Serving Size: 4 | **Total Time:** 25 minutes
2 tbsp olive oil
1 large onion, diced
3 garlic cloves, minced
2 celery stalks, diced
1 carrot, diced
2 tsp basil, chopped
1 tsp oregano, chopped
1 tsp rosemary, chopped
Salt and pepper to taste
14 oz can tomatoes, diced
5 curly kale, chopped
½ cup elbow macaroni
4 cups vegetable broth
14 oz can cannellini beans

Warm the olive oil in your Instant Pot on Sauté. Add in onion, garlic, celery, and carrot and cook for 5 minutes until tender. Stir in basil, oregano, rosemary, tomatoes, elbow macaroni, cannellini beans, and vegetable broth.
Seal the lid, select Manual, and cook for 6 minutes on High. Once done, perform a quick pressure release. Unlock the lid. Stir in kale and press Sauté. Cook for 4-5 minutes until it's wilted. Taste and adjust the seasoning.

Spicy Pumpkin Soup

Serving Size: 4 | Total Time: 25 minutes
2 tbsp butter
1 Vidalia onion, chopped
2 garlic cloves, chopped
2 carrots, diced
1 lb pumpkin, peeled, diced
½ tsp thyme
1 tsp cumin seeds
1 tbsp hot curry paste
4 cups vegetable broth
Salt and pepper to taste
1 cup heavy cream
2 tbsp cilantro, chopped

Melt the butter in your Instant Pot on Sauté. Add in onion, garlic, carrots, salt, and pepper and cook for 3 minutes. Stir in cumin seeds, thyme, hot curry paste, and pumpkin for 2 minutes and pour in vegetable broth.

Seal the lid, select Manual, and cook for 10 minutes on High. When ready, perform a quick pressure release. Blend the soup using an immersion blender and stir in heavy cream. Top with cilantro to serve.

Corn Soup with Chicken & Egg

Serving Size: 2 | Total Time: 25 minutes
1 tbsp cilantro, chopped
1 egg
½ lb chicken breasts
1 leek, chopped
1 tbsp sliced shallots
¼ tsp nutmeg
2 cups water
¼ cup corn kernels
¼ cup diced carrots
Salt and pepper to taste

Slice the chicken breasts into small cubes and place them in your Instant Pot. Add in corn kernels, water, shallots, salt, nutmeg, and black pepper. Seal the lid, select Pressure Cook, and cook for 15 minutes on High.

When done, allow a natural release and unlock the lid. Mix in carrots and leek and bring to a boil on Sauté. Beat the egg in a bowl. Once the Soup boil, pour in the beaten egg and toss until well combined and done. Divide between bowls, sprinkle with cilantro, and serve.

Mustard Carrot Soup

Serving Size: 4 | Total Time: 25 minutes
1 green bell pepper, diced
¼ cup butter
1 lb quartered carrots
3 cups chicken stock
1 tsp paprika
1 tsp ground cumin
2 tsp minced garlic
2 tbsp Dijon mustard
Salt and pepper to taste

Pour 1 cup of water into your Instant Pot; fit in a trivet. Place the carrots on the trivet and seal the lid. Select Manual and cook for 1 minute on High. When done, perform a quick pressure release; unlock the lid. Remove the carrots and pat dry the pot with a paper towel.

Melt butter in your Instant Pot on Sauté. Place the chicken stock, paprika, bell pepper, cumin, garlic, mustard, salt, black pepper, and cooked carrots. Seal the lid, select Manual, and cook for 4 minutes on High pressure.

When done, allow a natural release for 10 minutes and unlock the lid. Using an immersion blender, blend the soup until smooth and creamy. Serve right away.

Easy Veggie Soup

Serving Size: 4 | Total Time: 35 minutes
1 cup okra, trimmed
1 Carrot, sliced
1 cup Broccoli florets
1 green Bell Pepper, sliced
1 red Bell Pepper, sliced
1 Onion, sliced
2 cups vegetable broth
1 tbsp Lemon juice
4 Garlic cloves, minced
Salt and pepper to taste
2 tbsp Olive oil

Warm olive oil in your Instant Pot on Sauté. Place the onion and garlic and cook for 1 minute. Add in carrot, okra, broccoli florets, green bell pepper, and red bell pepper and cook for 5-10 minutes.

Stir in vegetable broth, salt, and black pepper and seal the lid. Select Meat/Stew and cook for 15 minutes on High pressure. When done, perform a quick pressure release and unlock the lid. Sprinkle with lemon juice and divide between bowls before serving.

Cheesy & Creamy Broccoli Soup

Serving Size: 4 | Total Time: 25 minutes
1 ½ cups grated Cheddar Cheese + extra for topping
2 tbsp cilantro, chopped
1 lb chopped Broccoli
3 cups Heavy Cream
3 cups Chicken Broth
4 tbsp Butter
4 tbsp Almond flour
1 red onion, chopped
3 garlic cloves, minced
1 tsp Italian Seasoning
Salt and pepper to taste
4 oz Cream Cheese

Melt butter in your Instant Pot on Sauté. Place the almond flour and stir until it clumps up. Slowly pour in heavy cream and stir until it gets a sauce. Remove to a bowl. Put the onions, garlic, chicken broth, broccoli, Italian seasoning, and cream cheese in the pot and stir.

Seal the lid, select Soup, and cook for 15 minutes on High pressure. When done, perform a quick pressure release and unlock the lid. Mix in butter sauce and cheddar cheese until the cheese melts. Divide between bowls and top with cheddar cheese. Serve topped with cilantro.

Gingery Carrot Soup

Serving Size: 2 | **Total Time:** 30 minutes
½ tsp red pepper flakes
2 cups chicken broth
½ lb carrots, chopped
½ tbsp Sriracha sauce
1 cup canned coconut milk
1 tbsp cilantro, chopped
1 tbsp unsalted butter
½ tsp fresh ginger, minced
1 garlic clove, minced
1 small onion, chopped

Place the butter and onion in your Instant Pot and cook for 2-3 minutes until soft on Sauté. Add in ginger and garlic and cook for 1 minute. Stir in carrots and cook for 2 minutes. Mix in coconut milk, chicken broth, red pepper flakes, and Sriracha and seal the lid.
Select Manual and cook for 6 minutes on High. When done, allow a natural release for 10 minutes; unlock the lid. Using an immersion blender, pulse the soup until purée. Serve topped with cilantro. Enjoy!

Carrot & Cabbage Soup

Serving Size: 4 | **Total Time:** 25 minutes
1 cup canned white beans
14 oz can diced tomatoes
1 head cabbage, chopped
3 tbsp Apple cider vinegar
4 minced garlic cloves
4 cup chicken broth
1 chopped celery stalk
3 chopped carrots
1 tbsp lemon juice
1 chopped onion

Place the chopped tomatoes, cabbage, apple cider vinegar, garlic, chicken broth, celery, carrots, lemon juice, and onion in your Instant Pot. Seal the lid, select Manual, and cook for 15 minutes on High pressure. When done, perform a quick pressure release and unlock the lid. Mix in white beans and cook for 2 minutes on Sauté. Serve.

Scallion Chicken & Lentil Soup

Serving Size: 4 | **Total Time:** 45 minutes
4 garlic cloves, sliced
6 oz skinless chicken thighs
½ lb dried lentils
½ chopped onion
4 cups water
¼ tsp paprika
½ tsp garlic powder
1 diced tomato
2 tbsp chopped cilantro
¼ tsp oregano
½ tsp cumin
1 chopped scallion
¼ tsp salt

Place the chicken thighs, dried lentils, onion, water, paprika, garlic powder, sliced garlic, tomato, cilantro, oregano, cumin, scallion, and salt in your Instant Pot. Seal the lid, select Soup, and cook for 30 minutes. When done, allow a natural release for 10 minutes and unlock the lid. Using a fork, shred the chicken before serving.

Tomato Shrimp Soup

Serving Size: 4 | **Total Time:** 40 minutes
½ cup coconut Cream
2 Tomatoes, sliced
2 oz Shrimp
4 cups Chicken broth
¼ cup Apple Cider Vinegar
2 Garlic cloves, minced
Salt and pepper to taste
1 tbsp Olive oil

Warm olive oil in your Instant Pot on Sauté. Place the garlic and cook for 1 minute. Add in shrimp and cook for 10 minutes. Stir in salt, black pepper, chicken broth, tomatoes, and apple cider vinegar.
Seal the lid, select Manual, and cook for 10 minutes on High pressure. When done, allow a natural release for 10 minutes and unlock the lid. Divide between 4 bowls and top each with coconut cream. Serve warm.

Mustard Potato Soup with Crispy Bacon

Serving Size: 4 | **Total Time:** 30 minutes
2 Yukon gold potatoes, chopped
2 tbsp olive oil
2 garlic cloves, minced
1 leek, diced
1 tbsp onion powder
1 green bell pepper, diced
4 cups chicken stock
Salt and pepper to taste
1 tbsp Dijon mustard
4 dashes hot pepper sauce
4 oz bacon, chopped
2 cups shredded mozzarella
1 cup milk

Warm olive oil in your Instant Pot on Sauté and cook the bacon for 5 minutes until crispy; set aside. Place garlic and leek in the pot and sauté for 3 minutes. Add in onion powder, potatoes, bell pepper, stock, salt, and pepper. Seal the lid, select Manual, and cook for 15 minutes.
When done, perform a quick pressure release. Mix in Dijon mustard, hot sauce, mozzarella cheese, and milk until thoroughly heated. Top with bacon and serve.

Curried Pumpkin Soup

Serving Size: 4 | **Total Time:** 20 minutes
1 tsp chili powder
2 tbsp Pumpkin seeds
2 tbsp Olive oil
1 onion, chopped
1 Carrot, chopped
2 garlic cloves, minced
2 tsp Curry powder
4 cups vegetable broth

Warm olive oil in your Instant Pot on Sauté. Place the onion and garlic and cook for 3 minutes until tender. Add in vegetable broth, pumpkin seeds, chili powder, curry powder, and carrots. Seal the lid, select Manual, and cook for 10 minutes on High. When done, allow a natural release for 10 minutes. Serve.

Nutmeg Broccoli Soup with Cheddar

Serving Size: 4 | **Total Time:** 25 minutes
2 garlic cloves, minced
1 tbsp butter
½ lb broccoli florets
¼ tsp nutmeg
½ tsp garlic powder
1 cup vegetable broth
¼ cup grated cheddar
¼ cup chopped onion
¼ tsp paprika
Salt and pepper to taste

Melt butter in your Instant Pot on Sauté. Place the onion and garlic and cook until wilted and aromatic. Put in vegetable broth, broccoli, black pepper, paprika, salt, nutmeg, and garlic powder. Seal the lid, select Manual, and cook for 5 minutes on High pressure.

When done, allow a natural release for 10 minutes and unlock the lid. Using an immersion blender, pulse the soup until smooth. Divide between bowls and serve.

Kielbasa Sausage Soup

Serving Size: 4 | **Total Time:** 60 minutes
12 oz Kielbasa smoked sausage, sliced
2 tbsp olive oil
1 yellow onion, chopped
1 celery stalk, chopped
1 carrot, chopped
2 tbsp parsley, chopped
3 garlic cloves, pressed
1 ripe tomato, pureed
1 cup pinto beans, soaked
Salt and pepper to taste
6 oz baby kale

Warm the olive oil in your Instant Pot on Sauté. Add in onion, garlic, celery, and carrot and cook for 4 minutes. Stir in smoked sausage for another 2 minutes and pour in pinto beans, salt, pepper, and 4 cups of water. Seal the lid, select Manual, and cook for 30 minutes on High.

When over, allow a natural release for 10 minutes and unlock the lid. Stir in baby kale and tomato and let it sit covered for 5 minutes. Serve sprinkled with parsley.

Chorizo & Bean Soup

Serving Size: 6 | **Total Time:** 55 minutes
2 tbsp olive oil
¾ lb chorizo sausage, sliced
1 cup white beans, soaked
1 sweet pepper, sliced
14 oz can diced tomatoes
1 clove garlic, minced
1 onion, diced
½ tsp dried oregano
1 tsp chili powder
6 cups chicken broth

Warm the olive oil in your Instant Pot on Sauté. Add in onion, garlic, chorizo, sweet pepper, chili powder, and oregano and cook for 4-5 minutes. Stir in chicken broth, tomatoes, and white bean and seal the lid. Select Manual and cook for 30 minutes. Once ready, perform a quick pressure release and let sit for 10 minutes. Serve warm.

Beet & Potato Soup

Serving Size: 4 | **Total Time:** 45 minutes
2 tbsp olive oil
2 garlic cloves, minced
1 carrot, chopped
3 potatoes, chopped
¾ lb beets, peeled, chopped
4 cups vegetable broth
1 onion, chopped
Salt and pepper to taste
¼ cup basil leaves, chopped

Heat the olive oil in your Instant Pot on Sauté. Place the onion, carrot, and garlic paste and cook for 3 minutes. Stir in vegetable broth, beets, and potatoes and seal the lid. Select Manual and cook for 25 minutes.

Once ready, allow a natural release for 10 minutes, then perform a quick pressure release and unlock the lid. Blend the soup using an immersion blender and adjust the seasoning. Serve topped with basil.

Vegan Tomato Soup

Serving Size: 4 | **Total Time:** 20 minutes
2 tbsp olive oil
2 (14-oz) cans tomatoes
1 tsp caraway seeds
1 cup vegetable broth
½ tsp thyme
1 large onion, diced
2 garlic cloves, sliced
Salt and pepper to taste
¾ cup almond milk

Warm the olive oil in your Instant Pot on Sauté. Add in onion, and garlic and cook for 5-6 minutes until lightly golden. Stir in caraway seeds for 1 minute and pour in tomatoes, thyme, and vegetable broth. Seal the lid, select Manual, and cook for 8 minutes on High. Once ready, perform a quick pressure release and unlock the lid. Stir in almond milk and adjust the seasonings. Purée the soup with an immersion blender.

Asian Tomato Soup

Serving Size: 8 | **Total Time:** 20 minutes
2 tbsp coconut oil
1 onion, diced
1 tbsp garlic-ginger puree
3 lb tomatoes, quartered
½ tsp ground cumin
1 tsp red pepper flakes
Pink salt to taste
3 ½ cups vegetable broth
1 cup coconut cream
2 tbsp cilantro, chopped

Heat the coconut oil in your Instant Pot on Sauté. Place the onion and garlic-ginger paste and cook for 3 minutes. Stir in tomatoes and cumin and Sauté for 3 more minutes.
Pour in the broth and salt and seal the lid. Select Manual and cook for 6 minutes. When done, perform a quick pressure release. Mix in coconut cream. Puree the soup with a stick blender until smooth. Serve topped with red pepper flakes and cilantro.

Tangy Pumpkin Soup

Serving Size: 4 | **Total Time:** 30 minutes
2 tbsp sesame oil
1 yellow onion, chopped
2 garlic cloves, minced
½ tbsp ginger, grated
1 lb pumpkin, cubed
Salt to taste
1 tbsp curry powder
1 tsp cayenne pepper
½ cup coconut milk
2 tbsp cilantro, chopped

Warm the sesame oil in your Instant Pot on Sauté. Add in onion and cook for 5 minutes. Stir in garlic and ginger and Sauté for 1 more minute. Stir in pumpkin, cayenne pepper, salt, and curry powder and 4 cups of water and seal the lid. Select Manual and cook for 20 minutes. Once ready, perform a quick pressure release and unlock the lid. Blend the soup using a stick blender and mix in coconut milk. Garnish with cilantro and serve.

Chicken Soup with Vegetables

Serving Size: 4 | **Total Time:** 35 minutes
½ lb chicken breasts, cubed
1 beet, chopped
1 carrot, diced
½ celery, diced
1 onion, chopped
1 cup mushrooms, sliced
5 cups chicken stock
2 garlic cloves, chopped
1 tsp thyme
1 tsp rosemary
2 bay leaves
2 tbsp olive oil
Salt and pepper to taste

Warm olive oil in your Instant Pot on Sauté. Place the carrots, beet, and onion and cook for 2-3 minutes. Add in garlic, celery, and mushrooms and cook for 3 minutes. Put in chicken breasts, chicken stock, thyme, rosemary, bay leaves, salt, and black pepper. Seal the lid, select Soup, and cook on Low pressure for 20 minutes. When done, perform a quick pressure release. Serve warm.

Celery & Oxtail Soup

Serving Size: 4 | **Total Time:** 30 minutes
4 cups vegetable broth
2 tbsp chopped' carrots
1 lb oxtails
1 tbsp chopped' celeries
¼ tsp nutmeg
Salt and pepper to taste

Place the oxtails, nutmeg, salt, and black pepper in your Instant Pot. Pour in vegetable broth and seal the lid. Select Pressure Cook and cook for 20 minutes on High.
When done, perform a quick pressure release and unlock the lid. Stir in chopped carrots and celeries and cook for 3 minutes until the carrots are tender on Sauté. Divide between bowls and serve.

Creamy Mushroom Soup with Chicken

Serving Size: 2 | **Total Time:** 20 minutes
1 celery stalk, chopped
¼ cup diced mushrooms
½ lb chicken breasts
¼ cup heavy cream
½ cup water
2 tbsp diced carrots
1 tsp minced' garlic
Salt and pepper to taste

Slice the chicken breast into small cubes and remove them to your Instant Pot. Add in celery, minced garlic, salt, black pepper, and water. Seal the lid, select Pressure Cook, and cook for 10 minutes on High pressure.
When done, perform a quick pressure release and unlock the lid. Stir in heavy cream, mushrooms, and carrots. Seal the lid, select Manual, and cook for 3 minutes on High pressure. When done, perform a quick pressure release and unlock the lid. Divide between bowls and serve.

Cheesy Cauliflower Soup

Serving Size: 4 | **Total Time:** 20 minutes
2 tbsp olive oil
1 carrot, chopped
¼ cup cream cheese
1 ½ cups cauliflower florets
1 cup vegetable broth
2 tsp minced garlic
¼ cup chopped onion
Salt and pepper to taste

Warm the olive oil in your Instant Pot on Sauté. Place the cauliflower florets, carrot, minced garlic, chopped onion, salt, and pepper and cook for 5 minutes until tender. pour in the vegetable broth. Seal the lid, select Manual, and cook for 6 minutes on High pressure.
When done, perform a quick pressure release and unlock the lid. Mix in cream cheese until well combined. Blend the soup until smooth with an immersion blender. Divide between bowls and serve.

Spicy Ground Beef Soup

Serving Size: 4 | **Total Time:** 30 minutes
2 tbsp butter
3 oz cream cheese
7-oz ground beef
4 cups beef broth
2 garlic cloves, minced
1 tsp chili powder
1 tsp ground cumin
½ cup heavy cream

Salt and pepper to taste

Melt butter in your Instant Pot on Sauté. Place the ground beef and cook for 5-7 minutes and strain excess fat. Add in cream cheese, garlic, chili powder, ground cumin, heavy cream, salt, black pepper, and beef broth.

Seal the lid, select Pressure Cook, and cook for 5 minutes on High pressure. When done, allow a natural release for 10 minutes and unlock the lid. Serve warm.

Hot Spinach Soup

Serving Size: 4 | **Total Time:** 50 minutes
1 onion, chopped
2 Garlic cloves, minced
1 cup baby Spinach
2 cups Vegetable broth
½ cup Almond Milk
½ tbsp Chili flakes
¼ cup sour cream
2 tbsp Olive oil

Place the garlic, onion, spinach, vegetable broth, almond milk, chili flakes, and olive oil in your Instant Pot. Seal the lid, select Manual, and cook for 25 minutes on High.

When done, allow a natural release for 10 minutes and unlock the lid. Using an immersion blender, blend until creamy and put it back to the pot and cook for 6 minutes on Sauté. Serve topped with sour cream.

Asian-Style Chicken Soup

Serving Size: 4 | **Total Time:** 35 minutes
1 tsp soy sauce
4 cups chicken broth
½ lb chicken breasts, cubed
1 tsp cinnamon
1 tsp cilantro, chopped
1 tbsp olive oil
1 tbsp fish sauce
1 tsp ginger
1 tbsp sugar
1 chopped onion
2 tsp minced garlic
Salt and pepper to taste

Place the olive oil, garlic, and onion in your Instant Pot and cook for 2-3 minutes until soft on Sauté. Stir in chopped chicken, ginger, cilantro, sugar, cinnamon, fish sauce, soy sauce, salt, pepper, and chicken broth. Seal the lid, select Manual, and cook for 15 minutes on High. When done, allow a natural release for 10 minutes. Serve.

Egg & Chicken Soup

Serving Size: 4 | **Total Time:** 35 minutes
1 carrot, chopped
2 Garlic cloves, minced
¼ lb chicken breasts, cubed
1 onion, chopped
2 Eggs, whisked
2 cups Chicken broth
2 cups Water
3 tbsp Almond flour

Salt and pepper to taste
2 tbsp Olive oil

Warm olive oil in your Instant Pot on Sauté. Place the carrot, garlic, and onion and cook for 1 minute. Add in chicken pieces and cook for 10 minutes. Put in salt, black pepper, and chicken broth and simmer for 15 minutes.

Meanwhile, combine water and almond flour in a bowl and pour it slowly into the pot and cook for 2 minutes. Add in eggs and cook for 2 more minutes. Divide between bowls and serve.

Cheesy Chicken Soup

Serving Size: 4 | **Total Time:** 30 minutes
2 garlic cloves, minced
1 green bell pepper, sliced
1 red bell pepper, sliced
½ cup chicken breast strips
1 tbsp canola oil
1 tsp dried oregano
1 onion, sliced
4 oz Provolone cheese, grated
4 cups Chicken broth
Salt and pepper to taste

Place the canola oil and chicken fillets in your Instant Pot and cook on Sauté. Mix in oregano, salt, black pepper, red bell pepper, green bell pepper, garlic, and onion and cook for 10 minutes. Pour in chicken broth and seal the lid. Select Manual and cook for 4 minutes on High pressure. When done, allow a natural release for 10 minutes and unlock the lid. Serve topped with cheese.

Brussel Sprout & Pork Soup

Serving Size: 4 | **Total Time:** 40 minutes
½ lb Brussels sprouts, shredded
1 cup carrot, shredded
½ tsp ground ginger
1 small onion, chopped
½ lb ground pork
4 cups chicken broth
1 tbsp soy sauce
2 tbsp olive oil
Salt and pepper to taste

Place the olive oil and ground pork in your Instant Pot and cook for 4-5 minutes until browned on Sauté. Stir in carrot, Brussels sprouts, ginger, onion, chicken broth, soy sauce, salt, and black pepper. Seal the lid, select Manual, and cook for 25 minutes on High pressure. When done, perform a quick pressure release. Serve and enjoy!

Tamarind Beef Soup

Serving Size: 2 | **Total Time:** 40 minutes
1 carrot, sliced
¼ cup green tomatoes
1 lb beef tenderloin
1 cup water
2 tsp tamarind
1 tsp soy sauce
2 tsp sliced garlic
2 tsp sliced shallots
2 tsp red chili flakes

½ tsp salt

Slice the beef tenderloin into medium pieces and place them in your Instant Pot. Add in garlic, carrot, shallots, red chili flakes, salt, green tomatoes, tamarind, soy sauce, and water. Seal the lid, select Manual, and cook for 22 minutes on High. When done, allow a natural release for 10 minutes and unlock the lid. Serve warm.

Cashew & Tomato Soup

Serving Size: 4 | Total Time: 15 minutes
½ ground cumin
15 oz tomato puree
15 oz diced tomatoes
4 tbsp cashew
2 cups vegetable stock
½ tbsp dried basil
1 ½ tbsp quick oats
2 minced garlic cloves
Salt and pepper to taste

Place the tomato puree, diced tomatoes, cashew, vegetable stock, dried basil, oats, cumin, and garlic in your Instant Pot. Seal the lid, select Manual, and cook for 4 minutes on High pressure. When done, allow a natural release. Using an immersion blender, pulse the soup until smooth. Sprinkle with salt and pepper before serving.

Pecorino Mushroom Soup

Serving Size: 4 | Total Time: 30 minutes
2 cups Pecorino, grated
3 cups Mushrooms, chopped
2 tbsp Butter
1 onion, chopped
2 Garlic cloves, minced
2 cups Thyme, chopped
2 tbsp Almond flour
3 cups Chicken stock

Place the butter and onion in your Instant Pot and cook for 2 minutes on Sauté. Mix in mushrooms, garlic cloves, thyme, chicken stock, and almond flour. Seal the lid, select Manual, and cook for 10 minutes on High. When done, allow a natural release for 10 minutes. Serve garnished with grated Pecorino cheese.

Creamy Chicken & Zucchini Soup

Serving Size: 4 | Total Time: 25 minutes
1 lb Zucchini, chopped
1 lb Chicken breasts, cubed
2 tbsp Butter
1 onion, chopped
2 Garlic cloves, minced
4 cups Chicken broth
2 tbsp Nutmeg powder
½ cup Half and Half

Melt butter in your Instant Pot on Sauté. Mix the zucchini, chicken broth, garlic, onion, nutmeg powder, chicken cubes, and half and half. Seal the lid, select Manual, and cook for 10 minutes on High pressure. When done, allow a natural release for 10 minutes and unlock the lid. Serve right away.

Quick Chicken Soup

Serving Size: 4 | Total Time: 25 minutes
½ cup mushrooms, chopped
½ lb Chicken Breasts
2 tbsp Olive oil
1 large Carrot, chopped
1 Celery Stalk, chopped
1 onion, chopped
2 garlic cloves, minced
1 Green Chili Pepper, sliced
Salt and pepper to taste
2 cups Chicken Broth

Warm olive oil in your Instant Pot on Sauté. Place the carrot, celery, onion, garlic, salt, pepper, and green chili pepper and cook for 3 minutes. Mix in broth, chicken breasts, mushrooms, and 2 cups of water. Seal the lid, select Soup, and cook for 10 minutes on High. Do a quick pressure release. Remove the chicken, shred it, and back it to the pot. Cook for 3 minutes on Sauté and serve.

Chicken & Noodle Soup

Serving Size: 2 | Total Time: 35 minutes
8 oz egg noodles
2 Carrots, sliced
1 tbsp Olive Oil
1 small onion, chopped
2 Celery Ribs, diced
1 Banana Pepper, minced
1 garlic clove, minced
1 small Bay Leaf
2 Chicken Breasts
3 cups Chicken Broth

Warm olive oil in your Instant Pot on Sauté. Place the onion, celery, carrots, garlic, and banana pepper and cook for 4 minutes. Add in bay leaf, chicken, and broth. Seal the lid, select Manual, and cook for 15 minutes on High. When done, perform a quick pressure release. Transfer the chicken onto a cutting board and shred it. Put the chicken back in the pot with the egg noodles and cook for 7-8 minutes on Sauté. Serve.

Simple Onion Cheese Soup

Serving Size: 4 | Total Time: 10 minutes
1 onion, chopped
2 tbsp all-purpose flour
4 cups vegetable broth
2 cups Monterey Jack, grated
2 cups milk
2 tbsp butter

Melt butter on Sauté and cook the onion and flour for 2 minutes. Gradually stir in the broth and milk. Seal the lid. Cook on High Pressure for 5 minutes. Do a quick pressure release. Stir in cheese until melted. Serve.

STEWS

Curried Sweet Potato Stew
Serving Size: 4 | **Total Time**: 15 minutes
1 cup almond milk
2 diced sweet potatoes
14 oz can diced tomatoes
½ diced bell pepper
½ diced zucchini
1 minced garlic clove
1 lime juice
½ tbsp minced ginger
1 diced onion
1 tbsp red curry paste
½ tsp turmeric
1 tsp curry powder
1 tbsp olive oil
½ tsp sea salt

Warm olive oil in your Instant Pot on Sauté. Place the onion and cook until translucent. Add in garlic and ginger and cook for 1 minute. Pour in milk, sweet potatoes, tomatoes, bell pepper, zucchini, lime juice, curry paste, turmeric, curry powder, and salt, seal the lid, select Manual, and cook for 5 minutes on High pressure. When done, perform a quick pressure release and unlock the lid. Mix well before serving.

Vegetable & Ground Pork Stew
Serving Size: 6 | **Total Time**: 30 minutes
1 ¼ lb ground pork
1 cup cabbage, shredded
½ cup chopped celery
2 red onions, chopped
2 large tomatoes, chopped
1 carrot, shredded
2 cups water
1 red bell pepper, chopped
1 green bell pepper, diced
1 yellow bell pepper, diced
¼ tsp cumin
1 tsp red pepper flakes
Salt and pepper to taste
2 tbsp cilantro, chopped

Coat with cooking spray. Add the pork and cook until browned on Sauté, 6 minutes. Stir in cabbage, celery, onions, tomatoes, carrot, water, bell peppers, cumin, red pepper flakes, salt, and black pepper. Seal the lid and set to Pressure Cook for 15 minutes. Do a quick pressure release. Sprinkle with cilantro and serve.

German-Style Sauerkraut & Pork Stew
Serving Size: 4 | **Total Time**: 30 minutes
1 lb ground pork
4 cups sauerkraut, shredded
1 cup tomato puree
1 cup vegetable stock
1 red onion, chopped
2 garlic cloves, minced
2 bay leaves
Salt and pepper to taste

Add onion, garlic, and cook until soft and fragrant, on Sauté. Add the pork and cook it until lightly browned. Stir in sauerkraut, tomato puree, stock, and bay leaves and season with salt and black pepper. Seal the lid and cook for 20 minutes on Meat/Stew on High. When done, release the pressure quickly. Discard the bay leaves.

Chicken Stew with Bacon & Cheese
Serving Size: 4 | **Total Time**: 25 minutes
1 ½ cups mozzarella cheese
10 oz Cream Cheese
10 Bacon Slices, chopped
1 lb Chicken Breasts
1 packet ranch Seasoning
½ cup Water

Place the cream cheese, chicken, Ranch seasoning, and water in your Instant Pot. Seal the lid, select Manual, and cook for 15 minutes on High. When done, perform a quick pressure release. Remove the chicken and shred it. Put the chicken back in the pot with bacon and mozzarella and cook on Sauté until the cheese melts.

Classic Goulash
Serving Size: 4 | **Total Time**: 15 minutes
1 celery stalk, chopped
1 cup diced tomatoes
½ lb cubed beef
3 oz egg noodles
1 chopped onion
1 tbsp olive oil
4 cup chicken broth
1 tbsp Hungarian paprika
1 tsp minced garlic
Salt and pepper to taste

Warm olive oil in your Instant Pot on Sauté. Place the garlic, celery, onion, and beef and cook until the meat browns. Stir in paprika, chicken broth, egg noodles, tomatoes, pepper, and salt. Seal the lid, select Manual, and cook for 5 minutes on High pressure. When done, perform a quick pressure release. Serve warm.

Kale, Potato & Beef Stew
Serving Size: 2 | **Total Time**: 55 minutes
1 green bell pepper, diced
2 potatoes, chopped
½ lb beef stew meat, cubed
1 tbsp hot sauce
1 small onion, chopped
1 celery stalk, chopped
1 tbsp olive oil
½ tsp garlic powder
2 carrots, chopped
1 cup kale, chopped
2 cups beef broth
Salt and pepper to taste

Warm olive oil in your Instant Pot on Sauté Place the meat and cook for 4-5 minutes until browned. Stir in potatoes, hot sauce, onion, celery, garlic powder, bell pepper, carrots, kale leaves, beef broth, salt, and black pepper. Seal the lid, select Meat/Stew, and cook for 40 minutes. When done, perform a quick pressure release.

Pea & Beef Stew

Serving Size: 6 | **Total Time:** 35 minutes
1 cup mixed wild mushrooms
1 cup green peas
1 cup diced potatoes
1 lb cubed beef
3 sliced carrots
1 tsp red pepper flakes
2 sliced garlic cloves
½ cup dry red wine
2 tbsp butter
1 diced onion
2 cups beef broth
14 oz can diced tomatoes

Melt the butter in your Instant Pot on Sauté. Place the onion and cook for 3 minutes until soft. Add in beef cubes and cook for 5-7 minutes until the meat browns. Add in garlic and cook for 1 minute until fragrant. Pour in red wine and scrape any brown bits from the bottom.
Put in potatoes, carrots, red pepper flakes, mushrooms, beef broth, diced tomatoes, and green peas. Seal the lid, select Manual, and cook for 15 minutes on High pressure. When done, perform a quick pressure release and unlock the lid. Serve immediately.

Cauliflower Beef Stew

Serving Size: 4 | **Total Time:** 60 minutes
½ head cauliflower, chopped
1 lb Beef stew meat
1 large quartered Onion
½ cup Beef or Bone broth
¼ cup Coconut aminos
2 tbsp Fish sauce
2 Garlic cloves, minced
1 tsp ground Ginger
½ tsp Salt
1 tbsp Coconut oil

Place the beef meat, onion, beef broth, coconut aminos, fish sauce, garlic, ginger, salt, and coconut oil in your Instant Pot. Seal the lid, select Manual, and cook for 35 minutes on High pressure. When done, perform a quick pressure release and unlock the lid. Put in cauliflower and simmer covered for 15 minutes on Sauté. Serve.

Rosemary Pork Belly Stew

Serving Size: 6 | **Total Time:** 50 minutes
3 lb sirloin pork roast
1 tbsp honey
1 tsp chili powder
1 tbsp rosemary
1 tbsp olive oil
Salt and pepper to taste

Combine chili powder, rosemary, salt, and pepper in a bowl and rub them onto the pork. Heat oil on Sauté and sear the pork on all sides. Stir in honey and seal the lid. Cook for 30 minutes on Meat/Stew. Do a natural pressure release for 10 minutes. Carefully unlock the lid.

Seafood Stew with Sausage

Serving Size: 4 | **Total Time:** 35 minutes
1 lb Andouille Sausages, sliced
1 lb halibut fillets, skinless and cut into 1-inch pieces
2 lb Mussels, debearded and scrubbed
1 lb Shrimp, peeled and deveined
1 tsp turmeric
2 (16 oz) cans Clam Juice
1 cup White Wine
Salt and pepper to taste
4 tbsp Olive oil
4 garlic cloves, minced
2 Fennel Bulb, chopped
4 Leeks, sliced
2 Bay Leaves
28 oz can Diced Tomatoes
2 tbsp chopped Parsley

Warm olive oil in your Instant Pot on Sauté. Place sausage, fennel, and leeks and cook for 5 minutes. Stir in garlic, turmeric, and bay leaves and cook for 30 seconds. Pour in white wine and cook for 2 minutes. Add in tomatoes, clam juice, and 3 cups of water; stir. Put in mussels, fish, and shrimp and slightly cover them with the sauce.
Seal the lid, select Meat/Stew, and cook for 15 minutes on High pressure. When done, perform a quick pressure release and unlock the lid. Discard bay leaves and sprinkle with parsley, salt, and black pepper. Serve right away.

Mushroom & Spinach Chicken Stew

Serving Size: 4 | **Total Time:** 40 minutes
1 ¼ lb White Button Mushrooms, halved
1 celery stalk, chopped
3 tbsp Olive oil
4 Chicken Breasts, diced
1 Onion, sliced
5 garlic cloves, minced
Salt and pepper to taste
1 ¼ tsp Arrowroot Starch
½ cup spinach, chopped
1 bay leaf
1 ½ cup Chicken Stock
1 tsp Dijon Mustard
1 ½ cup Sour Cream
3 tbsp Chopped Parsley

Warm olive oil in your Instant Pot on Sauté. Place the onion and cook for 3 minutes. Stir in mushrooms, chicken, celery, garlic, bay leaf, salt, black pepper, Dijon mustard, and chicken broth. Seal the lid, select Meat/Stew, and cook for 15 minutes on High. When done, allow a natural release for 10 minutes and unlock the lid.
Discard bay leaf. In a bowl, combine some cooking liquid with arrowroot starch until any lump left. Pour it into the pot and stir until the sauce thickens. Add in sour cream and spinach and let sit for 4 minutes. Divide between bowls and sprinkle with parsley. Serve with squash mash.

Green Pork Chili

Serving Size: 4 | **Total Time:** 90 minutes
- 1 lb Tomatillos, husks removed
- 1 tsp ground nutmeg
- 2 Green Chilies
- 1 onion, sliced
- 1 ½ lb Pork Roast, cubed
- 2 tbsp Olive oil, divided into
- 1 bulb Garlic, tail sliced off
- ½ cup Chicken Broth
- 1 Green Bell pepper, diced
- Salt and pepper to taste
- ½ tsp Cumin Powder
- 1 tsp dried Oregano
- 1 Bay Leaf
- 2 tbsp Cilantro, chopped

Preheat oven to 360°F. Place the garlic bulb, green bell peppers, onion, green chilies, and tomatillos on a baking tray and sprinkle with olive oil. Place the tray in the oven and roast for 25 minutes. Let cool the garlic before peeling. Place it in a blender with bell peppers, tomatillos, onion, and green chilies and pulse until slightly chunky.

Warm olive oil in your Instant Pot on Sauté. Sprinkle pork with salt and pepper and place it in the pot. Cook for 5 minutes until brown. Stir in oregano, nutmeg, cumin, bay leaf, green sauce, and broth. Seal the lid, select Manual, and cook for 35 minutes on High. When done, let sit for 10 minutes and allow a natural release for 5 minutes Stir in salt and pepper. Top with cilantro. Serve immediately.

Cheesy Turkey Stew

Serving Size: 4 | **Total Time:** 20 minutes
- 1 tbsp soy Sauce
- 1 lb Turkey Breast
- 1 ½ cups Chicken Broth
- 1 cup Sour Cream
- ¼ cup grated Parmesan
- 1 tsp Dijon Mustard
- ¼ tsp Garlic Powder
- Salt and pepper to taste

Place the turkey breast and chicken broth in your Instant Pot. Seal the lid, select Manual, and cook for 10 minutes on High pressure. When done, perform a quick pressure release. Transfer the turkey onto a cutting board and cut it into cubes. Discard the broth and wipe the pot out.

Mix in soy sauce, sour cream, Parmesan cheese, Dijon mustard, garlic powder, salt, black pepper, and cubed chicken and cook for 2 minutes on Sauté. Serve.

Chicken Stew with Potatoes & Broccoli

Serving Size: 4 | **Total Time:** 25 minutes
- 1 lb potatoes, chopped
- 2 tbsp Butter
- 3 Chicken Breasts, cubed
- 2 Onions, chopped
- 2 cups Chicken Broth
- Salt and pepper to taste
- ¼ tsp Red Chili Flakes
- 2 tbsp Dried Parsley
- 10 oz broccoli florets
- 1 cup cheddar cheese, grated

Sprinkle chicken breast with salt and pepper. Melt butter in your Instant Pot on Sauté. Place the chicken and cook for 8 minutes on both sides until browns. Add in onion and cook for 5 minutes, stirring often. Put chicken broth, black pepper, salt, red pepper flakes, potatoes, chicken, and parsley and seal the lid. Select Manual and cook for 4 minutes on High pressure.

When done, perform a quick pressure release and unlock the lid. Min in broccoli and cook until tender on Sauté. Serve right away topped with cheddar cheese.

Taco-Style Chicken Stew

Serving Size: 4 | **Total Time:** 25 minutes
- 2 tbsp butter
- 1 lb Chicken Breasts
- 1 Carrot, chopped
- 1 Celery stalk, chopped
- 1 Onion, chopped
- 3 garlic cloves, minced
- 3 tbsp Taco Seasoning
- Salt and pepper to taste
- 1 ½ cups Diced Tomatoes
- 1 lb cubed Butternut Squash
- 2 cups Chicken Broth
- 1 tsp Lime Juice
- 4 Lime Wedges
- 2 tbsp Chopped Cilantro

Melt butter in your Instant Pot on Sauté. Place the celery, onion, carrots, garlic, taco seasoning, black pepper, and salt and cook for 5 minutes, stirring often. Mix in chicken breast, tomatoes, butternut squash, broth, and lime juice. Seal the lid, select Soup and cook for 10 minutes.

When done, perform a quick pressure release. Transfer the chicken onto a cutting board and shred it. Put the chicken back in the pot and divide between bowls. Serve topped with cilantro and lime wedges.

One-Pot Sausages with Peppers & Onions

Serving Size: 4 | **Total Time:** 20 minutes
- 2 red bell peppers, cut into strips
- 4 pork sausages
- 1 sweet onion, sliced
- 1 tbsp olive oil
- ½ cup beef broth
- ¼ cup white wine
- 1 tsp garlic, minced
- Salt and pepper to taste

On Sauté, add the sausages and brown them for a few minutes. Remove to a plate and discard the liquid. Press Cancel. Wipe clean the cooker and heat the oil on Sauté. Stir in onion and bell peppers. Stir-fry them for 5 minutes until soft. Add garlic and cook for a minute. Add the sausages and pour in broth and wine. Season with salt and pepper. Seal the lid and cook for 5 minutes on High pressure. Once done, do a quick pressure release. Serve.

Cheesy Duck & Spinach Stew

Serving Size: 4 | **Total Time:** 25 minutes

1 onion, chopped
2 cups Spinach
1 lb Duck Breasts
¼ cup grated Parmesan
1 cup Heavy Cream
8 oz Cream Cheese
¼ cup Chicken Broth
1 tbsp Olive oil
1 tsp minced Garlic
Salt and pepper to taste

Warm olive oil in your Instant Pot on Sauté. Place the garlic and onion and cook for 1 minute. Add in duck breasts and cook for 6-8 minutes on both sides until golden brown. Remove to a plate and slice thinly. Mix the spinach, Parmesan cheese, heavy cream, cream cheese, broth, garlic, salt, and pepper in the pot and top with the sliced duck. Seal the lid, select Manual, and cook for 5 minutes on High pressure. When done, perform a quick pressure release and unlock the lid. Serve warm.

Sausage & Cannellini Bean Stew

Serving Size: 6 | Total Time: 35 minutes
1 cup cannellini beans
2 tbsp olive oil
1 lb Italian sausages, halved
1 celery stalk, chopped
1 carrot, chopped
1 onion, chopped
1 sprig fresh sage
1 sprig fresh rosemary
1 bay leaf
2 cups vegetable stock
3 cups fresh spinach
1 tsp salt

Warm oil on Sauté in your Instant pot. Add in sausage pieces and sear for 5 minutes until browned; set aside on a plate. To the pot, add celery, onion, bay leaf, sage, carrot, salt, and rosemary; cook for 3 minutes to soften slightly. Stir in vegetable stock and beans. Arrange seared sausage on top of the beans. Seal the lid, press Bean/Chili, and cook on High for 10 minutes. Release pressure naturally for 10 minutes. Get rid of bay leaf, rosemary, and sage. Mix in spinach and serve.

Tuscan Chicken Thighs

Serving Size: 4 | Total Time: 35 minutes
3 cups kale
6 Chicken Thighs
6 oz Cream Cheese
½ cup Sundried Tomatoes
2 tbsp Chicken Seasoning
½ cup Parmesan, grated
4 garlic cloves, minced
2 tsp Olive oil
2 cups Chicken Broth
1 ½ cups Milk
3 tbsp Heavy Cream
3 tsp Italian Seasoning
Salt and pepper to taste
2 tbsp chopped parsley

Sprinkle chicken thighs with salt, black pepper, and Italian seasoning. Warm olive oil in your Instant Pot on Sauté. Place the chicken and cook for 6 minutes. Add in milk, chicken stock, and chicken seasoning. Seal the lid, select Manual, and cook for 15 minutes on High.

When done, perform a quick pressure release. Remove the chicken to a plate. Put the tomatoes, heavy cream, cheese cream, Parmesan, kale, and garlic in the pot and cook for 5 minutes on Sauté. Put the chicken back to the pot and toss to combine. Serve topped with parsley.

Spicy Pumpkin Curry

Serving Size: 4 | Total Time: 30 minutes
4 spring onions, chopped into lengths
1 ½ lb pumpkin, chopped
4 cups chicken stock
½ cup buttermilk
2 tbsp curry powder
1 tsp ground turmeric
½ tsp ground cumin
¼ tsp cayenne pepper
2 bay leaves
Salt and pepper to taste
2 tbsp cilantro, chopped

In the pot, stir in pumpkin, buttermilk, curry, turmeric, spring onions, stock, cumin, and cayenne. Season with pepper and salt. Add bay leaves to the liquid and ensure they are submerged. Seal the lid, press Soup/Broth and cook for 10 minutes on High. Naturally release the pressure for 10 minutes. Discard bay leaves. Transfer the soup to a blender and process until smooth. Use a fine-mesh strainer to strain the soup. Garnish with cilantro before serving.

Vegetables with Veal & Pork

Serving Size: 4 | Total Time: 25 minutes
12 oz button mushrooms, sliced
1 lb veal cuts, cut into bite-sized pieces
1 lb pork tenderloin, cubed
3 carrots, chopped
2 tbsp butter, softened
2 tbsp olive oil
1 tbsp cayenne pepper
Salt and pepper to taste
3 oz celery root, chopped

Heat the olive oil and butter in the Instant Pot on Sauté. Add in veal, pork, mushrooms, carrots, salt, pepper, cayenne pepper, and celery, and cook for 5 minutes. Stir in 2 cups of water. Seal the lid and cook on High Pressure for 15 minutes. Do a quick release Open the lid and adjust the seasoning. Serve warm.

Aromatic Lamb Stew

Serving Size: 4 | Total Time: 60 minutes
1 ½ lb lamb stew meat, cubed
2 tbsp olive oil
3 garlic cloves, chopped
1 onion, chopped
3 cups mushrooms, sliced
1 celery stalk, chopped
1 carrot, chopped

28-oz can tomatoes, diced
3 cups chicken broth
½ cup pomegranate juice
½ tsp allspice
1 tsp ground cumin
½ tsp ground bay leaf
½ tsp curry powder
1 tsp ground coriander
Salt and pepper to taste

In a bowl, mix the allspice, ground cumin, ground bay leaf, curry powder, ground coriander, salt, and pepper and add in the lamb; toss to coat. Warm the olive oil in your Instant Pot on Sauté. Add in the lamb and cook for 5-6 minutes until browned. Add in garlic, onion, celery, carrot, and mushrooms and sauté for 5 minutes. Pour in tomatoes, pomegranate juice, and chicken broth.

Seal the lid, select Manual, and cook for 30 minutes on High pressure. When over, allow a natural release for 10 minutes, then perform a quick pressure release. Serve.

Flemish Beef Stew

Serving Size: 4 | **Total Time:** 60 minutes
1 ½ lb stew meat, cubed
2 tbsp olive oil
1 onion, chopped
2 garlic cloves, minced
1 cup beef broth
1 cup tomatoes, diced
1 tbsp yellow mustard
1 cup Belgian ale beer
2 sprigs thyme
Salt and pepper to taste

Warm the olive oil in your Instant Pot on Sauté. Place in meat and brown for 7 minutes on all sides, stirring occasionally. Add in onion and garlic and cook for another 3 minutes. Stir in beef broth, beer, mustard, bay leaf, thyme sprigs, salt, and pepper and seal the lid.

Select Manual and cook for 30 minutes on High pressure. When done, allow a natural release for 10 minutes, then a quick pressure release, and unlock the lid. Discard bay leaf and sprigs. Serve right away.

Grandma's Beef & Vegetable Stew

Serving Size: 6 | **Total Time:** 70 minutes
¼ cup flour
1 tsp paprika
2 lb beef chuck, cubed
2 tbsp olive oil
2 tbsp butter
1 onion, diced
3 garlic cloves, minced
1 cup dry red wine
2 cups beef stock
1 tbsp Italian seasoning
2 tsp Worcestershire sauce
4 cups potatoes, diced
2 celery stalks, chopped
3 cups carrots, chopped
3 tomatoes, chopped
2 bell peppers, chopped
Salt and pepper to taste
2 tbsp parsley, chopped

In a bowl, mix beef, flour, paprika, salt, and pepper. Toss the ingredients and ensure the beef is well-coated. Warm butter and oil on Sauté. Add in beef and cook for 8-10 minutes until browned. Set aside on a plate. To the same fat, add garlic, onion, celery, and bell peppers and cook for 4-5 minutes. Deglaze with wine, scrape the bottom to get rid of any browned beef bits.

Pour in beef stock, Worcestershire sauce, and Italian seasoning. Return beef to the pot; add carrots, tomatoes, and potatoes. Seal the lid, press Meat/Stew, and cook on High Pressure for 35 minutes. Release pressure naturally for 10 minutes. Taste and adjust the seasonings as necessary. Serve on plates and scatter over the parsley.

Chili Goose Stew

Serving Size: 6 | **Total Time:** 20 minutes
1 onion, chopped
1 cup Chicken Broth
1 lb Goose Breasts
3 tbsp Tamari Sauce
1 tbsp Sweetener
3 tbsp Chili Sauce
Salt and pepper to taste
½ cup water

Sprinkle goose breasts with salt and pepper. Place them in your Instant Pot. Mix the chicken broth, tamari sauce, sweetener, onion, chili sauce, salt. pepper, and water in a bowl and pour it over the goose. Seal the lid, select Manual, and cook for 15 minutes on High. Perform a quick pressure release. Serve topped with sauce.

Delicious Pork & Garbanzo Bean Chili

Serving Size: 10 | **Total Time:** 60 minutes
1 lb garbanzo beans, soaked overnight
1 tbsp olive oil
2 onions, finely chopped
2 ½ lb ground pork
1 jalapeño pepper, minced
6 garlic cloves, minced
¼ cup chili powder
2 tbsp ground cumin
Salt to taste
1 tsp smoked paprika
1 tsp dried oregano
1 tsp garlic powder
¼ tsp cayenne pepper
2 ½ cups beef broth
1 tbsp tomato puree

Add the beans and pour in cold water to cover 1 inch. Seal the lid and cook for 20 minutes on High Pressure. Release the pressure quickly. Drain beans and rinse with cold water. Set aside. Wipe clean the pot and set to Sauté. Warm olive oil, add the onions and sauté for 3 minutes until soft. Add jalapeño, pork, and garlic,

and stir-fry until it is cooked through, about 5 minutes.
Stir in chili powder, salt, garlic powder, paprika, cumin, oregano, and cayenne, and cook until soft, about 30 seconds. Pour in broth, beans, and tomato puree. Seal the lid and cook for 20 minutes on High Pressure. Release the pressure naturally. Open the lid, press Sauté, and cook as you stir until desired consistency is attained. Spoon chili into bowls and serve.

Red Wine Pork Stew with Tomatoes

Serving Size: 4 | **Total Time:** 45 minutes
1 lb pork tenderloin, cubed
1 onion, peeled, chopped
2 tbsp vegetable oil
4 tomatoes, peeled, diced
½ tbsp red wine
½ tbsp beef broth
A handful of fresh basil
Salt and pepper to taste

Heat oil and stir-fry the onion until translucent. Add the meat, salt, pepper, wine, tomatoes, and basil. Cook for 10 minutes. Pour in broth, seal the lid and cook on High Pressure for 25 minutes. Do a quick release. Serve.

Creamy Mushroom Chicken Stew

Serving Size: 4 | **Total Time:** 20 minutes
1 lb Button Mushrooms, sliced
2 tbsp butter
¼ tsp Garlic Powder
4 Chicken Breasts
1 cup Chicken Broth
1 can heavy Cream
2 tbsp Arrowroot
Salt and pepper to taste

Place the chicken broth in your Instant Pot. Add in butter, garlic powder, salt, and black pepper. Sprinkle chicken breasts with salt and black pepper and place it in the pot. Add in mushrooms and seal the lid. Select Manual and cook for 10 minutes on High pressure.
When done, perform a quick pressure release and unlock the lid. Remove the chicken to a plate. In a bowl, combine 2 tbsp water with arrowroot and pour it into the pot. Cook for 2 minutes until the sauce thickens on Sauté. Stir in heavy cream and put the chicken back and cook for 1 more minute. Serve warm.

Herby Whole Chicken Stew

Serving Size: 6 | **Total Time:** 50 minutes
1 tsp cumin
1 tbsp Butter
1 Lemon, halved
1 (3-lb) Chicken
1 ½ cups Chicken Broth
1 Onion, quartered
1 ½ tsp Ranch Seasoning
½ tsp Lemon Pepper
1 Rosemary Sprig
2 Garlic Cloves

Combine the Ranch seasoning and lemon pepper in a bowl. Brush the chicken with the mixture. Melt butter in your Instant Pot on Sauté. Place the chicken and sear on all sides until golden brown. Set aside.
Fill the chicken with lemon, onion, garlic, cumin, and rosemary and place it in the pot with chicken broth. Seal the lid, select Poultry, and cook for 30 minutes on High pressure. When done, perform a quick pressure release. Let chill for 10 minutes before serving.

Rabbit & Veggie Stew

Serving Size: 6 | **Total Time:** 55 minutes
1 rabbit, cut into chunks
4 tbsp olive oil
1 cup dry red wine
1 onion, chopped
2 garlic cloves, minced
1 carrot, chopped
1 cup mushrooms, sliced
1 zucchini, chopped
2 celery stalks, chopped
2 tomatoes, diced
1 tbsp tomato paste
1 bunch rosemary sprigs
1 bay leaf
3 cups chicken broth
Salt and pepper to taste
2 tbsp parsley, chopped

Sprinkle rabbit with salt and pepper. Warm the olive oil in your Instant Pot on Sauté. Place in rabbit chunks and cook for 5 minutes on all sides; reserve. Stir onion, garlic, carrot, celery, mushrooms, and zucchini for 4-5 minutes until tender. Add in red wine tomatoes, tomato paste, bay leaf, and rosemary and cook for 5 minutes.
Mix in chicken broth, return the rabbit, and seal the lid. Select Manual and cook for 15 minutes on High pressure. Once done, allow a natural release for 10 minutes, then perform a quick pressure release, and unlock the lid. Adjust season to taste and discard rosemary sprigs and bay leaf. Serve topped with parsley.

Thyme Chicken Pot with Cheese

Serving Size: 4 | **Total Time:** 30 minutes
1 carrot, chopped
1 lb Chicken breasts, cubed
1 Onion, chopped
3 Garlic cloves, minced
2 oz Parmesan cheese, grated

Salt and pepper to taste
¼ tbsp Thyme
2 tbsp Butter

Melt butter in your Instant Pot on Sauté. Add in onion and garlic and sauté for 2-3 minutes until translucent. Put in chicken breast and cook until golden brown, 6-8 minutes. Stir in carrot, salt, black pepper, thyme, and 3 cups of water. Seal the lid, select Manual, and cook for 20 minutes on High pressure. When done, perform a quick pressure release. Serve sprinkled with Parmesan.

Coconut & Cauliflower Curry

Serving Size: 4 | **Total Time**: 25 minutes
2 tbsp butter
1 onion, chopped
3 cups chicken broth
1 cup coconut milk
2 tbsp red curry paste
½ tsp cardamom
½ tsp cumin
1 head cauliflower, chopped
1 tbsp cilantro, chopped

Melt the butter in your Instant Pot on Sauté. Place the onion and cook for 4-5 minutes. Add in chicken broth, cauliflower, coconut milk, curry paste, cardamon, and cumin and seal the lid. Select Manual and cook for 10 minutes on High pressure. When ready, perform a quick pressure release and unlock the lid. Blend the soup using an immersion blender. Serve topped cilantro.

Pancetta & Cheese Chicken Thighs

Serving Size: 4 | **Total Time**: 30 minutes
4 Bacon Slices, cooked and crumbled
1 cup Chicken Broth
4 Chicken Thighs
8 oz Cream Cheese
½ cup shredded Cheddar
¼ tsp Garlic Powder
¼ tsp Italian Seasoning
Salt and pepper to taste
2 tbsp Arrowroot

Combine the chicken broth, cream cheese, garlic powder, Italian seasoning, salt, and black pepper in your Instant Pot. Add in chicken thighs and seal the lid. Select Manual and cook for 18 minutes on High pressure. When done, perform a quick pressure release and unlock the lid. Transfer the chicken to a plate. Add the arrowroot to the pot and cook for 2 minutes until the sauce thickens on Sauté. Mix in pancetta and chicken and serve right away.

Habanero Chicken Stew

Serving Size: 4 | **Total Time**: 25 minutes
1 habanero pepper, diced
2 tbsp Butter
½ cup Hot Sauce
1 ½ cups Chicken Broth
½ Onion, diced
2 Garlic Cloves, minced
1 cup Heavy Cream
2 cups shredded Cheddar
2 Chicken Breasts
1 Celery Stalk, diced
½ cup chopped Cauliflower
Salt and pepper to taste

Place the butter, hot sauce, chicken broth, onion, garlic, habanero pepper, chicken breasts, celery, cauliflower, salt, and pepper in your Instant Pot. Seal the lid, select Manual, and cook for 15 minutes on High. When done, perform a quick pressure release and unlock the lid. Mix in heavy cream and cheddar cheese. Serve.

Chinese-Style Chicken Stew with Broccoli

Serving Size: 4 | **Total Time**: 20 minutes
1 tsp Chinese Five-Spice seasoning
1 cup Coconut Aminos
4 Chicken Breasts
1 cup Chicken Broth
3 tbsp Olive oil
½ tsp Fish Sauce
1 inch Ginger, grated
1 garlic clove, minced
Salt and pepper to taste
4 cups Broccoli Florets
1 tbsp Sesame seeds
2 tbsp Arrowroot Flour

Place the chicken breasts, chicken broth, olive oil, garlic, ginger, coconut aminos, Chinese five-spice seasoning, black pepper, and salt in your Instant Pot. Seal the lid, select Manual, and cook for 8 minutes on High pressure.

When done, perform a quick pressure release. Whisk the arrowroot with 2 tbsp water in a bowl and pour it into the pot. Add in broccoli and cook for 5 minutes on Sauté. Stir in fish sauce. Serve garnished with sesame seeds.

Hot Beef Chili

Serving Size: 4 | **Total Time**: 35 minutes
1 lb ground beef
2 tbsp olive oil
1 red bell pepper, chopped
1 yellow bell pepper, diced
1 onion, chopped
2 cups tomatoes, chopped
2 carrots, chopped
1 tsp chili powder
2 tbsp Worcestershire sauce
2 tsp paprika
2 tbsp parsley, chopped
Salt and pepper to taste

Select Sauté and add the olive oil and ground beef. Cook the beef until it browns while stirring occasionally for about 8 minutes. Top it with the onion, bell peppers, tomatoes, carrots, chili powder, Worcestershire sauce, paprika, salt, and pepper. Stir the ingredients well. Seal the lid, and select Soup/Broth on High Pressure and cook for 20 minutes. Once the timer has ended, do a quick pressure release. Sprinkle with parsley and serve.

Delicious Thai Vegetable Stew

Serving Size: 4 | **Total Time:** 20 minutes
1 tbsp coconut oil
1 cup onion, chopped
1 tbsp fresh ginger, minced
2 garlic cloves, minced
3 carrots, chopped
1 red bell pepper, chopped
1 orange bell pepper, diced
1 (14-oz) can coconut milk
1 cup bok choy, chopped
½ cup water
2 tbsp red curry paste
Salt and pepper to taste

Melt coconut oil on Sauté. Add in onion, garlic, and ginger and cook for 3 minutes until soft. Mix in orange bell pepper, red bell pepper and carrots and cook for 3 minutes until the peppers become soft and tender.
Add curry paste, bok choy, coconut milk, and water and stir well to obtain a consistent color of the sauce. Seal lid. Cook for 1 minute on High Pressure. Release the pressure quickly. Adjust the seasoning and serve hot.

Garbanzo Stew with Onions & Tomatoes

Serving Size: 5 | **Total Time:** 35 minutes
1 lb chickpeas, soaked
3 purple onions, chopped
2 tomatoes, chopped
2 oz fresh parsley, chopped
3 cups vegetable broth
1 tbsp paprika
2 tbsp olive oil

Warm olive oil on Sauté and stir-fry the onions for 3 minutes. Add chickpeas, tomatoes, broth, parsley, and paprika. Seal the lid and cook on the Meat/Stew for 30 minutes on High. Do a quick release. Serve warm.

VEGAN & VEGETARIAN

Mashed Potato Balls with Tomato Sauce

Serving Size: 4 | **Total Time**: 55 minutes
2 potatoes, peeled
1 onion, peeled, chopped
1 lb spinach, torn
¼ cup mozzarella, shredded
2 eggs, beaten
Salt and pepper to taste
1 tsp dried oregano
1 cup whole milk
¼ cup flour
¼ cup cornflour
2 garlic cloves
TOMATO SAUCE:
1 lb tomatoes, chopped
1 onion, chopped
2 garlic cloves, minced
3 tsp olive oil
¼ cup white wine
1 tsp sugar
1 tsp dried rosemary
½ tsp salt
1 tsp tomato paste

Place the potatoes in your Instant Pot and add enough water to cover. Seal the lid and cook on High Pressure for 13 minutes. Do a quick release. Add 1 cup of milk and mash with a potato masher. Whisk in eggs, add onion, spinach, mozzarella, salt, pepper, oregano, flour, cornflour, and garlic, and mix with hands. Shape into balls and set aside. Press Sauté, warm olive oil, and stir-fry onion and garlic until translucent.

Stir in tomatoes and cook until tender, about 10 minutes. Pour in the wine and add sugar, rosemary, and salt. Stir in 1 tsp of tomato paste and mix well. Cook for five more minutes. Place the potato balls in the cooker and seal with the lid. Cook on High Pressure for 5 minutes. Do a natural release for 10 minutes. Ser

Weekend Burrito Bowls

Serving Size: 4 | **Total Time**: 30 minutes
2 tbsp olive oil
1 onion, chopped
2 garlic cloves, minced
1 tbsp chili powder
2 tbsp ground cumin
2 tbsp paprika
Salt and pepper to taste
¼ tbsp cayenne pepper
1 cup quinoa, rinsed
14.5-oz can diced tomatoes
1 (14.5-oz) can black beans
1 ½ cups vegetable stock
1 cup frozen corn kernels
2 tbsp chopped cilantro
2 tbsp cheddar, grated
1 avocado, chopped

Warm oil on Sauté. Add in onion and stir-fry for 3-5 minutes until fragrant. Add garlic and Sauté for 2 more minutes until soft and golden brown. Add in chili powder, paprika, cayenne pepper, salt, cumin, and black pepper and cook for 1 minute until spices are soft. Pour quinoa into onion and spice mixture and stir to coat quinoa thoroughly in spices. Add tomatoes, black beans, vegetable stock, and corn; stir to combine.

Seal the lid and cook for 7 minutes on High Pressure. Release the pressure quickly. Open the lid and let sit for 6 minutes until flavors combine. Use a fork to fluff quinoa and season with pepper and salt. Stir in cilantro and divide into plates. Top with cheese and avocado slices and serve.

Plant-Based Indian Curry

Serving Size: 4 | **Total Time**: 20 minutes
1 tsp butter
1 onion, chopped
2 cloves garlic, minced
1 tsp ginger, grated
1 tsp ground cumin
1 tsp red chili powder
1 tsp salt
½ tsp ground turmeric
1 (15-oz) can chickpeas
1 tomato, diced
1/3 cup water
2 lb collard greens, chopped
½ tsp garam masala
1 tsp lemon juice

Melt butter on Sauté. Add in the onion, ginger, cumin, turmeric, red chili powder, garlic, and salt and cook for 30 seconds until crispy. Stir in tomato. Pour in ⅓ cup of water and chickpeas. Seal the lid and cook on High Pressure for 4 minutes. Release the pressure quickly. Press Sauté. Into the chickpea mixture, stir in lemon juice, collard greens, and garam masala until well coated. Cook for 2 to 3 minutes until collard greens wilt on Sauté. Serve over rice or naan.

Spicy Vegetable Pilaf

Serving Size: 4 | **Total Time**: 40 minutes
3 tbsp olive oil
1 tbsp ginger, minced
1 cup onion, chopped
1 cup green peas
1 cup carrots, chopped
1 cup mushrooms, chopped
1 cup broccoli, chopped
1 tbsp chili powder
½ tbsp ground cumin
1 tbsp garam masala
½ tbsp turmeric
1 cup basmati rice
2 cups vegetable broth
1 tbsp lemon juice
Salt and pepper to taste

Warm 1 tbsp olive oil on Sauté. Add in onion and ginger and cook for 3 minutes. Stir in broccoli, green peas, mushrooms, and carrots and cook for 5 minutes. Stir in the turmeric, chili powder, garam masala, salt, pepper, and cumin for 1 minute. Add ¼ cup broth and scrape the bottom to get rid of any browned bits. Add the remaining broth and rice. Seal the lid and cook for 20 minutes on High Pressure. Release the pressure quickly. Drizzle with lemon juice and serve.

Quick Farro with Greens & Pine Nuts

Serving Size: 6 | **Total Time:** 20 minutes
6 oz spinach, chopped
6 oz collard greens, torn
3 oz Swiss chard, chopped
3 tbsp parsley, chopped
1 leek, chopped
1 ½ cups farro
2 tbsp olive oil
2 ¼ cups vegetable broth
1 tbsp salt
½ cup toasted pine nuts

Add farro and vegetable broth to the Instant Pot. Season with salt and seal the lid. Cook on Manual for 9 minutes on High. Do a quick release and open the lid. Fluff the farro with a fork and set aside. Wipe the pot clean.
Warm the olive oil in the pot on Sauté. Add the leek and stir-fry for 4-5 minutes until slightly caramelized. Add in the spinach, Swiss chard, and salt and sauté for another 4-5 minutes until the greens are wilted. Toss in the farro, sprinkle with pine nuts, and serve.

Quinoa with Brussels Sprouts & Broccoli

Serving Size: 2 | **Total Time:** 25 minutes
1 cup quinoa, rinsed
Salt and pepper to taste
1 beet, peeled, cubed
1 cup broccoli florets
1 carrot, chopped
½ lb Brussels sprouts
2 eggs
1 avocado, chopped
¼ cup pesto sauce
Lemon wedges, for serving

In the pot, mix 2 cups of water, salt, quinoa and pepper. Set trivet over quinoa and set steamer basket on top. To the steamer basket, add eggs, Brussels sprouts, broccoli, beet cubes, carrots, pepper, and salt. Seal the lid and cook for 1 minute on High Pressure. Release pressure naturally for 10 minutes. Remove the steamer basket and trivet from the pot and set the eggs in a bowl of ice water. Peel and halve the eggs. Use a fork to fluff the quinoa. Divide quinoa, broccoli, avocado, carrots, beet, Brussels sprouts, eggs between two bowls, and top with a pesto dollop. Serve with lemon wedges.

Vegetarian Green Dip

Serving Size: 4 | **Total Time:** 15 minutes
10 oz canned green chiles, drained, liquid reserved
2 cups broccoli florets
1 green bell pepper, diced
¼ cup raw cashews
¼ cup soy sauce
½ tsp sea salt
¼ tsp chili powder
¼ tsp garlic powder
¼ tsp cumin

In the pot, add cashews, broccoli, green bell pepper, and 1 cup water. Seal the lid and cook for 5 minutes on High Pressure. Release the pressure quickly. Carefully unlock the lid. Drain water from the pot. Add reserved liquid from canned green chiles, salt, garlic powder, chili powder, soy sauce, and cumin. Use an immersion blender to blitz the mixture until smooth. Stir in chiles and serve.

Cauliflower & Potato Curry with Cilantro

Serving Size: 4 | **Total Time:** 40 minutes
1 tbsp vegetable oil
10 oz cauliflower florets
1 potato, peeled and diced
1 tbsp ghee
2 tbsp cumin seeds
1 onion, minced
4 garlic cloves, minced
1 tomato, chopped
1 jalapeño pepper, minced
1 tbsp curry paste
1 tbsp ground turmeric
½ tsp chili pepper
Salt and pepper to taste
2 tbsp cilantro, chopped

Warm oil on Sauté. Add in potato and cauliflower and cook for 8 to 10 minutes until lightly browned; season with salt. Set the vegetables in a bowl. Add ghee to the pot. Mix in cumin seeds and cook for 10 seconds until they start to pop; add onion and cook for 3 minutes until softened. Mix in garlic and pepper; cook for 30 seconds.
Add in tomato, curry paste, chili pepper, jalapeño pepper, and turmeric; cook for 4 to 6 minutes. Return potato and cauliflower to the pot. Stir in 1 cup water. Seal the lid and cook on High Pressure for 4 minutes. Quick-release the pressure. Unlock the lid. Top with cilantro and serve.

Parmesan Topped Vegetable Mash

Serving Size: 6 | **Total Time:** 15 minutes
3 lb Yukon gold potatoes, chopped
2 cups cauliflower florets
1 carrot, chopped
1 cup Parmesan, shredded
¼ cup butter, melted
¼ cup milk
1 tsp salt
1 garlic clove, minced
2 tbsp parsley, chopped

Into the pot, add potatoes, cauliflower, carrot and salt; cover with enough water. Seal the lid and cook on High Pressure for 10 minutes. Release the pressure quickly. Drain the vegetables and mash them with a potato masher. Add garlic, butter, and milk. Whisk until well incorporated. Top with Parmesan cheese and parsley.

Steamed Artichokes with Lime Aioli

Serving Size: 4 | **Total Time:** 20 minutes

2 large artichokes
2 garlic cloves, smashed
½ cup mayonnaise
Salt and pepper to taste
Juice of 1 lime

Using a serrated knife, trim about 1 inch from the top of the artichokes. Into the pot, add 1 cup of water and set trivet over. Lay the artichokes on the trivet. Seal lid and cook for 14 minutes on High Pressure. Release the pressure quickly. Mix the mayonnaise, garlic, and lime juice. Season with salt and pepper. Serve artichokes on a platter with garlic mayo on the side.

Buttery Mashed Cauliflower
Serving Size: 4 | Total Time: 15 minutes
2 cups water
1 head cauliflower
1 tbsp butter
Salt and pepper to taste
¼ cup heavy cream
1 tbsp parsley, chopped

Into the pot, add water and set trivet on top. Lay cauliflower head onto the trivet. Seal the lid and cook for 8 minutes on High Pressure. Release the pressure quickly. Remove trivet and drain the liquid from the pot. Take back the cauliflower to the pot. Add heavy cream, butter, salt, and pepper. Use an immersion blender to blend until smooth. Top with parsley and serve.

Vegetarian Chili with Lentils & Quinoa
Serving Size: 4 | Total Time: 45 minutes
28-oz can diced tomatoes
1 cups cashew, chopped
1 cup onion, chopped
½ cup red lentils
½ cup red quinoa
2 chipotle peppers, minced
2 garlic cloves, minced
1 tsp chili powder
1 tsp salt
1 cup carrots, chopped
1 (15-oz) can black beans
¼ cup parsley, chopped

In the pot, mix tomatoes, onion, chipotle peppers, chili powder, lentils, cashew, carrot, quinoa, garlic, and salt. Cover with water. Seal the lid, Press Soup/Stew, and cook for 30 minutes on High Pressure. Release the pressure quickly. Add in black beans. Simmer on Sauté until heated through. Top with parsley and serve.

Minestrone Soup with Green Vegetables
Serving Size: 4 | Total Time: 15 minutes
2 tbsp olive oil
10 oz broccoli florets
4 celery stalks, chopped
1 leek, chopped thinly
1 zucchini, chopped
1 cup green beans
2 cups vegetable broth
2 cups chopped kale

Add broccoli, leek, beans, zucchini, and celery. Mix in vegetable broth, oil, and enough water to cover. Seal the lid and cook on High Pressure for 4 minutes. Release pressure naturally for 5 minutes, then release the remaining pressure quickly. Stir in kale on Sauté and cook until tender. Serve.

Homemade Gazpacho Soup
Serving Size: 4 | Total Time: 2 hours 20 minutes
1 lb trimmed carrots
1 lb tomatoes, chopped
1 cucumber, peeled, cubed
¼ cup olive oil
2 tbsp lemon juice
1 red onion, chopped
2 cloves garlic
2 tbsp white wine vinegar
Salt and pepper to taste

Add carrots, salt, and enough water to cover the carrots. Seal the lid and cook for 10 minutes on High Pressure. Do a quick release. In a blender, add carrots, cucumber, red onion, pepper, garlic, oil, tomatoes, lemon juice, vinegar, 4 cups of water, and salt. Blend until very smooth. Place gazpacho into a serving bowl, chill while covered for 2 hours. Serve and enjoy!

Easy Tahini Sweet Potato Mash
Serving Size: 4 | Total Time: 15 minutes
1 cup water
2 lb sweet potatoes, cubed
2 tbsp tahini
¼ tsp ground nutmeg
2 tbsp chopped chives
Salt and pepper to taste

Into the cooker, add 1 cup water and insert a steamer basket. Put potato cubes into the steamer basket. Seal the lid and cook for 8 minutes at High Pressure. Release the pressure quickly. In a bowl, add cooked sweet potatoes and slightly mash. Using a hand mixer, whip in nutmeg and tahini until the sweet potatoes attain desired consistency. Add salt and pepper and top with chives.

Parsley Lentil Soup with Vegetables
Serving Size: 4 | Total Time: 20 minutes
1 tbsp olive oil
1 onion, chopped
1 cup celery, chopped
2 garlic cloves, chopped
3 cups vegetable stock
1 ½ cups lentils, rinsed
4 carrots, halved lengthwise
½ tsp salt
2 tbsp parsley, chopped

Warm olive oil on Sauté. Add in onion, garlic, and celery and sauté for 5 minutes until soft. Mix in lentils, carrots, salt, and stock. Seal the lid and cook on High Pressure for 10 minutes. Release the pressure quickly. Serve topped with parsley.

Simple Cheese Spinach Dip
Serving Size: 6 | Total Time: 20 minutes
2 cups cream cheese

1 cup baby spinach
1 cup mozzarella, grated
Salt and pepper to taste
½ cup scallions
1 cup vegetable broth

Place cream cheese, spinach, mozzarella cheese, salt, pepper, scallions, and broth in a mixing bowl. Stir well and transfer to your Instant Pot. Seal the lid and cook on High Pressure for 5 minutes. Release the steam naturally for 10 minutes. Serve with celery sticks or chips.

Savory Spinach with Mashed Potatoes

Serving Size: 6 | Total Time: 20 minutes
3 lb potatoes, peeled
½ cup milk
⅓ cup butter
2 tbsp chopped chives
Salt and pepper to taste
2 cups spinach, chopped

Cover the potatoes with salted water in your Instant Pot. Seal the lid and cook on High Pressure for 8 minutes. Release the pressure quickly. Drain the potatoes, and reserve the liquid in a bowl. Mash the potatoes. Mix with butter and milk; season with pepper and salt. With reserved cooking liquid, thin the potatoes to attain the desired consistency. Put the spinach in the remaining potato liquid and stir until wilted; Season to taste. Drain and serve with potato mash. Garnish with chives.

Coconut Milk Yogurt with Honey

Serving Size: 6 | Total Time: 15 hours
2 cans coconut milk
1 tbsp gelatin
1 tbsp honey
1 tbsp probiotic powder
Zest from 1 lime

Into the pot, stir in gelatin and coconut milk until well dissolved. Seal the lid, Press Yogurt until the display is reading "Boil". Once done, the screen will then display "Yogurt". Ensure milk temperature is at 180°F. Remove steel pot from Pressure cooker base and place into a large ice bath to cool milk for 5 minutes to reach 112°F.

Remove the pot from the ice bath and wipe the outside dry. Into the coconut milk mixture, add probiotic powder, honey, and Lime zest, and stir to combine. Return steel pot to the base of the Instant Pot. Seal the lid, press Yogurt, and cook for 10 hours. Once complete, spoon yogurt into glass jars with rings and lids; place in the refrigerator to chill for 4 hours to thicken.

Tofu with Noodles & Peanuts

Serving Size: 4 | Total Time: 15 minutes
1 package tofu, cubed
8 oz egg noodles
2 bell peppers, chopped
¼ cup soy sauce
¼ cup orange juice
1 tbsp fresh ginger, minced
2 tbsp vinegar
1 tbsp sesame oil
1 tbsp sriracha
¼ cup roasted peanuts
3 scallions, chopped

In the Instant Pot, mix tofu, bell peppers, orange juice, sesame oil, ginger, egg noodles, soy sauce, vinegar, and sriracha. Cover with enough water. Seal the lid and cook for 2 minutes on High Pressure. Release the pressure quickly. Divide the meal between 4 plates and top with scallions and peanuts to serve.

Mushroom & Gouda Cheese Pizza

Serving Size: 4 | Total Time: 30 minutes
4 oz button mushrooms, chopped
½ cup grated gouda cheese
1 pizza crust
½ cup tomato paste
1 tbsp sugar
1 tbsp dried oregano
2 tbsp olive oil
12 olives
1 cup arugula

Grease the bottom of a baking dish with one tbsp of olive oil. Line some parchment paper. Flour the working surface and roll out the pizza crust to the approximate size of your Instant Pot. Gently fit the dough in the previously prepared baking dish.
In a bowl, combine tomato paste, ¼ cup water, sugar, and oregano. Spread the mixture over the crust, make a layer with button mushrooms and grated gouda. Add a trivet inside the pot and pour in 1 cup water. Seal the lid and cook for 15 minutes on High Pressure. Do a quick release. Sprinkle the pizza with the remaining oil and top with olives and arugula. Serve.

Chickpea Stew with Onion & Tomatoes

Serving Size: 4 | Total Time: 40 minutes
6 oz chickpeas, soaked
2 tomatoes, chopped
1 red onion, chopped
1 tbsp cumin seeds
2 cups vegetable broth
2 tbsp olive oil
2 tbsp butter
2 tbsp parsley, chopped
Salt and pepper to taste

To the Instant Pot, add olive oil, tomatoes, onion, cumin seeds, chickpeas, and pour in the broth. Seal the lid and set the steam handle. Cook on Manual for 30 minutes on High. Do a quick release and set aside to cool for a while.
Transfer the soup to a food processor and season with salt and pepper. Process until pureed and spoon onto a serving bowl. Stir in 2 tbsp of butter. Top with freshly chopped parsley and serve.

One-Pot Swiss Chard & Potatoes

Serving Size: 4 | Total Time: 15 minutes
1 lb Swiss chard, chopped
2 potatoes, peeled, chopped
¼ tsp oregano
1 tsp salt

1 tsp Italian seasoning
Add Swiss chard and potatoes to the pot. Pour water to cover all and sprinkle with salt. Seal the lid and select Manual. Cook for 3 minutes on High. Release the steam naturally for 5 minutes. Transfer to a serving plate. Sprinkle with oregano and Italian seasoning and serve.

Green Bean Salad with Cheese & Nuts
Serving Size: 6 | **Total Time**: 15 minutes
Juice from 1 lemon
2 lb green beans, trimmed
1 cup toasted pine nuts
1 cup feta, crumbled
6 tbsp olive oil
Salt and pepper to taste
Add water and set rack over the water and the steamer basket on the rack. Loosely heap green beans into the steamer basket. Seal lid and cook on High Pressure for 5 minutes. Release pressure quickly. Drop green beans into a salad bowl. Top with olive oil, feta cheese, salt, lemon juice, black pepper, and pine nuts.

Power Green Soup with Lasagna Noodles
Serving Size: 4 | **Total Time**: 25 minutes
1 tsp olive oil
1 cup leeks, chopped
2 garlic cloves minced
1 cup tomato paste
1 cup tomatoes, chopped
1 carrot, chopped
½ lb broccoli, chopped
¼ cup dried green lentils
2 tsp Italian seasoning
Salt to taste
2 cups vegetable broth
3 lasagna noodles
Warm olive oil on Sauté. Add garlic and leeks and cook for 2 minutes until soft; add tomato paste, carrot, Italian seasoning, broccoli, tomatoes, lentils, and salt. Stir in vegetable broth and lasagna noodles. Seal the lid and cook on High Pressure for 3 minutes. Release pressure naturally for 10 minutes. Divide into bowls and serve.

Stuffed with Rice Grape Leaves
Serving Size: 4 | **Total Time**: 50 minutes
32 wine leaves
1 cup long grain rice
½ cup olive oil
2 garlic cloves, crushed
¼ cup lemon juice
Salt and pepper to taste
In a bowl, mix rice with 3 tbsp of olive oil, garlic, salt, and pepper. Place 1 wine leaf at a time on a working surface and add 1 tbsp of filling at the bottom. Fold the leaves over the filling towards the center. Bring the 2 sides in towards the center and roll them up tightly.
Grease the Instant Pot with 2 tbsp olive oil. Make a layer of wine leaves. Transfer the previously prepared rolls. Add the remaining olive oil, 2 cups water, and lemon juice. Seal the lid and cook on High Pressure for 30 minutes. Do a natural release for 10 minutes. Remove the dolmades from the pot and chill overnight.

Spanish-Style "Tortilla de Patatas"
Serving Size: 3 | **Total Time**: 40 minutes
5 eggs, beaten
1 cup spinach, torn
1 potato, chopped
1 cup heavy cream
Salt and pepper to taste
1 tbsp olive oil
In a bowl, mix eggs, heavy cream, and potato. Sprinkle with salt and pepper and stir to combine. Heat olive oil on Sauté and cook the spinach for 3 minutes or until wilted. Remove the spinach to the egg mixture.
Transfer all to an oven-safe dish. Add 1 cup of water, insert the trivet, pour 1 cup of water, and place the oven-safe dish on top. Seal the lid and cook on High for 20 minutes. Release the steam naturally for 10 minutes.

Parsnip & Cauliflower Mash with Chives
Serving Size: 8 | **Total Time**: 15 minutes
1 ½ lb parsnips, cubed
10 oz cauliflower florets
2 garlic cloves
Salt and pepper to taste
¼ cup sour cream
¼ cup grated Parmesan
1 tbsp butter
2 tbsp minced chives
In the pot, mix parsnips, garlic, 2 cups water, salt, cauliflower, and pepper. Seal the lid and cook on High Pressure for 4 minutes. Release the pressure quickly. Drain parsnips and cauliflower and return to pot. Add Parmesan, butter, and sour cream. Use a potato masher to mash until the desired consistency is attained. Top with chives and place to a serving plate. Serve.

Traditional Italian Pesto
Serving Size: 4 | **Total Time**: 20 minutes
3 zucchini, peeled, chopped
1 eggplant, peeled, chopped
3 red bell peppers, chopped
½ cup basil-tomato juice
½ tbsp salt
2 tbsp olive oil
Add zucchini, eggplant, bell peppers, basil-tomato juice, salt, and olive oil to the pot and give it a good stir. Pour 1 cup of water. Seal the lid and cook on High Pressure for 15 minutes. Do a quick release. Set aside to cool completely. Serve as a cold salad or a side dish.

Mozzarella & Eggplant Lasagna
Serving Size: 2 | **Total Time**: 30 minutes
1 large eggplant, chopped
4 oz mozzarella, chopped
3 oz mascarpone cheese

2 tomatoes, sliced
¼ cup olive oil
Salt and pepper to taste

Grease a baking dish with olive oil. Slice the eggplant and make a layer in the dish. Cover with mozzarella and tomato slices. Top with mascarpone cheese. Repeat the process until you run out of ingredients. In a bowl, mix olive oil, salt, and pepper. Pour the mixture over the lasagna, and add ½ cup of water. In your pot, pour 1 cup of water and insert a trivet. Lower the baking dish on the trivet, seal the lid and cook on High Pressure for 4 minutes. Do a natural release for 10 minutes.

Mushroom & Ricotta Cheese Manicotti

Serving Size: 4 | **Total Time:** 35 minutes
6 oz button mushrooms, chopped
8 oz pack manicotti pasta
12 oz spinach, torn
3 oz ricotta cheese
¼ cup milk
3 oz butter
¼ tbsp salt
1 tbsp sour cream

Melt butter on Sauté and add mushrooms. Cook until soft, 5 minutes. Add spinach and milk and continue to cook for 6 minutes. Stir in cheese and season with salt. Line a baking dish with parchment paper. Fill manicotti with spinach mixture. Transfer them on the baking sheet. Pour 1 cup water into the Instant Pot and insert a trivet. Lay the baking sheet on the trivet. Seal the lid and cook on High Pressure for 15 minutes. Do a quick release. Top with sour cream and serve.

Mixed Vegetables Medley

Serving Size: 4 | **Total Time:** 20 minutes
10 oz broccoli florets
16 asparagus, trimmed
10 oz cauliflower florets
5 oz green beans
2 carrots, cut on bias
Salt to taste

Add 1 cup of water and set trivet on top. Place a steamer basket over the water. In an even layer, spread green beans, broccoli, cauliflower, asparagus, and carrots in the steamer basket. Seal the lid and cook on Steam for 3 minutes on High. Release the pressure quickly. Remove basket from the pot and season with salt.

Carrot & Chickpea Boil with Tomatoes

Serving Size: 4 | **Total Time:** 25 minutes
½ cup button mushrooms, chopped
1 cup canned chickpeas
1 onion, peeled, chopped
1 lb string beans, trimmed
1 apple, cubed
½ cup raisins
2 carrots, chopped
2 garlic cloves, crushed
4 cherry tomatoes
1 tbsp grated ginger
½ cup orange juice

Place mushrooms, chickpeas, onion, beans, apple, raisins, carrots, garlic, cherry tomatoes, ginger, and orange juice in the Instant Pot. Pour enough water to cover. Cook on High Pressure for 8 minutes. Do a natural release for 10 minutes. Serve warm.

Amazing Vegetable Paella

Serving Size: 4 | **Total Time:** 25 minutes
½ cup green peas
2 carrots, chopped
1 cup fire-roasted tomatoes
1 cup zucchini, chopped
3 oz celery root, chopped
1 tbsp turmeric
2 cup vegetable broth
1 cup long-grain rice

Place green peas, carrots, tomatoes, zucchini, celery, turmeric, and broth in the Instant Pot. Stir well and seal the lid. Cook on Manual for 15 minutes on High. Do a quick release, open the lid, and stir in the rice. Seal the lid and cook on High pressure for 3 minutes. When ready, release the pressure naturally for about 10 minutes.

Delicious Mushroom Goulash

Serving Size: 4 | **Total Time:** 50 minutes
6 oz portobello mushrooms, sliced
1 cup green peas
1 cup pearl onions, minced
2 carrots, chopped
1 celery stalk, chopped
2 garlic cloves, crushed
2 potatoes, chopped
1 tbsp apple cider vinegar
1 tbsp rosemary
Salt and pepper to taste
2 tbsp butter
4 cups vegetable stock

Melt butter on Sauté and stir-fry onions, carrots, celery stalks, and garlic for 2-3 minutes. Season with salt, pepper, and rosemary. Add mushrooms, peas, potatoes, vinegar, and stock and seal the lid. Cook on High Pressure for 30 minutes. When ready, release the pressure naturally.

Stuffed Peppers with Rice & Mushrooms

Serving Size: 4 | **Total Time:** 40 minutes
4 bell peppers, seeds and stems removed
6 oz button mushrooms, chopped
1 onion, peeled, chopped
2 garlic cloves, minced
2 tbsp olive oil
½ cup rice
½ tbsp paprika
2 cups vegetable stock

Warm the olive oil on Sauté. Add onion, garlic, and mushrooms, and stir-fry until tender for about 5 minutes. Press Cancel and set aside. In a bowl, combine rice with the mixture from the pot. Sprinkle with paprika.
Stuff each bell pepper with this mixture. Place them in the Instant Pot, filled side up, and pour in the stock.

Seal the lid and cook on High Pressure for 15 minutes. Release the pressure naturally for about 10 minutes.

Celery & Red Bean Stew

Serving Size: 4 | **Total Time**: 25 minutes
6 oz red beans, cooked
2 carrots, chopped
2 celery stalks, chopped
1 onion, chopped
2 tbsp tomato paste
1 bay leaf
2 cups vegetable broth
3 tbsp olive oil
1 tbsp salt
2 tbsp parsley, chopped
1 tbsp flour

Warm olive oil on Sauté and stir-fry the onion for 3 minutes. Add celery and carrots. Cook for 5 more minutes. Add red beans, bay leaf, salt, and tomato paste. Stir in 1 tbsp of flour and pour in the vegetable broth. Seal the lid and cook on High Pressure for 5 minutes. Do a natural release for about 10 minutes. Sprinkle with some fresh parsley and serve warm.

Penne Pasta with Shiitake & Vegetables

Serving Size: 4 | **Total Time**: 20 minutes
6 oz shiitake mushrooms, chopped
6 oz penne pasta
2 garlic cloves, crushed
1 carrot, chopped into strips
6 oz zucchini cut into strips
6 oz finely chopped leek
4 oz baby spinach
3 tbsp oil
2 tbsp soy sauce
1 tbsp ground ginger
½ tbsp salt

Heat oil on Sauté and stir-fry carrot and garlic for 3-4 minutes. Add mushrooms, penne, zucchini, leek, spinach, soy sauce, ginger, and salt and pour in 2 cups of water. Cook on High Pressure for 4 minutes. Quick-release the pressure and serve.

Thyme Asparagus Soup

Serving Size: 4 | **Total Time**: 15 minutes
1 carrot, chopped
2 cups sour cream
½ lb Asparagus, chopped
1 sliced Onion
3 Garlic cloves, minced
3 tbsp Coconut oil
½ tsp dried Thyme
5 cups Bone broth
1 Lemon, juiced, zested

Melt coconut oil in your Instant Pot on Sauté. Place the onions and garlic and cook for 2 minutes, stirring often. Add in thyme and cook for 1 minute. Put in bone broth, asparagus, carrot, and lemon zest and seal the lid. Select Manual and cook for 5 minutes on High pressure. When done, perform a quick pressure release and unlock the lid. Mix in sour cream and serve.

Gingery Butternut Squash Soup

Serving Size: 6 | **Total Time**: 25 minutes
1 lb peeled and diced Butternut Squash
2 garlic cloves, minced
1 tbsp Ginger powder
4 cups Chicken broth
1 cup Heavy cream
2 tbsp vegetable oil
Salt and pepper to taste

Place the vegetable oil and half of the butternut squash cubes and cook for 5 minutes until browns on Sauté. Add in the remaining cubes, garlic, ginger powder, chicken broth, heavy cream, salt, and black pepper. Seal the lid, select Manual, and cook for 10 minutes on High pressure. When done, perform a quick pressure release and unlock the lid. Using an immersion blender, pulse until purée. Serve immediately.

Vegan Lentil & Quinoa Stew

Serving Size: 4 | **Total Time**: 35 minutes
10 sun-dried tomatoes, chopped
1 cup quinoa
1 cup tomatoes, diced
1 cup lentils
1 tsp garlic, minced
4 cups vegetable broth
1 tsp salt
1 tsp red pepper flakes

Add sun-dried tomatoes, quinoa, tomatoes, lentils, garlic, broth, salt, and red pepper flakes to your Instant Pot. Seal the lid and adjust the steam release handle. Cook on High Pressure for 20 minutes. Release the steam naturally for about 10 minutes. Carefully unlock the lid.

Spinach Tagliatelle with Mushrooms

Serving Size: 4 | **Total Time**: 25 minutes
8 oz spinach tagliatelle
6 oz mixed mushrooms
3 tbsp butter
¼ cup feta cheese
¼ cup grated Parmesan
2 garlic cloves, crushed
¼ cup heavy cream
1 tbsp Italian seasoning

Melt butter on Sauté and stir-fry the garlic for a minute. Stir in feta, Italian seasoning, and mushrooms. Add the tagliatelle, 2 cups water, and heavy cream. Cook on High Pressure for 4 minutes. Quick-release the pressure. Top with Parmesan cheese. Serve and enjoy!

Pasta Orecchiette with Broccoli & Tofu

Serving Size: 4 | **Total Time**: 25 minutes
1 (9 oz) pack orecchiette
16 oz broccoli, chopped
2 garlic cloves
3 tbsp olive oil
1 tbsp grated tofu
Salt and pepper to taste

Place the orecchiette and broccoli in your Instant Pot. Cover with water and seal the lid. Cook on High

Pressure for 10 minutes. Do a quick release. Drain the broccoli and orecchiette. Set aside. Heat the olive oil on Sauté. Stir-fry garlic for 2 minutes. Stir in broccoli, orecchiette, salt, and pepper. Cook for 2 minutes. Stir in tofu to serve.

English Vegetable Potage
Serving Size: 4 | Total Time: 50 minutes
1 lb potatoes, cut into bite-sized pieces
2 carrots, peeled, chopped
3 celery stalks, chopped
2 onions, peeled, chopped
1 zucchini, sliced
A handful of celery leaves
2 tbsp butter, unsalted
3 tbsp olive oil
2 cups vegetable broth
1 tbsp paprika
Salt and pepper to taste
2 bay leaves

Warm olive oil on Sauté and stir-fry the onions for 3-4 minutes until translucent. Add carrots, celery, zucchini, and ¼ cup of broth. Continue to cook for 10 more minutes, stirring constantly. Stir in potatoes, paprika, salt, pepper, bay leaves, remaining broth, and celery leaves. Seal the lid and cook on Meat/Stew for 30 minutes on High. Do a quick release and stir in butter.

Spicy Split Pea Stew
Serving Size: 4 | Total Time: 40 minutes
2 cups split yellow peas
1 cup onion, chopped
1 carrot, chopped
2 potatoes, chopped
2 tbsp butter
2 garlic cloves, crushed
1 tbsp chili pepper
4 cups vegetable stock

Melt butter on Sauté and stir-fry the onion for 3 minutes. Add peas, carrot, potatoes, and garlic and cook for 5-6 minutes until tender. Stir in chili pepper. Pour in the stock and seal the lid. Cook on Meat/Stew for 25 minutes. Do a quick release. Serve.

Speedy Mac & Goat Cheese
Serving Size: 4 | Total Time: 20 minutes
1 lb elbow macaroni
2 oz goat's cheese, crumbled
½ cup skim milk
1 tsp Dijon mustard
1 tsp dried oregano
1 tsp Italian seasoning
2 tbsp olive oil
5 oz olives, sliced

Add macaroni in the Instant Pot and cover with water. Seal the lid and cook on High Pressure for 4 minutes. Do a quick release. Drain the macaroni and set aside. Press Sauté on the pot and add the olive oil, mustard, milk, oregano, and Italian seasoning. Cook for 3 minutes. Stir in macaroni and cook for 2 minutes. Top with fresh goat's cheese and olives and serve.

Two-Cheese Carrot Sauce
Serving Size: 4 | Total Time: 25 minutes
1 carrot, shredded
1 cup cream cheese
½ cup Gorgonzola cheese
3 cups vegetable broth
1 cup Gruyere, crumbled
Salt and pepper to taste
1 tsp garlic powder
1 tbsp parsley, chopped

Combine carrot, cream cheese, gorgonzola cheese, broth, gruyere, salt, pepper, garlic powder, and parsley in a large bowl. Pour in the Instant Pot, seal the lid and cook on High Pressure for 8 minutes. Do a natural release for 10 minutes. Store for up to 5 days.

Curly Kale Soup
Serving Size: 4 | Total Time: 20 minutes
4 cups curly kale
2 tbsp Ginger, minced
4 Garlic cloves, minced
1 tbsp Mustard seeds
1 tbsp Olive oil
1 cup Heavy cream
2 cups vegetable broth
1 tbsp Cumin powder

Warm olive oil in your Instant Pot on Sauté. Place the mustard seeds, garlic, ginger, cumin powder, vegetable broth, curly kale, and heavy cream. Seal the lid, select Manual, and cook for 10 minutes on High pressure. When done, perform a quick pressure release and unlock the lid. Serve warm.

Cauliflower Rice with Peas & Chili
Serving Size: 2 | Total Time: 20 minutes
10 oz cauliflower florets
2 tbsp olive oil
Salt to taste
1 tsp chili powder
¼ cup green peas
1 tbsp chopped parsley

Add 1 cup water, set rack over water and place the steamer basket onto the rack. Add cauliflower into the steamer basket. Seal the lid and cook on High Pressure for 1 minute. Release the pressure quickly. Remove rack and steamer basket. Drain water from the pot. Set it to Sauté and warm oil. Add in cauliflower and stir to break into smaller pieces like rice. Stir in chili powder, peas and salt. Serve the cauliflower topped with parsley.

Sweet Potato Medallions with Garlic
Serving Size: 4 | Total Time: 25 minutes
1 tbsp fresh rosemary
1 tbsp garlic powder
4 sweet potatoes
2 tbsp butter
Salt to taste

Add 1 cup water and place a steamer rack over the water. Use a fork to prick sweet potatoes all over and set onto the steamer rack. Seal the lid and cook on High Pressure for 12 minutes. Release the pressure quickly. Transfer sweet potatoes to a cutting board.

Peel and slice them into ½-inch medallions. Melt butter in the on Sauté. Add in the medallions and cook each side for 2 to 3 minutes until browned. Season with salt and garlic powder. Serve topped with rosemary.

Steamed Artichokes & Green Beans

Serving Size: 4 | **Total Time**: 20 minutes
4 artichokes, trimmed
½ lb green beans, trimmed
1 lemon, halved
1 tbsp lemon zest
1 tbsp lemon juice
3 cloves garlic, crushed
½ cup mayonnaise
Salt to taste
2 tbsp parsley, chopped

Rub the artichokes and green beans with lemon. Add 1 cup water into the pot. Set steamer rack over water and set steamer basket on top. Add in artichokes and green beans and sprinkle with salt. Seal lid and cook on High Pressure for 10 minutes.
Release the pressure quickly. In a mixing bowl, combine mayonnaise, garlic, lemon juice, and lemon zest. Season to taste with salt. Serve with warm steamed artichokes and green beans sprinkled with parsley.

Stuffed Potatoes with Feta & Rosemary

Serving Size: 4 | **Total Time**: 50 minutes
1 cup button mushrooms, chopped
6 whole potatoes
¼ cup olive oil
3 garlic cloves, minced
¼ cup feta cheese
1 tsp rosemary, chopped
½ tsp dried thyme
1 tsp salt

Rub the potatoes with salt and place them in the Instant Pot. Add enough water to cover and seal the lid. Cook on High Pressure for 30 minutes. Do a quick release and remove the potatoes. Let chill for a while. In the pot, mix oil, garlic, rosemary, thyme, and mushrooms. Sauté until the mushrooms soften, 5 minutes on Sauté. Stir in feta. Cut the top of each potato and spoon out the middle. Fill with cheese mixture and serve.

Grandma's Asparagus with Feta & Lemon

Serving Size: 4 | **Total Time**: 20 minutes
1 lb asparagus spears
1 tbsp olive oil
Salt and pepper to taste
1 lemon, cut into wedges
1 cup feta cheese, cubed

Into the pot, add 1 cup of water and set trivet over the water. Place steamer basket on the trivet. Place the asparagus into the steamer basket. Seal the lid and cook on High Pressure for 1 minute. Release the Pressure quickly. Add olive oil in a bowl and toss in asparagus until well coated. Season with pepper and salt. Serve with feta and lemon wedges.

Turmeric Stew with Green Peas

Serving Size: 4 | **Total Time**: 35 minutes
2 cups green peas
1 onion, chopped
4 cloves garlic, minced
3 oz of olives, pitted
1 tbsp ginger, shredded
1 tbsp turmeric
1 tbsp salt
4 cups vegetable stock
3 tbsp olive oil

Heat olive oil on Sauté. Stir-fry the onion and garlic for 2-3 minutes, stirring a few times. Add peas, olives, ginger, turmeric, salt, and stock and press Cancel. Seal the lid, select Manual, and cook on High Pressure for 20 minutes. Once the timer goes off, do a quick release before opening the lid. Serve with a dollop of yogurt.

Spicy Shiitake Mushrooms with Potatoes

Serving Size: 4 | **Total Time**: 45 minutes
1 lb shiitake mushrooms
2 potatoes, chopped
3 garlic cloves, crushed
2 tbsp olive oil
1 tsp garlic powder
1 tbsp cumin seeds
½ tbsp chili powder
1 large zucchini, chopped
1 cup onions
2 cups vegetable stock
1 cup tomato sauce

Warm olive oil on Sauté. Stir-fry cumin seeds for one minute. Add onions, chili powder, garlic, and garlic powder. Cook for 3 minutes, stirring constantly. Add mushrooms and continue to cook on Sauté for 3 more minutes. Add potatoes, zucchini, stock, and tomato sauce and seal the lid. Cook on High Pressure for 20 minutes. When done, release the pressure naturally. Serve warm.

Creamy Turnips Stuffed with Cheese

Serving Size: 4 | **Total Time**: 20 minutes
½ cup chopped roasted red bell pepper
4 small turnips
¼ cup whipping cream
¼ cup sour cream
1 tsp Italian seasoning
1 ½ cups grated mozzarella
4 green onions, chopped
1/3 cup grated Parmesan

Pour 1 cup of water into the pot and insert a trivet. Place the turnips on top. Seal the lid and cook on High for 10 minutes. Do a quick pressure release. Remove the turnips to a cutting board and allow cooling. Cut the turnips in half. Scoop out the pulp into a bowl and mash it with a potato mash. Mix in the whipping and sour cream until smooth. Stir in the roasted bell pepper.
Add in Italian seasoning and mozzarella cheese. Fetch out 2 tbsp of green onions and put into the turnips. Fill the turnip skins with the mashed mixture and sprinkle with Parmesan cheese. Arrange on a

greased baking dish and place on the trivet. Seal the lid and cook on High pressure for 3 minutes. Do a quick pressure release. Top with the remaining onions to serve.

Sautéed Spinach with Roquefort Cheese
Serving Size: 2 | **Total Time:** 10 minutes
½ cup Roquefort cheese, crumbled
9 oz fresh spinach
2 leeks, chopped
2 red onions, chopped
2 garlic cloves, crushed
3 tbsp olive oil
Grease the inner pot with oil. Stir-fry leeks, garlic, and onions for about 5 minutes on Sauté. Add spinach and give it a good stir. Press Cancel, transfer to a serving dish, and sprinkle with Roquefort cheese. Serve right away.

Roman Stewed Beans with Tomatoes
Serving Size: 6 | **Total Time:** 30 minutes
2 cups cranberry beans
2 onions, chopped
3 carrots, chopped
3 tomatoes, peeled, diced
3 tbsp olive oil
2 tbsp parsley, chopped
2 cups water
Salt and pepper to taste
Heat olive oil on Sauté, and stir-fry the onions for 3-4 minutes until translucent. Add in carrots and tomatoes. Stir well and cook for 5 minutes. Stir in beans, salt, black pepper and water, and seal the lid. Cook on High Pressure for 15 minutes. Do a quick release and serve hot sprinkled with fresh parsley.

Cannellini Beans with Garlic & Leeks
Serving Size: 4 | **Total Time:** 45 minutes
1 lb cannellini beans
1 onion, chopped
2 large leeks, finely chopped
3 garlic cloves, whole
Salt and pepper to taste
TOPPING
2 tbsp vegetable oil
2 tbsp flour
1 tbsp cayenne pepper
Add beans, onion, leeks, garlic, salt, and pepper to the Instant Pot. Press Manual/Pressure Cook and cook for 20 minutes on High. Heat the vegetable oil in a skillet. Add flour and cayenne pepper. Stir-fry for 2 minutes and set aside. When done, do a quick release. Pour in the cayenne mixture and give it a good stir. Let it sit for 15 minutes before serving.

Stuffed Avocado Bake
Serving Size: 2 | **Total Time:** 20 minutes
1 avocado, halved
2 eggs
3 tbsp butter, melted
1 tbsp dried oregano
Salt and pepper to taste
1 tomato, chopped
Grease a baking dish with butter. With a spoon, remove some of the avocado flesh to create more space for the eggs. Reserve the flesh for garnish. Place the avocado in the baking dish. Crack an egg into each avocado half. Season with salt and oregano. Add 1 cup of water and place the trivet in the pot. Lower the baking dish on top.
Seal the lid, select Manual, and cook on High Pressure for 10 minutes. When done, do a quick release before opening the lid. Mix the reserved avocado flesh with the tomato, season with salt and pepper and serve with the baked avocado.

Corn & Lentil Hummus with Parmesan
Serving Size: 6 | **Total Time:** 45 minutes
1 lb lentils, cooked
1 cup sweet corn
2 tomatoes, diced
3 tbsp tomato paste
½ tbsp dried oregano
2 tbsp Parmesan cheese
1 tbsp salt
½ tbsp red pepper flakes
3 tbsp olive oil
¼ cup red wine
Heat olive oil on Sauté and add tomatoes, tomato paste, and ½ cup of water. Sprinkle with salt, pepper flakes, and oregano and stir-fry for 5 minutes. Add lentils, sweet corn, and red wine. Pour in ½ cup of water and seal the lid. Cook on High Pressure for 2 minutes. Do a quick release. Set aside to cool completely and refrigerate for 30 minutes. Sprinkle with Parmesan cheese before serving.

Indian Dhal with Veggies
Serving Size: 4 | **Total Time:** 35 minutes
1 cup lentils
2 tbsp almond butter
1 carrot, peeled, chopped
1 potato, peeled, chopped
1 bay leaf
¼ tbsp parsley, chopped
½ tbsp chili powder
2 tbsp ground cumin
1 tbsp garam masala
3 cups vegetable stock
Melt almond butter on Sauté. Add carrots, potatoes, and bay leaf. Stir and cook for 10 minutes. Add lentils, chili powder, cumin, garam masala, and stock and press Cancel. If the mixture is very thick, add a bit of water. Seal the lid, select Manual, and cook on High Pressure for 15 minutes. Once the timer goes off, do a quick release. Serve sprinkled with parsley.

Acorn Squash with Sweet Glaze
Serving Size: 4 | **Total Time:** 15 minutes
1 lb acorn squash, cut into 2-inch chunks
3 tbsp honey
2 tbsp butter
1 tbsp dark brown sugar
1 tbsp cinnamon
Salt and pepper to taste

In a small bowl, mix 1 tbsp honey, butter and ½ cup water. Pour into the pot. Add in acorn squash, seal the lid and cook on High Pressure for 4 minutes. Release the pressure quickly. Transfer the squash to a serving dish.
Set on Sauté. Mix sugar, cinnamon, the remaining 2 tbsp honey and the liquid in the pot. Cook as you stir for 4 minutes to obtain a thick consistency and turn caramelized and golden. Spread honey glaze over squash; add pepper and salt to taste.

Vegan Sloppy Joe's
Serving Size: 6 | **Total Time:** 40 minutes
3 tbsp olive oil
1 chopped onion
1 red bell pepper, diced
3 cups vegetable broth
1 cup green lentils
14 oz can diced tomatoes
1 tsp chili powder
1 tbsp mustard powder
1 tbsp brown sugar
Salt and pepper to taste
6 hamburger buns
3 dill pickles, sliced
Warm the olive oil in your Instant Pot. Place in onion and bell pepper and cook for 5 minutes. Stir in vegetable broth, lentils, tomatoes, mustard powder, chili powder, brown sugar, salt, and pepper. Seal the lid, select Manual, and cook for 15 minutes on High pressure. Once over, allow a natural release for 10 minutes and unlock the lid. To assemble, toast each bun and top with lentil mixture and a dill slice. Serve right away.

Sweet Polenta with Pistachios
Serving Size: 4 | **Total Time:** 20 minutes
½ cup honey
5 cups water
1 cup polenta
½ cup heavy cream
¼ tsp salt
¼ cup pistachios, toasted
Set your Instant Pot to Sauté. Place honey and water and bring to a boil, stirring often. Stir in polenta. Seal the lid, select Manual, and cook for 12 minutes on High.
When ready, perform a quick pressure release and unlock the lid. Mix in heavy cream and let sit for 1 minute. Sprinkle with salt to taste. Top with pistachios and serve.

Almond & Cherry Millet
Serving Size: 4 | **Total Time:** 25 minutes
½ cup chopped dried cherries
1 cup millet
½ cup almond milk
2 tbsp coconut oil
2 tbsp shaved almonds
Place millet, milk, 2 cups of water, cherries, and coconut oil in your Instant Pot. Seal the lid; select Manual, and cook for 10 minutes on High. Once done, allow a natural release for 10 minutes. Top with almonds and serve.

Basil Parmesan Sauce
Serving Size: 4 | **Total Time:** 10 minutes
1 cup fresh basil, torn
1 cup cream cheese
2 tbsp Parmesan, shredded
1 tbsp olive oil
Salt and pepper to taste
2 cups vegetable broth
In the Instant Pot, stir basil, cream cheese, Parmesan, oil, salt, pepper, and broth. Seal the lid and cook on High Pressure for 5 minutes. Do a quick pressure release and unlock the lid. Serve immediately.

Coconut Milk Millet Pudding
Serving Size: 4 | **Total Time:** 25 minutes
1 cup millet
1 cup coconut milk
4 dried prunes, chopped
Maple syrup for serving
Place the millet, milk, and prunes in your Instant Pot. Stir in 1 cup water. Seal the lid, select Manual, and cook for 10 minutes on High pressure. When ready, allow a natural release for 10 minutes. Drizzle with maple syrup.

Blueberry & Quinoa Porridge
Serving Size: 4 | **Total Time:** 20 minutes
½ cup quinoa
1 ½ cups milk
2 tbsp honey
½ tsp vanilla extract
3 tbsp blueberries
Place the quinoa, vanilla extract, milk, and ½ cup of water in your Instant Pot and stir. Seal the lid, select Manual, and cook for 1 minute on High pressure. Once ready, allow a natural release for 10 minutes and unlock the lid. Top with honey and blueberries and serve.

Carrot & Sweet Potato Thick Soup
Serving Size: 4 | **Total Time:** 40 minutes
4 sweet potatoes, cut into bite-sized pieces
2 carrots, chopped
1 onion, chopped
6 tbsp olive oil
2 tbsp tomato sauce
1 tbsp celery, chopped
1 tbsp parsley, chopped
Salt and pepper to taste
Heat olive oil on Sauté. Add onion, carrots, celery, and potatoes. Stir-fry for 2 minutes. Stir in 4 cups of water and tomato sauce. Seal the lid and cook for 25 minutes on High Pressure. Do a quick release. Open the pot and add celery, parsley, salt, and pepper. Seal again, and cook for 5 minutes on High. Do a quick release.

Coconut Millet Porridge
Serving Size: 2 | **Total Time:** 25 minutes
½ cup millet

½ cup coconut milk
2 tbsp coconut flakes
1 tbsp honey

Place millet, milk, and 1/2 cup of water in your Instant Pot. Seal the lid, select Manual, and cook for 10 minutes on High pressure. When over, allow a natural release for 10 minutes and unlock the lid. Drizzle with honey, top with coconut flakes, and serve.

Cheddar Cheese Sauce with Broccoli

Serving Size: 4 | **Total Time**: 15 minutes
1 cup broccoli, chopped
1 cup cream cheese
1 cup cheddar, shredded
3 cups chicken broth
Salt and pepper to taste
2 tsp dried rosemary

Mix broccoli, cream cheese, cheddar, broth, salt, pepper, and rosemary in a large bowl. Pour the mixture into the Instant Pot. Seal the lid and cook on High Pressure for 8 minutes. Do a quick release. Store for up to 5 days.

Hot Tofu Meatballs

Serving Size: 4 | **Total Time**: 35 minutes
1 lb tofu, crumbled
2 tbsp butter, melted
¼ cup almond meal
1 garlic clove, minced
2 tbsp olive oil
3 tbsp hot sauce
2 tbsp chopped scallions
Salt to taste

Mix the almond meal, tofu, garlic, salt, and scallions in a bowl. Make meatballs out of the mixture. Warm olive oil in your Instant Pot on Sauté. Place the meatballs and cook for 10 minutes until browned. In the meantime, microwave the butter and hot sauce in a bowl. Combine and set aside. Place the meatballs in the pot and top with hot sauce and 1 cup of water. Seal the lid, select Manual, and cook for 15 minutes on High pressure. When done, perform a quick pressure release and unlock the lid. Serve immediately.

DESSERTS & DRINKS

Vanilla Cheesecake with Cranberry Filling
Serving Size: 8 | **Total Time:** 1 hour + chilling time
- 1 cup coarsely crumbled cookies
- 2 tbsp butter, melted
- 1 cup mascarpone cheese
- ½ cup sugar
- 2 tbsp sour cream
- ½ tsp vanilla extract
- 2 eggs
- 1/3 cup dried cranberries

Fold a 20-inch piece of aluminum foil in half lengthwise twice and set on the Instant Pot. In a bowl, combine butter and crumbled cookies. Press firmly to the bottom and about 1/3 of the way up the sides of a cake pan. Freeze the crust. In a separate bowl, beat mascarpone cheese and sugar to obtain a smooth consistency. Stir in vanilla and sour cream. Beat one egg and add into the cheese mixture to combine well. Do the same with the second egg. Stir cranberries into the filling. Transfer the filling into the crust. Into the pot, add 1 cup water and set the steam rack. Center the springform pan onto the prepared foil sling. Use the sling to lower the pan onto the rack.

Fold foil strips out of the way of the lid. Seal the lid, press Manual, and cook on High Pressure for 40 minutes. Release the pressure quickly. Transfer the cheesecake to a refrigerator for 3 hours. Use a paring knife to run along the edges between the pan and cheesecake to remove the cheesecake and set to the plate.

Orange New York Cheesecake
Serving Size: 6 | **Total Time:** 1 hour + freezing time
FOR THE CRUST
- 1 cup graham crackers crumbs
- 2 tbsp butter, melted
- 1 tsp sugar

FOR THE FILLING
- 2 cups cream cheese
- ½ cup sugar
- 1 tsp vanilla extract
- Zest from 1 orange
- A pinch of salt
- 2 eggs

Fold a 20-inch piece of aluminum foil in half lengthwise twice and set on the Instant Pot. Grease a parchment paper and line it to a cake pan. In a bowl, combine melted butter, sugar, and graham crackers. Press into the bottom and about ⅓ up the sides of the pan. Transfer the pan to the freezer as you prepare the filling.

In a separate bowl, beat sugar, cream cheese, salt, orange zest, and vanilla until smooth. Beat eggs into the filling, one at a time. Stir until combined. Add the filling over the chilled crust in the pan. Add 1 cup water and set a trivet into the pot. Put the pan on the trivet.

Seal the lid, press Cake, and cook for 40 minutes on High. Release the pressure quickly. Cool the cheesecake and then transfer it to the refrigerator for 3 hours. Use a paring knife to run along the edges between the pan and cheesecake to remove the cheesecake and set to the plate.

Pie Cups with Fruit Filling
Serving Size: 6 | **Total Time:** 40 minutes + chilling time
FOR THE CRUST:
- 2 cups flour
- ¾ tsp salt
- ¾ cup butter, softened
- 1 tbsp sugar
- ½ cup ice water

FOR THE FILLING:
- ½ fresh peach
- ½ cup apples, chopped
- ¼ cup cranberries
- 2 tbsp flour
- 1 tbsp sugar
- ½ tsp cinnamon
- 1 egg yolk, for brushing

Place flour, salt, butter, sugar, and water in a food processor and pulse until dough becomes crumbly. Remove to a lightly floured work surface. Divide among 4 equal pieces and wrap in plastic foil. Refrigerate for an hour. Place apples, peach, cranberries, flour, sugar, and cinnamon in a bowl. Toss to combine and set aside. Roll each piece into 6-inch round discs. Add 2 tablespoons of the apple mixture at the center of each disc and wrap to form small bowls. Brush each bowl with egg yolk and gently Transfer to an oiled baking dish. Pour 1 cup of water into the pot and insert the trivet. Place the pan on top. Seal the lid, and cook for 25 minutes on High Pressure. Release the pressure naturally. Serve cool.

Homemade Lemon Cheesecake
Serving Size: 6 | **Total Time:** 1 hour + chilling time
CRUST:
- 4 oz graham crackers
- 1 tsp ground cinnamon
- 3 tbsp butter, melted

FILLING:
- 1 lb mascarpone cheese, softened
- ¾ cup sugar
- ¼ cup sour cream, at room temperature
- 2 eggs
- 1 tsp vanilla extract
- 1 tsp lemon zest
- 1 tbsp lemon juice
- A pinch of salt
- 1 cup strawberries, halved

In a food processor, beat cinnamon and graham crackers to attain a texture almost same as sand; mix in melted butter. Press the crumbs into the bottom of a 7-inch springform pan in an even layer. In a stand mixer, beat sugar, mascarpone cheese, and sour cream for 3 minutes to combine well and have a fluffy and smooth mixture. Scrape the bowl's sides and add eggs, lemon zest, salt, lemon juice, and

vanilla. Carry on to beat the mixture until you obtain a consistent color and all ingredients are completely combined. Pour filling over crust.
Into the inner pot, add 1 cup water and set in a trivet. Place the springform pan on the trivet. Seal the lid, press Cake, and cook for 40 minutes on High. Release the pressure quickly. Remove the cheesecake and let it cool. Garnish with strawberry halves on top. Use a paring knife to run along the edges between the pan and cheesecake to remove it and set it to a plate. Serve.

Classic French Squash Tart
Serving Size: 6 | **Total Time:** 35 minutes
15 oz mashed squash
6 fl oz milk
½ tsp cinnamon, ground
½ tsp nutmeg
½ tsp salt
3 large eggs
½ cup granulated sugar
1 pack pate brisee

Place squash puree in a large bowl. Add milk, cinnamon, eggs, nutmeg, salt, and sugar. Whisk together until well incorporated. Grease a baking dish with oil. Gently place pate brisee creating the edges with hands. Pour the squash mixture over and flatten the surface with a spatula. Pour 1 cup of water into the pot and insert the trivet. Lay the baking dish on the trivet. Seal the lid, and cook for 25 minutes on High Pressure. Do a quick release. Transfer the pie to a serving platter. Refrigerate.

Walnut & Pumpkin Tart
Serving Size: 6 | **Total Time:** 70 minutes
1 cup packed shredded pumpkin
3 eggs
½ cup sugar
1 cup flour
½ cup half-and-half
¼ cup olive oil
1 tsp baking powder
1 tsp vanilla extract
1 tsp ground cinnamon
½ tsp ground nutmeg
½ cup chopped walnuts
2 cups water
FROSTING:
4 oz cream cheese, room temperature
8 tbsp butter
½ cup confectioners sugar
½ tsp vanilla extract
½ tsp salt

In a bowl, beat eggs and sugar to get a smooth mixture. Mix in oil, flour, vanilla extract, cinnamon, half-and-half, baking powder, and nutmeg. Stir well to obtain a fluffy batter. Fold walnuts and pumpkin through the batter. Add batter into a cake pan and cover with aluminum foil. Into the pot, add 1 cup water and set a trivet. Lay cake pan onto the trivet. Seal the lid, select Manual, and cook on High Pressure for 40 minutes. Release pressure naturally for 10 minutes. Beat cream cheese, confectioners' sugar, salt, vanilla, and butter in a bowl until smooth. Place in the refrigerator until needed. Remove cake from the pan and transfer to a wire rack to cool. Over the cake, spread frosting and apply a topping of shredded carrots.

Cottage Cheesecake with Strawberries
Serving Size: 6 | **Total Time:** 35 minutes +cooling time
10 oz cream cheese
¼ cup sugar
½ cup cottage cheese
1 lemon, zested and juiced
2 eggs, cracked into a bowl
1 tsp lemon extract
3 tbsp sour cream
1 cup water
10 strawberries, halved to decorate

Blend with an electric mixer, the cream cheese, quarter cup of sugar, cottage cheese, lemon zest, lemon juice, and lemon extract until a smooth consistency is formed. Adjust the sweet taste to liking with more sugar. Add the eggs. Fold in at low speed until incorporated. Spoon the mixture into a greased baking pan. Level the top with a spatula and cover with foil. Fit a trivet in the pot and pour in water. Place the cake pan on the trivet.
Seal the lid. Select Manual and cook for 15 minutes. Mix the sour cream and 1 tbsp of sugar. Set aside. Once the timer has gone off, do a natural pressure release for 10 minutes. Use a spatula to spread the sour cream mixture on the warm cake. Let cool. Top with strawberries.

Yogurt Cheesecake with Cranberries
Serving Size: 6 | **Total Time:** 45 minutes + chilling time
2 lb Greek yogurt
2 cups sugar
4 eggs
2 tsp lemon zest
1 tsp lemon extract
1 cheesecake crust
FOR TOPPING:
7 oz dried cranberries
2 tbsp cranberry jam
2 tsp lemon zest
1 tsp vanilla sugar
1 tsp cranberry extract
¾ cup lukewarm water

In a bowl, combine yogurt, sugar, eggs, lemon zest, and lemon extract. With a mixer, beat well until well-combined. Place the crust in a greased cake pan and pour in the filling. Flatten the surface with a spatula. Leave in the fridge for 30 minutes. Combine cranberries, jam, lemon zest, vanilla sugar, cranberry extract, and water in the pot. Simmer for 15 minutes on Sauté. Remove and wipe the pot clean. Fill in 1 cup water and insert a trivet. Set the pan on top of the trivet and pour cranberry topping. Seal the lid and cook for 20 minutes on High Pressure. Do a quick release. Run a sharp knife around the edge of the cheesecake. Refrigerate. Serve and enjoy!

Lemon-Apricot Compote

Serving Size: 6 | **Total Time:** 20 minutes
2 lb fresh apricots, sliced
1 lb sugar
2 tbsp lemon zest
1 tsp ground nutmeg
10 cups water

Add apricots, sugar, water, nutmeg, and lemon zest. Cook, stirring occasionally until half of the water evaporates, on Sauté. Press Cancel and transfer the apricots and the remaining liquid into glass jars. Let cool. Refrigerate.

Banana Chocolate Bars

Serving Size: 6 | **Total Time:** 25 minutes
½ cup almond butter
3 bananas
2 tbsp cocoa powder

Place the bananas and almond butter in a bowl and mash finely with a fork. Add the cocoa powder and stir until well combined. Grease a baking dish. Pour the banana and almond butter into the dish. Pour 1 cup water into the cooker and lower a trivet. Place the baking dish on the trivet and seal the lid. Select Pressure Cook for 15 minutes on High. When it goes off, do a quick release. Let cool for a few minutes before cutting into squares.

Cherry & Chocolate Marble Cake

Serving Size: 6 | **Total Time:** 45 minutes
1 cup flour
1 ½ tsp baking powder
1 tbsp powdered stevia
½ tsp salt
1 tsp cherry extract
3 tbsp butter, softened
3 eggs
¼ cup cocoa powder
¼ cup heavy cream

Combine flour, baking powder, stevia, and salt in a bowl. Mix well to combine and add eggs, one at a time. Beat well with a dough hook attachment for one minute. Add heavy cream, butter, and cherry extract. Continue to beat for 3 more minutes. Divide the mixture in half and add cocoa powder in one-half of the mixture. Pour the light batter into a greased baking dish. Drizzle with cocoa dough to create a nice marble pattern. Pour in one cup of water and insert the trivet. Lower the baking dish on top. Seal the lid and cook for 20 minutes on High Pressure. Release the pressure naturally for 10 minutes.

Chocolate Glazed Cake

Serving Size: 6 | **Total Time:** 40 minutes + chilling time
3 cups yogurt
3 cups flour
2 cups granulated sugar
1 cup oil
2 tsp baking soda
3 tbsp cocoa
FOR THE GLAZE:
7 oz dark chocolate
10 tbsp sugar
10 tbsp milk
5 oz butter, unsalted

In a bowl, combine yogurt, flour, sugar, oil, baking soda, and cocoa. Beat well with an electric mixer. Transfer a mixture to a large springform pan. Wrap the pan in foil. Insert a trivet in the Instant Pot. Pour in 1 cup water and place the pan on top. Seal the lid and cook for 30 minutes on High Pressure. Do a quick release, remove the pan, and unwrap. Chill well. Microwave the chocolate and whisk in butter, milk, and sugar. Beat well with a mixer and pour the mixture over the cake. Refrigerate for at least two hours before serving.

Molten Chocolate Cake

Serving Size: 6 | **Total Time:** 40 minutes
1 cup butter
4 tbsp milk
2 tsp vanilla extract
1 ½ cups chocolate chips
1 ½ cups sugar
Powdered sugar to garnish
7 tbsp flour
5 eggs
1 cup water

Grease the cake pan with cooking spray and set aside. Fit the trivet at the pot, and pour in water. In a heatproof bowl, add the butter and chocolate and melt them in the microwave for about 2 minutes. Stir in sugar. Add eggs, milk, and vanilla extract and stir again. Finally, add the flour and stir it until smooth. Pour the batter into the greased cake pan and use a spatula to level it. Place the pan on the trivet, inside the pot, seal the lid, and select Manual at High for 15 minutes.
Do a natural pressure release for 10 minutes. Remove the trivet with the pan on it and place the pan on a flat surface. Put a plate over the pan and flip the cake over onto the plate. Pour the powdered sugar in a fine sieve and sift over the cake. Cut the cake into slices and serve.

Best Tiramisu Cheesecake

Serving Size: 6 | **Total Time:** 35 minutes + chilling time
1 ½ cups ladyfingers, crushed
1 tbsp Kahlua liquor
1 tbsp granulated espresso
1 tbsp butter, melted
16 oz cream cheese
8 oz mascarpone cheese
2 tbsp powdered sugar
½ cup white sugar
1 tbsp cocoa powder
1 tsp vanilla extract
2 eggs

In a bowl beat the cream cheese, mascarpone, and white sugar. Gradually beat in the eggs, the powdered sugar, cocoa powder, and vanilla. Combine Kahlua liquor, espresso, butter, and ladyfingers, in another bowl. Press the ladyfinger crust at the bottom. Pour the filling on a greased cake pan. Cover the pan with aluminum foil. Pour 1 cup of water into your pressure cooker and lower a trivet. Place the pan inside and seal the lid. Select Manual and set to 25 minutes at High pressure. Release the pressure quickly. Allow cooling completely.

Catalan-Style Crème Brûlée
Serving Size: 4 | Total Time: 15 minutes
5 cups heavy cream
8 egg yolks
1 cup honey
4 tbsp sugar
1 vanilla extract
1 cup water
In a bowl, combine heavy cream, egg yolks, vanilla, and honey. Beat well with an electric mixer. Pour the mixture into 4 ramekins. Set aside. Pour water into the pot and insert the trivet. Lower the ramekins on top. Seal the lid and cook for 10 minutes on High Pressure. Do a quick pressure release. Remove the ramekins from the pot and add a tablespoon of sugar to each ramekin. Burn evenly with a culinary torch until brown. Chill well and serve.

Simple Apple Cinnamon Dessert
Serving Size: 6 | Total Time: 30 minutes
TOPPING:
½ cup rolled oats
½ cup oat flour
½ cup granulated sugar
¼ cup olive oil
FILLING:
5 apples, cored, and halved
2 tbsp arrowroot powder
½ cup water
1 tsp ground cinnamon
¼ tsp ground nutmeg
½ tsp vanilla paste
In a bowl, combine sugar, oat flour, rolled oats, and olive oil to form coarse crumbs. Spoon the apples into the Instant Pot. Mix water with arrowroot powder in a bowl. Stir in nutmeg, cinnamon, and vanilla. Toss in the apples to coat. Apply oat topping to the apples. Seal the lid and cook on High Pressure for 10 minutes. Release the pressure naturally for 10 minutes.

Easy Lemon Cake
Serving Size: 6 | Total Time: 30 minutes
2 eggs
2 cups sugar
1 cup vegetable oil
½ cup flour
1 tsp baking powder
LEMON TOPPING:
1 cup sugar
1 cup lemon juice
1 tbsp lemon zest
1 lemon, sliced
In a bowl, combine eggs, sugar, oil, and baking powder. Gradually add flour until the mixture is thick and slightly sticky. Shape balls with hands and flatten them to half-inch thick. Place in a baking pan. Pour 1 cup of water, insert a trivet, and lower the pan onto the trivet. Cover the pan with foil and seal the lid. Cook on High Pressure for 20 minutes. Do a quick release. Let cool at room temperature. Add sugar, lemon juice, lemon zest, and lemon slices to the Instant Pot. Press Sauté and stir until the sugar dissolves. Pour the hot topping over the cake.

Honey Homemade Almond Milk
Serving Size: 4 | Total Time: 15 minutes
1 cup raw almonds, peeled
2 dried apricots, chopped
2 tbsp honey
1 vanilla bean
½ tsp almond extract
In the Instant Pot, mix a cup of water with almonds and apricots. Seal the lid and cook for 1 minute on High. Release the pressure quickly. The almonds should be soft and plump, and the water should be brown and murky. Use a strainer to drain almonds and apricots. Rinse with cold water. To a blender, add the rinsed almonds and apricots, almond extract, vanilla bean, honey, and 4 cups water. Blend for 2 minutes until well combined and frothy. Line a cheesecloth to the strainer. Place the strainer over a bowl and strain the milk. Use a wooden spoon to press milk through the cheesecloth and get rid of solids. Place almond milk in an airtight container and refrigerate.

Amazing Fruity Cheesecake
Serving Size: 6 | Total Time: 35 minutes
1 ½ cups graham cracker crust
1 cup raspberries
3 cups cream cheese
1 tbsp fresh orange juice
3 eggs
½ stick butter, melted
¾ cup sugar
1 tsp vanilla paste
1 tsp orange zest
Insert the tray into the pressure cooker, and add 1 cup of water. Grease a springform. Mix in graham cracker crust with sugar and butter in a bowl. Press the mixture to form a crust at the bottom. Blend the raspberries and cream cheese with an electric mixer. Crack in the eggs and keep mixing until well combined. Mix in orange juice, vanilla paste, and orange zest. Pour this mixture into the pan, and cover the pan with aluminum foil. Lay the springform on the tray. Select Pressure Cook and cook for 20 minutes on High. Once the cooking is complete, do a quick pressure release. Refrigerate the cheesecake.

Chocolate Quinoa Bowl
Serving Size: 4 | Total Time: 15 minutes
12 squares dark chocolate, shaved
2 tbsp cocoa powder
1 cup quinoa
2 tbsp maple syrup
½ tsp vanilla
A pinch of salt
1 tbsp sliced almonds

Put the quinoa, cocoa powder, maple syrup, vanilla, 2 ¼ cups water, and salt in your Instant Pot. Seal the lid, select Manual, and cook for a minute on High pressure. When ready, allow a natural release for 10 minutes and unlock the lid. Using a fork, fluff the quinoa. Top with almonds and dark chocolate and serve.

Simple Apple Cider with Orange Juice

Serving Size: 6 | **Total Time**: 20 minutes
6 green apples, chopped
¼ cup orange juice
2 cinnamon sticks
In a blender, add orange juice, apples, and 3 cups water and blend until smooth; use a fine-mesh strainer to strain and press using a spoon. Get rid of the pulp. In the pot, mix the apple puree and cinnamon sticks. Seal the lid and cook for 10 minutes on High Pressure. Release the Pressure naturally. Strain again and do away with the solids.

Spiced & Warming Mulled Wine

Serving Size: 6 | **Total Time**: 20 minutes
3 cups red wine
2 tangerines, sliced
¼ cup honey
6 whole cloves
6 whole black peppercorns
2 cardamom pods
8 cinnamon sticks
1 tsp fresh ginger, grated
1 tsp ground cinnamon
Add red wine, honey, cardamom, 2 cinnamon sticks, cloves, tangerine slices, ginger, and peppercorns. Seal the lid and cook for 5 minutes on High Pressure. Release pressure naturally for 10 minutes. Using a fine mesh strainer, strain the wine. Discard spices. Divide the warm wine into glasses. Garnish with cinnamon sticks to serve.

Walnut & Dark Chocolate Brownies

Serving Size: 6 | **Total Time**: 30 minutes
2 eggs
1/3 cup granulated sugar
¼ cup olive oil
1/3 cup flour
1/3 cup cocoa powder
1/3 cup dark chocolate chips
1/3 cup chopped walnuts
1 tbsp milk
½ tsp baking powder
1 tbsp vanilla extract
Add 1 cup of water and set a steamer rack into the cooker. Line a parchment paper on the steamer basket. In a bowl, beat eggs and sugar to mix until smooth. Stir in oil, cocoa, milk, baking powder, chocolate chips, flour, walnuts, vanilla, and sea salt. Transfer the batter to the prepared steamer basket. Arrange into an even layer. Seal the lid, press Cake, and cook for 20 minutes on High. Release the pressure quickly. Let cool before cutting into squares. Use powdered sugar to dust and serve.

APPENDIX : RECIPES INDEX

A

Acorn Squash with Sweet Glaze 146
Almond & Cherry Millet 147
Almond & Raisin Quinoa 97
Amazing Fruity Cheesecake 152
Amazing Vegetable Paella 142
Apple Pork Chops 51
Apricot Steel Cut Oats 101
Aromatic Lamb Stew 132
Arroz con Pollo 92
Arugula & Wild Mushroom Risotto 91
Arugula Salad with Sweet Potatoes & Eggs 106
Asian Pork & Noodle Soup 60
Asian Tomato Soup 125
Asian-Style Chicken Soup 127
Asian-Style Lamb Curry 77
Asparagus & Mushrooms with Bacon 24
Asparagus & Tomato Tart 16
Asparagus Wrapped in Parma Ham 62
Authentic German Salad with Bacon 106
Authentic Neapolitan Sauce 107
Avocado & Cherry Tomato Jasmine Rice 91
Avocado Fajitas 25
Awesome Chicken in Tikka Masala Sauce 30
Awesome Herby Pork Butt with Yams 56
Awesome Pork & Celery Soup 61

B

Baby Carrot & Onion Pork Chops 55
Baby Spinach & Gruyère Gratin 16
Baby Spinach with Beets & Cheese 16
Bacon & Potato Brussels Sprouts 60
Balsamic Lamb 78
Banana Chocolate Bars 151
Barley & Smoked Salmon Salad 100
Basil Clams with Garlic & White Wine 87
Basil Parmesan Sauce 147
BBQ Pork Lettuce Cups 55
Bean Pasta with Vegetables 89
Beef & Bean Chili 72
Beef & Brussels Sprout Rice 93
Beef & Butternut Squash Chili 73
Beef & Jasmine Rice Porridge 63
Beef & Lentil Stew 72
Beef & Potatoes Moussaka 67
Beef & Root Vegetable Pot 72
Beef & Vegetable Stew 72
Beef Arancini with Potatoes 66
Beef Bones with Beans & Chili Pepper 67
Beef Fillets with Onions 63
Beef Garam Masala with Rice 89
Beef Goulash with Cabbage & Potatoes 66
Beef Gyros with Yogurt & Dill 63

Beef Lasagna with Eggplant & Almonds 65
Beef Layer Tart with Yogurt 104
Beef Meatballs with Tomato-Basil Sauce 73
Beef Neapolitan Ragù 73
Beef Ragù Bolognese 71
Beef Steak with Mustard Sauce 70
Beef Tikka Masala 69
Beef with Potatoes & Mushrooms 67
Beef with Snow Peas 68
Beer-Braised Beef Short Ribs 68
Beer-Braised Pork 55
Beer-Steamed Mussels 87
Beet & Potato Soup 125
Bell Pepper & Chicken Stew 32
Best Italian Chicken Balls 26
Best Pork Chops with BBQ Sauce & Veggies 56
Best Tiramisu Cheesecake 151
Black Bean & Corn Chicken Soup 109
Black Squid Ink Tagliatelle 86
Black-Eyed Pea Soup 120
Blueberry & Quinoa Porridge 147
Boeuf Bourguignon 73
Breakfast Frittata 12
Broccoli & Cauliflower Pork Sausages 53
Broccoli & Cherry Tomato Salad 15
Broccoli & Egg Salad 15
Broccoli & Ham Risotto 93
Broccoli Couscous 101
Brussel Sprout & Pork Soup 127
Brussels Sprouts & Zucchini Chicken 31
Brussels Sprouts with Cranberries 20
Buffalo Chicken with Blue Cheese Sauce 37
Buffalo Turkey Chili 43
Bulgur Pilaf with Roasted Bell Peppers 99
Butter & Wine Lobster Tails 86
Butter-Braised Cabbage 23
Butternut Squash & Beef Stew 63
Butternut Squash & Cheese Risotto 92
Butternut Squash & Kale Pot 20
Butternut Squash with Rice & Feta 91
Buttery Mashed Cauliflower 139
Button Mushroom Risotto 93

C

Cabbage & Pork Soup 116
Cajun Orange Pork Shoulder 61
Cajun Pork Carnitas 54
Calf's Liver Venetian-Style 68
Cannellini Beans with Garlic & Leeks 146
Caprese Sauce with Goat Cheese 107
Caribbean Turkey Wings 43
Caribean-Style Pork with Mango Sauce 46
Carrot & Beet Medley 22

Carrot & Broccoli Salad with Hazelnuts 15
Carrot & Cabbage Soup 124
Carrot & Chickpea Boil with Tomatoes 142
Carrot & Sweet Potato Thick Soup 147
Carrot Casserole with Beef & Potato 65
Cashew & Tomato Soup 128
Catalan-Style Crème Brûlée 152
Cauliflower & Kale Curry 21
Cauliflower & Potato Curry with Cilantro 138
Cauliflower & Potato Soup with Parsley 110
Cauliflower Beef Stew 130
Cauliflower Cheese Soup 122
Cauliflower Rice with Peas & Chili 144
Celery & Oxtail Soup 126
Celery & Red Bean Stew 143
Cheddar Cheese Sauce with Broccoli 148
Cheesy & Creamy Broccoli Soup 123
Cheesy Cauliflower Soup 126
Cheesy Chicken Soup 127
Cheesy Duck & Spinach Stew 131
Cheesy Jalapeño Sweet Potatoes 19
Cheesy Polenta with Sundried Tomatoes 102
Cheesy Potatoes with Herbs 17
Cheesy Shrimp Scampi 85
Cheesy Tuna 79
Cheesy Turkey Stew 131
Cheesy Vegetable Medley 15
Cherry & Chocolate Marble Cake 151
Chicken & Bacon Cacciatore 39
Chicken & Broccoli Rice 92
Chicken & Lima Bean Soup 120
Chicken & Noodle Soup 128
Chicken & Pepper Cacciatore 35
Chicken & Potato Soup 117
Chicken & Spinach Soup 118
Chicken & Tomato Curry 36
Chicken & Vegetable Stew 30
Chicken & Zucchini Pilaf 27
Chicken Alla Italiana 27
Chicken Drumsticks in Sriracha Sauce 27
Chicken Drumsticks with Hot Sauce 104
Chicken Fricassee 34
Chicken Gumbo 37
Chicken in Creamy Mushroom Sauce 39
Chicken Sausage & Navy Bean Chili 29
Chicken Soup with Vegetables 126
Chicken Stew with Bacon & Cheese 129
Chicken Stew with Potatoes & Broccoli 131
Chicken Thighs with Mushrooms & Garlic 31
Chicken Wings in Yogurt-Garlic Sauce 34
Chicken Wings with Worcestershire Sauce 28
Chicken with Chili & Lime 38
Chicken with Honey-Lime Sauce 26
Chicken with Port Wine Sauce 40

Chickpea & Jalapeño Chicken 96
Chickpea & Lentil Soup 97
Chickpea Stew with Onion & Tomatoes 140
Chili & Lemon Chicken Wings 35
Chili Beef & Turnip Stew 64
Chili Coconut Potatoes 18
Chili Corn On the Cob 21
Chili Cream of Acorn Squash Soup 110
Chili Goose Stew 133
Chili Poached Eggs with Leeks 104
Chili Soup with Avocado & Corn 112
Chili Squid 87
Chili Steamed Catfish 81
Chili-Braised Pork Chops with Tomatoes 54
Chimichurri Chicken 32
Chinese Beef with Bok Choy 67
Chinese Shrimp with Green Beans 85
Chinese-Style Chicken Stew with Broccoli 135
Chipotle & Garlic Mashed Potatoes 18
Chipotle Pumpkin Soup 109
Chipotle Shredded Beef 74
Chive & Truffle Potato Mash 18
Chocolate Glazed Cake 151
Chocolate Quinoa Bowl 152
Chorizo & Bean Soup 125
Chorizo & Lentil Stew 98
Chorizo & Tomato Pork Chops 56
Chorizo & Veggie Quinoa 98
Chorizo Soup with Roasted Tomatoes 110
Chorizo with Macaroni & Cheddar Cheese 54
Chowder with Broccoli, Carrot & Tofu 109
Christmas Ham with Honey-Mustard Glaze 46
Cilantro & Coconut Chicken Soup 118
Cilantro & Spring Onion Quinoa 98
Cilantro Pork with Avocado 59
Cinnamon BBQ Pork Ribs 56
Clam & Corn Chowder 88
Classic Beef Stroganoff 69
Classic French Squash Tart 150
Classic Goulash 129
Classic Mushroom Beef Stroganoff 66
Coconut & Cauliflower Curry 135
Coconut Cherry Steel Cut Oats 102
Coconut Chicken Soup 118
Coconut Milk Millet Pudding 147
Coconut Milk Yogurt with Honey 140
Coconut Millet Porridge 147
Coconut Pumpkin Chili 22
Coconut Rice Breakfast 94
Colorful Quinoa with Red Salsa 97
Colorful Vegetable & Chicken Rice 31
Corn & Lentil Hummus with Parmesan 146
Corn & Mackerel Chowder 81
Corn & Sweet Potato Soup with Chicken 29

Corn Soup with Chicken & Egg 123
Cottage Cheesecake with Strawberries 150
Country Chicken with Vegetables 33
Couscous with Lamb & Vegetables 101
Crab Pilaf with Broccoli & Asparagus 86
Cranberry Millet Pilaf 100
Cranberry Orange Sauce 107
Cranberry Turkey with Hazelnuts 41
Creamed Butternut Squash Soup 121
Creamed Lentils 99
Creamy Bean & Potato Soup 115
Creamy Beef & Cauliflower Chili 65
Creamy Broccoli-Gorgonzola Soup 113
Creamy Celery & Green Pea Soup 115
Creamy Chicken & Zucchini Soup 128
Creamy Mascarpone Chicken 36
Creamy Mushroom Chicken Stew 134
Creamy Mushroom Soup with Chicken 126
Creamy Potatoes 18
Creamy Turnips Stuffed with Cheese 145
Creole Chicken with Rice 38
Creole Seafood Gumbo 83
Creole Shrimp with Okra 84
Crushed Potatoes with Aioli 17
Cuban Mojo Chicken Tortillas 38
Cumin Chicken with Capers 39
Curly Kale Soup 144
Curried Chicken with Mushrooms 35
Curried Pumpkin Soup 124
Curried Sweet Potato Stew 129
Curried Tofu with Vegetables 24

D

Date & Apple Risotto 91
Delicious Broccoli & Cauliflower Salad 106
Delicious Chicken & Potato Soup 112
Delicious Mushroom Goulash 142
Delicious Pork & Garbanzo Bean Chili 133
Delicious Pork & Vegetables Soup 61
Delicious Thai Vegetable Stew 136
Delicious Turkey Burgers 40
Dijon Catfish Fillets with White Wine 80
Dijon Mustard Chicken Breast 33
Dill Marinated Gherkins 103
Dill Potatoes with Butter & Olives 17
Dilled Salmon Soup 116
Duck Breasts with Honey-Mustard Glaze 45

E

Easy Camembert Cakes 105
Easy Chicken with Capers & Tomatoes 26
Easy Italian Chicken Stew with Potatoes 32
Easy Lamb & Spinach Soup 74
Easy Lemon Cake 152
Easy Pork Balls with Apple Sauce 50
Easy Pork Fillets with Peachy Sauce 51

Easy Primavera Chicken Stew 33
Easy Red Lentil Dhal with Spinach 98
Easy Seafood Paella 82
Easy Tahini Sweet Potato Mash 139
Easy Veggie Soup 123
Easy Wax Beans with Ground Beef 64
Effortless Tomato-Lentil Soup 115
Egg & Chicken Soup 127
Egg Pancake with Spinach & Herbs 104
Eggplant & Beef Stew with Parmesan 66
English Vegetable Potage 144

F

Fall Beef Steak with Vegetables 68
Fall Vegetable Mash 21
Fall Vegetable Soup 111
Famous Chicken Adobo 36
Farro & Vegetable Chicken Soup 111
Fennel & Rosemary Pork Belly 58
Fennel Chicken with Tomato Sauce 37
Fennel Lamb Ribs 77
Fennel Pork Butt with Mushrooms 51
Festive Chicken with Bacon 33
Feta & Onion Layered Potatoes 17
Feta & Potato Salad 105
Feta & Vegetable Faro 100
Feta Cheese Turkey Balls 40
Filipino-Style Chicken Congee 36
Flemish Beef Stew 133
Four Cheeses Party Pizza 103
French Cheese & Spinach Quiche 12
French Onion Soup 122
Friday Night BBQ Pork Butt 53
Fruity Pork Steaks 56

G

Galician-Style Octopus 88
Garam Masala Parsnip & Red Onion Soup 111
Garbanzo Stew with Onions & Tomatoes 136
Garden Vegetable Soup 112
Garlic & Herbed Potatoes 104
Garlic & Thyme Pork 61
Garlic Chicken 33
Garlic Eggplants with Parmesan 23
Garlic Lamb with Thyme 76
Garlic Mashed Potatoes with Sausages 52
Garlic Mushroom Polenta 102
Garlic Pork Meatloaf with Ketchup Glaze 49
Garlic Red Bell Pepper Sauce 107
Garlicky Herb-Rubbed Beef Brisket 72
Garlic-Spicy Ground Pork with Peas 54
German Pork with Sauerkraut 58
German-Style Red Cabbage with Apples 62
German-Style Sauerkraut & Pork Stew 129
Ginger & Garlic Crab 86
Gingered Beef Pot Roast 65

Gingery Butternut Squash Soup 143
Gingery Carrot Soup 124
Gingery Squash & Leek Soup 115
Gluten-Free Porridge 100
Goat Cheese & Beef Steak Salad 105
Grandma's Asparagus with Feta & Lemon 145
Grandma's Beef & Vegetable Stew 133
Grandma's Egg Salad 106
Greek Chicken with Potatoes & Okra 36
Greek Yogurt with Honey & Walnuts 13
Greek-Style Fish Soup 120
Greek-Style Navy Beans 96
Greek-Style Pasta Salad 106
Greek-Style Stuffed Peppers 74
Green Bean Salad with Cheese & Nuts 141
Green Immune-Boosting Soup 109
Green Pea & Beef Ragout 66
Green Pork Chili 131
Green Soup 121
Green Vegetables with Tomatoes 24
Grilled Chicken Drumsticks with Salad 28
Ground Beef & Eggplant Casserole 63
Gruyere Mushroom & Mortadella Cups 62

H

Habanero Chicken Stew 135
Haddock with Edamame Soybeans 79
Ham & Peas with Goat Cheese 101
Harissa Chicken Thighs 36
Harissa Chicken with Fruity Farro 100
Harvest Vegetable Soup with Pesto 121
Hawaiian Rice 92
Hazelnut Brown Rice Pilaf 94
Hazelnut Brussels Sprouts with Parmesan 20
Healthy Kale & Egg Muffins 105
Hearty Beef Soup 117
Herbed Squash Sauce 107
Herby Chicken with Peach Gravy 34
Herby Crab Legs with Lemon 86
Herby Whole Chicken Stew 134
Hoisin Spare Pork Ribs 55
Homemade Braised Pork Belly 50
Homemade Chicken Puttanesca 37
Homemade Gazpacho Soup 139
Homemade Honey Applesauce 108
Homemade Lemon Cheesecake 149
Homemade Turkey Pepperoni Pizza 41
Homemade Veggie Quinoa 97
Homemade Winter Soup 113
Honey Butternut Squash Cake Oatmeal 12
Honey Coconut Rice 93
Honey Homemade Almond Milk 152
Honey Oat & Pumpkin Granola 102
Honey-Glazed Turkey 44
Hot Beef Chili 135

Hot Chicken with Coriander & Ginger 26
Hot Chicken with Garlic & Mushrooms 29
Hot Paprika & Oregano Lamb 75
Hot Pork Chops with Cheddar Cheese 57
Hot Shrimp & Potato Chowder 84
Hot Spinach Soup 127
Hot Tofu Meatballs 148
Hungarian-Style Turkey Stew 43

I

Indian Dhal with Veggies 146
Indian Prawn Curry 85
Indian-Style Chicken 38
Italian Egg Cakes 12
Italian Roast Beef 69
Italian Sausage & Lentil Pot 53
Italian Steamed Sea Bream with Lemon 79
Italian-Style Brussels Sprouts 20

J

Jalapeño Chicken Soup with Tortilla Chips 116
Jalapeño Shrimp with Herbs & Lemon 84
Jamaican Chicken with Pineapple Sauce 36
Jamaican Cornmeal Porridge 102
Japanese-Style Pork Tenderloin 57
Juicy Pork Butt Steaks 57

K

Kale & Parmesan Pearl Barley 99
Kale, Bean & Pancetta Soup 119
Kale, Potato & Beef Stew 129
Kielbasa Sausage Soup 125
Kimchi Ramen Noodle Soup 112
Kiwi Steel Cut Oatmeal 102
Korean-Style Chicken 35

L

Lamb Chops with Mashed Potatoes 77
Lamb Chorba 78
Lamb Shanks with Garlic & Thyme 75
Lamb Stew with Lemon & Parsley 76
Lamb with Tomato & Green Peas 75
Leftover Beef Sandwiches 71
Leg of Lamb with Garlic and Pancetta 76
Lemon & Leek Tilapia 80
Lemon & Thyme Chicken 39
Lemon-Apricot Compote 151
Lentil & Carrot Soup 115
Lentil & Chorizo Chili 99
Lentil & Pork Shank Soup 117
Light & Fruity Yogurt 13
Lime & Honey Scallops 88
Lime Brown Rice 92
Lime Bulgur with Olives 99

M

Mackerel with Potatoes & Spinach 81
Mango & Pumpkin Porridge 21
Maple Beef Teriyaki 68

Maple Pork Carnitas 49
Mascarpone Mashed Turnips 22
Mashed Potato Balls with Tomato Sauce 137
Mediterranean Beef Stew with Olives 70
Mediterranean Carrot & Chickpea Soup 110
Mediterranean Duck with Olives 44
Mediterranean Lamb 76
Mediterranean Meatballs with Mint Sauce 103
Mediterranean Soup with Tortellini 121
Mediterranean Tomato Sauce 107
Mediterreanean Asparagus 19
Merlot Pork Chops 53
Mexican Bean Soup 120
Mexican Pork Chili Verde 57
Millet & Beef Soup 116
Minestrone Soup with Green Vegetables 139
Minestrone with Fresh Herbs 122
Minty Lamb 75
Mixed Vegetables Medley 142
Modern Minestrone with Pancetta 114
Molten Chocolate Cake 151
Mom's Black-Eyed Peas with Garlic & Kale 101
Mom's Meatball Soup 118
Moroccan Beef & Cherry Stew 64
Moroccan Lentil Soup 121
Moroccan-Style Chicken 38
Mozzarella & Eggplant Lasagna 141
Mushroom & Bell Pepper Casserole 24
Mushroom & Gouda Cheese Pizza 140
Mushroom & Pork Stroganoff 59
Mushroom & Ricotta Cheese Manicotti 142
Mushroom & Spinach Chicken Stew 130
Mushroom-Potato Hash Casserole 16
Mussels With Lemon & White Wine 87
Mustard Carrot Soup 123
Mustard Potato Soup with Crispy Bacon 124

N

Navy & Pinto Bean Pot 96
Navy Bean & Zucchini Soup 119
North African Turkey Stew 44
Nutmeg Broccoli Soup with Cheddar 125
Nutty Potatoes 19

O

Octopus & Shrimp with Collard Greens 88
Old-Fashioned Apple Pie 105
One-Pot Mexican Rice 95
One-Pot Sausages with Peppers & Onions 131
One-Pot Swiss Chard & Potatoes 140
Orange & Thyme Beet Wedges 23
Orange Glazed Carrots 22
Orange New York Cheesecake 149
Oregano Pork with Pears & Dijon Mustard 52

P

Pancetta & Cheese Chicken Thighs 135
Pancetta Kale with Chickpeas 50
Pancetta with Garbanzo Beans 96
Paprika Pulled Pork Fajitas 56
Parmesan Topped Vegetable Mash 138
Parsley & Lemon Turkey Risotto 41
Parsley Creamy Tomato Soup 115
Parsley Lentil Soup with Vegetables 139
Parsley New Potatoes with Radishes 18
Parsley Noodle Soup with Chicken 113
Parsley Pork with Savoy Cabbage 59
Parsnip & Cauliflower Mash 21
Parsnip & Cauliflower Mash with Chives 141
Party Apple-Glazed Pork Ribs 52
Party Shrimp with & Rice Veggies 83
Pasta Orecchiette with Broccoli & Tofu 143
Pea & Beef Stew 130
Pea & Garbanzo Bean Soup 122
Pea & Rice Chicken with Paprika & Herbs 29
Pear & Cider Pork Tenderloin 57
Pearl Barley Sloppy Joes 99
Peasant Bean Soup 122
Pecorino Mushroom Soup 128
Penne Pasta with Shiitake & Vegetables 143
Penne with Beef & Tomato Sauce 64
Peppered Chicken with Chunky Salsa 39
Pesto Beef Sandwiches with Pepperoncini 65
Pesto Chicken with Green Beans 30
Picante Chicken with Lemon 28
Pie Cups with Fruit Filling 149
Pilau Brown Rice 95
Pino Noir Beef Pot Roast 68
Piri Piri Chicken Soup 114
Pizza with Tuna & Goat Cheese 79
Plant-Based Indian Curry 137
Poached Eggs with Watercress 104
Pollock & Tomato Stew 80
Pomegranate Rice with Vegetables 94
Pork Belly with Tamari Sauce 52
Pork Carnitas Wraps with Lime & Cilantro 47
Pork Chops & Mushrooms with Tomato Sauce 54
Pork Chops in Cinnamon Apple Sauce 50
Pork Chops on Puréed Butternut Squash 48
Pork Chops with Brussels Sprouts 46
Pork Loin with Apples & Rutabaga 47
Pork Loin with Pineapple Sauce 47
Pork Meatloaf with Chili Tomato Sauce 50
Pork Medallions with Porcini Sauce 58
Pork Rice Porridge 93
Pork Shoulder with Honey & Ginger 48
Pork Sirloin Chili 56
Pork Soup with Cabbage & Beans 117
Pork Tenderloin with Balsamic & Butter 47
Pork Tenderloin with Cherries & Apples 52

Pork with Onions & Cream Sauce 51
Potato & Broccoli Soup with Rosemary 113
Potato & Carrot Puree 18
Potato & Cauliflower Turkey Soup 44
Potato & Salmon Salad 15
Potato Skins with Shredded Turkey 42
Potato, Green Bean & Egg Salad 15
Potatoes & Tuna Salad with Pickles 105
Potatoes with Creamy Arugula Sauce 17
Potato-Leek Soup with Tofu 112
Power Green Soup with Lasagna Noodles 141
Prawn Basmati Rice 94
Provençal Ratatouille 21
Provençal Rice 93
Prune & Shallot Pork Tenderloin 59
Pulled BBQ Beef 73
Pulled Pork Tacos 60
Pulled Pork with Homemade BBQ Sauce 48
Pumpkin & Potato Mash 18
Pumpkin & Wild Rice Cajun Chicken 25
Punjabi Chicken in Lemon-Honey Gravy 30

Q

Quick Beef Soup 116
Quick Chicken Soup 128
Quick Farro with Greens & Pine Nuts 138
Quick French-Style Lamb with Sesame 76
Quick Mushroom-Quinoa Soup 112
Quick Pork & Vegetable Rice 59
Quick Shrimp Gumbo with Sausage 84
Quick Swiss Chard & Chicken Stew 33
Quick Zucchini Sauce with Greek Yogurt 107
Quinoa Bowls with Broccoli & Pesto 97
Quinoa Pilaf with Chicken 31
Quinoa with Brussels Sprouts & Broccoli 138

R

Rabbit & Veggie Stew 134
Ranch Potatoes with Ham 62
Red Wine Beef & Vegetable Hotpot 67
Red Wine Pork Stew with Tomatoes 134
Red Wine Squid 86
Rice & Chicken Soup 95
Rice & Lentil Chicken with Parsley 28
Rice & Red Bean Pot 95
Rice Chowder with Bacon & Green Peas 46
Rich Beef & Vegetable Casserole 71
Rich Millet with Herbs & Cherry Tomatoes 100
Rich Shrimp Risotto 85
Ricotta & Potato Breakfast 13
Rigatoni with Turkey & Tomato Sauce 40
Risotto with Broccoli & Grana Padano 91
Risotto with Spring Vegetables & Shrimp 90
Roast Goose with White Wine 45
Roast Lamb Leg with Potatoes 75
Roman Stewed Beans with Tomatoes 146
Rosemary Braised Beef in Red Wine 71
Rosemary Chicken with Asparagus Sauce 28
Rosemary Pork Belly Stew 130
Rosemary Potato Fries 19
Rosemary Sweet Potatoes with Butter 17
Rustic Soup with Turkey Balls & Carrots 113

S

Saffron Quinoa Pilaf 98
Sage Chicken in Orange Gravy 32
Sage Turkey & Red Wine Casserole 41
Salmon & Spinach Couscous 101
Salmon & Tomato Farfalle 90
Sambal Beef Noodles 69
Saucy Baby Back Ribs 46
Saucy Barbecue Baby Back Ribs 53
Saucy Carrots with Crispy Bacon 103
Saucy Chicken Marsala 33
Saucy Clams with Herbs 87
Sausage & Cannellini Bean Stew 132
Sausage & Red Bean Stew 96
Sautéed Spinach with Roquefort Cheese 146
Savory Chicken Chili with Chickpeas 26
Savory Herb Meatloaf 70
Savory Irish Lamb Stew 77
Savory Pork Chops with Brussel Sprouts 53
Savory Spinach with Mashed Potatoes 140
Savory Tropical Chicken 29
Scallion Chicken & Lentil Soup 124
Scrambled Eggs with Cranberries & Mint 103
Seafood & Fish Stew 81
Seafood Chowder with Oyster Crackers 82
Seafood Hot Pot with Rice 83
Seafood Medley with Rosemary Rice 82
Seafood Pilaf 82
Seafood Stew with Sausage 130
Seafood Traditional Spanish Paella 82
Short Ribs with Wine Mushroom Sauce 49
Shrimp Boil with Chorizo Sausages 83
Shrimp with Chickpeas & Olives 83
Shrimp with Okra & Brussels Sprouts 84
Sicilian Seafood Linguine 89
Simple Apple Cider with Orange Juice 153
Simple Apple Cinnamon Dessert 152
Simple Beef with Rice & Cheese 67
Simple Black Bean Soup 96
Simple Carrot & Oregano Soup 111
Simple Cheese Spinach Dip 139
Simple Onion Cheese Soup 128
Simple Roast Lamb 76
Sirloin Steaks with Red Wine 63
Smoked Ham & Potato Soup 117
Smoked Salmon & Egg Muffins 12
Smoky Chipotle Beef Brisket 70
Smoky Shredded Pork with White Beans 60

South American Pot 93
Southern Cheese Grits 102
Spanish-Style "Tortilla de Patatas" 141
Speedy Mac & Goat Cheese 144
Speedy Soft-Boiled Eggs 13
Spiced & Warming Mulled Wine 153
Spiced Chicken Thighs with Garlic 32
Spiced Mexican Pork 60
Spiced Pork with Garbanzo Beans 60
Spiced Pork with Orange & Cinnamon 47
Spicy Cauliflower Cakes 20
Spicy Chicken Thighs 32
Spicy Garlic Pork 48
Spicy Green Sauce 108
Spicy Ground Beef Soup 126
Spicy Ground Turkey Chili with Vegetables 42
Spicy Haddock with Beer & Potatoes 79
Spicy Honey Chicken 35
Spicy Indian Rice 95
Spicy Lamb & Bean Chili 77
Spicy Mussels & Anchovies with Rice 87
Spicy Okra & Eggplant Dish 23
Spicy Pasta with Seafood 83
Spicy Pork Sausage Ragu 58
Spicy Pumpkin Curry 132
Spicy Pumpkin Soup 122
Spicy Red Kidney Bean Soup 114
Spicy Rice Noodles with Tofu & Chives 89
Spicy Shiitake Mushrooms with Potatoes 145
Spicy Split Pea Stew 144
Spicy Sweet Potato Soup 116
Spicy Tomato Soup with Rice 109
Spicy Turkey Casserole with Tomatoes 41
Spicy Vegetable Pilaf 137
Spinach & Anchovy Fusilli 89
Spinach & Feta Pie with Cherry Tomatoes 13
Spinach & Kidney Beans 96
Spinach & Potato Gratin 16
Spinach & Shrimp Fusilli 84
Spinach Chicken Thighs 34
Spinach Tagliatelle with Mushrooms 143
Spinach, Garlic & Mushroom Pilaf 90
Spring Chicken Vermicelli Soup 119
Spring Onion & Pork Egg Casserole 48
Spring Onion Buffalo Wings 34
Spring Risotto 92
Squash Soup with Yogurt & Cilantro 111
Steamed Artichokes & Green Beans 145
Steamed Artichokes with Lime Aioli 138
Steamed Artichokes with Salsa Roquefort 22
Steamed Asparagus with Salsa Verde 22
Steamed Cauliflower with Cheese 20
Steamed Halibut Packets 81
Steamed Leek with Parmesan Topping 103

Steamed Red Cabbage with Crispy Bacon 46
Steamed Sweet Potatoes with Cilantro 19
Steamed Vegetables with Chile Butter 20
Stewed Beef with Potatoes 65
Sticky Chicken Wings 35
Sticky Teriyaki Chicken 37
Strawberry Jam 13
Stuffed Avocado Bake 146
Stuffed Mushrooms with Rice & Cheese 90
Stuffed Peppers with Rice & Mushrooms 142
Stuffed Potatoes with Feta & Rosemary 145
Stuffed Tench with Herbs & Lemon 80
Stuffed with Rice Grape Leaves 141
Sumac Red Potatoes 19
Sunday Turkey Lettuce Wraps 40
Sweet & Spicy BBQ Chicken 37
Sweet & Spicy Pork Ribs 55
Sweet & Spicy Pulled Pork 49
Sweet Chicken Carnitas in Lettuce Wraps 25
Sweet Mustard Pork Chops with Piccalilli 54
Sweet Polenta with Pistachios 147
Sweet Potato Medallions with Garlic 144

T

Taco-Style Chicken Stew 131
Tamarind Beef Soup 127
Tandoori Pork Butt 58
Tangy Pumpkin Soup 126
Tangy Shrimp Curry 85
Tarragon & Garlic Chicken 27
Tarragon Apple Pork Chops 56
Tarragon Baby Carrots with Parsnips 22
Tarragon Whole Chicken 31
Tasty Asparagus Soup 115
Tasty Buckwheat & Pork Stew 49
Tasty Cajun Pork Chops 52
Tasty Chicken Breasts 27
Tasty Chicken Breasts with BBQ Sauce 25
Tasty Indian Chicken Curry 25
Tasty Spicy Beef 66
T-Bone Steaks with Basil & Mustard 65
Thai Beef Short Ribs 70
Thai Chicken 34
Thai-Style Chili Pork 55
Thyme & Garlic Potatoes 19
Thyme Asparagus Soup 143
Thyme Chicken Pot with Cheese 134
Thyme Chicken with White Wine 26
Thyme Ground Beef Roll 68
Thyme Pork Loin with Apples & Daikon 51
Thyme Sea Bass with Turnips 80
Tilapia Fillets with Hazelnut Crust 80
Tilapia with Basil Pesto & Rice 80
Tofu Hash Brown Breakfast 13
Tofu with Noodles & Peanuts 140

Tomato & Feta Pearl Barley 100
Tomato & Mozzarella Egg Scramble 103
Tomato & Mushroom Rotini 89
Tomato Shrimp Soup 124
Traditional American Beef Meatloaf 69
Traditional Cheesy Onion Soup 113
Traditional Indian Lentil Soup 98
Traditional Italian Pesto 141
Traditional Italian Vegetable Soup 109
Traditional Lamb with Vegetables 76
Traditional Turkish Dolma (Stuffed Peppers) 64
Tuna & Pasta Bake 79
Turkey & Black Bean Chili 42
Turkey Cakes with Ginger Gravy 40
Turkey Meatball Soup with Rice 43
Turkey Sausage with Brussels Sprouts 43
Turkey Soup with Noodle 42
Turkey Stew with Salsa Verde 42
Turkey with Rice & Peas 44
Turkish-Inspired Lentil Soup 119
Turkish-Style Roasted Turkey 41
Turmeric Butternut Squash Soup 114
Turmeric Stew with Green Peas 145
Tuscan Chicken Thighs 132
Tuscan Vegetable Chicken Stew 31
Two-Cheese Carrot Sauce 144

U

Ukrainian-Style Borscht 118

V

Vanilla Cheesecake with Cranberry Filling 149
Veal Chops with Greek Yogurt 74
Vegan Lentil & Quinoa Stew 143
Vegan Sloppy Joe's 147
Vegan Tomato Soup 125
Vegetable & Ground Pork Stew 129
Vegetable & Lamb Casserole 78
Vegetable Beef Soup 113

Vegetable Casserole with Smoked Bacon 51
Vegetable Green Biryani 94
Vegetable Paella 94
Vegetables with Veal & Pork 132
Vegetarian Chili with Lentils & Quinoa 139
Vegetarian Green Dip 138
Vegetarian Lentil Soup with Nachos 110
Vegetarian Soup with White Beans 114
Vegetarian Wild Rice with Carrots 90
Veggie & Elbow Pasta Soup 119
Vietnamese Beef 74
Vietnamese Fish & Noodle Soup 81

W

Walnut & Dark Chocolate Brownies 153
Walnut & Pumpkin Strudel 12
Walnut & Pumpkin Tart 150
Warm Spinach Salad With Eggs & Nuts 104
Weekend Burrito Bowls 137
Weekend Turkey with Vegetables 44
White Cabbage & Beetroot Borscht Soup 110
White Peas with Jalapeño & Bacon 50
White Wine Marinated Squid Rings 86
White Wine Oysters 88
Wild Rice Pilaf 94
Wine Pork Butt with Fennel & Mushrooms 49
Winter Root Vegetables with Feta 23

Y

Yellow Beef Soup 114
Yogurt Cheesecake with Cranberries 150
Yogurt Eggplant Dip 23
Yummy Mexican-Style Rice & Pinto Beans 91
Yummy Vegetable Soup 24

Z

Za'atar Chicken with Baby Potatoes 38
Zucchini & Bacon Cheese Quiche 16
Zucchini with Asparagus 21
Zuppa Toscana 120